W9-BFZ-148

MONTREAL & QUEBEC CITY

Fourth Edition © 2004 by **ACCESS®** PRESS. All rights reserved. No portion of this publication may be reproduced or transmitted in any form or manner by any means, including, but not limited to, graphic, electronic, and mechanical methods, photocopying, recording, taping, or any informational storage and retrieval systems without explicit permission from the publisher. **ACCESS®** is a registered trademark of HarperCollins Publishers Inc.

The extraordinary geographic diversity of Quebec, Canada's oldest and largest (600,000 square miles) province, is reflected in its confluence of cultures. In the 16th and 17th centuries, French explorers, looking for a shortcut to China via the **St. Lawrence River**, were met by resident Algonquin and Iroquois Indians, fisherfolk, and hunters, who lived off the land. After 2 centuries of acrimonious encounters between the natives and Europeans, New France took root. For a while the fledgling colony was a major trading center for the mother country, but the advent of the Seven Years' War pitted England against France, and in 1763 Canada was ceded to Britain. Relations between the leaders of the former New France and its new sovereign often strained the reins of diplomacy. The cultural tug-of-war between British, French, and native peoples continues: *La Belle Province* (the Beautiful Province—Quebec's sobriquet) is perpetually at odds with its Canadian–British context, and the issue of Quebecois independence fuels ongoing, heated debate.

Nonetheless, Quebec's two major cities (home to more than half of its 7,293,100 total inhabitants) are enriched by this diverse heritage. **Montreal** is an au courant, cosmopolitan city that boldly flirts with the future; **Quebec City**'s character is more romantic than urbane—the town remains proud of its history and customs.

Measuring 31 miles long and 10 miles wide, the island of Montreal is linked to the mainland by one tunnel and 15 bridges. Its location at the junction of the St. Lawrence and **Ottawa Rivers**—the head of the mighty waterway connecting the Great Lakes to the Atlantic—has made the city a capital of commerce, a strategic military site, and a formidable political power. This multicultural metropolis is the second-largest French-speaking city in the world

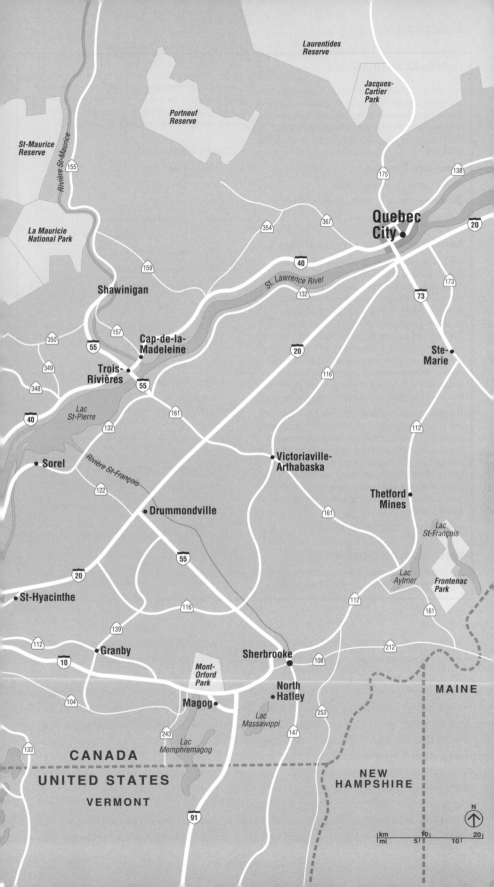

How to Read This Guide

ACCESS MONTREAL/QUEBEC CITY is arranged so you can see at a glance where you are and what is around you. The numbers next to the entries in the following chapters correspond to the numbers on the maps. The text is color-coded according to the kind of place described:

Restaurants/Clubs: Red

Hotels: Purple | **Shops: Orange**

Outdoors: Green | **Sights/Culture: Blue**

♿ Wheelchair accessible

RATING THE RESTAURANTS AND HOTELS

The restaurant star ratings take into account the quality, service, atmosphere, and uniqueness of the restaurant. An expensive restaurant doesn't necessarily ensure an enjoyable evening; a small, relatively unknown spot could have good food, professional service, and a lovely atmosphere. Therefore, on a purely subjective basis, stars are used to judge the overall dining value (see the star ratings at right). Keep in mind that chefs and owners often change, which sometimes drastically affects the quality of a restaurant. The ratings in this guidebook are based on information available at press time.

The price ratings, as categorized, apply to restaurants and hotels. These figures describe general price-range relationships among other restaurants and hotels in the area. The restaurant price ratings are based on the average cost of an entrée for one person, excluding tax and tip. Hotel price ratings reflect the base price of a standard room for two people for one night during the peak season. At press time, the exchange rate was $1.65 Canadian to $1 US.

All prices are in Canadian dollars.

WHEELCHAIR ACCESSIBILITY

An establishment (except a restaurant) is considered wheelchair accessible when a person in a wheelchair can easily enter a building (i.e., no steps, a ramp, a wide-enough door) without assistance. Restaurants are deemed wheelchair accessible *only* if the above applies *and* if the rest rooms are on the same floor as the dining area and their entrances and stalls are wide enough to accommodate a wheelchair.

RESTAURANTS

★	Good
★★	Very Good
★★★	Excellent
★★★★	Extraordinary Experience
$	The Price Is Right (less than $15)
$$	Reasonable ($15-$20)
$$$	Expensive ($20-$30)
$$$$	Big Bucks ($30 and up)

HOTELS

$	The Price Is Right (less than $125)
$$	Reasonable ($125-$200)
$$$	Expensive ($200-$275)
$$$$	Big Bucks ($275 and up)

MAP KEY

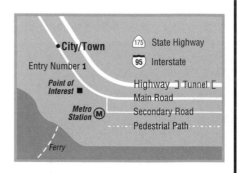

after Paris, the second-largest city in Canada (with a metropolitan population of more than three million) after Toronto, and the second-largest port in North America after New York.

The ambiance of Montreal is remarkably footloose. In warm weather, Montreal bares its Latin soul with a host of international festivals of fireworks, jazz, film, and theater. And bilingual punch lines are standard when the largest comedy competition in the world, **Just for Laughs/Juste Pour Rire**, is staged in July. Even winter doesn't dampen the spirit of the citizenry. Impromptu ice castles and igloos pop up in parks and yards. Toboggans zip down the slopes of **Mont-Royal**, skaters glide over frozen lakes and canals, and fiddles fire the blood at Quebecois *veillées*–lively evenings of traditional music and dance.

Let it be said that Montrealers are also avid restaurant-goers (savoring a gastronomic cornucopia of nearly 5,000 eateries) as well as incurable night owls. Neither whiteouts (snowstorms) nor workdays stay them from their favorite late-night haunts: the jazz clubs on **Rue St-Denis**, funky **Boulevard St-Laurent**, and the pedestrian zones of **Rues Prince Arthur, Duluth, Bernard,** and **Crescent.** And when they're ready for a break from urban life, Montrealers head for their choice of mountains, lakes, and rivers within just a few hours' drive from the city center.

In contrast to the modernity and Anglophile influences of Montreal, Quebec City—or at least the **Old City**—remains stubbornly, gloriously provincial and Gallic. Its 17th- and 18th-century architecture hasn't lost its luster; the scent of coffee and croissants wafts through the winding, narrow streets; and hurdy-gurdy players stand on street corners to serenade passersby with rousing French folk tunes.

French is the mother tongue of 95% of the metropolitan area's 603,000 inhabitants, many of whose ancestors hail from Normandy and Brittany. Indeed, Quebec City's cobblestoned *quartiers* (neighborhoods) seem slightly incongruous surroundings for a contemporary seat of government.

Compact and laced with a maze of narrow streets that makes driving difficult, the city is best explored on foot, whether you're wandering through the **Château Frontenac** in **Old Quebec's Upper Town**, exploring the elegant **Dufferin Terrace** high above the St. Lawrence River, poking around the antiques district in **Lower Town** or the open-air market at the **Old Port**, or taking in the cafés and 19th-century mansions on **Grande Allée**, Quebec City's Champs-Elysées. The city's history, art, and culture are also celebrated in its museums and historic sites, among them the **Citadel, Musée du Quebec,** and **Musée de la Civilisation.** And the rolling hills and country inns of rural Quebec along the **North** and **South Shores** of the St. Lawrence River can be explored in one or more quick day trips.

FYI

Climate

In Quebec's short summer and long winter seasons, temperatures can rise and drop significantly over a few hours. The mean temperature from June to August is 70 degrees, but during *les canicules* (heat waves) temperatures soar into the humid 90s. Winters are cold, with temperatures between 20 degrees and 0 degrees. In urban areas, snow removal is immediate and efficient.

Customs and Immigration

US citizens traveling in Quebec must carry proof of citizenship, such as a valid passport or voter's registration card. Permanent US residents who are not citizens must show Alien Registration Cards. When clearing customs, all food items and plant material must be declared. No handguns or automatic weapons may be brought into the country. Canada doesn't restrict the entry of cats, but dogs must have certificates of vaccination against rabies to be allowed in. The standard stay limit is 3 months, but you may be asked to show a minimum amount of money and credit cards for such an extended visit. For further information, call **Canadian Customs** at 514/283.9900.

Dress

In Montreal and Quebec City, dress depends first on the weather and second, your own mood. Winter requires good snow boots, warm gloves, and hats, whereas the cool evenings of summer call for sweaters and light jackets. Dressing in layers and wearing comfortable shoes are good ideas in any season. Formal dress suits the big, fancy hotels, but the general style in Montreal and Quebec City is casual elegance.

Drinking

The minimum legal drinking age is 18. The provincial government controls the sale of wine and liquor in **Société des Alcools** stores (M-W, Sa; Th-F, 9:30AM-9PM; Su, noon-7PM). Neighborhood *dépanneurs* (corner stores) offer a limited selection of wine and beer. Restaurants displaying the sign *license complète* sell cocktails as well as wine and beer. Those that have no license often allow you to bring your own bottle.

> The 1837–1838 Patriots Rebellion began when French members of the legislature were more adamant than their English counterparts about wresting control of spending from the British government. The short-lived rebellion resulted in the death or exile of many patriots but ultimately helped point the way to responsible government in Canada.

Driving

US citizens and residents must carry a US driver's license, proof of vehicle registration and insurance, or car rental papers. Visitors can bring their own cars into the country for up to 6 months. The minimum age for renting a car is 21.

The Canadian Automobile Association (CAA) is the Canadian branch of the American Automobile Association (AAA), which provides services to US visitors upon presentation of an AAA membership card. The CAA office in Montreal is at 1180 Rue Drummond, between Boulevard René Lévesque and Rue Ste-Catherine (514/861.7111). The location of the CAA office in Quebec City is 444 Rue Bouvier at Boulevard de la Capitale (418/624.0708). For 24-hour emergency road service, call 800/336.HELP.

A good rule of thumb is that drivers in the province of Quebec generally travel well over the speed limit. Road signs are usually easy-to-interpret pictograms, but some are in French only. The most common are

Arrêt—Stop

Cul-de-sac—Dead end

Priorité de virage au clignotement du feu vert—Make turn on flashing green light

Ligne d'arrêt—Stop at line

Rue barrée—Street closed

The speed limit is 100 kilometers per hour (62 miles per hour) on highways, 90 kph (55 mph) on secondary roads, and 50 kph (30 mph) in the city. Seat belts are mandatory, and hefty fines are levied on those who don't comply.

Nonresidents driving a vehicle in Quebec are as fully covered as a Quebecer in the event of an accident in Quebec. The Société de l'Assurance Automobile du Québec (888/810.2525) has more information.

Holidays

Banks, government offices, and post offices in both Montreal and Quebec City are closed on the following days: New Year's Day, Good Friday, Easter Monday, Fête de Dollard (third Monday in May), St-Jean-Baptiste Day (24 June), Canada Day (1 July), Labor Day (first Monday in September), Thanksgiving Day (second Monday in October), Christmas, and Boxing Day (26 December).

Language

More than 92% of Montreal's residents speak French, some with accents from their French-speaking countries of origin such as Haiti, Vietnam, and French Guiana. About 60% of Montrealers speak English, and conversations between bilinguals ricochet from one tongue to the other. With immigrants from about 150 countries around the world, Montreal has become an ethnic crucible where you can hear as many as 50 different languages. As for Quebec City and the rest of the province, English is spoken much less often, but usually understood.

If you're eager to try out your school-learned French, you may find yourself as confused as some Parisians who arrive in Montreal and hear unfamiliar French words. Having been marooned away from the mother country for more than 2 centuries, Quebecers speak a French peppered with 18th-century words and expressions, Anglicisms, and neologisms reflecting North American influences.

M. Blum

Notre-Dame Basilica, Montreal

Money

For a better exchange rate, wait until you arrive in Canada to change money. The basic unit of currency in Quebec is the Canadian dollar, worth approximately 65 US cents at press time. There are no 1-dollar bills, only coins. Other coins come in the same denominations as US currency. Bills are issued in denominations of $2, $5, $10, $50, and $100. Automatic teller machines (ATMs) throughout the province operate 24 hours a day, dispensing Canadian cash. Major credit cards are accepted throughout Quebec, in most hotels, restaurants, department stores, and service stations.

Rest Rooms

Museums, historic sites, and tourist areas offer free, clean public rest rooms. If you're discreet, it's all right to venture into a restaurant or hotel just to use the rest room.

Smoking

Although French Quebecois are big smokers, the anti-smoking effort has made tremendous progress since the passing of the Tobacco Act on 17 December 1999. Smoking is now prohibited in most public areas (check the signs); it is prohibited in restaurants except in certain areas (smoking sections may not exceed 40% of the space, the rooms, or the places available). The Tobacco Act does not apply to bars, taverns, or casinos—yet. Smoking is permitted in taxis if the driver and all of the passengers agree. In addition, an operator may decide to totally prohibit smoking in his or her establishment or vehicles, whether or not they are covered by the act.

Street Smarts

Downtown Montreal and Quebec City are remarkably safe. However, don't invite trouble by meandering aimlessly at night, walking alone in deserted areas, or conspicuously carrying expensive purses and cameras. Always lock your car, keeping valuables out of view, and park in well-lighted areas at night.

Taxes

Taxes in the province of Quebec are high; some would say inexplicably so. As do locals, visitors to Quebec must pay the 7.5% provincial sales and services tax (the TVQ) and the 7% goods and services tax (GST). The traveler will find that few items are exempt from either tax. With proof of expenditure, foreign visitors can request a rebate of the federal GST (but not the TVQ) on accommodations and most consumer goods to be taken out of the country. For rebate applications, call 800/668.4748 within Canada or 800/267.5177 from the United States (613/952.3741 from elsewhere) or visit www.ccra.gc.ca/forms/ for order forms online. In addition, the forms can be found at Dorval International Airport and many hotels.

Telephones

Quebec has three area codes: 514 for Montreal and environs; 418 for Quebec City, eastern Quebec, and the Gaspé Peninsula; and 819 for Estrie (Eastern Townships), Hull, and northern Quebec. Local calls cost 25 cents at public pay phones. To make credit card and collect long-distance calls from pay phones, dial 0 before the area code and number. Most public phones now use phone cards, available in various denominations at newsstands, convenience stores, machines at airports and train stations, and most hotel gift shops. Local information is 411, and all operators are bilingual.

Time Zones

Quebec City and Montreal are located in the Eastern Standard time zone. Daylight saving time is observed from the first Sunday in April to the last Saturday in October.

Tipping

Tips are not included in restaurant bills; leave 15%. Give taxi drivers 15%, baggage carriers and bellhops $1 per suitcase, and hotel porters $1 for hailing a cab.

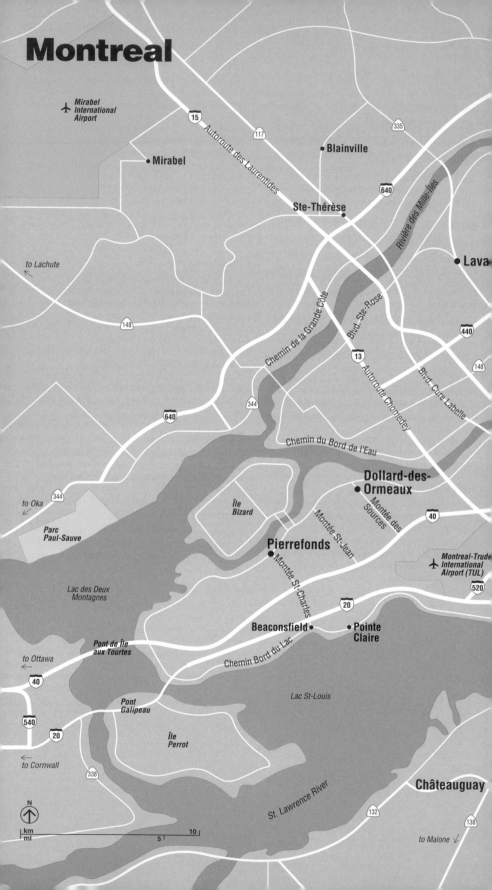

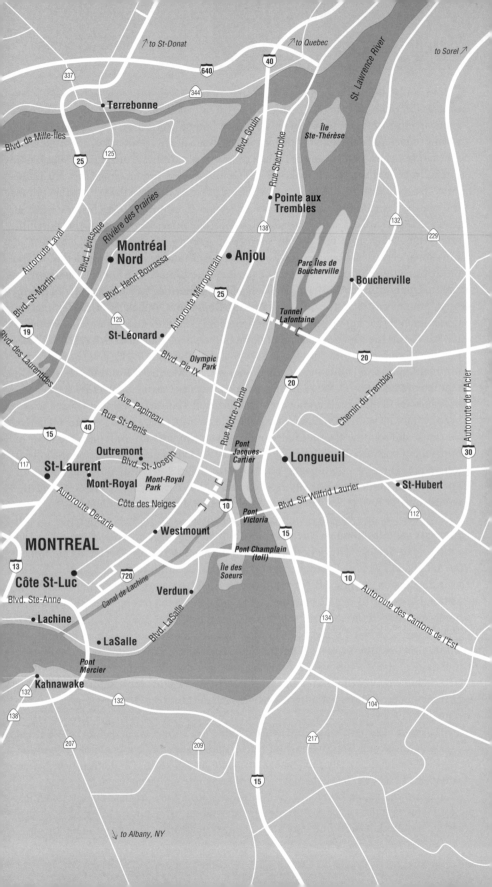

Set on an island in the middle of the **St. Lawrence River**, Montreal is indeed a place apart—in more than a geographic sense. Often called the most European of North American cities, it is a vigorous blend of its two founding cultures, French and English, factions that continually joust with each other linguistically, politically, and otherwise. Settled in 1642 by a small group of French missionaries, Montreal today has a population topping three million, which makes it the second-largest French-speaking city in the world. In recent years it has been adopted by a polyglot of more than 100 other ethnic groups as well, including sizable Jewish and Asian communities. The historic heart of the city is **Old Montreal**, a 95-acre neighborhood of cobblestoned streets and authentic architecture, where the city began more than 350 years ago. East meets West in **Chinatown**, settled in the late 1800s by immigrant laborers after completion of the Transcontinental Railroad. Shoppers favor **Rue Sherbrooke** and the vast network of stores in **Underground Montreal**. The bohemian enclave encompassing **Plateau Mont-Royal, Boulevard St-Laurent**, and **Rue St-Denis** and the **Latin Quarter** has an international flavor and is popular with Francophiles and trendy types, whereas lively **Rue Ste-Catherine** clings to its reputation as the street that never sleeps. The **1976 Summer Olympic Games** left Montreal with the **Olympic Park**, now home to the **Montreal Expos** baseball team, the **Biodome**, and the **Montreal Botanical Garden**. Go to the top of **Mont-Royal**, the 764-foot peak that Jacques Cartier named for King Francis I of France in 1535, for a literal overview of the city. The surrounding 494-acre park—only a 20-minute walk from downtown—was laid out by Central Park designer Frederick Law Olmsted. From the **Grand Chalet** lookout, you can peer not only into the heart of Montreal but outward for a sweeping view of the **St. Lawrence Seaway** and the hills of Montérégie. The city's landmarks—**Buckminster Fuller**'s geodesic dome designed for **Expo '67**, the giraffe-necked **Olympic Stadium**, the Art Deco clock tower, and the **Jacques-Cartier Bridge**—embellish the skyline with their eclectic geometries.

Downtown is at your feet: gleaming, mirrored skyscrapers; venerable **McGill University**; and fashionable Rue Sherbrooke in the center of an area often referred to as the golden **Square Mile**, where at the turn of the 19th century, residents controlled 70% of Canada's wealth. Off to the right, you'll spot the spires of the neo-Gothic **Notre-Dame Basilica** on the **Place d'Armes** in Old Montreal, the core of the original city. The Basilica, famed for its ornate pre-Raphaelite interior, stands on the spot where Paul de Chomedey founded the settlement of **Ville-Marie** in 1642.

The narrow, cobbled streets of Old Montreal are chockablock with well-preserved architectural treasures from the French regime. The stone buildings now house museums, offices, cafés, and restaurants. Trace the evolution of the city—from the Iroquois village of **Hochelaga** to maritime and banking hub to hotbed of contemporary separatist sentiment—at the **Pointe-à-Callière Museum** and the **Montreal History Center** in **Place d'Youville**.

The Jacques-Cartier Bridge, created for Expo '67, connects the island of Montreal with the mini-islands **Ste-Hélène** and **Notre-Dame**. They offer a pastoral playground replete with gardens, an Olympic-size pool, an old British arsenal and military museum, a Grand-Prix racetrack, and the wild rides of **La Ronde** amusement park.

Circle around to the other side of Mont-Royal for a view of the Olympic Stadium, which looms over the 182-acre **Botanical Garden** (home to the largest Ming-style garden outside Asia); the **Biodome** natural sciences museum, with four walk-through ecosystems replicated under one roof; and the **Insectarium**, home to a quarter of a million creepy crawlies.

In the northeastern section of the city rise the brightly painted turrets and cupolas of Montreal's most colorful *quartier*, **Plateau Mont-Royal**, a haven for creative types. To the west sit the dignified brownstones of **Westmount**, a distinctly English district. As for the rest of the city's cultural mosaic, **Little Italy, Chinatown, Little Portugal**, and dozens of other ethnic enclaves offer days of good eating and exploring.

Making the rounds of all these areas is a cinch via the clean and quiet Metro system. Each of the 65 stations is artistically outfitted with tile, stained glass, and enameled-steel installations. One stop—**Place d'Armes**—even has a small display of archeological artifacts.

Transit is by no means the only reason to go underground in Montreal; 19 miles of pedestrian passageways link more than 1,700 department stores and shops, theaters, cinemas, and restaurants—very handy in winter.

If the urban excesses of museum-hopping, boutique-browsing, and bistro-going (above or below ground) exhaust you, the nearby environs offer myriad Arcadian antidotes. Pick your pleasure: whitewater rafting on the **Rouge River**, wine tasting in the vineyards of Montérégie, or hiking in the **Eastern Townships**. And for those interested in skiing, the **Laurentians**, known as Quebec's Alps, provide excellent alpine skiing and are just a short jaunt to the north.

Area code 514 unless otherwise noted.

Getting to Montreal

Airports

Montreal-Trudeau International Airport (YUL)

At 22.5 kilometers (14 miles) from downtown Montreal, **DIA** handles all regular international and continental flights (394.7377; 633.5235 for Canadian Immigration; 633.7700 for Canadian Customs). Driving to Montreal from the airport, follow signs to Route 20, then take the Autoroute Ville Marie (720 East). The trip downtown via taxi or by bus takes 20 to 30 minutes. Buses to the city center cost $12; they depart every 30 minutes daily between 7AM and 1AM from the **Aérobus Station** at 777 Rue de la Gauchetière W (Aérobus, 931.9002). Taxi fare will run about $28. Make sure you have Canadian money; otherwise, the exchange rate is left to the discretion of the driver.

Mirabel International Airport (MIA)

At 55 kilometers (34 miles) northwest of the city or 45 minutes by car, **MIA** handles all charter and cargo flights (394.7377; 476.2976 for Canadian Immigration; 476.2963 for Canadian Customs). Leaving the airport, follow signs to Route 20 and then take the Autoroute Ville Marie (720 East) to Montreal. A taxi from **Mirabel** to downtown will cost approximately $55. For **Aérobus** bus service, call 931.9002. Schedules vary; the one-way fare is $22.

Note that Montreal airports tap outbound passengers for so-called Airport Improvement Fees. Be prepared to part with $15 at Dorval and $10 at Mirabel on departure (as a sign that these fees aren't going away anytime soon, there are sleek fee-processing counters and fee ticket machines, both of which accept credit cards). You must pay the fee before clearing security.

Airlines

Air Canada/Canadien International	393.3333, 888/247.2262
American	800/433.7300
British Airways	888/247.9297
Delta	337.5520, 800/361.1970
Northwest/KLM	800/225.2525
United Airlines	800/241.6522
US Air	800/432.9768

Rental Cars

Avis	866.7906, 800/879.2847
Budget	937.9121, 800/268.8900
Hertz	842.8537, 800/263.0678
Pelletier	281.5000, 877/281.5001

Bus Terminal

Greyhound buses to and from US cities stop at the **Station Centrale**, located at 505 Boulevard de Maisonneuve East. For further information, call 842.2281.

Phone Book

EMERGENCIES

Ambulance/Fire/Police 911
Police 280.2222
Dental...342.4444
Emergency Road Service
(CAA/AAA Montreal) 861.7575
Lost Passports..398.9695
Poison Control 800/463.5060
Rape Hot Line 278.9383

OTHER IMPORTANT NUMBERS

Postal Service 800/267.1177
Road Conditions 284.2363
Veterinary Services 731.9442
VIA Rail Station 989.2626
Station Central (bus terminal) 842.2281
Weather 800/463.4311, 283.3010

TRAIN STATION

All trains from the US and other Canadian provinces terminate at the **Gare Centrale** on Rue de la Gauchetière between Rues Université and Mansfield. The **Gare Centrale** is at the **Bonaventure** Metro stop. Call 989.2626 or 888/VIARAIL (888/842.7245).

Getting around Montreal

BUS/METRO

A car isn't a necessity in Montreal. You'll save time and avoid traffic and parking hassles by using the clean and convenient **Metro** and the city bus network (288.6287). The climate-controlled subway system has 65 stops and operates between 5:30AM and 1AM. Each station connects with one or more bus routes; transfers from the subway to buses are available from machines near the ticket booths. Bus drivers offer bus-to-**Metro** transfers and bus-to-bus transfers, making the most of your $2.25 (per ticket) investment. A strip of six tickets costs $9.50, and the STCUM Tourist Card, which gives unlimited access to the system for one day, costs $7 (a 3-day card is $14). Get a free subway map at ticket booths.

DRIVING

Although there's no need to brave traffic in downtown Montreal, if you do decide to drive, it's best to avoid the narrow one-way streets of Old Montreal. Directional and parking signs are in French (see page 6 of the main orientation). If you plan to drive in or around the city, a pocket dictionary may come in handy. Parking is permitted on the street at metered spots, but if you intend to sightsee in a popular area like Old Montreal or Rue Sherbrooke, go early and be sure to read the parking restrictions on the street signs. For road conditions, call 284.2363.

TAXIS

Montreal taxicabs come in a rainbow of colors and styles, but they all start the meter at $2.50 and add $1 per kilometer (and 44 cents per minute waiting time). Cabs are easily hailed on the street; when the sign on the roof is lit, the cab is available. Taxi companies include **Co-op Taxi** (725.9885), **Diamond Taxi** (273.6331), and **Taxi Lasalle** (277.2552).

FYI

CONSULATES

UK ....1000 Rue de la Gauchetière West, at Rue Mansfield, 866.5863
US ....1155 Rue St-Alexandre, at Blvd René Lévesque, 398.9695

HOSTELS

Downtown Montreal has about a dozen hostels, including the **Auberge de l'Hotel de Paris** at 901 Rue Sherbrooke E (522.6861, 800/567.7217); **YWCA** on Boulevard René Lévesque West at Rue Crescent (866.9941); and student residences at the **Université de Montréal** (343.6531), **McGill University** (398.6367), and the **Royal Victoria College** (398.6378).

FURNISHED APARTMENTS

For those who seek a more independent (and often less expensive) alternative to hotels, furnished apartments can be an enjoyable option. **Appartements Touristiques du Centre-Ville** offers Montreal's choicest selection of furnished apartments. The apartments vary in size, but all are fully equipped and located in cheerful, modern buildings close to the city center. Two-person studios start at $95 a day or $600 a week; one-bedroom apartments, which can comfortably accommodate up to five people, start at $125 a day or $800 a week. Monthly rates are also available. Most apartment stays include daily complimentary continental breakfast. For those occasions when style is a consideration, the company also offers a small selection of more spacious luxury apartments. 845.0431; fax 845.0262. www3.sympatico.ca/app

HOURS

Opening hours of shops, attractions, and so forth are listed with entries wherever possible. Most shops in Montreal are open Monday to Wednesday, 10AM-6PM; Thursday and Friday, 10AM-9PM; Saturday, 10AM-5PM; and Sunday, noon-5PM. However, hours can fluctuate according to the season and to owners' whims. If you're intent on visiting a listed shop that's not part of one of the major shopping centers, call ahead to avoid disappointment.

MONEY

Banks are generally open weekdays between 9:30AM and 3:30PM, and some are also open Saturday mornings. ATMs are placed throughout the city, many of them in local grocery stores. Most machines are connected to the PLUS System and Interac.

For the best exchange rates, don't change money in shops or restaurants. You can find foreign exchange services at the following locations:

Currencies International: 1250 Rue Peel, 392.9100

Downtown Currency Exchange: 2000 Avenue McGill College, 844.1414

Montreal Currency Exchange Ltd.: 1257 Rue Peel, 866.0227

National Bank of Canada: 1140 Sherbrooke Street West, 500 Place d'Armes, Gare Centrale; 394.5555, 888/835.6281

PUBLICATIONS

Montreal's French daily newspapers are *Le Devoir*, *La Presse*, and *Le Journal de Montréal*. The French free weekly paper is *Voir*. The English daily is the *Montreal Gazette*, and two free weekly alternative papers in English that are good sources for entertainment information are *Hour* and the *Mirror*. The *New York Times*, *Wall Street Journal*, *USA Today*, and other major US newspapers are available in Montreal at outlets of **Maison de la presse** and large newsstands.

TOURS

Guided tours vary from standard bus excursions to specialty tours on foot or in a van. Here's a sampling: **Gray Line** (934.1222) runs daily bus tours from Dorchester Square, with pickups at major hotels. They include stops at several main attractions and are great for a general overview of the city. Walking tours are also available. **Tours Imperial** (871.4733) offers guided tours on London-style double-decker buses. **Heritage Montreal** (286.2662) organizes walks around the neighborhoods of Montreal on weekends from June to September. Run by a preservationist group, the tours emphasize architecture and history.

VISITOR INFORMATION

Tourisme Montréal is the city's official tourist office. The telephone is 844.5400; fax is 844.5757. On the Web, visit www.tourisme-montreal.org.

The *Official Tourist Guide* is a trove of valuable information (including maps), and it's free. Pick it up first thing from **Infotouriste**, 1001 Dorchester Square (873.2015), or call toll-free (800/363.7777) and have it mailed to you before your trip.

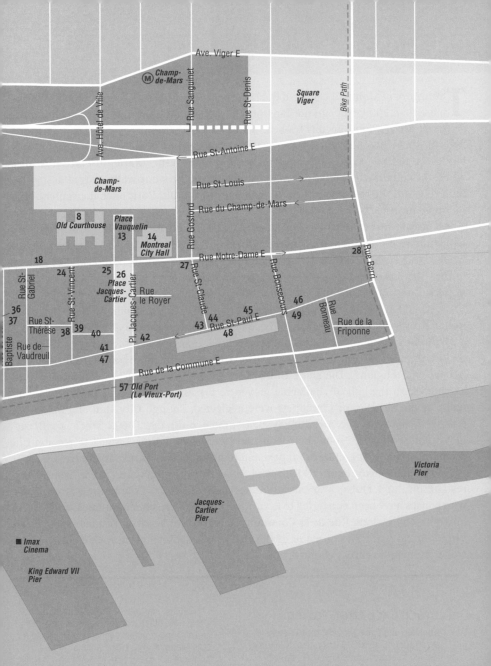

Ave. Viger E

M Champ-de-Mars

Square Viger

Ave. Hôtel-de-Ville

Rue Sanguinet

Rue St-Denis

Bike Path

Rue St-Antoine E

Champ-de-Mars

Rue St-Louis

Rue du Champ-de-Mars

Rue Gosford

8
Old Courthouse

Place Vauquelin

13

14
Montreal City Hall

Rue Notre-Dame E

28

Rue Berri

18

27

Rue St-Claude

24

25

26
Place Jacques-Cartier

Rue le Royer

Rue Bonsecours

Rue St-Gabriel

Rue St-Vincent

Pl. Jacques-Cartier

46

45

49

Rue Bonneau

36

37

Rue St-Thérèse

38 **39**

40

43 **44**

Rue St-Paul E

48

Rue de la Friponne

Baptiste

Rue de Vaudreuil

41

47

42

Rue de la Commune E

57 Old Port
(Le Vieux-Port)

Victoria Pier

Jacques-Cartier Pier

■ Imax Cinema

King Edward VII Pier

St. Lawrence River

OLD MONTREAL

The history of Montreal begins in Old Montreal, where the first settlers put down roots more than 350 years ago not far from the site of an old Iroquois settlement on the slopes of **Mont-Royal**. In this 95-acre historic quarter, Montreal's past can be traced from the spot where 53 French pioneers, led by Paul de Chomedey, Sieur de Maisonneuve, landed in 1642 and christened their newfound home **Ville-Marie**, to **Place d'Armes**, where the colonists battled the Iroquois, to the site of the stone walls, now almost gone, built to guard the settlement in 1716, and back to the **Old Port**, once the center of the lucrative fur trade.

Montreal's first colonists were sponsored by **La Société de Notre-Dame de Montréal**, a missionary group intent on converting Canada's native residents to Christianity. But when France realized the fur-trading potential of the colony, which stood at the gateway to the Great Lakes and the continent's interior, missionary zeal took a backseat to economics. Constant skirmishes with the Iroquois hobbled the settlement's progress until 1701, when France signed a peace treaty with the Five Nations Indians. So began a period of prosperity that saw Montreal become the business capital of New France.

With the signing of the Treaty of Paris in 1763, France ceded the territory of Quebec to Britain, and Old Montreal suddenly overflowed with immigrants from Scotland, Ireland, and England. The stone fortifications were torn down to enable the city to expand. Soon the hub of commerce moved to present-day downtown Montreal, and many of the old quarter's buildings were neglected. Though **City Hall** and the courts remained, much of the area slowly deteriorated until the 1960s, when a citizens' movement led to the establishment of the Viger Commission, formed to reclaim Old Montreal's forgotten architectural past and to promote and protect its future.

Today, many of the quarter's 18th- and 19th-century buildings are home to museums, restaurants, and clubs, and busy outdoor cafés line the cobblestone streets. Old warehouses have been converted to luxurious, ultramodern condominiums, and the Old Port, stretching along **Rue de la Commune**, bustles with activity. Summer and winter, Old Montreal is the site of many of the city's festivals, including the Fête des Neiges winter carnival in early February.

---

1 STOCK EXCHANGE TOWER

Opening onto Place Victoria, this 47-story skyscraper, built in 1964, is one of Canada's few reinforced concrete high-rises, though most visitors are more interested in the glass sculpture that graces the travertine lobby. The artificial stalactite plunges three stories from the ground floor toward the Metro level and is made of 3,000 glass elements, each hand-blown in Murano, Italy. The **Montreal Stock Exchange**, Canada's oldest, was founded in 1874 and occupies the fourth floor of the building. At the time of its move here some 30 years ago, it was the first stock exchange to use an electronic quotation board to cover trading. If you would like to follow the action on the floor, 1-hour weekday tours (admission charged) are given at 9:30AM and 1:30PM. For reservations, call 871.2424. A number of boutiques and other specialty stores, as well as a post office, occupy the lower and Metro levels, and a tunnel connects the building to the Metro. ♦ 800 Place Victoria (at Rue Université). 875.5170

2 HOTEL INTER-CONTINENTAL MONTREAL

$$$$ This 26-story castle with a conical turret is Old Montreal's only major hotel. Opened in 1991 as the latest property in the luxury chain, it adds a whimsical touch to the commercial district and provides posh comfort throughout its 357 rooms (including 22 suites), which are decorated in soft green, cream, and sienna. An executive business center offers secretarial and translation services and a private lounge, and the 10th-floor health club offers a full-service gym with

sauna, steambath, massage room, and lap pool opening onto a terrace garden. ♦ 360 Rue St-Antoine (between Rues St-Pierre and McGill). 987.9900, 800/361.3600; fax 847.8550

Within the Hotel Inter-Continental Montreal:

CHEZ PLUME

★$ This bistro-style room facing Rue St-Jacques offers a fast lunch or dinner of sandwiches, stews, salads, or quiche, with draft beer and wine by the glass. To reach the restaurant, just stroll across the **World Trade Center**'s atrium bridge to the restored **Nordheimer Building**. The 3-foot walls here are actually 18th-century basement foundations, unearthed for the complex. ♦ Continental ♦ M-F Lunch and dinner. 987.9900

3 PLACE VICTORIA

Ⓟ Formerly a hay market, this is now a beautifully landscaped public square that serves as the frontage for the **Stock Exchange Towers**. The square, which stretches across Rue St-Antoine, was named in 1860 both for Queen Victoria and to commemorate that year's inauguration of **Victoria Bridge**, the first to span the St. Lawrence. Marshall Wood's bronze statue of the queen on the northern side of the square was erected in 1872. Now, in true dual-culture style, this monument to the British ruler watches over a Metro entrance donated to Montreal by the City of Paris in 1966. It dates to 1900 and is in the elaborate, entwining *nouille*, or "noodle," style. The southern side of the square was laid out in 1964 and has been continually under construction or repair since 1986. When the fountain is working, its spraying jets and surrounding beds of petunias and geraniums are a welcome oasis on a hot day. ♦ Bounded by Rues McGill and Université and by Rue St-Jacques and Ave Viger

4 WORLD TRADE CENTER

Rue St-Jacques, once the financial heart of Canada and called St. James Street, has needed a boost for decades, ever since many of its financial institutions left for downtown high-rises or Toronto. This international trade complex was built in 1992 to revitalize the old financial district. It combines state-of-the-art engineering with 19th-century façades both to preserve Old Montreal's character and to attract business back to the area. The soaring, sunlit atrium (which bridges Fortifications Lane, site of the city's old stone walls) has an airy lobby and a peaceful pool presided over by a statue entitled *Amphitrite* (the Greek goddess of the sea). Encircling this space is a 500,000-square-foot multipurpose complex

planned to provide luxurious quarters for government, finance, and commerce. The **Hotel Inter-Continental** connects with the center via the atrium, and the restored **Nordheimer Building**, a former music hall where Sarah Bernhardt performed in 1880, has been incorporated into the complex. A smaller number of boutiques and restaurants border the atrium on the ground level. Daily, 7AM-7PM. 747 Square-Victoria. 982.9888 ♦ Bounded by Rues St-Pierre and McGill and by Rues St-Jacques and St-Antoine W

5 HOTEL ST. JAMES

$$$$ Was that Catherine Zeta-Jones darting into the elevator? (The door of which, by the way, comes from the original Waldorf-Astoria.) Very possibly, but the discreet staff at Montreal's most unabashedly luxurious hotel, in the former Merchant's Bank building, neither confirm nor deny the rumors of their illustrious guests in residence. But if it is true that the Rolling Stones once reserved the entire hotel for themselves, who can fault them? None of the 61 rooms and suites are exactly alike, but each is sumptuously decorated with European antiques, faithful reproductions, and original works of art. Thoughtful touches include Denon vertical-loading CD players and bedside command-center phones from which you can check the temperature inside or out, dim the lights, or turn on your plasma TV screen. Bath amenities are by Penhaglion's and Hermès, and turndown service comes with chocolates and a complimentary bottle of chilled Fiji water. With such extreme attention to detail—and levels of service to match—it's no wonder many hotel guests need nudging to actually leave the building. ♦ 55 Rue St-Jacques (at Rue St-Pierre), 841.3111, 866/841.3111; fax 841.1232

6 EGGSPECTATION

★$ There is something particularly appealing about the Old Montreal location of this Canadian breakfast chain, which like the others features myriad egg and omelette dishes as well as waffles, sandwiches, and hamburgers. If at first glance the eggcentric menu strikes you as American, you'll be in for a few surprises: an example is the banana pancakes, which come with the fruit sliced on top of, rather than cooked into, the flapjacks, Perhaps you'd be better off with a muffin "eggsplosion." Whatever you choose, portions tend to be not simply big, but huge, so come hungry. There's also an attractive range of fruit juices and fresh fruit smoothies. ♦ Canadian ♦ Daily, lunch and dinner. 201 Rue St-Jacques W (at Rue St-François-Xavier). 282.0019

Restaurants/Clubs: Red | Hotels: Purple | Shops: Orange | Outdoors/Parks: Green | Sights/Culture: Blue

THE BEST

Sophie Desbiens

Development Coordinator, Montreal International Jazz Festival/Festival Montréal en Lumière/FrancoFolies de Montréal

What makes Montreal my favorite city is its people. Montrealers are what make the city so warm, welcoming, and comfortable. People smile and are helpful, but mostly there is an open-mindedness to the whole city that shows in every aspect, especially in its culture. There is a sense of discovery about every activity the Montrealer undertakes.

My favorite time in the city is the summer. I have been a Montrealer for the past 12 years and attend the Montreal International Jazz Festival every summer. In a city known for its festivals, this one is undoubtedly the best, mostly because you can make discoveries every day. The programming is so eclectic that everyone finds something to fit their tastes. I love the atmosphere it gives to the whole city and wouldn't miss it for the world.

HÔTEL   PLACE   D'ARMES

7   HÔTEL PLACE D'ARMES

$$$ The 48 rooms and suites in this renovated 1870 building opposite **Notre-Dame Basilica** are clean and modern, but small, awkwardly shaped lobby, ill-maintained bathroom fixtures, and thinning towels can take the ginger out of a sojourn here. Street noise can also be problematic, especially on weekends, and (at least at press time) disorganized service can border on the intrusive. There is an in-house restaurant, **Aix**. ◆ 701 Côté de la Place-d'Armes (at Rues St-Urbain and St-Jacques). 842.1887, 888/450.1887; fax 842.6469

8   LUCIEN SAULNIER BUILDING (OLD COURTHOUSE)

For some 100 years, civil cases were heard in this Greek Revival–style courthouse built in 1856 by architects **John Ostell** and **Henri-Maurice Perreault**. The building's impressive dome, neoclassical columns, and portico are all that remain, as courtrooms and chambers have been converted into a warren of municipal offices for City Hall, next door. However, the building did have a few glamorous years as headquarters of the **Olympic Organizing Committee** for the **1976 Montreal Summer Games**. ◆ M-F. 155 Rue Notre-Dame E (at Rue St-Vincent)

9   ROYAL BANK OF CANADA

Designed in 1926 by New York architects **York & Sawyer**, this impressive building with Art Deco brass doors formerly housed the bank's head office. The interior is Renaissance Italian, with a richly decorated central dome and vaulted ceiling. This branch operates a foreign exchange counter. ◆ 360 Rue St-Jacques (at Rue St-Pierre)

10   MOLSON BANK

Considered the oldest bank building on the street (1866), this edifice was built for the wealthy brewing family of the same name, whose international businesses still operate out of Montreal. The handsome white marble interior provides an attractive backdrop for the Spanish mahogany woodwork and furnishings. It's now an international business center. ◆ 288 Rue St-Jacques (at Rue St-Pierre)

11   5 HOTEL XIX SIÈCLE

$$ Located in a renovated Second Empire–style building, this hotel offers good value in a neighborhood of pricey lodgings. Rooms are elegantly appointed, if not particularly fancy, and most have large windows and tall ceilings. You won't find amenities such as a minibar or room service, but there are in-room CD players, and a generous continental breakfast is served in a pleasant room near the lobby. ◆ 262 Rue St-Jacques W (at Rue St-Jean). 282.0019. www.hotelxixsiecle.com

12   PLACE D'ARMES

Begin at this square for an excellent overview of the two hearts of Old Montreal—the historic and the modern. Commanding the top of a steep rise between Rues St-Antoine and Notre-Dame, the area was for many years considered the "upper" town, as the stone fortifications began just a few yards away. At the square's center is **Maisonneuve Monument**, which commemorates the many battles the French and Iroquois fought around this site. It was here in 1644 that founding father Maisonneuve was wounded and an Iroquois chief was killed. The event is chronicled in a plaque on the wall of the building at **105 Rue St-Jacques**. If a tour of the area in a horse-drawn carriage appeals to you, you'll find carriages waiting on the square's south side, facing **Notre-Dame Basilica**, in all but the very worst weather and deep winter. Tours last between 30 minutes and 2 hours. ◆ Bounded by Côté de la Place-d'Armes and Rue de la Place d'Armes and by Rues Notre-Dame W and St-Jacques

On Place d'Armes:

MAISONNEUVE MONUMENT

Unveiled in 1895, this monument-fountain was created by sculptor Philippe Hébert to commemorate the 250th anniversary of the city. The figure of Maisonneuve holding aloft a banner tops the pedestal, and at the base stand representations of Jeanne Mance, founder of the colony's first hospital, caring for an Iroquois child; Major Lambert Closse, defender of the colony, and his dog Pilote, who warned settlers of a crucial Iroquois attack; colonist Charles Le Moyne; and an Iroquois warrior.

BANK OF MONTREAL

Neoclassical columns grace the portico of the bank, a landmark on Côté de la Place-d'Armes since 1847. The original domed building was designed as the bank's headquarters by **J. Wells**; in 1905, the New York architectural firm **McKim, Mead & White** added on to the building and redesigned the interior. The immense lobby is embraced by 32 Corinthian columns of green syenite topped by gold-plated bronze capitals. Interested visitors should stop in at the tiny museum just off the main hall, where they can peruse such oddities as a check written on beaver pelt, a piggy bank collection, and antique currency. ♦ Museum: M-F, 10AM-noon, 1PM-4PM. Bank: M-F. 129 Rue St-Jacques (at Côté de la Place-d'Armes). Museum: 877.6892. Bank: 877.7373

PREVOYANCE BUILDING

Formerly the **Aldred Building**, this skyscraper, designed in Art Deco style by **Barott & Blackader** in 1930, bears a faint resemblance to the Empire State Building in New York City. ♦ 501-507 Place d'Armes (at Rue Notre-Dame)

NEW YORK LIFE COMPANY BUILDING

That's the name on the wall plaque, though New York Life no longer exists. This neo-Roman Scottish sandstone edifice next door to the **Prevoyance** now houses a variety of businesses. Montreal's first skyscraper, the building was erected in 1887. ♦ 511 Place d'Armes (at Rue St-Jacques)

13 PLACE VAUQUELIN

Stretching between the **Old Courthouse** and **City Hall**, this expansive square was originally a fiefdom awarded to Maisonneuve's right-hand man, Lambert Closse, in 1658. It became a public square 200 years later and is now one of the loveliest in the city, with its fountain and sweeping view of the recently landscaped **Champ-de-Mars**. The latter was a military parade ground between 1814 and 1924, but it was paved over for a parking lot. Now restored to its original grassy state, it resembles a 19th-century promenade. During excavation, parts of the old stone fortifications were found and left uncovered, delineating the boundaries of the former walled city. The site is named for Lieutenant Jean Vauquelin, the naval defender of New France, whose memory is also commemorated by a statue at the northern end of the square. The sculpture, by artist Eugene Benet, recently had a face-lift and looks much as it did when it was unveiled in 1930. Convenient to many Old Montreal landmarks, the square is the main rendezvous for guided walking tours of the area. ♦ Rue Notre-Dame E (across from Place Jacques-Cartier)

14 MONTREAL CITY HALL

This Second Empire building dominates Place Vauquelin and Place Jacques-Cartier with its elaborate façade, mansards, turrets, and bell tower. The pillared front balcony on the third story is the famous perch where General Charles de Gaulle, then president of France, made his controversial pronouncement *"Vive le Québec libre"* (Long live a free Quebec) on an official visit during Canada's centennial celebrations.

The first city hall was designed in 1876 by **Henri-Maurice Perreault** and **Alexander Cowper Hutchison** on the site of Jesuit gardens. After fire gutted the structure in 1922, architect **J. Omer Marchand** added the upper story and the copper roof. The current structure reopened in 1929, and there were no further renovations until Mayor Jean Dore, elected in 1986 but no longer in office, ordered a multimillion-dollar restoration to bring the building up to code. Dore encouraged free public exhibitions in the columned marble and travertine **Hall of Honour**. Guarding the hall entrance are the handsome sculptures *Woman with a Pail* and *Sower* by Alfred Laliberté, a popular Quebec artist who died in 1953.

Greeting a French person from Montreal can be confusing for visitors. The customary way to greet friends in Montreal is to kiss them on both cheeks, starting with the right. Canadians in other provinces tend to keep a distance of about 3 feet and simply shake hands.

Restaurants/Clubs: Red | Hotels: Purple | Shops: Orange | Outdoors/Parks: Green | Sights/Culture: Blue

JusteChock-Full of Fêtes

Montrealers like nothing better than showing off their city to visitors, a pastime dating back to the **1967 World's Fair** and the **1976 Summer Olympics**. Today they indulge that civic pride—along with their own penchant for the pleasures of urban street life—by holding a wealth of indoor and outdoor festivals between early February and August.

February

You can't hide from winter, so you might as well enjoy it. Each year, starting on the first weekend in February, the 3-week **Fête des Neiges** offers snow-castle building, ice sculpture contests, family skating parties, and more. Events are staged in central locations on **Notre-Dame** and **Ste-Hélène Islands** and in the city's **Old Port**. For information, call 514/872.6093.

The **Festival Montréal en Lumière** is a culinary festival that takes place over the course of three weekends in February.

May–June

Since 1989, the **Festival de Théâtre des Amériques** has been bringing some of the best American and European theater companies to town with provocative and innovative new drama. Performances run during the last week of May and first week of June at various venues downtown. For information, call 514/842.0704.

In mid-June, the glamour and excitement of Formula One racing takes over the city with the kickoff of the **Grand Prix Molson du Canada**. Quebecers are passionate about motor sports, and this event—the only Canadian stop on the international circuit—is an occasion to commemorate a major folk hero: Formula One driver Gilles Villeneuve, who died while racing in Italy in 1982. The **Grand Prix** is held on a course named in his honor on Notre-Dame Island. For information, call 514/392.0000.

June–July

During the **International Fireworks Competition**, gunpowder artists from around the world light up the sky over **La Ronde** amusement park, creating a dazzling extravaganza for spectators in the Old Port area and beyond. The festival usually takes place Wednesday and Saturday evenings between around 20 June and the end of July. For information, call 514/790.1245 or visit www.montrealfeux.com.

The **Festival International de Jazz de Montréal** is considered one of the world's best. For 10 days in late June to early July, the likes of the Shirley Horn Trio,

Ornette Coleman, and Montreal's own Oscar Peterson perform more than 500 concerts, 350 of which are staged outdoors free of charge. If you don't care for jazz, don't despair: Recent festivals have also included the likes of Stereolab, Manu Chao, and Prince. Yet what really sets this festival apart is the spontaneous street jam sessions that spring up throughout the city's Latin Quarter along Rue St-Denis (between Rue Ste-Catherine and Rue Rachel), featuring talent from Pat Metheny to virtuoso unknowns. For information, call 515/871.1881 or 888/515.0515.

Buster Keaton, Dan Aykroyd, Rick Moranis (of *Honey, I Shrunk the Kids*)—without question, Canada has turned out some of this century's funniest comedians. So it's only natural that the international **Just for Laughs/Juste Pour Rire Festival** has caught on as a prime showcase for laugh-masters from all over the world. For 1 week in mid-July, more than 500 artists, from street jugglers to top comics like the US's Jon Stewart, pack 'em in and keep 'em howling at various venues on Rue St-Denis. For information, call 514/845.3155.

The lyrics may be in French, but the language of music is universal, and that's what makes **Les FrancoFolies de Montréal** such a uniquely enjoyable festival. Beginning the last Thursday in July and continuing for 10 days thereafter, some of the best-known names in French music as well as rising stars from a dozen countries give more than 200 concerts, 150 of which are staged outdoors free of charge (many in and around the Place des Arts). In 2001 notable performers included Juliette Gréco, Arthur H., and Vanessa Paradis. For information, call 514/876.8989 or visit www.francofolies.com.

August

Les Fêtes Gourmandes Internationales de Montréal lets your palate travel the globe without leaving the confines of Notre-Dame Island. This immense outdoor bazaar, held midmonth, features cuisine from such far-flung areas as the West African republic of Togo, along with exotic Asian and European treats. For information, call 514/861.8241.

One of the major showcases for artistic new cinema—yet no less festive than its Hollywood-style counterpart in Toronto—the **Montreal World Film Festival** is the only competitive film festival in North America that's recognized by the prestigious International Federation of Film Producers Association, an influential organ for movie marketing and distribution. At any of 13 theaters throughout the month, audiences can preview films months before their general release and sometimes hear from the stars and directors themselves. For information, call 514/848.3883.

A plaque on the southwest corner of the building honors Montreal's first mayor, Jacques Viger, who took office in 1833. The journalist, historian, and archivist was a founding father of both the Quebec nationalist organization Société St-Jean Baptiste and the Montreal Historical Society. Viger also designed the coat of arms, still in use today, and authored Montreal's motto, "Concordia Salus," or "Salvation through Concord." Guided tours are available on request. ♦ Free. M-F. 275 Rue Notre-Dame E (at Place Jacques-Cartier). 872.3355

15 CHEZ DELMO

★★★★$$$$ Locals who enjoy good food and company have made this restaurant an Old Montreal tradition for 90 years. Two marble-and-wood counters stretch the length of the front room, where judges and journalists sit side by side with regular folk. Congenial host Roland Perisset, in a crisp white jacket, patrols every lunch hour, making sure his guests are happy and occasionally stopping to chat. The only time they're not happy is when the wait for a seat at the counters is long. (It's best to arrive before noon or around 1:45PM.) Menus feature fresh halibut, sole, lobster, oysters, mussels, and shrimp. Try the curried shrimp to warm up on a cold day. The back dining room, a cozy spot with charming landscape paintings enhancing the yellow-papered walls, is reserved for quieter lunches and evening suppers. ♦ French/seafood ♦ M-Sa, lunch and dinner; closed mid-July. Reservations recommended for dinner. 211-215 Rue Notre-Dame W (between Rues St-François-Xavier and St-Jean). 849.4061

16 MCDONALD'S

★$ This is the only one in the franchise built on a landmark site—the former homestead of Antoine Laumet de Lamothe, Sieur de Cadillac, founder of Detroit and Governor of Louisiana, according to the plaque on the south wall. ♦ Fast food ♦ Daily, breakfast, lunch, and dinner. 1 Rue Notre-Dame W (at Blvd St-Laurent). 285.8720

17 PALAIS DE JUSTICE (COURTHOUSE)

When it was built in 1971, this stark gray and brown provincial courthouse was not considered an aesthetic addition to Old Montreal. But now that the neighborhood has learned to live in the shadow of the 18-story high-rise, many feel it adds contrast to the surrounding graystone buildings. Some 220 provincial judges hear both civil and criminal cases in the courthouse, an unusual situation occasioned by Quebec's continued adherence

to the Napoleonic Civil Code. Marriages are also performed here, not at City Hall. There's a Viennese-style café on the fifth floor. ♦ M-F. 1 Rue Notre-Dame E (at Blvd St-Laurent). 393.2721

18 MARGUERITE DE BOURGEOYS SQUARE

Ⓟ The lawn and fountain dedicated to Ste-Marguerite de Bourgeoys, who founded the congregation of Notre-Dame and was the colony's first teacher, separate the new courthouse from the old one. The bronze sculpture-fountain unveiled in 1988 portrays Marguerite de Bourgeoys helping two children over stepping-stones across the basin of the fountain. ♦ Rue Notre-Dame E (between Place Vauquelin and Blvd St-Laurent)

19 TRIPP'S

Designer clothes at bargain prices are the mainstay of this discount boutique. You'll find such labels as Ralph Lauren and Anne Klein mixed in with a jumble of less illustrious tags on the racks, so keep a keen eye. ♦ M-W; Th, 10AM-8PM; F, 10AM-sundown. 389 Rue Notre-Dame W (at Rue McGill). 871.8895

20 AU CEPAGE

★★$$ The bar here is a favorite with journalists from the nearby Gazette, while the basement restaurant is popular with businesspeople and with theatergoers before and after performances at the Centaur Theater down the street. The décor varies—the front room is Art Deco, whereas the spacious back room is contemporary, with a highly polished floor and bright prints on the walls. In summer, a walled terrace makes for another relaxing spot. Owner Steve Morse cheerfully oversees the noontime rush, happy hour, candlelit evenings, and Sunday brunch. The avocado stuffed with shrimp is a good choice for starters, and the rack of lamb Provençale (roasted with a light touch of garlic) is among the fine dinner selections. ♦ Continental ♦ M, lunch; Tu-F, lunch and dinner. 482 Rue St-François-Xavier (at Rue Notre-Dame W). 845.5436

20 CENTAUR THEATER COMPANY

Montreal's only English-language theater company was founded in 1968 by Maurice Podbrey, its present director. Performances are staged in the former stock exchange building, designed in the early 1900s by American architect George B. Post, whose New York Stock Exchange was under construction at the same time. French-language plays, dance productions, and

---

Restaurants/Clubs: **Red** | Hotels: **Purple** | Shops: **Orange** | Outdoors/Parks: **Green** | Sights/Culture: **Blue**

lectures are also featured here. ◆ Box office: M, noon-5PM; Tu-Sa, noon-8:30PM; Su, noon-7PM. 212 Rue Notre-Dame W (southwest corner of Rue St-François-Xavier). Box office: 288.3161

21 SULPICIAN SEMINARY

This rough-fieldstone building is Montreal's oldest, dating back to 1685, when it was both a residence for the Sulpicians who governed the island of Montreal and the administrative center of the colony. The seminary is now used as a private retirement home for the religious community, so visitors are not permitted, but you can still have a good look at it through the wrought-iron grille at the tiny front garden. The bell tower, symmetrical gabled windows, and curbed pediment are all typical of 17th-century Quebec architecture, and the outdoor clock (1710) over the main entrance is reputedly the oldest in North America. Also visible is the order's coat of arms on the gate leading to the seminary. ◆ 130 Rue Notre-Dame W (between Rues St-Sulpice and St-François-Xavier)

22 LA SOROSA

★$ Wicker doll carriages, wooden sleighs, dolls, toys, and other treasures from Grandma's attic decorate the broad ceiling beams and exposed brick walls of this restaurant. But there's nothing old-fashioned about the menu, which lists gourmet pizzas, several kinds of pasta, and generous salads that overflow their attractive seashell platters. Pizzas are kept hot at the table atop pedestals with chafing dishes. ◆ Italian ◆ Daily, lunch and dinner. 56 Rue Notre-Dame W (between Blvd St-Laurent and Rue St-Sulpice). 844.8595

23 DESMARAIS & ROBITAILLE

Though this boutique is one of the few places where local priests can purchase vestments and church ornaments, the beautifully worked crèches, local handcrafts, religious books, and hand-painted ceramics and greeting cards bring in customers beyond the religious community. ◆ M-Sa (Labor Day-23 June); M-Su (24 June-Labor Day). 60 Rue Notre-Dame W (between Blvd St-Laurent and Rue St-Sulpice). 845.3194

Seventy-five percent of Internet communications in North America travel over transmission equipment manufactured in Montreal.

The first non-Catholic place of worship in Montreal was the Spanish and Portuguese Synagogue now on Rue St-Kevin, founded in 1768.

24 ERNEST CORMIER BUILDING

Built in 1926 on the south side of Rue Notre-Dame, this courthouse was designed by Montreal architect **Ernest Cormier**, best known for his bronze doors at the United Nations. Cormier blended the neoclassical style used in the colonnaded portico with Art Deco touches, as seen in the lamp stands at the imposing copper doors. The building is now the property of the Quebec Ministry of Cultural Affairs and home to the **Music Conservatory**. Free cultural exhibitions and student concerts are often held in the rotunda. ◆ M-F. 100 Rue Notre-Dame E (between Rues St-Vincent and St-Gabriel)

25 TOURIST INFORMATION KIOSK

Housed in a restored building erected in 1803 and once known as the **Silver Dollar Saloon** for the 350 American silver dollars embedded in the floor, this tourist office gives out advice and free brochures and maps. A computerized reservations system is also available. ◆ Daily. 174 Rue Notre-Dame E (at Place Jacques-Cartier). 873.2015

26 PLACE JACQUES-CARTIER

Now a tourism hub, this square honoring the city's first visitor began as a marquis's garden, then became a marketplace in 1804 that teemed with life throughout the 19th century. For most of the 20th century, it has been a popular meeting place, especially among those who live or work in this neighborhood of limestone commercial buildings interspersed with fieldstone houses. The hustle of the market has been replaced by street performers and tourists exploring restaurants and boutiques on either side of the central mall. A flower market beneath **Nelson's Column** adds to the colorful atmosphere. ◆ Between Rues St-Paul E and Notre-Dame E

On Place Jacques-Cartier:

NELSON'S COLUMN

The figure of British naval admiral Lord Horatio Nelson gazes over Rue Notre-Dame atop the city's oldest monument, designed by Robert Mitchell. Erected in 1809 to commemorate the admiral's victory at Trafalgar, it's the world's oldest column honoring Nelson. The sculpture atop the Tuscan column is a fiberglass reproduction of the original, which was repeatedly vandalized in the 1970s. Bas-reliefs of Nelson's victories at Aboukir and Copenhagen encircle the base.

CARTIER HOUSE

★$$ A fine example of the work of 19th-century Montreal stonemason Amable Amyot, this typical Quebec house is now a restaurant. Every summer the backyard is transformed into one of the most delightful spots on Place Jacques-Cartier, **Le Jardin du Nelson**, a courtyard dining room in the shade of a spreading chestnut tree. Alfresco diners are serenaded by a chamber orchestra from the nearby **Music Conservatory**. Crepes, in some 50 combinations, are the specialty for both the main course and dessert. ♦ Continental ♦ Daily, lunch and dinner. 407 Place Jacques-Cartier (at Rue St-Paul E). 861.5731

LE FRIPON

★★$$$ A great place to watch the world go by, this bistro bar and outdoor café features hearty *croques monsieur*—toasted ham sandwiches with melted cheese—in summer. The main dining room offers a broad range of classic French cuisine, with a nod to fresh trout and lobster, mussels in season, and the catch of the day. ♦ French ♦ Daily, lunch and dinner in summer; W-Su, lunch and dinner in winter. 436 Place Jacques-Cartier (between Rues St-Paul E and Notre-Dame E). 861.1386

LA MAREE

★★★★$$$$ Located in the **Del Vecchio House**, where Pierre Del Vecchio operated a bar during the early 19th century, this elegant restaurant offers a memorable dining experience and gives its patrons a real sense of history. As part of the Viger Commission's plan to revitalize Old Montreal, **Canadian Industries Ltd.** painstakingly restored the rubble masonry building to its original 1807 condition, including the Louis XIII colonial décor, exposed stone walls, and deep-set casements. The seafood—much of it flown in daily from France—is considered among the best in Montreal, shining in such dishes as *homard brunetière* (mushrooms and slices of lobster served in the shell), braised fillet of salmon, and trout stuffed with crabmeat. The wines and such desserts as strawberries in Grand Marnier complement the gourmet experience. ♦ French ♦ M-F, lunch and dinner; Sa-Su, dinner. Reservations recommended. 404 Place Jacques-Cartier (at Rue St-Amable). 861.9794

27 CHÂTEAU RAMEZAY MUSEUM

Montreal Governor Claude de Ramezay had this château built for his growing family of 16 children in 1705, commissioning one of the best architects of the era, master mason **Pierre Couturier**, to design a Norman-style country home with a rounded tower. The château became a social mecca at the height of the French regime. After Quebec passed into British hands in 1763, it served as a residence for English governors of Canada; and in 1775, when American revolutionaries captured Montreal, it was used as military headquarters by generals Benedict Arnold and Richard

Montgomery and, later that year, by Benjamin Franklin. Various governmental and civic activities were carried out in the house until 1895, when the city of Montreal acquired the property for the Antiquarian and Numismatic Society and turned it into a museum. Restored closely to period, the furnished rooms display such items as a Louis XIII-style clerk's table, a provincial pine cradle, a candle mold and snuffer from 1830, costumes, and portraits. The basement kitchen shows what the 18th-century cook had to contend with, whereas the upstairs ballroom (not original to the house) gives an idea of how the local 19th-century bourgeoisie entertained. There are also exhibits of native art and life. ♦ Admission. 1 June-30 Sept, daily, 10AM-6PM; 1 Oct-31 May, Tu-Su, 10AM-4:30PM. 280 Rue Notre-Dame E (at Rue St-Claude). 861.3708

28 SIR GEORGE-ETIENNE CARTIER HOUSE

Off the beaten path, east along Notre-Dame, this former home is a worth a detour. Sir George-Etienne Cartier, a Quebec statesman, helped to negotiate the Canadian Confederation while living in the semidetached house between 1848 and 1871. The second floor features audiovisual displays that describe pre-Confederation Canada. Upstairs, many of the rooms have been furnished to period, and visitors can push a button on the guardrail to hear the simulated voice of a 19th-century maid filling them in on Cartier family life. A tour of the bedroom, salon, and dining room proves that Victorian clutter—heavy draperies, busy floral rugs, and crowded mantelpieces—was as popular in the British colony as it was at home. A National Historic Park property, the museum is run by Canadian Heritage. ♦ Admission. Daily, 10AM-6PM. 458 Rue Notre-Dame E (at Rue Berri). 283.2282

29 LUNA D'ORO

$ This small but bright eatery is the perfect place for a quick pick-me-up, whether it's a gourmet panini sandwich (try the tuna or roasted red peppers and goat cheese) or any of the freshly made pastas. ♦ Italian ♦ M-F, breakfast and lunch. 469 Rue St-François-Xavier (between Rues de l'Hôpital and Notre-Dame W). 288.1999

Restaurants/Clubs: Red | Hotels: Purple | Shops: Orange | Outdoors/Parks: Green | Sights/Culture: Blue

30 NOTRE-DAME BASILICA

Ville-Marie's first real parish church was **Notre-Dame**, built in 1627 to the specifications of the religious order that administered the colony's affairs. Today's imposing neo-Gothic structure, constructed in 1829, replaced the original but on a much grander scale. Protestant architect **James O'Donnell**, who designed the basilica, was so taken with the project that he converted to Catholicism and at his death was buried in the church basement (epistle side).

Soaring 227 feet over Place d'Armes are the basilica's twin towers **Temperance** and **Perseverance**, which were added in 1842. The **Gros Bourdon Jean-Baptiste**, a 10.9-ton bell that can be heard 15 miles away, is housed in the western tower. Architect **John Ostell** added the presbytery around 1850, and further improvements were made to the interior between 1870 and 1929, resulting in the finely sculpted woodwork, the rose windows in the ceiling, the gilded stars shining down from the vaulted blue ceiling, and the 14 French stained-glass windows that trace the history of Ville-Marie. The organ, once the most powerful in North America, has 5,772 pipes. With seating capacity for 5,000 people, the church frequently hosts concerts, such as the Mozart Plus Festival every summer. **PBS** viewers will recognize the church from the traditional Luciano Pavarotti Christmas Concert filmed here.

In 1978, a fire leveled the **Sacred Heart Chapel** (sometimes called simply the **Wedding Chapel**) at the back of the basilica, but it was quickly reconstructed. When it reopened to the public, many were jarred by the modern additions, such as the reredos: some 32 bronze panels created by Quebec artist Charles Daudelin. A small museum displays various religious artifacts, paintings, and vestments. ♦ Nominal admission to museum; basilica is free. Museum: Sa-Su. Basilica: daily, 7AM-6PM, Labor Day-24 June: daily, 7AM-8PM, 25 June-Labor Day. Guided tours: daily. 116 Rue Notre-Dame W (between Rues St-Sulpice and St-François-Xavier). Basilica and museum: 842.2925

31 AUBERGE BONAPARTE

$$ This small hotel in a quiet street features 31 spacious, soundproofed, and reasonably priced rooms. The décor features polished wood floors, bronze lamps, and large French dormer windows. When making a reservation—which is highly advisable—you might want to request a top-floor room with private terrace. A generous breakfast, served in a restaurant on the premises, is included in all room rates. As an added plus, the staff is very friendly. ♦ 447 Rue St-François-Xavier (between Rues de l'Hôpital and Notre-Dame W). 844.1448

32 BORIS BISTRO

★★★$$ One of the best dining bets in Old Montreal is this very relaxed, new-fashioned restaurant, which handsome owner Jean-Marc Lebeau named after his beloved Labrador. The dining area is a pleasant, upbeat blend of stained wood and varnished or painted concrete, with contemporary artwork by Montreal artist Corno. In any season, the kitchen, overseen by Montreal chef Jason Duffy, turns out a variety of succulent and refreshingly priced bistro dishes, such as an appetizer of caponata and warm goat cheese or *pommes frites* with Boris's zesty mayonnaise, or entrées of lacquered chicken salad and braised fennel, three-deck duck sandwich with salad, and grilled trout with caramelized walnuts on a bed of fresh baby spinach. All pastries are made on the premises and include the likes of iced chocolate and pistachio fondant with butterscotch cream and lime tart. Even beverages shine here, from the ample selection of inexpensive wines by the glass to Boréale blond beer with sparkling apple juice (a house specialty) and Earl Grey iced tea, home-brewed with lemon and a touch of sugar. In summer the wide terrace, separated from the street by a formidable old stone façade, is a highly prized chill-out zone. ♦ French/contemporary ♦ June-Aug, daily, lunch and dinner; Sept-May, Tu-Sa, lunch and dinner, and M, lunch. Reservations recommended. 465 Rue McGill (between Rues le Moyne and des Récollets). 848.9575

33 HOTEL GAULT

$$$$ If you ever wondered what it was like to live in a hip Soho loft, look no further. A considerate and highly qualified staff combined with a winning makeover of a dignified 19th-century commercial building make this small hotel a destination unto itself. The owner is

---

When explorer Jacques Cartier sailed up the St. Lawrence River to Quebec in 1535, he saw the sun glittering on the rocks above him and thought they were diamonds—hence the name Cap-Diamant, or Cape Diamond.

The first high-ranking member of the British royal family to visit Canada was the Prince of Wales, who arrived in Montreal on 25 August 1860. The future King Edward VII, then 19 years old, opened the Victoria Bridge, linking the city with the south shore of the St. Lawrence River. The bridge's mile-and-a-half span was then the longest in the world; it required the work of 3,000 men and over 10 years to complete.

Daniel Langlois, founder of the futuristic Ex-Centris moviehouse (page 94), and his team obviously knows its away around a design showroom. The discreet street entrance leads to a lobby with polished concrete floors, slender cast-iron columns, and brightly colored high-tech furniture, making for a stylish, you-have-arrived ambiance that can't be beat. That feeling extends to the 30 unusually spacious guestrooms and loft-style suites, which feature white oak built-ins replete with CD players, more high-profile furniture such as re-editions of Harry Bertoia chairs, sleek bathrooms with peerless Toto toilets separated by movable partitions, and large windows you can actually open. The overall effect is minimalist but luxurious. A generous, made-to-order breakfast can be enjoyed in the rooms or the lobby bar and, unlike at so many hotels in the area, is included in the room price. ♦ 449 Rue Saint-Hélène (at Rue des Récollets). 904.1616, 866/904.1616; fax 904.1717. www.hotelgault.com

34 JENNIFER SCOTT

Behind the glass windows of this chic boutique is displayed a selection of Jennifer Scott's stylish handbags, part of her original line of accessories that has earned a loyal following among both local and celebrity crowds. ♦ M-Sa. ♦ 438 Rue St-Pierre (at Rue des Récollets). 844.2255

35 TITANIC

★$ In touristy Old Montreal, sometimes it pays to go where the locals go, especially when it's this capacious and cheerful basement-level luncheonette. Come here for cheap, fresh homemade salads, sandwiches, and cakes and pies. ♦ Canadian ♦ Daily, breakfast and lunch. 445 Rue St-Pierre (between Rues St-Sacrament and Notre-Dame W). 849.0894

36 MARRIOTT SPRINGHILL SUITES

$$ This new hotel features 124 suites, many with balconies or terraces. The décor is functional, catering more to business travelers than itinerant fashionistas, but comfortable and modern. All the suites include pantry and work areas and pull-out sofa beds. Other suite-style amenities include free local calls and access to a coin-operated laundry. There's also a complimentary buffet breakfast, exercise room and pool, and direct access through the elegant lobby to the Auberge Le Vieux Saint-Gabriel restaurant (for lunch and dinner), which also provides the hotel's room service. ♦ 445 Rue St-Jean-Baptiste (between Rues St-Paul E and Notre-Dame E). 875.4333, 866/875.4333; fax 875.4331

37 AUBERGE LE VIEUX SAINT-GABRIEL

★★★$$$$ Billed as the oldest inn in North America, this immense fieldstone house dates back to 1754. In 1769, it became the first British North American hostelry to obtain a liquor license. The rough-hewn fireplace and ceiling beams in the main dining room, the elegant **Sabrevoix** room, recall the days of New France, when trappers stored their furs in vaults just like the one in the bistro bar, reached via a stone-walled tunnel. Today Marie-Noëlle Allard and Marc Bolay bring one of the finest dining experiences in Montreal to these storied and atmospheric surroundings, now with such contemporary flourishes as a glassed-in wine cellar near the entrance. Start with pan-fried scallops St. Jacques with saffron and seasonal vegetables before moving on to such succulently prepared entrées as halibut pavé with Parmesan gratin and truffle risotto and duck cutlet with roasted pear infused with star anise and served with raspberry sauce. Popular dessert options include homemade gourmet Bilboquet ice creams and a tangy lemon coconut tart. Homemade truffles add a finishing touch. ♦ French ♦ Daily, lunch and dinner. Reservations recommended. 426 Rue St-Gabriel (between Rues St-Paul E and Notre-Dame E). 878.3561

38 ASTOR WAREHOUSE

Built in 1759, this stone warehouse is one of the oldest structures in the province. Original owner John Jacob Astor used it to store the furs of his famous New York family. ♦ 94 Rue Ste-Thérèse (at Rue de Vaudreuil)

39 LA MAISON BEAUDOIN

Encompassing three buildings joined by a coat of white plaster, this historic monument, dating back to the early 18th century, houses a tavern and two restaurants. The structure began as a boardinghouse for lawyers and journalists working at the nearby courts. Rue St-Vincent was the heart of legal and intellectual life in 19th-century Montreal, and many lawyers and writers kept their offices here. ♦ 27 Rue St-Vincent (at Rue Ste-Thérèse)

Restaurants/Clubs: Red | Hotels: Purple | Shops: Orange | Outdoors/Parks: Green | Sights/Culture: Blue

40 RUE ST-AMABLE

This narrow cobblestoned alley mimics Quebec City's Rue de Trésor, a street of artists and portraitists that teems with activity all summer. You'll find little great art here, but it's fun to sit for a fast portrait by one of Montreal's local painters or to peruse the handcrafted silver jewelry. ♦ Between Place Jacques-Cartier and Rue St-Vincent

On Rue St-Amable:

LE ST-AMABLE

★★★$$$$ Located on tiny Rue St-Amable, this French restaurant par excellence could easily be missed, and that would be a pity. The beige stone house with bright yellow awnings is where Montrealers splurge on special occasions. Classically trained chefs produce such gastronomic treats as *chateaubriand grillé Henri IV* for two; center-cut filet mignon grilled and served with Béarnaise sauce and a *bouquetière* of fresh vegetables; sweetbreads braised in vermouth; and tender medallions of veal. The wine list is quite sophisticated, and the enticing dessert menu features assorted house sorbets, cherries jubilee, and mille-feuille. The intimate dining room is best appreciated by evening candlelight, while lingering over a cognac. ♦ French ♦ M-F, lunch and dinner; Sa-Su, dinner. Jacket required for dinner; reservations required. 188 Rue St-Amable (at Place Jacques-Cartier). 866.3471

41 LA MAISON DU PATRIOTE

Built around 1775, this graystone house with white wood trim was originally part of the Viger family estate. No one knows why it was called the **House of the Patriot**; the two favored theories are that it was because the Vigers espoused "patriotic" Quebec causes and that a long-ago tobacconist had a carved wooden figure of a *patriote* standing outside. Offices of OXFAM Quebec, a nonprofit international assistance organization, now occupy the house. ♦ 169 Rue St-Paul E (between Place Jacques-Cartier and Rue St-Vincent)

42 JARDIN NELSON

★★$ Strolling by the old stone façade on Rue St-Paul on a warm summer afternoon, you can't help but be taken by the scene of diners lazily enjoying salads, crepes, and ample drinks on the huge terrace abloom with hibiscus and oleander, serenaded by a chamber group. Enter around the corner and wait for a table, because the food is surprisingly good, portions are generous, and the prices fair. Service can be slow, but this is a great spot to unwind and listen to the music. A classical trio performs at lunch daily, while jazz is served Thursday to Sunday evenings and weekend afternoons. The terrace is open from April to November. ♦ M-F, lunch and dinner; Su, brunch and dinner. ♦ 407 Pl Jacques-Cartier (at Rue St-Paul). 861.5731

43 RASCO'S HOTEL

Head west on Rue St-Paul to find this former hotel that hosted Charles Dickens and his wife in 1842. The British author stayed here to see one of his plays performed at the **Théâtre Royale**, which stood across the street on the site now occupied by the west wing of **Bonsecours Market**. Designed by architect-mason **Vital Gibeau** for hotelier Francesco Rasco in 1834, this was one of the more cosmopolitan hostelries in North America in its day. The upscale Italian restaurant **La Scala** is on the ground floor of the building. ♦ 281 Rue St-Paul E (between Rue St-Claude and Place Jacques-Cartier)

Within Rasco's Hotel:

CHEZ L'ÉPICIER
N°311
ET ST-PAUL EST MTL AVIN
BAR À

44 RESTAURANT CHEZ L'ÉPICIER

★★★$$$ From refreshing start to surprising finish, this restaurant and wine bar offers one of the most appealing dining experiences in Old Montreal. The space itself is inviting, a warm synthesis of old rough stone and brick walls complemented by clean contemporary touches. And true to its name, the restaurant also incorporates a small and tasteful gourmet grocery. The theme continues with chef-owner Laurent Godbout's *cuisine du marché*, which one orders off a blackboard or cleverly designed paper-bag menus. For entrées, try any of the original soups or the scallop seviche with fresh asparagus salad, green olive vinaigrette, and smoked salmon. For the main course, the black rice risotto with asparagus on a bed of diced carrots, served with tomatoes à la Grecque (peeled and marinated in balsamic vinaigrette and thyme), does nicely, as does salmon simmered in mustard and fresh mint and clove-perfumed duck stew. Desserts are outstanding: Try the fresh-fruit tacos with citrus salsa and mint sour cream or the pineapple split, drizzled to taste with sauces of warm caramel, chocolate, and strawberry. ♦ French/contemporary ♦ Daily, lunch and dinner. Reservations recommended. 311 Rue St-Paul E (at Rue St-Claude). 878.2232

45 AUBERGE BONSECOURS

$ The existence of this small inn, tucked into a quiet interior courtyard, comes as a delightful surprise. Seven clean, traditionally furnished rooms are housed in a renovated stable. ◆ 353 Rue St-Paul E (between Rues Bonsecours and St-Claude). 396.2662

46 HOSTELLERIE PIERRE DU CALVET

$$ This historic house-turned-inn, once the residence of wealthy merchant and justice of the peace Pierre du Calvet, dates from 1725 and is considered one of the finest examples of domestic design surviving from the French regime. Du Calvet was imprisoned by the British for many years for collaborating with American General Richard Montgomery during the American occupation of the city in 1775—during which time Benjamin Franklin stayed here. After inspecting the delightfully evocative red wooden façade, note the firebreaks—typical of fire-prone colonial Quebec—that extend beyond the roof, windows that diminish in size toward the top story, and cut-stone door and window frames. Friendly Gaëtan Trottier and his family preside over the inn's nine inviting guestrooms, which, though modernized, feature thick stone walls, antique furnishings, and fireplaces. Classic French and French Canadian cuisine is served in the atmospheric **Les Filles du Roy** restaurant; a greenhouse replete with plants, a fountain, and perky parrots serves as a breakfast room. ◆ 405 Rue Bonsecours (at Rue St-Paul E). 282.1725, 866/544.1725; fax 282.0456

47 LE ROUET METIERS D'ART INC.

The main store for this Quebec crafts chain sells a wide variety of items, including hand-painted ceramics, wooden toys, original-design woven shawls, and pewter jewelry. ◆ Summer: M-W, 10AM-9PM; Th-Su, 10AM-11PM. In winter: M-W, Sa-Su, 10AM-6PM; Th-F, 10AM-9PM. 136 Rue St-Paul E (between Place Jacques-Cartier and Rue St-Vincent). 875.2333

48 LE MARCHÉ BONSECOURS (BONSECOURS MARKET)

A large, silver-domed edifice facing the Old Port just east of Jacques-Cartier Pier, this market has had a long and varied history. Designed by **William Footner** and **George Browne** in 1850 to resemble a Roman temple—note the Doric portico and columns imported from England—the market was built on the site of a colonial official's palace, which seems fitting, because it served first as **Montreal City Hall**. The municipal council met here between 1852 and 1878, and for a while, so did the united parliaments of Upper and Lower Canada after a fire destroyed their chambers in 1849. When the municipal government decamped to the present city hall, the building became a market. Then, in 1964, it was renovated and converted into municipal offices. For Montreal's 350th anniversary celebrations, the market underwent another face-lift to accommodate special exhibitions, and today it also houses 15 boutiques offering the wares of Quebec and Canadian craftsmen and artisans, the **Auberge les Filles de Roy** restaurant, and a currency exchange office. ◆ 24 June-3 Sept, daily, 10AM-9PM; 4 Sept-23 June, Sa-W, 10AM-6PM, and Th-F, 10AM-9PM. 350 Rue St-Paul E (at Rue Bonsecours). 872.7730

49 NOTRE-DAME-DE-BONSECOURS CHAPEL

Affectionately known as the sailors' church because it served seafaring folk for so long, this little chapel has unfortunately begun to deteriorate, though votive offerings of model ships still decorate the nave, gifts of appreciation from the many sailors who found comfort here. On the orders of Ste-Marguerite de Bourgeoys, founder of the Notre-Dame congregation of nuns, the original structure was built in 1657. The present building dates from 1772. Its most arresting feature is the rooftop statue of *Our Lady*, her arms reaching out to welcome returning sailors. The steeple shelters an unusual chapel overlooking the St. Lawrence that was used to bless ships and their crews gathered below in the harbor. Access to the chapel lies through the museum (see below). An observation deck reached by a winding stairway—not for the faint of heart—gives a panoramic view of the port. ◆ Daily, 10AM-3PM, Nov–May; daily, May–Nov. 400 Rue St-Paul E (at Rue Bonsecours). 845.9991

Within the Notre-Dame-de-Bonsecours Chapel:

MARGUERITE DE BOURGEOYS MUSEUM

Located in the basement of the church, this museum commemorates Canada's first woman saint, who was canonized in 1982. Ste-Marguerite de Bourgeoys was the colony's first teacher and went on to found both the Notre-Dame congregation and the church. A quaint display depicts her story with 58 tiny scenarios and small dolls. ◆ Nominal admission. Mid-March through April, daily, 11AM-3:30PM; May–Oct, daily, 10AM-5PM. 282.8670

50 ST. PAUL HOTEL

$$$$ One of the newest boutique hotels to open in a rapidly revitalizing Old Montreal, the St. Paul features 120 rooms and suites in a

large and completely renovated old Beaux Arts office building. Floors are broken into two categories, conceptually speaking: earth rooms and sky rooms. The stylistic idiosyncrasies of these two elements are played to the hilt, resulting in rooms that score high points for chic but that generally lack warmth. The usual boutique hotel amenities, such as CD players, voice mail–equipped phones, and modem hookups are all here. ♦ 355 Rue McGill (at Rue St-Paul W). 380.2222, 866/380.2202; fax 380.2200

Within the St. Paul Hotel:

CUBE

★★$$$$ No, you haven't stumbled into a SoHo art gallery, but with the ocean of white paint and impossibly sleek tables and chairs at this high-profile hotel eatery, you could be forgiven for thinking you had. The studied simplicity of the room provides a counterpoint to a small but complicated menu. Appetizers include the likes of asparagus soup with a lobster "cake" and coriander, salmon three ways (tartare, marinated, and carpaccio), and a mushroom tart with aged cheddar, arugula, and truffle oil. Among the entrées are wild sea bass with young leeks, bacon, and herbs; braised Quebec lamb au jus; porcini mushrooms and tomato tatin; and lacquered duck breast with cauliflower and passion fruit. ♦ Canadian/eclectic ♦ Daily, lunch and dinner. 876.2823

51 WANT STIL

Blink as you walk past this narrow, stylish ("Stil," by the way, is Swedish for style) boutique and you might miss it altogether, but that would be a shame for anyone remotely interested in the world of modern Scandinavian design. On the right you'll find fashion by Swedish designers, including Action Jeans and Nudie Jeans, while the left side is reserved for contemporary interior design products, including glassware by the Finnish maker Iittala and flatware by Antonio Citterio and Koskinen. ♦ M-Sa. ♦ 231 Rue St-Paul W (between Rues St-Eloi and St-Nicholas). 499.8549

52 GANDHI

★★$$ A small red sign with gold lettering announces one of Montreal's best Indian restaurants. Attentive service, elegant décor, and sensible spicing make this a choice spot among locals and tourists alike for tandoori chicken, biryanis, and other staples from the subcontinent. Indian. ♦ Daily lunch and dinner. ♦ 230 Rue St-Paul W (between Rues St-Eloi and St-Nicholas)

53 STASH

★★$$ Burned out of its original home in the shadow of **Notre-Dame Basilica**, this popular Polish café has found a new home on Rue St-Paul, where it continues to serve great pierogi and carrot cake. The flames spared the polished pine banquettes that were transferred to the new dining room, distinguished by exposed brick walls, hanging plants, and a cozy bar. ♦ Polish ♦ Daily, lunch and dinner. 220 Rue St-Paul W (at Rue St-François-Xavier). 845.6611

54 SITE OF MAISONNEUVE'S HOME

Rue St-Paul is named for the city's founding father, Paul de Chomedey, later Sieur de Maisonneuve, who lived here, to the north of what is now **151 Rue St-Paul**, until returning to France in 1665. History buffs and other interested visitors must go through a porte cochere and into a dingy courtyard to find the plaque marking his long-gone home. ♦ 151 Rue St-Paul W (between Rues St-Sulpice and St-François-Xavier)

55 PLACE ROYALE

Like so many other places in Old Montreal, this square, which dates back before the city's founding, has served a number of purposes. Owing to its location and its access to the St. Lawrence River, the site was a natural harbor, and in 1611 French explorer Samuel de Champlain made use of it and named it **Place Royale**. Three decades later, the first colonists used the spot as a military square and called it **Place d'Armes**. In 1706, it was a large marketplace, **Place du Marché**, where the town crier made official proclamations, colonial delinquents sat in the stocks, and hardened criminals were hanged at the gallows.

In 1825, the opening of the Lachine Canal brought more foreign trade to the growing port. By the 1880s, as the customs business was booming, **John Ostell**, an architect, engineer, and surveyor, began work on the customshouse. The building's fine stonework, Tuscan-design pilasters, sash windows, and triangular pediment are excellent examples of neoclassical architecture popular at the time.

During most of the 1980s, the customshouse was closed to the public because of archaeological digs. Today, the building is part of **Pointe-à-Callière**, the **Museum of Archaeology and History**, where the first French colonists landed. An underground tunnel links it to the museum's newer structure. ♦ Bounded by Rues St-Sulpice and St-François-Xavier and by Rues de la Commune and St-Paul W

56 HOTEL NELLIGAN

$$$ What a little hype can do—or not—is exemplified by the popularity of this property, where cigar smoke from the restaurant wafts into the cramped lobby, furnishings are uninspired (and sometimes clumsily arranged), and lack of soundproofed windows means the clank of trash hitting a Dumpster may wake you before your alarm clock does. Exposed brick walls in most of the 35 rooms and 28 suites along with comfortable beds and a polite staff offset but do not completely erase these flaws. The Nelligan, otherwise stated, is a property that jumped on the boutique hotel bandwagon but often misses the mark. It is well-situated in a buzzing part of Old Montreal, but inattention to details can add up to a less-than-stellar stay. A restaurant, **Verses,** serves contemporary French cuisine. ♦ 106 Rue St-Paul W (at Rue St-Sulpice). 788.2040, 877/788.2040; fax 788.2041. www.hotelnelligan.com

57 OLD PORT

🅟 A sense of merriment has filled the air around the old harbor since the spring of 1992, when the area was overhauled in preparation for the city's 350th anniversary. The port is now a central attraction in Old Montreal and is still growing rapidly. No matter when you visit, it has something for just about everyone—even movies and places to shop. A rolling green lawn with picnic tables overlooks the harbor, a pedestrian mall stretches the length of the port, and a bicycle path follows the port to the Lachine Canal and beyond for some 6 miles. There are various futuristic exhibits to explore, as well as sporting activities for sheer fun, including summer bicycling and winter ice skating on a rink that curves around an old freighter slip. First-time visitors who come unprepared to cycle or skate can rent equipment at the site.

Quadricycle International (849.9953) at the Place Jacques-Cartier entrance rents a vehicle that's a cross between a rickshaw and a bicycle, with seating for up to nine people. During winter, the chalet at the skating rink between Jacques-Cartier and Victoria Piers, equipped with changing rooms and washrooms, rents skates and sharpens blades.

For those who want to explore the vicinity at a more leisurely pace, horse-drawn *calèches* (carriages with double facing seats and a driver's seat set high in front) wait patiently for passengers around the main entrance at Place Jacques-Cartier and Rue de la Commune.

Between mid-May and mid-October, a variety of boat cruises leave the westernmost Alexandra Pier as well as the Jacques-Cartier

and Victoria Piers at the east end of the port. The glass-topped **Bateau-Mouche** (849.9952) leaves Jacques-Cartier Pier for 1.5-hour excursions through the locks and along the restored section of the Lachine Canal between mid-May and mid-October. Or opt for a 3-hour dinner cruise, with gourmet meals catered by the Queen Elizabeth Hotel. The **Island Shuttle** (281.8000) departs every half hour from Jacques-Cartier Basin between 10AM and 9PM for the 10-minute crossing to **Parc des Îles**, a recreational parkland with a beach, cycle paths, and picnic grounds on the former site of **Expo '67.** For a hovercraft ride to Verchères or all the way to Quebec City, head to the kiosk of **Les Dauphins du St-Laurent** (288.4499), also on the Jacques-Cartier Pier.

More adventurous navigators might want to try the heart-stopping tour of the Lachine Rapids with **Saute-Moutons** (literally, "sheep jumpers")—custom-designed, jet-propelled boats built to take on pounding rapids. Be prepared to get soaked by the churning waves, even with the yellow mackintoshes and hoods the guides provide. Trips set out daily from the Clock Tower Pier at the Rue Berri entrance every 2 hours between 10AM and 6PM. For special tours, call 284.9607. Traditional harbor tours with **Croisières AML** depart the Victoria Pier (Bonsecours entrance) every day. There are 1- to 2-hour guided trips (plus daylong jaunts to Sorel on Saturday and Sunday), guided tours of the harbor, evening dance and/or dinner cruises, and theme trips, in addition to full charter services. Make reservations over the phone (842.3871) or in person at the wharf.

In addition to the main entrance at Place Jacques-Cartier, other entrances to the port are along Rue de la Commune at Rue McGill, Boulevard St-Laurent, and Rue Bonsecours. A tourist information center is located in the **Lock-keeper's Hut** (daily, 10AM-10PM, mid-May to mid-September; 496.7678) near the Rue McGill entrance to the west of Place Jacques-Cartier. This former control tower for barges on the Lachine Canal houses a snack bar and informative displays on the canal system. ♦ Along Rue de la Commune, between Rues Berri and McGill. 496.7678

Within the Old Port:

THE MONTREAL SCIENCE CENTER

This family-oriented interactive science and entertainment complex is housed in a large, modern structure right on the waterfront. It encompasses a variety of multimedia exhibitions, the IMMERSION Interactive Cinema with three interactive screens, and an **IMAX** theater that presents both two-dimensional and three-dimensional features such as

---

Restaurants/Clubs: Red | Hotels: Purple | Shops: Orange | Outdoors/Parks: Green | Sights/Culture: Blue

SAY FROMAGE: THE SAVORY WORLD OF QUEBEC'S CHEESES

Ample countryside and the right weather in *la belle province* spell more than beautiful changes of season: they also mean great cheese. In recent years the cheeses of Quebec have achieved a solid reputation both in the province and internationally. There are some 80 fine cheeses, in flowery, pressed, and washed-rind varieties. Here is a sampling of some of the artisanal Quebec cheeses you can expect to find on restaurant menus in Montreal and throughout Quebec:

Perron cheddar from the Saguenay-Lac-Saint-Jean region

Migneron from Maurice Dufour of Baie-Saint-Paul (Charlevoix)

Three-year-old goat's cheese from the Tournevent cheese factory in the Bois-Francs region

Casimir from the P'tit train du nord cheese factory in the Laurentians

Victor et Berthold, perfumed with cinnamon-laced hot cider, from the du Champ à la Meule cheese factory in the Lanaudière region

Bleu Bénédictin, a Roquefort-style cheese, from the monks of the Abbaye de Saint-Benoît-du-Lac in the Eastern Townships

Creamy Riopelle, named for the Quebec artist, from the Île-aux-Grues cheese factory in the Chaudière-Appalaches region

Le Gré des Champs from Montérégie's dairy region

Pied-de-Vent and **Joli-Cœur** from the Magdalen Islands

In addition, cheese lovers will be happy to learn that the Montreal restaurant **Les Chèvres** (1201 Ave Van Horne, 270.1119) offers a selection of 30 to 40 fine cheeses from Quebec.

Dolphins and *Amazing Caves.* There are also seven fast-food restaurants, including **Le Taboulé** and **Queues de Castor/Jus Moozoo**, and a variety of boutiques housed in refitted red freight containers. ◆ Admission. IMMER-SION, 18 June-9 Sept, Su-W, 10AM-6PM, and Th-Sa, 10AM-9PM; until 17 June, daily, 10AM-6PM. IMAX, every hour between 10:15AM and 7:15PM. King Edward VII Pier (at Blvd St-Laurent). 496.4724, www.montrealsciencecenter.com

58 PLACE D'YOUVILLE

Located just past the triangular Pointe-à-Callière, where the archaeology museum stands, this square was one of the first civic centers in Montreal. Landscaped in the 19th century over the dry riverbed of the Little St-Pierre, this was the place for people to greet passengers on the ships that moored along Rue de la Commune and to stroll on Sundays. The middle of the square was first occupied by an open-air fish market; then **Ste-Anne's Market** was constructed, and that building served briefly as parliament, beginning in 1844, when the Upper and Lower Canadas were united—an unpopular move, resulting in the burning of the new chamber by rioters in 1849. **Central Fire Station No. 1** was erected on the spot in 1906, and that building is now home to the **Montreal History Center** (under renovation at press time). ◆ Between Rues de Callière and McGill

On Place d'Youville:

GIBBY'S RESTAURANT

★★★★$$$$ Montrealers and visitors alike are drawn to this restaurant, which looks out over the courtyard and peaceful garden of **Youville Stables**, a picturesque complex of graystone warehouses built in 1825 by merchants Jean and Tancrede Bouthillier. Note the overhanging dormers where pulleys were attached to haul merchandise upstairs. Today, the low structure, with its sloping roofs and porte cochere, invites passersby to linger in the courtyard and perhaps enjoy a cocktail on the shady patio. Inside, pine armoires and other Quebec furnishings highlight exposed stone walls and beamed ceilings. Steaks and grills are the restaurant's specialties, and seafood choices include lobster Newburg and oysters Rockefeller. The salads and baked potatoes are usually sprinkled with Gibby's own bacon bits, and housemade sorbet freshens the palate between the salad and main courses. ◆ Continental ◆ Daily, dinner. Reservations recommended. 298 Place d'Youville (between Rues du Port and St-Pierre). 282.1837 ♿

59 CALIFORNIA DREAM

★★★$$$$ If diversity of restaurants is one measure of a city's sophistication, then this gorgeous spot can only boost Montreal's aspirations to be a world-class city. Part of the reason is conceptual: to open a restaurant in the heart of Old Montreal that takes its inspiration from a place 3,000 miles to the west is audacious in the best sense of the word; that it's a beautiful spot to boot only adds to the appeal. Judging from the space—tall ceilings, huge windows, and acrylic blue Philippe Starck chairs—you'd never guess this was the site of Montreal's first hospital. With such entrées as blackened grouper with new potatoes and roasted lamb with old grain mustard crust, the fare may be heartier than typical Californian, but the wine list is exclusively Californian and even the breezy white bar is nonsmoking. ♦ Californian ♦ Tu-F, lunch and dinner; Sa, dinner. 355 Place d'Youville (at Rue St-Pierre). 288.8999

60 GREY NUNS' HOSPITAL

Just off Place d'Youville is the site of the colony's second hospital. Begun in 1694 by the Charon brothers, it was taken over in 1747 by Marguerite d'Youville, a very religious, wealthy widow who later founded the Sisters of Charity, or Grey Nuns. Chartered in 1753 by Louis XV, the congregation was dedicated to caring for orphans and the sick, poor, and elderly of the colony. A visit to the wing in which Mother d'Youville died can be arranged by calling 842.9411. ♦ 138 Rue-St-Pierre (between Rue d'Youville and Place d'Youville)

61 OBELISK

This 30-foot obelisk was erected in 1894 to commemorate the city's 250th anniversary (2 years late). The granite monument listing the names of the first colonists stands on a pedestrian island near the eastern end of the point. ♦ Rue St-François-Xavier (at Place d'Youville)

62 POINTE-À-CALLIÈRE MUSEUM OF ARCHAEOLOGY AND HISTORY

On 17 May 1642, four French ships sailed up the St. Lawrence River from Quebec City, bringing some 53 colonists to this spot at the mouth of the Little St-Pierre River. The new arrivals put up a wooden stockade to enclose their tiny community, which consisted of a few houses, a store, a chapel, barracks, and a hospital. A cemetery had to be added the following year for Guillaume Boissier, the first colonist to die because of the harsh winter. Some 40 years later, Louis-Hector de Callière, governor of Montreal between 1684 and 1698, had his house built here; the area has borne his name ever since, in recognition of his negotiating the treaty of 1701, which ended the war with the Iroquois.

Those historical years are chronicled in the starkly modern **Eperon** building, the main section of the museum. Actually three exhibition centers in one, it combines the customshouse, a modern structure with a multimedia theater, and a crypt believed to date back to the first cemetery. The underground tunnel between the customshouse and the Eperon building leads visitors through Old Montreal foundations (most date back 100 years) and even over a sewer outlet where what's left of the Little St-Pierre River still runs. Audiovisual displays introduce visitors to an 18th-century innkeeper and his wife and other early Montrealers, and scale-model villages portraying the area at various points in its history are ingeniously displayed in Plexiglas panels beneath the floor. The Eperon's subterranean showcases are filled with 17th- to 20th-century artifacts found during the archaeological excavations. The "archaeological crypt" is actually a spooky alcove surrounded by stone foundations encircling excavated grave sites.

Upstairs, the future takes over to explain the past. A multimedia presentation turns Sieur de Maisonneuve, Montreal's founding father, into a holographic talking head that floats above visitors and comments on Montreal past and present, while earphones at each seat translate his words into English and French.

The Eperon building, named for the insurance company that once stood on this spot and whose foundations are preserved in the basement, boasts a rooftop lookout as well as the bright café **L'Arrivage** one level below. In 1992, the federal, provincial, and municipal governments joined forces to create this museum in honor of Montreal's 350th birthday ♦ Admission. Tu-F, 10AM-5PM; Sa-Su, 11AM-5PM (until 6PM in July and Aug). 350 Place Royale (between Rue de la Commune and Place d'Youville). 872.9150

63 LE CARTET

★★$$ The look is a cross between colonial and functional at this gourmet market and corner bistro on the first floor of an old office building, where you can find all the makings of a delicious picnic or lunch with the locals around one of two big communal tables. Market cuisine's the thing here, and portions are generous. ♦ Canadian ♦ M-F, breakfast, lunch, and dinner; Sa, breakfast and lunch. 106 Rue McGill (between Rues William and Wellington). 871.8887.

PLACE DES ARTS/CHINATOWN/THE VILLAGE

Impromptu performances by comedians and street musicians herald the beginning of Montreal's two major summertime fêtes, **Just for Laughs/Juste Pour Rire Festival** and the **Montreal International Jazz Festival**, which bring color, life, and crowds to East Downtown Montreal, a neighborhood that otherwise takes itself rather seriously. Hundreds of government employees report to work here each day, disappearing into their huge bureaucratic towers. But they share the neighborhood with some of the city's main attractions.

The enormous **Complexe Desjardins**, for instance, has more than a hundred boutiques and restaurants, along with four office towers. Gurgling waterfalls and luxuriant hanging vines encourage visitors to linger in the complex's interior court rather than venture outdoors, especially in inclement weather. Linked to the office and shopping complex via a vast network of underground passages is the **Palais des Congrès** convention center and the posh **Meridien Hotel**. Although the underground walkways are a blessing in the snow and cold, stay aboveground during the warmer months to enjoy East Downtown's street theater. Relax on a bench near **Place des Arts**, Montreal's major musical and theatrical venue, or the lively and sometimes controversial **Museum of Contemporary Art** and watch a colorful cast of characters parade along the esplanade. Just a few blocks away is **Boulevard St-Laurent**, the dividing line between West and East Montreal, and **Rue St-Denis**, with its lineup of eclectic shops, bistros, and outdoor cafés.

Montreal's **Chinatown** may be small—a quarter-mile area bounded by Boulevard St-Laurent on the east, **Rue Jeanne-Mance** on the west, **Avenue Viger** on the south, and **Boulevard René Lévesque** on the north—but it's an important symbol of survival and

pride for the city's sizable Chinese community. Although only about 400 of Montreal's approximately 60,000 Chinese actually live in Chinatown, many commute in from the suburbs and other neighborhoods to frequent the restaurants and shops—as do legions of Laotians, Vietnamese, Koreans, and other Asians who are part of the city's diverse ethnic mix.

For its inhabitants at the turn of the 19th century, though, Chinatown was both home and haven against pervasive racial discrimination. Most had come to western Canada in the late 1800s to help build the **Transcontinental Railway** and later migrated east to Montreal (then Canada's largest city) in search of economic opportunities and a new life. Since then, Chinese immigrants have arrived in Montreal in distinct waves. Today's Chinatown is a colorful, aromatic, and flavorful part of the city. Try to explore the area around mealtime and treat yourself to some pungent and delicious cuisine.

Farther east is where the Village, also known as the Gay Village, starts. The nucleus of this neighborhood, which at press time was somewhere between seedy and up-and-coming in terms of both atmosphere and appearance, is Rue Ste-Catherine East between Rue Amherst and Avenue Papineau (the exterior of the Beaudry Metro station, roughly in the middle, is decked out in the colors of the rainbow flag). Other than a number of restaurants, bars, and other establishments catering to a gay clientele, the neighborhood is largely residential and at its most animated Friday and Saturday nights. The exception to that is summer, particularly July and August, when no one in Montreal seems to sleep and the sidewalks of Ste-Catherine are crowded all night, every night, with partygoers and pleasure-seekers of every stripe.

1 CHURCH OF ST. JOHN THE EVANGELIST

The city's main Anglo-Catholic church (commonly known as the church with the red roof) is 125 years old, and though its yellow-and redbrick interior is something of an attraction, the rood screen in the main sanctuary is even more noteworthy. It was carved in Oberammergau, Germany, site of the Passion Play every decade since 1634. The artist, Robert Reid, portrayed Christ in the 1898 version of the German reenactment of the Crucifixion. Services are held daily with the traditional liturgy. ♦ Services: M-Tu, Th-F, 5:45PM; W, 7:30AM, 9:30AM; Sa, noon; Su, 8:30AM, 9:45AM, 10:30AM. 137 Ave du President-Kennedy (at Rue St-Urbain). 288.4428

2 BUST OF PRESIDENT JOHN F. KENNEDY

The bronze bust of the late US president was erected in 1986 by the Henry Birks and Sons retail chain "in tribute to the citizens of Montreal." The artist was P. Lanc. ♦ Traffic island between Blvd de Maisonneuve W and Ave du President-Kennedy (east of Rue Jeanne-Mance)

3 LE PARKING

This large gay disco and bar, lodged in the former Cox Garage, is one of the Gay Village's most popular. Appropriately enough, an automotive theme prevails, but despite an excellent sound system and light set, expect more grunge than glamour. A sizable leather crowd adds to the fun. Wednesday and Thursday unite gay and lesbian youths with house, techno, and hip-hop music, while Fridays and Saturdays are reserved for gay men. The bar on the first floor (open nightly) is especially popular with a hip after-work crowd. ♦ 1295 Rue Amherst (between Blvd de Maisonneuve and Rue Robin). 522.2766

4 PLACE DES ARTS

The definitive center for the performing arts in Montreal provides lovers of theater, music, opera, and dance with a gourmet repast for the senses. It's actually Canada's only cultural complex devoted to both the performing and visual arts. Over the years, such major stars as Placido Domingo, Philip Glass, and Frank Sinatra have taken the stage, and productions of Broadway shows such as *Kiss of the Spider Woman* and *Phantom of the Opera* have played to Montreal audiences. The **Montreal Symphony Orchestra**, led by conductor

Restaurants/Clubs: Red | Hotels: Purple | Shops: Orange | Outdoors/Parks: Green | Sights/Culture: Blue

Charles Dutoit, performs regularly at the center, often hosting internationally renowned classical musicians, and performances are scheduled throughout the year. During the **Montreal International Jazz Festival** in the summer, jazz greats congregate at the center for the city's most memorable shows. The complex contains five halls: **Salle Wilfred-Pelletier** (seats 2,982), **Théâtre Maisonneuve** (seats 1,460), **Théâtre Jean-Duceppe** (seats 755), the intimate **Théâtre Café de la Place** (seats 138), and **La Cinquième Salle** (seats 400). An underground mall houses a branch of the (largely Francophone) music and book emporium **Archambault,** the boutique of the Museum of Contemporary Art, and other shops. The parking lot entrance is off Rue St-Urbain. ♦ Montreal Symphony Orchestra, 842.9951; Opéra de Montréal, 985.2222. General box office: M-Sa, noon-8PM (260 Blvd de Maisonneuve W). Rue Ste-Catherine E (at Rue Jeanne-Mance). 842.2112. www.pda.qc.ca

A R E A

5 AREA

★★$$$ The preparation is French, but the flavors stray across Mediterranean as well as a few Far Eastern borders at this trendy eatery in the heart of the Gay Village. Young chef Ian Perreault's creative touch begins with the appetizers: Try the arugula salad with vanilla-flavored poached tomato, diced citrus fruits, lemon thyme, olive oil, and coarse salt or the cold yellow tomato soup with tarragon-flavored oil and fresh onion chutney seasoned with saffron and cinnamon sticks. Stand-out entrées include any fresh fish as well as the standard saddle of salmon with grilled asparagus, roasted garlic oil–flavored mushrooms, and reduced lemon-flavored whipped egg yolks. There's also curried shrimp tempura with mango salsa, papayas, and lime, or for carnivores, Quebec piglet braised in red wine with carrots and parsnip. Portions are large, but save room for one of the tasty desserts, which include Nicolas Jongleux–style molten chocolate cake topped with pistachio ice cream, and banana cake with fresh lime, mint, and roasted pistachios. Only one drawback here: Service can be slow. ♦

The many silver-spired churches along the shores of the St. Lawrence River were not only centers of worship. Sailors and fishermen used them as navigational aids before the days of lighthouses.

What did Montreal do with the tons of earth excavated to make the city's Metro system? Enlarged Ste-Hélène Island.

Eclectic ♦ Tu-Fri, lunch and dinner; Sa-Su, dinner. Reservations recommended. 1429 Rue Amherst (between Rues St-Catherine E and Maisonneuve). 890.6691

Librairie
L'ANDROGYNE
La librairie gaie et lesbienne
de Montréal depuis 1973

6 L'ANDROGYNE

This is the leading gay and lesbian bookstore in Montreal and features an extensive range of both English and French fiction and nonfiction, with a total of more than 5,000 titles. There are also current gay-oriented magazines and videos from the US, Canada, and France. ♦ Daily, 10AM-midnight. 1436 Rue Amherst (between Rues St-Catherine E and Maisonneuve). 842.4765

7 MUSEUM OF CONTEMPORARY ART

First founded in 1964 by the Quebec government, this museum was located in three places around (and off) the island before moving to its current 44,000-square-foot, multilevel space on Rue Ste-Catherine in 1992. Over the past 3 decades, the museum's nearly 600 exhibitions of contemporary art have attracted more than 1.6 million visitors. The museum schedules seasonal shows of both international and Canadian artists' work. ♦ Admission; student discount; children under 12 free; free to all W, 6PM-9PM. Tu, Th-Su, 11AM-6PM; W, 11AM-9PM. 185 Rue Ste-Catherine W (at Rue St-Urbain). 847.6226

Within the Museum of Contemporary Art:

LA ROTONDE

★★$$ The menu of this restaurant offers the delightful flavors of Provence, such as fish soup with a savory rouille and breast of duck in lavender honey. As expected of a museum eatery, the décor is gallery like, with contemporary-style chairs, tables, and artwork. Pre-theater and festival crowds provide a ready-made clientele here, and in summer they can dine alfresco on the sunny terrace. ♦ French ♦ Daily, lunch in summer; lunch Tu-Su in winter; dinner evenings when concerts are scheduled at Place des Arts. 847.6900

GAY MONTREAL

Rue St. Catherine East is without question the locus of gay nightlife in Montreal, especially the blocks between St-Hubert and Dorion streets—the heart of the Gay Village. The Beaudry metro station is even decorated with the colors of the rainbow flag. While generally a safe neighborhood, if a bit quirky, revelers and casual strollers alike should be aware that the "village" is still part of the larger city and as such has its fair share of homeless and delinquent youth problems. Take shelter from the not-always-gay chaos of the street inside one of the neighborhood's many cafés and bars. Night crawlers should keep in mind that bigger is not necessarily better—particularly as it applies to bars and clubs. A sizable one that seems to please just about everyone is **Unity** (no. 1171; 523.4429). The main bar is on the first floor, which also features a small stage area used for drag performances on certain nights. The top floors are where the discos are (count on techno and house music), and in summertime the rooftop terrace is open for drinks and sophisticated lounging. The dance floor is the main draw at the decidedly fashionable **Sky Club and Pub** (no. 1474), though it is also popular for its evening and Sunday-afternoon bar scene. **Le Drugstore** (no. 1360) is a complex of eight bars and cafés. Inside the **Bourbon Complex** (no. 1578), a Village nexus of gay and lesbian leisure owned by Norman Chamberlain, a former Montreal police officer, is **Le Cajun**, a bar, and the tri-level disco **La Track** (521.1419), particularly popular on Wednesdays and Sundays. The complex also has a 24-hour restaurant, 37-room hotel with sauna, ice cream parlor and wedding chapel.

Give your partying skills a tune-up—literally—at **Le Parking** (1296 Amherst St; 522.2766), a bi-level space housed in the former Cox Garage. The very popular disco on the first floor is mainly a weekend affair, but the Cruising Bar upstairs is open nightly. Gay strip clubs are something of a Montreal specialty; two popular ones are **Stock** (1278 Rue St-André; 842.1336) and **Campus** (1111 Rue St-Catherine E; 526.3616). Shifting genders, **Sisters** (no. 1333, second floor; 522.4717) is a lesbian bar and dance club with an avid following. Dancing is the sine qua non at **Stereo** (no. 858), a club with a mixed crowd and (according to everyone) the best sound system in Montreal. Hearty partiers should remember that while the last call at bars and clubs is generally 3AM, there is a growing after-hours scene with clubs such as Stereo open until 10AM. Check flyers for the latest club news and events.

The best source of listings for gay bars, clubs, and other establishments, plus a wealth of other useful information, is the bilingual monthly magazine **Fugues** (www.fugues.com). It is available at many record stores, bars, and retail outlets throughout Montreal. The Montreal tourist office is another resource; visit www.tourism-montreal.org/gay for gay news and information.

Of the two major annual gay fêtes in Montreal, the first is **Divers Cité** (www.divercite.com), a weeklong celebration of gay, lesbian, bisexual, and transgender pride that begins the first weekend in August. The weeklong **Black and Blue Festival** (www.bbcm.org) starts the first weekend in October and culminates in the rollicking Black and Blue Ball in the Olympic Stadium.

8 ARCHAMBAULT

This music and book emporium is Montreal's *très* French answer to Virgin Megastore. Whether you're looking for an obscure Serge Gainsbourg album, soundtracks to French movies old and new, or the latest from Daft Punk or Etienne Daho (like George Michael, but cuter), this is the place. Although the merchandise is definitely geared toward the French-speaking market—the bookstore stocks French-language titles exclusively—the music department is quite international. ◆ M-W, 9:30AM-6PM; Th-F, 9:30AM-9PM; Sa, 11AM-5PM; Su, noon-5PM. 500 Rue Ste-Catherine E (at Rue Berri). 849.6201. Also at 175 Rue Ste-Catherine W (Place des Arts). M-W, 9:30AM-8PM; Th-F, 9:30AM-9PM; Sa, 11AM-6PM; Su, noon-5PM. 281.0367

9 THÉÂTRE DU NOUVEAU MONDE

Though vaudeville shows were popular here during the 1920s and 1930s, this French-language theater now presents the works of Shakespeare, Goldoni, Gorki, Racine, Michel Tremblay, and other renowned contemporary and classical playwrights. The building was erected in the early 1900s, with renovations in 1950 and recently in 1995. The theater once had its own regular troupe but found it less expensive to hire actors on a per-production basis; freelance actors are now engaged from across the country. The seating capacity is 866. ◆ 84 Rue Ste-Catherine W (at Rue St-Urbain). 866.2252

Within the Théâtre du Nouveau Monde:

LE CAFÉ DU NOUVEAU MONDE

★$ This always lively café-restaurant is a popular spot for theatergoers and non-theatergoers alike, who are united in their appreciation of such tasty dishes as grilled trout with spinach salad and red pepper-mango chutney, a simple but well-made spaghetti, or panini sandwiches. For dessert, try the pear or mango sorbet. ◆ French/eclectic ◆ Daily, lunch and dinner. 866.8669

10 COMPLEXE DESJARDINS

Owned by the massive **Mouvement Desjardins** financial organization, this enormous complex opened in 1976, the year the separatist Parti Québécois took power in Quebec. The building houses provincial government offices, more than 100 boutiques, four cinemas, travel and car-rental agencies, walk-in dental and medical clinics, and several small bistros and eateries. The huge plaza provides a venue for such cultural and social events as circuses, banquets, and exhibitions and retail outlets that include everything from **Excellence Sports** and **Caleçons Vos Gouts . . . ?** (a men's undergarments shop) to **Daskalidès Chocolatier.** An impressive food court, **Les Restos de la Grande Place,** includes such eateries as **La Friterie, Paradis Panini,** and **Basha** (Lebanese). A $25 million renovation currently under way will add new boutiques and beautify the whole complex, making it the largest mall in the downtown area. ♦ Shopping mall: M-W, 9:30AM-6PM; Th-F, 9:30AM-9PM; Sa, 10AM-5PM; Su, noon-5PM. Bounded by Rues St-Urbain and Jeanne-Mance, Blvd René Lévesque W, and Rue Ste-Catherine W. 281.1870

Linked to Complexe Desjardins:

WYNDHAM MONTRÉAL

$$$ The 600-room hotel, formerly the Meridien, is a standout in a city with plenty of fine accommodations, thanks in part to the sauna, sundeck, full-size pool, whirlpool, and fitness center. All of the rooms and 34 suites have cable TV and modern décor, with carpets and drapes in warm earth tones. ♦ 1255 Rue Jeanne-Mance. 285.1450, 800/361.8234; fax 285.1243 ᴄ

Canadian Pacific trains heading west once left from the former Dalhousie Station at 514-522 Rue Notre-Dame East, which was built as a major Canadian Pacific hub in 1883. In 1898, it was closed and replaced by the castlelike Viger Station (now municipal offices) on nearby Rue St-Antoine. Although the Dalhousie edifice endured a long period of neglect, Montreal urban planners bought and recycled it for a purpose that Canadian Pacific railroad tycoons would never have imagined. Since 1989, the École Nationale du Cirque (the National Circus School) has occupied the building. This school trains young people from all over the world to be professional acrobats, tumblers, trapeze artists, and contortionists. The popular Cirque du Soleil draws performers from the school, and a number of its cast also teach there.

Within the Wyndham Montréal:

LE CAFÉ FLEURI

★★★$$$ The lavish Sunday buffet is arguably the best in the city, with such offerings as roast beef, smoked salmon, eggs, and waffles (and some irresistible desserts). A pre-theater table d'hôte begins at 5:30PM 7 days a week and includes an entrée, a glass of wine, dessert, and coffee that you can savor in a dining room rife with exotic plants or on the outdoor terrace on warm-weather days. ♦ Continental ♦ M-Sa, breakfast, lunch, and dinner; Su, brunch and dinner. Reservations recommended. 285.1450

11 DEER GARDEN

★★$ Here's one of the best little restaurants in Chinatown—favored for its friendly, no-nonsense service and prices, to be sure, but mostly for the delicious food. Anything on the menu is a good bet, but the braised ginger chicken and sautéed shrimp in black bean sauce in particular win accolades. You can order plain rice vermicelli as a side dish instead of white rice—a tasty entrée mix-in. There's no wine, but you can bring your own. ♦ Chinese ♦ Daily, lunch and dinner. 1162 Blvd St-Laurent (between Blvd René Lévesque and Rue Ste-Catherine E). 861.1056

12 LE LATINI

★★★★$$$$ Considered one of the city's finest Italian restaurants, this class act owes its success to dishes that are as appealing to the eye as they are to the palate. The menu changes daily, with more than a thousand recipes in its gastronomic repertoire. Entrées have included such delicacies as sweetbreads laced with balsamic vinegar on a *feuilletage* served with arugula, and roast quails nestled on yellow peppers in a delicately seasoned sauce. In season, the split lobster topped with linguine is a popular choice. The dessert menu covers several octaves (traditional standbys include tiramisù, profiteroles, and zabaglione), hitting the high notes with adventurous choices such as fresh figs with roasted pine nuts in a mascarpone–caramel sauce. The outstanding wine cellar's 80,000 bottles span 850 labels and 500 Italian vineyards. All of the above are served by attentive staffers in a split-level dining room amid marble columns. The patio is popular with summer diners. ♦ Italian ♦ M-F, lunch and dinner; Sa, dinner. Reservations recommended. 1130 Rue Jeanne-Mance (at Blvd René Lévesque W). 861.3166 ᴄ

13 COMPLEXE GUY-FAVREAU

Like **Complexe Desjardins**, this place owes its almost decade-long existence to civil servants who work for Health and Welfare, Human Resources Development, and other

FIDDLERS ON THE LOOSE

You happen on a wild fest of fiddles, harmonicas, melodeons, and raucous singing, occasionally spiced with saxophone and contrabass and, for rhythm, clacking spoons and clogging feet flying back and forth so fast they turn into a blur. Welcome to your first encounter with traditional Quebecois music.

Quebec's traditional music incorporates Irish rhythm and French melody and lyrics, with traces of Scottish structure and American bluegrass. Irish immigrants brought their fiddles, jigs, reels, and hornpipes to bear on the French working songs, waltzes, quadrilles, and laments beloved by those who came from Brittany and Normandy. Over the last 50 years, the music has evolved through the technical skill and original compositions of such Quebecois virtuosos as violinists Joseph Allard, Jean Carignan, and Louis Boudreault, accordionist Philippe Bruneau, and singer and *conteur* (storyteller) Michel Faubert. The resulting music, colorful and robust, has won admirers even among traditional musicians in Ireland, some of whom play and record Quebecois music. Despite the presence of exciting contemporary music, traditional music and dance are alive and well from **Hudson Bay** to the **Gaspé Peninsula**. On almost any weekend of the year, you can attend an old-fashioned *veillée*, a congenial evening of traditional music and rollicking jigs and reels. As long as you understand the difference between *main droite* and *main gauche* (right hand and left hand), you can get around the dance floor. Festivals, music competitions, concerts, and *rencontres* (musical get-togethers that may last for days) keep the tunes flowing.

Quebecois dances are based on French quadrilles and resemble American square dances with groups of four couples forming squares, grand chains, and promenades. Although many dances are called (directions are given) in French, just as many are called in English.

The songs express everything in the culture—from the sacred to the bawdy: work songs and tunes of sorrow, seduction, and political rebellion. Lilting, a complicated rhythmic mouth music composed of nonsense syllables, often accompanies the dance music of fiddles and accordions or may be interjected into verses of songs. As with the music of Ireland, Brittany, and Acadia, the sounds and oral traditions of Quebec reflect a communal spirit, sense of humor, triumph, and joie de vivre.

To find out where and when traditional Quebecois dances are held in the greater Montreal area and all over Quebec, contact the **Society for the Promotion of Traditional Quebecois Music and Dance** at 514/273.0880.

federal government departments. The architects of this low-profile office building (designed to look like a university campus) were actually part of a consortium called **Larose Laliberté Petrucci**, which has since become part of the architectural firm **Webb Zerafat Menkes Housden**. The east, west, and north towers house offices; the south tower comprises residential apartments. The most sought-after feature, however, is a veritable secret garden on the lobby level, with trees, water fountains, and benches, all completely hidden from the street. (Ask directions, or you risk wandering inside for hours.) The complex also contains an all-purpose grocery store, a hair stylist, travel agent, and **Tilden Rent-a-Car**, as well as a branch of the **YMCA** (open 7 days a week) and other commercial establishments. Two small sit-down snack bars, **A.L. Van Houtte** and **Casse-Croûte**, provide more than adequate nourishment for those on the go. ♦ Passport office: M-F, 7:30AM-5PM. Other government offices: daily. Stores: hours vary. 200 Blvd René Lévesque W (between Rues St-Urbain and Jeanne-Mance). 283.6289

14 **PLACE DU QUARTIER**

This residential and commercial complex, with 98 condominium units and the Romanian consulate, has 15 stores (including gift shops, a grocery, and a florist), a brasserie with beer on tap, and a pizzeria. ♦ 1081 Rue St-Urbain (at Blvd René Lévesque W). 878.0673

15 **WAI JIAN INC.**

Should your stomach start to hurt from your overindulging in Chinatown's culinary finest, you might want to try some traditional Chinese medicine. Patrons line up at this herb shop (especially on weekends), seeking ancient remedies for fatigue, colds, and all sorts of other maladies. Essence of chicken and deer tail extract are just some of the medicinal offerings, ground fine in a potion or an herbal tea. It's fascinating to stand and watch the action. ♦ Daily. 1127 Rue Clark (at Blvd René Lévesque). 866.6156

16 **RUE DE LA GAUCHETIÈRE**

Bordered by the large plaza behind **Palais des Congrès** (at Place d'Armes Metro

Restaurants/Clubs: Red | Hotels: Purple | Shops: Orange | Outdoors/Parks: Green | Sights/Culture: Blue

THE BEST

Marian Kahn

Founder and Coordinator, Bed & Breakfast '88 Montreal

Schwartz's Deli—no visit to Montreal is complete without a visit to this deli (now Greek-owned) to sample Montreal's famous (and best) smoked-meat sandwiches. Diners sit at tables for six, and lines are common.

Desserts? Try **La Tulipe Noire** café in the **Maison Alcan** atrium and **Café Cherrier**.

See Montreal from its heights—the lookouts in **Mont-Royal Park** or the tower of the **Olympic**

Stadium. From its depths—**Underground Montreal**, 29 km of passages filled with boutiques, restaurants, banks, cinemas, and even a branch of the public library. Come here to escape rain, snow, or heat. Or from the water—try white-water rafting on the **Lachine Rapids** (20 minutes from downtown Montreal, in **Lachine**) or take a cruise around the island of Montreal.

Rent a bicycle—and enjoy the many cycle paths, especially through **Old Montreal**.

Sure, there's the **Ritz-Carlton Kempinski** hotel, but if that's too staid, try the hospitality of a bed-and-breakfast stay. Private homes in and near downtown provide comfort, security, information, great breakfast, and reasonable rates.

station), this is Chinatown's Main Street—though it has actually had many ethnic incarnations. Before the Chinese made it their own in the 1920s, this thoroughfare was by turns distinctively French, English, Irish, Jewish, Italian, Ukrainian, and Russian. Today, Vietnamese and Korean newcomers have added to the Asian flavor. The few blocks extending from Boulevard St-Laurent to Rue Jeanne-Mance—redesigned in the 1980s as an outdoor pedestrian-only mall—have been the heart of Chinatown since its early days. Two successive ceremonial archways, unveiled in 1983, were crafted by local artists and architects. In the brick pathways between them, six inset bronze medallions are inscribed with dragons, which are traditional Chinese symbols of life, fortune, and strength. ♦ Between Blvd St-Laurent and Rue Jeanne-Mance

17 PASTRY MAXIM

Tucked away in a basement, this bakery is popular with Chinese students and families as a fast-food emporium. Selections include egg tarts, barbecue pork buns, winter melon (quite similar to candied watermelon rind), and lotus-seed cake. ♦ M-Th, Su; F-Sa, 9AM-9PM. 1050 Rue Clark (at Rue de la Gauchetière W). 398.9696

18 LA MAISON VIP

★★★$ If you're still around Chinatown after dark, make it a point to join the lineup here,

Smoked meat—a cousin of pastrami—has something of a cult following in Montreal. Originally introduced to the city by Jewish immigrants from Romania, it has become a Quebecois specialty. Tons of it are sold each week in restaurants on Boulevard St-Laurent, and it's actually smuggled out of the country in suitcases going to Miami, London, and Hong Kong, and even sent to prisons and criminals in exile.

where the real action doesn't start before 11PM. Although the restaurant is open for lunch and dinner earlier on, those in the know say the best cooks work the late-night shift, as evidenced by the crowd of other restaurant workers from all over the city who flock here after hours. Though the décor is unremarkable, the house chow mein and mixed-seafood hot pot are unforgettable. The service can be a bit abrupt, but the food and the prices will make up for the annoyance. After midnight, this eatery is Montreal at its best: slightly tipsy, delicious, fun. ♦ Chinese ♦ Daily, lunch and dinner. 1077 Rue Clark (between Rue de la Gauchetière W and Blvd René Lévesque). 861.1943

19 MARCHÉ KIM-PHAT

The selection of edibles from far-flung lands at this grocery is a shining example of what makes Montreal's Chinatown so uniquely cosmopolitan in flavor. Shelves are stocked with items from other Asian and Southeast Asian cultures, including *galanga* (a gingerlike root used in Thai and Laotian cooking) and kaffir lime leaves (used in Thai soups). ♦ Tu-W, Su, 9:30AM-7:30PM; Th-Sa, 9:30AM-8:30PM. 1057 Blvd St-Laurent (between Rue de la Gauchetière W and Blvd René Lévesque). 874.0129

20 LA CONCIERGERIE

$ Two adjoining Victorian houses make up this charming gay inn of 17 rooms (of which nine have private bathrooms) on the edge of the Gay Village. A large rooftop terrace with jacuzzi makes for an unexpected urban escape in summertime. ♦ 1019 Rue Hubert (between Rue de la Gauchetière E and Blvd René Lévesque E). 289.9297; fax 289.0845

21 WING BUILDING

The oldest building in Chinatown is also the home of **Wing Noodles**, Canada's largest manufacturer of Chinese noodles and fortune cookies (and a supplier, under different names, to many Asian food companies in the US). Headquartered at this location since 1965, the operation is headed by Gilbert Lee, a third-generation Montrealer whose grandfather ran a local grocery store and whose father founded the noodle business. Lee says visitors are welcome to come in and purchase a bag of noodles, soy sauce, wonton covers, or almond cookies. But the building is of historical interest as well. Erected in 1826, it's the only local structure, besides **Notre-Dame Basilica** in Old Montreal, to survive the fire that devastated this part of the city in 1852. (Curiously, both buildings were designed by US architect **James O'Donnell**.) Originally, the building housed the **British and Canadian School**, a progressive trade school for boys and girls. ◆ 1009 Rue Côté (at Rue de la Gauchetière W). 861.5818

22 KEUNG KEE

★★$$ Though less elaborate than **Chez Chine**, this Cantonese restaurant is much classier than the average Chinatown eatery. Owned and staffed by newcomers form Hong Kong, the restaurant posts daily specials in Chinese on vertical paper menus on the wall, which waiters will cheerfully translate. There's a definite bent toward healthy eating: soups with mustard greens, lamb with spinach, fresh fish, and lots of fresh vegetables. ◆ Cantonese ◆ Daily, lunch and dinner. 70 Rue de la Gauchetière W, second floor (at Rue Clark). 393.1663

22 DR. SUN YAT SEN PARK

Named after the father and first provisional president of the Republic of China (Taiwan), this tranquil spot is marked only by benches and a mound of rocks—a symbol of peace and harmony to the Chinese. There are no swings or slides, but children love to scale the rocks, and passersby often pause here to people-watch while munching on a treat from one of the nearby pastry shops. ◆ Daily, sunrise-sunset. Rues de la Gauchetière W and Clark

22 PATISSERIE C. J. REGENT

East meets West in this bakery: Traditional Chinese sweets are laid out next to French pastries. ◆ Daily. 68 Rue de la Gauchetière W (at Rue Clark). 866.1628

23 PALAIS DES CONGRÈS

Montreal's major convention center has 32 high-tech meeting rooms and 100,000 square feet of exhibition space, enough to handle some 10,000 delegates at once (6,000 in the same room). To reach the center, take the enclosed walkway from **Complexe Guy Favreau**. ◆ 201 Ave Viger W (between Rues St-Urbain and Chenneville). 871.3170

24 HOLIDAY INN

$$$ This nondescript, nonthematic hotel chain broke all its own rules in 1991 when it opened its **Jardin Sinomonde** in Chinatown—topped by twin pagodas and decorated with calligraphy conceived by Aisin-Gioro Pu Cheih, the surviving brother of the last emperor of China. The 235-room inn offers a serendipitous blending of Western comfort with authentic Eastern architecture and food, plus a convenient location, near the **Palais des Congrès** convention center. It also has an executive floor with a lounge for business meetings. ◆ 99 Ave Viger W (at Rue St-Urbain). 878.9888, 800/HOLIDAY; fax 878.6341

Within the Holiday Inn:

CHEZ CHINE

★★★$$$ The most elegant restaurant in Chinatown captures the atmosphere of a serene Chinese garden, complete with a miniature lake swirling with a rainbow of exotic fish. (It's worth a peek even if you don't eat here.) The tables are beautifully set—heavy linen cloths, blue and white porcelain, ivory chopsticks on individual silver holders—and the food, mostly Cantonese, is excellent, plentiful, and, to the uninitiated, daring (pigeon is a specialty). Bite-size dim sum is served every day at lunch, though in an atypical format: Rather than the customary tableside service from an assortment on a wheeled cart, the restaurant offers only a few unusual dim sum items cooked to order (try the shark's fin dumpling), each presented in its own covered dish. ◆ Cantonese ◆ Daily, lunch and dinner. Reservations recommended. 878.9888

UNDERGROUND MONTREAL

Neither winter blizzards nor the hot and humid dog days of summer can frazzle Montrealers, thanks to Underground Montreal, a temperature-controlled subterranean city linking shopping centers and offices via pedestrian corridors and the Metro. Underground Montreal is one of the largest of its kind in the world, used by more than 500,000 people each day. It began in 1962 with the completion of the **Place Ville Marie** office and shopping complex, the first building in Montreal to have an underground shopping mall, which proved to be a hit, and in turn attracted a slew of private developers, who in hodgepodge fashion created this gargantuan city within a city. Today, the primary underground axis runs along the **Bonaventure, McGill,** and **Peel** Metro lines, connecting such important city landmarks as Place Ville Marie, the **Queen Elizabeth Hotel, Place Bonaventure,** the **IBM Marathon Building,** and the **Promenades Cathédrale.**

But Underground Montreal does have plenty of detractors. Although the original planners of Place Ville Marie liked to say they modeled their vision after Leonardo da Vinci's plans for a subterranean city, critics argue that a better comparison would be a velvet painting of Elvis. They complain that the tunnels, though lined with tile, brick, and stone, are long and uninteresting, despite designated areas for musicians and street artists. And they feel that the commercial malls, awash in shoe stores, pretend to be public spaces but are really private, and force pedestrians along confusing and circuitous routes to gain maximum exposure for merchants while luring people away from the traditional aboveground shopping streets such as **Rue Ste-Catherine.** Despite the naysayers, Underground Montreal keeps on growing, with developers ever eager to be connected to it. There are now more than 19.2 miles of underground pedestrian walkways linking 10 subway stations, 60 buildings, seven major hotels, 2,727 apartments, 349 restaurants, 929 boutiques, 19 movie theaters, five universities, six bus and train stations, and 10 performing arts centers. Undeniably convenient, it still has enough interesting shops and sights, including the eye-catching designs of the Metro stations, to make a walk through more than just a detour to avoid inclement weather.

1 PEEL METRO STATION

One of the most aesthetically interesting stations in the city was designed by artist Jean-Paul Mousseau in 1966. Considered revolutionary at the time, multicolored circular patterns run along the walls in dramatic swirls of tinted glass, creating the impression of movement. ♦ Rue Peel and Blvd de Maison-neuve

2 McGILL METRO STATION

How many other subway stations have their own library or a sign flashing information on the quality of the air outside? The Montreal Urban Community air-quality index provides continuous readings of general air quality and individual data on everything from dust to carbon monoxide to ozone. A good general reading is below 25, acceptable is below 50, and a bad reading of more than 50 is enough

to keep people in the tunnels. Situated in the station right above the tracks is the tiny **City of Montreal Library**, where commuting book-worms check out an average of 15,000 books weekly in French and English. The station is decorated with five immense glass panels, painted by artist Nicolas Sollogoub with illus-trations of 19th-century life in Montreal. ♦ Blvd de Maisonneuve and Rue Université

3 LES COURS MONT-ROYAL

When the **Mount Royal Hotel** opened on this site in 1922, it was the largest in the British Empire, with 1,046 rooms. The hotel closed in 1983 and was converted into 175 shops, an office building, and luxury condominiums. Once the hotel's most stunning feature, the huge lobby was replaced by a multistory atrium with a winding staircase. Still here is the original chandelier, which once hung from the ceiling of a casino in Monte Carlo. Fast-

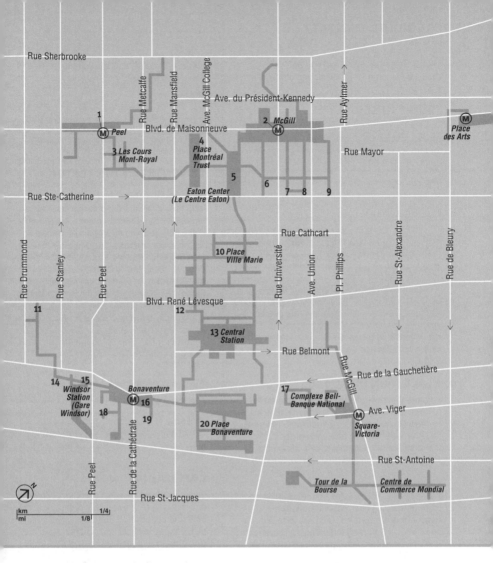

food joints dominate the Metro level of the shopping center, whereas prestigious boutiques occupy the upper floors. To get to the mall, follow signs from **Peel Metro**, or head through what used to be the basement of the now defunct Simpson department store in **Place Montreal Trust**. ♦ M-W, 10AM-6PM; Th-F, 10AM-9PM; Sa, 10AM-5PM; Su, noon-5PM. 1455 Rue Peel (between Rue Ste-Catherine and Blvd de Maisonneuve). 842.7777

Within Les Cours Mont-Royal:

BAGEL PLACE

This is one of only two places downtown (**Le Faubourg Ste-Catherine** is the other) where you can stock up on authentic Montreal bagels baked in a wood-burning oven. ♦ M-W, Sa; Th-F, 9:30AM-9PM; Su, noon-5PM. 848.1802

GIORGIO EMPORIO

Not to be confused with Emporio Armani, this upper-end clothing boutique carries such high-profile designer labels as Donna Karan, Gianfranco Ferre, Thierry Mugler, and Dolce & Gabbana. There are two nearly adjacent stores, one for men and one for women.

GUY & DODO MORALI

★★$$$ This husband-and-wife team prepares such French classics as beef Wellington as well as slightly less traditional dishes. Other good bets are cream of spinach soup, marinated shrimp and scallop salad, salmon in puff pastry with sorrel sauce, and rack of lamb with five sauces. For dessert, try the pan-fried apples with pistachios. With fresh roses atop white linen tablecloths, muted lighting, and dark wood trim, the atmosphere is elegantly cozy. Don't be surprised if the chef visits

---

Restaurants/Clubs: Red | Hotels: Purple | Shops: Orange | Outdoors/Parks: Green | Sights/Culture: Blue

your table to ask if you're happy with your meal. ◆ French ◆ Daily, lunch and dinner. 842.3636

HARRY ROSEN

The Montreal outpost of this Canadian menswear chain is a real looker: 22,000 square feet of designer labels from Armani to Zegna, on two attractive levels. 284.3315

PR'ALINE

Delicious, authentic—and expensive—Belgian chocolates flown in directly from Belgium by owner Michel Daras are available at this small counter. ◆ M-W, Sa; Th-F, 9:30AM-9PM; Su, noon-5PM. No phone

STYLEXCHANGE

This busy bi-level shop pulsates to a techno beat and specializes in street chic for hip young ladies and gentlemen, and the goods can take the form of anything from bright dyed jeans and ready-to-wear to the latest club-remix CDs and trendy housewares. 282.6500

4 PLACE MONTREAL TRUST

Perhaps the most popular underground mall to open in the city in the last 5 years, this five-level complex has 120 shops and restaurants, an eye-catching antique bronze fountain, and a breathtaking central atrium. Annoyingly (but strategically) placed, the only escalators are at either end, so you must walk the mall's entire length before you can reach the next level. Follow signs from **McGill Metro** or enter the mall directly from the **Eaton Center**. ◆ M-W, Sa; Th-F, 9:30AM-9PM; Su, noon-5PM. 1500 Ave McGill College (between Rue Ste-Catherine and Blvd de Maisonneuve). 843.8000

Within Place Montreal Trust:

INDIGO

With its immense bilingual selection, this multilevel book and music emporium is Montreal's answer to Barnes & Noble—though it arguably has more character. Stop in at the café if you need to refuel for serious browsing. Unlike the other stores in the **Place Montreal Trust**, this one has extended hours. ◆ Daily, 9AM-11PM. 281-5549

LES PALMES

★$$ Opening directly onto the mall and crowded with palm trees, this restaurant features California cuisine and an excellent view of the mall's atrium. ◆ California ◆ Daily, lunch. Level 3. 499.9903

MEXX

A department store unto itself, this sleek 17,000-square-foot space on three floors showcases collections for women, teens, and children. 288.6399

ZARA

The trendy Spanish retailer's large Montreal outpost is practically a department store unto itself and includes sections for men, women, and children. ◆ 281.2001

5 LE CENTRE EATON (EATON CENTER)

With four levels of boutiques surrounding an impressive open atrium under a skylight, this is the largest commercial mall downtown. It replaced **Les Terrasses**, a hopelessly confusing shopping mall that left visitors lost and grumbling. To reach the mall, follow signs from **McGill Metro**, or take the new tunnel from **Place Ville Marie**. (The tunnel is open Monday to Friday between 6AM and 1AM and Saturday and Sunday between 7AM and 1AM.) ◆ Store hours: M-F, 10AM-9PM; Sa, 10AM-5PM; Su, noon-5PM. 705 Rue Ste-Catherine (between Rue Université and Ave McGill College). 288.3708

Within Eaton Center (Le Centre Eaton):

GEOMANIA

Minerals, shells, crystals, and fossils are turned into art at this store. There's also a good selection of Inuit soapstone carvings. ◆ 842.0446

CAFÉMANIA

Select from a wide variety of coffee beans while enjoying a fresh-brewed cup at this complete, one-stop coffee shop. Coffee machines and all the paraphernalia a java connoisseur would ever need are also sold. ◆ 894.0197

CHOCOLATIER DASKALIDÈS

Pick out some chocolate truffles for a friend or colleague, then splurge for yourself with some gourmet caramels, raspberry chocolate bars, or whatever other varieties of chocolates on offer strike your fancy. ◆ 847.0043

CRÊPES DE GÉRARD

Superb French crêpes are the specialty at this tiny takeout counter. ◆ 845.5502

LA CABINE TÉLÉPHONIQUE

Phones in every conceivable shape fill this store, from Coca-Cola bottles to dress shoes to hamburgers to Batmobiles. You'll also find more conventional answering machines, cordless phones, fax machines, and accessories. ◆ 282.2063

ÉDITION LIMITÉE MORGAN

Collectors flock to this sports card and comic-book store for everything from autographed

Mario Lemieux and Wayne Gretzky hockey sweaters to original comic-book art. ♦ 849.0394

6 COMPLEXE LES AILES

The cornerstone of this shopping complex, adjacent to Eaton Center, is the attractive, upscale **Les Ailes de La Mode** department store, a showcase of such international designer labels as Hugo Boss, Giorgio Armani, Max Mara, Teenflo, and Helena Rubenstein. The four-story emporium, which occupies the site of the old Eaton department store, has such modern touches as a sushi counter, cloakroom for greater winter shopping ease, and a Clairins Beauty Institute. ♦ M-W, 10AM-6PM; Th, F, 10AM-9PM; Sa, 10AM-5PM; Su, noon-5PM. ♦ 677 Rue Ste-Catherine W (at Rue Université). 282.4537

Within Complexe Les Ailes:

SAQ SIGNATURE MONTREAL

This wine and liquor store is so elegant and impressively stocked you'd never guess it was run by the provincial government. There are occasional wine tastings. 282.9445

7 PROMENADES CATHÉDRALE

Located below **Christ Church Cathedral**, this 100-store shopping mall is part of **Place de la Cathédrale**, an office tower that is known as the "Batman building" or "cat ears building" because of the shape of its roof. Built in the late 1980s, **Place de la Cathédrale** stirred up controversy because designs showed its 34 stories would overpower the historic cathedral. The glitzy underground shopping mall was considered by some inappropriate. But the church ultimately agreed to lease its land and air rights to the developers. Perhaps in keeping with the cathedral above, the shopping mall's Gothic concrete ceiling makes it darker and more subdued than other malls. ♦ Store hours: M-W, 10AM-6PM; Th-F, 10AM-9PM; Sa, 9AM-5PM; Su, noon-5PM. 625 Rue Ste-Catherine W (between Ave Union and Rue Université). 849.8230

Within the Promenades Cathédrale:

LINEN CHEST

The huge selection of linens and kitchenware make this department store popular for bridal registries. It stocks an assortment of gifts and home accessories from Royal Doulton china to music boxes. ♦ 282.9525

MONTREAL

Not your run-of-the-mill watch store, this boutique carries an unusually large selection of relatively inexpensive but trendy watches. The name is also a play on words: *montre* is French for "watch." ♦ 288.6834

ALDO

This chain store has an extensive selection of fashionable, reasonably priced Italian shoes for men and women. ♦ 848.0566

LE PARCHEMIN

★★★$$$ Linked to **Place de la Cathédrale** by a corridor, this restaurant used to be the parish house of **Christ Church Cathedral**. The building (completed in 1876 and classified as a historic monument) was dismantled during the construction of the office tower and shopping mall, then rebuilt stone by stone in 1988 and turned into this three-story restaurant. The cuisine is equal to the beautiful setting. Try the fine seafood crepes. For dessert, the crème caramel with fruit is delicious. After your meal, venture outside to the **Cloister Garden**, a small park between the church and the office tower. This flower garden, mostly hidden from the street, is one of the best-kept secrets in the city. ♦ French ♦ Daily, lunch and dinner. 1333 Rue Université (between Rue Ste-Catherine and Blvd de Maisonneuve). 844.1619

8 CHRIST CHURCH CATHEDRAL

This historic Protestant church is open for prayer every day and also features regular afternoon choral and organ concerts. Built in 1859, it was the first structure in Montreal to be faced in the limestone, or graystone, from local quarries that now graces so many homes in the city. The tower of the church appears to be made of stone as well, but it's actually an aluminum replica of the original stone tower, which had to be replaced in the 1920s when it threatened to topple beneath its own weight. ♦ Daily. 1440 Ave Union (between Rue Ste-Catherine and Blvd de Maisonneuve). 288.6421

9 LA BAIE (THE BAY)

During the winters of 1610 and 1611, when Henry Hudson visited the shoreline of what was to become Hudson Bay, he traded two beaver pelts for the land before him. That was the genesis for a trading company that would evolve into **Hudson's Bay Company**, one of Canada's largest department store chains. Construction of this flagship store, originally called **Morgan's**, in 1890 heralded commercial development on Rue Ste-Catherine. This store has moderately priced merchandise, including its famous striped Hudson's Bay

---

Restaurants/Clubs: Red | Hotels: Purple | Shops: Orange | Outdoors/Parks: Green | Sights/Culture: Blue

coats, as well as fashionable clothing. To reach the store, follow signs from **McGill Metro**; it's also connected underground to the **Promenades Cathédrale**. ♦ M-W, Sa; Th-F, 10AM-9PM; Su, noon-5PM. 585 Rue Ste-Catherine (between Pl Phillips and Ave Union). 281.4422

10 PLACE VILLE MARIE

Developed at a cost of $105 million, Montreal's most famous office building rises above an open plaza that's three times the size of New York City's Rockefeller Center and contains more rentable space than the Empire State Building. The brainchild of swashbuckling US developer William Zeckendorf, the building covers what used to be a large, ugly tract of railway yards lying in a trench extending from the **Queen Elizabeth Hotel** and **Central Station** to the commuter railway tunnel beneath Mont-Royal. After securing air rights to the site, Zeckendorf, backed by Donald Gordon of the **Canadian National Railway**, hired architect **I.M. Pei** to design the tower, which was built in the shape of a cross to commemorate the wooden cross erected by the French-Catholic founders of the original settlement. The design is strikingly appropriate—Montreal was the largest Catholic city in North America north of Mexico, originally founded as a mission for the conversion of Indian allies. It is symbolic of the boom years leading to **Expo '67**, when the golden word in Montreal was *development*. You can enjoy the view from the restaurant **Altitude 737**, on the forty-sixth floor, or from the terrace lounge two flights below (397.0737). To symbolize the tower's new dominance—and as a way to ward off airplanes at night—a rotating beacon whose light can shine across 35 miles was installed on its roof.

At first, retailers considered the underground shopping mall a folly, but its proximity to tens of thousands of office workers and to commuters coming through nearby Central Station guaranteed success. Also linked to the Queen Elizabeth Hotel, the complex set the standard for what was to become the city's underground network. In 1988, shopping corridors were renovated, and skylights, arched ceilings with indirect lighting, and marble tile floors, as well as a fast-food court to keep pace with a new generation, were added. ♦ Shopping mall: M-W, 9:30AM-6PM; Th-F, 9:30AM-9PM; Sa, 9:30AM-5PM; Su, noon-5PM. Blvd René Lévesque and Rue Université. 866.6666

Within Place Ville Marie:

CHAUSSURES BROWNS

This outlet in the men's and women's shoe store chain is one of the largest and best in the city. It's pricey, but aren't your feet worth it? ♦ 861.8925

DANS UN JARDIN

This shops purveys an attractive selection of fragrant soaps, bath gels, perfumes, and cosmetics, many from France. ♦ 954.1284

LAURA SECORD

Some say that if it weren't for this store, the War of 1812 might have been won by the Americans. Secord overheard some American soldiers planning a surprise attack on a British outpost and walked 30 miles through wilderness to warn the Brits. As a result, the Yanks were the ones surprised, and hundreds surrendered. Laura's heroism is now "honored" by this nationwide chain of chocolates stores, which sells a variety of sweets. ♦ 861.7867

11 IBM–MARATHON BUILDING

Unlike most Montreal high-rises, this one has a designer label, that of the New York firm of **Kohn, Pederson, Fox**. Built in 1991, the 1-million-square-foot building is considered the most innovative downtown skyscraper since **Place Ville Marie** was completed in 1962. The asymmetrical design consists of 45 stories of granite and glass that curve up the east side of the building and the west side is squared off for a dramatic contrast. From the **Bonaventure Metro**, follow the "1250 Blvd René Lévesque" sign. ♦ 1250 Blvd René Lévesque (between Rues Stanley and Drummond)

12 FAIRMONT QUEEN ELIZABETH HOTEL

$$$$ Forty-four years old, but not looking a day over 18 (at least not from the inside), this grande dame of Montreal hotels still reigns as the largest hotel in the city. It has had its fair share of boldfaced names in residence at one time or another, including John Lennon, who held his famous "bed-in" with Yoko Ono here in 1969 (it was in **suite 1742**). Offering excellent service in fine style, the 1,050-room hostelry has a wide range of facilities, including a day-care center for children up to age 12, and a fully equipped health club and aquatic center. The rooms are modern in décor, many with bright, pastel accents of mauve, light green, or lilac. **Entrée Gold**, a sort of hotel within the hotel, offers guests a private lounge, concierge service, and an executive boardroom on the eighteenth and nineteenth floors. Guests are whisked there by a private, glass-walled elevator, providing a panoramic view of the city, and met by a concierge. There's also an executive level on the third floor. To reach the hotel, follow the signs from **Place Ville Marie**. ♦ 900 Blvd René Lévesque (at Rue Mansfield). 861.3511, 800/441.1414; fax 954.2256

THE BEST

George Balcan

Former Morning Radio Host, CJAD Radio, Montreal

The best sensation is a jet boat ride through the **Lachine Rapids** on the **St. Lawrence River**. Save this one for a sizzling July or August afternoon; you won't mind getting soaked to the skin, even through the gear they make you wear.

The best naval-gazing is at **Old Port**, where you'll see Canadian Navy vessels (and sometimes other countries' ships, too). You'll be welcomed aboard.

The best free music is the bagpiper with kilt and full regalia who walks the five floors of the **Oglivy** department store every day, starting about noon.

The best smoked meat (not to be confused with pastrami) can be found at **Schwartz's Deli** . . . on **Boulevard St-Laurent**.

Les Halles on **Rue Crescent** has the best French dining because host-owner Jacques Landurie still gives you the finest food and service. Leave room for Paris Brest, a dessert originally served on trains between these two French cities.

The best sushi is at **Mikado** on **Laurier** (nice shopping street, too). Ask for "Steve's Roll"—if Kimyo has the time, they'll make it for you.

The best approach to the city (by car) at night is over the **Champlain Bridge** from the south, where you can catch the city reflected in the St. Lawrence, including the skyline, the outline of **Mont-Royal** in the center of the city, and the illuminated cross on its eastern slope. Don't do it on Sunday night or you'll be caught in the usual 2-hour traffic jam of Montrealers coming home after a weekend in the **Eastern Townships** and Vermont.

The best summer festivals are part of the **International Jazz Festival**, usually held the first 10 days of July, which features some 2,000 jazz performers (two thirds of the shows are free); in 1992, it attracted 1.3 million people. Next up is the **Just for Laughs/Juste Pour Rire Festival**, held during the middle 10 days of July, attracting over 250 performers (lots of free street acts, including mimes) and some of the biggest comedy names. Get hotel reservations early.

Within the Fairmont Queen Elizabeth Hotel:

BEAVER CLUB

★★★★$$$$ From the classical haute cuisine to the quality of the wine cellar, this restaurant ranks among the best in Canada. Created in 1785, it's named after a 19th-century fraternity of Scottish and French Canadian fur traders, who included New Yorker John Jacob Astor as an honorary member. Originally, animal furs lined the wooden interior, lending an aura of the early days of the fur trade. In recent years, however, the furs have been replaced with paintings by Canadian artists, accenting the traditional décor with a gallery-like setting. Fresh flowers, soft lighting, and white table linens offer an air of elegance. The excellent menu includes such dishes as roast prime rib of beef au jus and a terrine of duckling with pistachios and onions. This is also the only restaurant in Montreal that offers cigars after your meal. It still hosts an annual banquet, a high-society affair in which everyone dresses in fur-trader garb. ◆ French/Canadian ◆ M-F, lunch and dinner; Sa, dinner; Su, brunch and dinner. 861.3511

13 CENTRAL STATION

The home of Canada's passenger rail line, **VIA Rail Canada**, this is also the point of departure of **Amtrak** and commuter trains. Busy travelers can grab a quick bite in the fast-food corridor, which is decorated like an old-fashioned train station. Even the **McDonald's** sports a railway motif. ◆ Blvd René Lévesque and Rue Mansfield. VIA Rail Canada, 871.1331; Amtrak, 800/872.7245

14 MOLSON CENTER

This state-of-the-art sports complex with a 21,000-seat capacity next to **Windsor Station**, several blocks east of the old **Montreal Forum**, is home to the **Montreal Canadiens** hockey team. The stadium is accessible by two Metro stops (**Lucien L'Allier** and **Bonaventure**) and via Montreal's extensive underground pedestrian city. The enormous complex doubles as a concert hall–theater with more than 225 concessions, 38 snack bars, and 3 restaurants, including a 300-seat brasserie. ◆ 1260 Rue de la Gauchetière (bordered by Rues Peel, de la Montagne, and St-Antoine). 989.2841

Within the Molson Center:

LA BOUTIQUE DES CANADIENS

A paradise for hockey fans and collectors of **Montreal Canadiens** memorabilia, this store has anything you can think of that could hold a monogram—from sweaters, cups, and pens to miniature replicas of the **Stanley Cup**. ◆ M-W, Sa; Th-F, 9:30AM-9PM. 989.2836

Restaurants/Clubs: Red | Hotels: Purple | Shops: Orange | Outdoors/Parks: Green | Sights/Culture: Blue

SWEET RITE OF SPRING

"A la cabane! Sortez le violon!" ("Everybody to the sugar shack! Get out the fiddle!") In Quebec, the arrival of spring is celebrated with maple-syrupy feasts, accompanied by traditional music and dance to work off the calories. Between mid-March and late April, after the sap in the maple trees has risen, Quebecers head to their local *cabanes-à-sucre* ("sugar shacks") to fill up on treats soaked, sopped, drenched, and doused in syrup. A few sugar shacks are open year-round.

Traditional sugar-shack menus feature crispy deep-fried pancakes drizzled with maple syrup, oblong slivers of salted pork rind fried into *oreilles de crisse* (Christ's ears), fried eggs in puddles of syrup, crocks of maple-flavored baked beans, and fried ham. For dessert, there's maple sugar pie, maple pudding, and—everybody's favorite—a group binge called *tire sur la neige* ("pull on the snow"): Boiling syrup is dribbled over a long, shallow trough filled with fresh snow, and everybody stabs and pulls at it with forks, stretching it into a golden taffy. Although *cabanes* once were literally shacks, most today are informal restaurants, many resembling barns, where people gather at long tables for a communal sugar rush.

Quebec—Canada's biggest syrup-producing province—provides the rest of the country with 92% of its maple products. Although the **Beauce** region is the heart of Quebec's sugar country, there are *sucreries* scattered throughout **Montérégie**, the **Laurentians**, **Lanaudière**, the **Eastern Townships**, and **Coeur-du-Québec**.

The old-fashioned way of collecting the syrup—by tapping the trees, catching the sap in buckets, and gathering the buckets with draft horses—has largely been replaced by a system of tubes that connects each tree to a sophisticated boiling room. But old-timers insist that the taste of today's maple syrup lacks the spunk of the dark, coarse stuff that came from hours of boiling outdoors, where the wind would blow leaves and ashes into the kettles, or cinders would fall into the mixture—all imparting a little extra flavor. This crude method of making syrup may seem more romantic, but hauling around 35-pound pails of sap and boiling it through the night was exhausting. Even with modern methods, making maple syrup is labor intensive: One quart of pure syrup requires boiling down 40 quarts of sap.

According to the legends of native North Americans, it wasn't always difficult to get sweet, thick syrup from the trees. Once upon a time, the sap that dripped from maple trees was almost pure syrup, but the Ottawa Indian god Ne-naw-Bo-zhoo found its taste too delicious. Not wanting his human "nephews" to undervalue it, he diluted the sap until its sweetness was barely discernible. Other legends and superstitions involving maple syrup have flowed through Beauce over the years, persisting into modern times. It was once believed that working in the sugar bush (woods of sugar maples) on Good Friday would make your trees drip blood instead of sugar. Beaucerons also thought that an owner who died before receiving payment for the sale of his sugar bush would haunt the sap boilers at their nightly work. And people still remember when *cabanes* served as hideouts for men fleeing conscription during World War II, and when a night spent in charge of the sugar bush constituted a youth's rite of passage to manhood.

Generations of Amerindians have practically worshiped the maple sugar tree, which, they said, "cried sugar with tears of crystal." Just as the Indians eagerly awaited springtime and the Festival of the Maple Moon, when they could fortify themselves by drinking the sap, today's Quebecers' mouths water at the approach of the vernal season.

15 GARE WINDSOR (WINDSOR STATION)

Completed in 1889, this historic train station was originally the eastern terminal and head office of the **Canadian Pacific Railway**. Long the hub for much Canadian commerce and travel, and a major transit hub for immigrants and soldiers on their way to war, it plays a less glorious role today as the terminal for one of Montreal's suburban commuter rail systems. During more than a century of operation, the station has expanded several times, the most spectacular addition being a long, glass-roofed concourse that was added in 1913. ♦ Rues de la Gauchetière and Peel

Within Gare Windsor:

LA RÔTISSERIE ST-HUBERT

★$$ This immense restaurant is the urban flagship of a popular Quebec chain and serves just about every conceivable cut of chicken, plus such nonpoultry items as ribs. The place is attractive enough, but don't expect anything too gourmet, as the menu caters to families and Canadiens fans who may appreciate the proximity to Molson Center as much as a good chicken dinner. ♦ Canadian ♦ Daily, lunch and dinner. 1180 Rue de la Gauchetière W (at Rue Peel). 866.0500

16 BONAVENTURE METRO STATION

Montreal's Metro, unlike most subway systems, is a delight to the eye and the ear: Each station is individually designed, and some, like this one, are quite dramatic; and the French-designed trains, which run on rubber tires, are much quieter than those with steel wheels. The station was inaugurated in 1966, during a busy period of preparation for **Expo '67**. One of the system's original stations, it was built in a dug-out pit rather than a tunnel, which allowed for the construction of large, concrete-vaulted spaces that make the station reminiscent of an underground basilica. This is among the most important Metro stations in the city, because it connects **Windsor** and **Central Stations**, **Place Bonaventure**, the **Marriott Château Champlain**, and the **IBM–Marathon** and **1000 de la Gauchetière** office buildings. It also gives access to the **Molson Center** sports complex. ♦ Rues de la Cathédrale and de la Gauchetière

17 Aérobus Station

Situated in the **Canadian National** building, to the south of **Central Station**, this shuttle terminal alleviates the hassle of traveling to and from Montreal's airports. The one-way fare to Dorval is $12 and $20 to Mirabel. Money exchange, snacks, newspapers, and duty-free shopping are also available. ♦ 777 Rue de La Gauchetière (at Rue Université). 394.7369, 931.9002

18 Marriott Château Champlain

$$$ An elevator is the only link between the hotel and the underground city. Completed in 1966, this 611-room hotel is affectionately known as the Cheese Grater because each of the windows is recessed inside a convex arch. Each room is traditional in décor, with mahogany furnishings and fluffy down comforters and brightened by floor-to-ceiling arched windows. Follow signs from the **Bonaventure Metro**. ♦ 1 Place du Canada (between Rues de la Cathédrale and Peel). 878.9000, 800/200.5909; fax 878.6761 ఉ

19 1000 Rue de la Gauchetière

If swimming outdoors during winter at the **Montreal Bonaventure Hilton** doesn't suit your taste, perhaps you'd prefer a few cool turns around this office tower's indoor skating rink in the middle of summer. Inspired by the skating rink at Rockefeller Center, the 10,000-square-foot **L'Amphithéâtre Bell Rink** (395.0555) is bathed in natural sunlight and open year-round to the public, providing skate rentals, skate sharpening, and changing rooms. Fast-food restaurants surround the rink, along with seating for 1,600 for the occasional ice show. The rink can also accommodate parties and conventions by covering the ice with a wood floor. In the building's basement is a bus terminal for transit to the communities on the south shore of the St. Lawrence River and a link to the Metro. Both this and the **IBM–Marathon Building** claim to be Montreal's tallest. Although each is no higher than 232 meters (approximately 760 feet)—because no building in Montreal can be taller than **Mont-Royal**—1000 de la Gauchetière might get the nod because it's built on lower ground. Follow signs from the **Bonaventure Metro**. ♦ Between Rues Mansfield and de la Cathédrale

20 Place Bonaventure

Some call this immense, 13-story concrete cube, occupying an entire 6-acre block, an example of architectural brutalism. On the inside, the complex houses a shopping mall, two cavernous exhibition halls (which host more than 60 major trade shows and exhibitions annually), and a merchandise mart. The surprisingly intimate 400-room **Hilton** hotel on the roof surrounds a charming garden. To reach the complex, follow signs from **Central Station**. ♦ 901 Rue de la Gauchetière (at Rue Université). 397.2355

Within Place Bonaventure:

Montreal Bonaventure Hilton

$$$$ Where else can you enjoy a winter swim in an outdoor pool surrounded by snowbanks and guests bundled against the cold? The hotel's exterior rooftop swimming pool is heated, as is the air around it, allowing guests to swim outside even when it's −40 degrees with the windchill factor. Afterward, retreat to one of the 393 cozy guest rooms to curl up in an overstuffed chair and enjoy a spectacular view of the city. Each room is done in soft pastels and boasts newly renovated bathrooms—all with marble fixtures. In summer, the snowbanks give way to a charming and lush waterfall rock garden, home to ducks, pheasants, and goldfish. There's an executive floor and lounge offering concierge service and complimentary continental breakfast. ♦ 878.2332, 800/445.8667; fax 878.3881

Within the Montreal Bonaventure Hilton:

Le Castillon

★★★$$$$ Stunning views of the hotel's rooftop gardens are just one of the highlights of this luxurious restaurant, where the wine cellar is renowned and the haute cuisine is oh so French. Especially good is the fresh salmon prepared in a pastry with spinach and lobster cream sauce, or poached with leeks and served with a watercress sauce. The dining room is elegant, with chandeliers and velvet-paneled high-backed chairs. ♦ French ♦ M-F, lunch and dinner; Sa-Su, dinner. 878.2332

Restaurants/Clubs: Red | Hotels: Purple | Shops: Orange | Outdoors/Parks: Green | Sights/Culture: Blue

STE-CATHERINE

ong after other Canadian cities have turned out the lights for the night, Montreal is just warming up, especially around Rue Ste-Catherine, where 3AM traffic jams are not uncommon. Although this vibrant and colorful sweep of street is home to some of Montreal's most popular bars and restaurants by night, it's also the city's business core, with shops and office complexes keeping the action rolling by day. Rue Ste-Catherine is the street of choice for major festivities as well, including the Stanley Cup Parades for the beloved, oft-victorious **Montreal Canadiens** and the lively St. Patrick's Day Parade.

The street got its name between 1801 and 1817, but historians are still arguing over whether it was meant to honor St. Catherine of Alexandria, St. Catherine of Siena, or another St. Catherine. Most do agree, however, that it has never been particularly saintly and has definitely become less so in recent years. Strip joints with names such as **Super Sexe** have proliferated, to the embarrassment of Montreal's city council, which has tried without success to force club owners to take down their gaudy, sexist signs. In addition, fast-food restaurants, chain stores, and pinball arcades threaten to homogenize the area, leaving only the French-language signs that Quebec law requires to set it apart from every other commercial street in North America.

A number of retailers were hard hit by the increase in underground shopping malls. Rue Ste-Catherine is still holding its own, however, thanks in part to recent developments on adjoining streets. In the 1980s, **Avenue McGill College** between **Place Ville Marie** and **McGill University** was widened in an attempt to turn it into Montreal's Champs-Elysées, and it's now lined with glitzy office towers. Nearby at **Boulevard René Lévesque** and **Rue Stanley** is the new **IBM–Marathon Building** (see page 44), the most

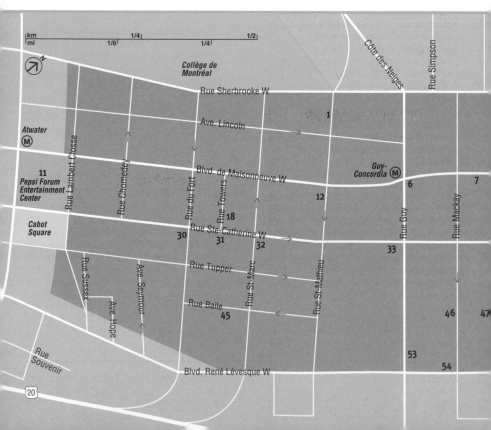

striking addition to the city's skyline since Place Ville Marie was built 30 years ago. Popular bars and restaurants have moved into the classic graystone houses on **Rues Crescent, Bishop,** and **de la Montagne. Le Faubourg Ste-Catherine,** the bustling new market at the corner of Rues Ste-Catherine and Guy, is a favorite with shoppers and moviegoers. Nearby, the **Shaughnessy Village** area draws architecture enthusiasts, who come to visit the new **Canadian Centre for Architecture** and to stroll through the neighborhood and look at the lovingly restored graystone homes.

Although the Rue Ste-Catherine area is ideal for walking, pedestrians should take note that downtown Montreal is notorious for having some of the most maniacal drivers in North America, as well as very aggressive pedestrians. Despite the fact that crosswalks seem to be a signal for motorists to speed up, pedestrians tend to cross at any time regardless of the light. If you wait at a red light when there's no traffic, Montrealers will think you're from Toronto. Jaywalking is a local pastime, and residents treat the rare police crackdowns with bemusement.

1 AU BISTRO GOURMET

★★$$$ The welcome is warm and the ambiance friendly at this charming little bistro. The menu, a simple sheet of modified table d'hôte, or full-course meals, includes soup or appetizer, a main dish, and vegetables. The delicious, thick cream soups, the veal kidneys with mustard sauce, and *tournedos du gourmet* are outstanding. Don't pass up the housemade, open-fruit flans. ◆

French ◆ M-F, lunch and dinner; Sa-Su, dinner. Reservations recommended. 2100 Rue St-Mathieu (between Ave Lincoln and Rue Sherbrooke W). 846.1553 &

2 TROÏKA

★★★$$$ Opened in 1962, the old-country flavor of this delightful Russian restaurant is enhanced by the musicians dressed as gypsies who stroll among the tables playing

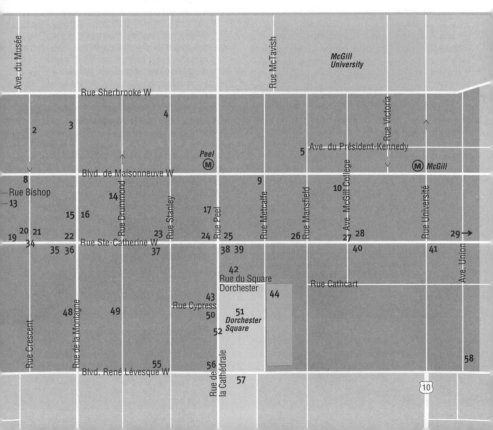

traditional violin or accordion tunes, and the waitstaff dressed in Russian clothing from czarist days. Begin with imported vodka and fresh caviar, for which the restaurant is famous. Then dig into one of the fine authentic main dishes—chicken Kiev is a favorite, as are hot or cold borscht, beef Stroganoff, and wild boar. ♦ Russian ♦ Daily, lunch and dinner. Reservations recommended on Saturdays and Sundays. 2171 Rue Crescent (between Blvd de Maisonneuve W and Ave Lincoln). 849.9333 &

2 GALERIE D'ARTS CONTEMPORAINS

In this gallery you'll find original works by both Canadian and European artists, including Riopelle, Miró, Pellan, Bellefleur, Thibault, and Castelli. ♦ M-F, 10AM-6PM; Sa, 11AM-5PM. 2165 Rue Crescent (between Blvd de Maisonneuve W and Rue Sherbrooke W). 844.6711

3 KATSURA

★★$$$$ Kimono-clad waitresses add to the atmosphere of this classy—and expensive—Japanese restaurant. Slip off your shoes and enjoy the excellent sushi at one of the low-lying tatami bars, which can accommodate groups between 4 and 30. If you prefer to be closer to the action, the restaurant also has a sushi bar. ♦ Japanese ♦ M-F, lunch and

When the army of the Continental Congress occupied Montreal during the winter of 1775-1776, Benjamin Franklin attempted to convince Canadians to support the US cause against the British by bringing a bilingual printer (Fleury de Mesplet) from Philadelphia to produce persuasive political pamphlets in French and English. After the British defeated them in Quebec, the Americans hurried home, leaving poor Mesplet with his expensive and cumbersome press. As he had never been paid for his expenses or services, Mesplet also needed to earn some money. In 1778, turning to his sole asset, he began printing the French-language *La Gazette de Commerce et Littéraire*, a broadsheet that evolved into the English-language *Gazette*, Montreal's oldest newspaper and its only enduring English daily.

Montreal has a booming film industry, employing approximately 9,000 people and pumping more than $1.5 billion into the local economy.

Montreal is a world leader in special-effects software for film. Movies such as *Titanic*, *Jurassic Park*, and *Godzilla* all used software designed in Montreal.

dinner; Sa-Su, dinner. 2170 Rue de la Montagne (between Blvd de Maisonneuve W and Rue Sherbrooke W). 849.1172 &

4 LE TAJ

★★$$ The *tandoor* (a traditional clay oven used to bake meats, poultry, and fresh *nan* bread) is glassed in to let you see the chef preparing the food in this Indian restaurant. Lamb chops and a variety of curry and vegetarian dishes are served on sizzling cast-iron platters. ♦ Indian ♦ M-Sa, lunch and dinner. 2077 Rue Stanley (between Blvd de Maisonneuve W and Rue Sherbrooke W). 845.9015

HÔTEL LE GERMAIN

5 HÔTEL LE GERMAIN

$$$$ Montreal's first genuine boutique hotel, perched in a quiet spot in downtown near Rue Sherbrooke, is also one of its most popular. The nondescript façade of a former office building conceals a small but chic lobby with easygoing staff members clad in uniforms designed by Montreal designer Philippe Dubuc. The Lemay-Michaud décor in the 101 rooms is defined by dark natural woods that contrast with earth-tone fabrics and soft, natural-fiber linens that adorn uncommonly comfortable beds. The high-ceilinged rooms have comfortable, oversize furniture and lamps on tripods, and a glass wall separates the shower from the bedroom (there are curtains). State-of-the-art televisions, CD players, and Internet connections are some of the added touches that give the rooms the atmosphere of a chic urban loft. A small mezzanine-level restaurant features a small bistro menu; it's also here where guests can enjoy a top-flight continental breakfast, included in the room rate. ♦ 2050 Rue Mansfield (at Ave du Président-Kennedy). 849.2050, 877/333.2050; fax 849.1437 &

6 PLACE NORMAN BETHUNE

Near the end of the 1930s, Norman Bethune, a Montreal doctor, helped tend to the wounded and dying of Mao Tse Tung's army in China, where he is considered a national hero. The Chinese government donated the monument that honors him, which now graces this tiny square. ♦ Blvd de Maisonneuve W and Rue Guy

7 CINÉMATHÈQUE CANADA (THE CONSERVATORY OF CINEMATOGRAPHIC ART)

The conservatory screens a range of classic, experimental, and obscure European films—from Soviet releases to Oscar winners for best foreign-language film—at less than half the price of first-run movies. The conservatory is located in a 200-seat auditorium at **Concordia University** in the **J. W. McConnell Building**, a stunning library that was completed in 1992. Two-month schedules are available for free; call 848-4779 for information. ♦ 1400 Blvd de Maisonneuve W (between Rues Bishop and Mackay)

NEWTOWN

8 NEWTOWN

★★★$$ Formula One racing champ Jacques Villeneuve translated his name into English and gave it to this high-profile, tri-level restaurant, bar, and club. The overall effect of the polished wood floors, textured walls, and tones of black, white, and above all gray throughout, combined with the always upbeat music, may be more Miami than Montreal, but no matter: This has rapidly become *the* place to see and be seen on Rue Crescent. With its prominent bar and outdoor terrace, the focus of the first floor (the lounge) is libations, but a bistro menu offers such dishes as black bean and chili–rubbed chicken and steak au poivre with fries. The formal restaurant occupies the second floor and offers an upscale surf-and-turf menu: Try the salmon in parchment paper with julienned vegetables and vermouth or espresso-crusted filet of beef with sweet-potato purée and Brussels sprouts. The third-floor terrace, open to the stars in summer, offers a light menu similar to the first-floor lounge. There's also a disco in the basement level that, like the lounge and terrace, plays host to local and visiting DJs. ♦ Eclectic ♦ Daily, lunch and dinner. Reservations recommended. 1476 Rue Crescent (at Blvd de Maisonneuve W). 284.6555

9 BENS

★$ In 1908, Ben Kravitz made his first smoked-meat sandwich based on his Lithuanian mother's recipe. Today both the smoked-meat sandwich and the restaurant he opened have become Montreal institutions. Unchanged since the 1940s, the décor consists of vinyl booths, yellow Formica counters, green tiled floors, neon lighting, and walls covered with faded publicity shots of the famous, the once-famous, and the never-famous. The low-lying building holds its own among high-rises, because the Kravitz family has steadfastly refused to sell its storefront to developers. Canadian novelist Hugh MacLennan once called this deli the nearest thing Montreal has to Delphi—the ancient Greek shrine of peace—a place where everybody from students and tourists to separatist politicians can meet and exchange ideas over a sandwich. Definitely try the smoked-meat sandwiches, blintzes, French onion soup, or a cheap breakfast. But avoid the more inventive combinations such as smoked-meat egg rolls, Chinese fried rice with smoked meat, and smoked-meat spaghetti. ♦ Deli ♦ Daily, breakfast, lunch, and dinner. The restaurant closes only for a few hours around 5AM. 990 Blvd de Maisonneuve W (at Rue Metcalfe). 844.1000

10 PARAGRAPHE

One of Montreal's most literary bookstores, it's known for its esoteric selection, good sales of remainders, and literature section. The café within the bookstore serves light fare, and you're welcome to read a book from the shelves while you eat—as long as you watch the crumbs. (It's one of the only cafés in Montreal that doesn't allow smoking.) ♦ M-W, 9:30AM-8PM; Th-F, 9:30AM-9PM; Sa-Su. 2220 Ave McGill College (between Rue Ste-Catherine and Blvd de Maisonneuve W). 845.5811

11 PEPSI FORUM ENTERTAINMENT CENTER

Formerly the legendary **Montreal Forum**, home of the **Montreal Canadiens** hockey team (now based at the **Molson Center** downtown), this venerable venue has been transformed into a sleek entertainment megaplex with a 22-screen movie theater center (with a total of 4,300 seats) managed by AMC, three floors of themed-restaurant dining and interactive games, **Jillians** for pool or bowling, and an indoor climbing wall. *Legends of the Forum*, a free multimedia show from a 360-degree perspective that touches on some of the greatest moments of the building's past, is presented eight times daily. Outside the building is a Walk of Fame that includes the legendary 24 Stanley Cup championships. ♦ 2313 Rue Ste-Catherine W (at Ave Atwater). 933.6786

12 BOCCA D'ORO

★★★$$$ Everyone from prime ministers to mayors has sampled the excellent food at this Italian restaurant housed in an old Victorian duplex. Sprawling over three levels, it includes a basement with a pasta bar, a main-floor dining room with a plant-filled courtyard, and a more intimate second story, all of which can seat 150 people. Owner Rocco DiLiddo recently added some innovative new dishes to his solid menu of Italian classics, including pasta entrées without a trace of cream or tomato. Among the old favorites are the superb osso buco Milanese, served with an excellent risotto, *delizia di melanzane* (stuffed eggplant with ricotta cheese and spinach),

---

Restaurants/Clubs: Red | Hotels: Purple | Shops: Orange | Outdoors/Parks: Green | Sights/Culture: Blue

and *scallopini bocca d'oro* (veal with wild mushrooms). ◆ Italian ◆ M-Sa, lunch and dinner. Reservations recommended for dinner on Fridays and Saturdays. 1448 Rue St-Mathieu (between Rue Ste-Catherine W and Blvd de Maisonneuve W). 933.8414

13 MEXICALI ROSA'S

★★$$ **Montreal Expos** players used to wail and moan about the lack of good Mexican restaurants in Montreal, and the more sympathetic wives would go on missions of mercy across the border to nearby Plattsburgh, New York, to stock up on nachos and burritos. This is one of several decent Mexican restaurants to have come to the rescue in the last few years. Try the spicy Texan chili, *nachos con pollo* topped with sour cream, or the excellent gringo hamburgers with crispy french fries. For dessert, ask for an apple cinnamon burrito, a concoction that also includes honey and cheese or ice cream and is covered in granola. ◆ Mexican ◆ Daily, lunch and dinner. 1425 Rue Bishop (between Rue Ste-Catherine W and Blvd de Maisonneuve W). 284.0344

14 MOUNT STEPHEN CLUB

★★$$$$ The classic French restaurant of this private club opens its doors to nonmembers for a few months each year. The menu changes frequently, but such haute cuisine as fillet of beef with balsamic vinegar and shallots, scallop mousse, or salmon in a light saffron sauce can be enjoyed in the elegant dining room. The magnificent Renaissance-style mansion was once the home of George Stephen, president of the Bank of Montreal and the **Canadian Pacific Railway**. Architect **W. T. Thomas** designed the building, which took craftsmen from Europe 3 years to construct during the 1880s. Named a historic site by the Canadian government, the mansion was bought by the private Mount Stephen Club in 1920. The interior woodwork and staircase are particularly noteworthy. In summer, Monday through Friday, guided tours of the mansion are offered by reservation only. ◆ French ◆ Su, brunch; call for months open to public. Reservations required; jacket and tie required. 1440 Rue Drummond (between Rue Ste-Catherine W and Blvd de Maisonneuve W). 849.7338

15 HOTEL DE LA MONTAGNE

$$$ A business crowd frequents this posh, 135-room (including 9 suites) hotel with Baroque décor, though the opening of the **Hotel Vogue** across the street has taken away some of its clientele. In summer the rooftop swimming pool and bar are open to the public—offering a superb view of downtown. Both the rooftop bar and the piano bar offer live entertainment nightly. Inside the hotel is

Le **Lutetia**, a French bistro serving light fare daily. As an added attraction, the hotel is linked by tunnel to **Thursday's**, a popular restaurant and club on Rue Crescent, which is under the same ownership. ◆ 1430 Rue de la Montagne (between Rue Ste-Catherine W and Blvd de Maisonneuve W). 288.5656, 800/361.6262; fax 288.9658

16 HOTEL VOGUE

$$$$ What was once a **Texaco Canada** office building is now home to the city's fanciest and trendiest hotel. Most of the rooms are bright, airy, and modern, with mahogany furnishings and blue and crème accents. If you require a telephone and a TV in your bathroom, along with marble accoutrements and a whirlpool, this is the place to stay. Naturally, there are fax machines, briefcase-size electronic safes, and Internet hookups in each of the 154 rooms. Most of the 16 suites have boardrooms, and the concierge service is excellent. ◆ 1425 Rue de la Montagne (between Rue Ste-Catherine W and Blvd de Maisonneuve W). 285.5555, 800/465.6654; fax 849.8903

Within the Hotel Vogue:

CHEZ GEORGES

★★$$$ This welcoming, traditional Parisian-style bistro replaces the former **Société Café**. Among the many menu offerings are vichyssoise; pan-fried sirloin steak with Armagnac, Béarnaise, or *forestière* (wild mushroom) sauce; frog legs à la Provençale; and a delicious signature lobster crêpe. ◆ French ◆ Daily, breakfast, lunch, and dinner. 1415 Rue de la Montagne. 288.6181 ⚅

17 CARLOS & PEPE'S

★★$ Another student hangout, this Mexican restaurant has a pleasant pastel décor and the requisite cacti. The food is good and cheap, the margaritas require two hands, and nachos and salsa are complimentary. The tacos are a steal. ◆ Mexican ◆ Daily, lunch and dinner. 1420 Rue Peel (between Rue Ste-Catherine W and Blvd de Maisonneuve W). 288.3090 ⚅

17 ALEXANDRE

★★$$ This restaurant has evolved into a three-level entertainment complex. The first floor is a French bistro with a terrace, where the food ranges from mussels and pasta to *croques monsieur* (a glorified grilled ham and cheese sandwich); the second floor is an authentic British pub with dozens of imported ales, ports, and malts; and the basement is home to **Le Paradis**, a disco with a British pub–Club Med atmosphere, where owner Alain Creton launched the lambada craze. Dress is corporate casual, except for those in suits and ties who didn't bother to go home after work. ♦ French/Italian/British ♦ Daily lunch and dinner. 1454 Rue Peel (between Rue Ste-Catherine W and Blvd de Maisonneuve W). 288.5105

17 FERREIRA

★★$$$ Stepping into this Portuguese restaurant is like walking into a ray of sunshine. Curvy blue chairs nestle up to a white stucco wall encrusted with broken Portuguese ceramics, creating a montage of blue and white in perfect harmony with the sun-inflected music. A variety of fresh fish, the mainstay of Portuguese cuisine, is grilled to perfection in the open kitchen. Try the grilled cod with caramelized onions. Oenophiles will be pleased by a wine list that is some 15,000 bottles strong. ♦ Portuguese ♦ M-F, lunch and dinner; Sa, dinner. 1446 Rue Peel (between Rue Ste-Catherine W and Blvd de Maisonneuve W)

18 ROTISSERIE ITALIENNE

★★$ Waiters and waitresses are nowhere to be found at this informal Italian restaurant, where customers place their order at a counter, then pick it up when called. The pasta is good and the prices even better. ♦ Italian ♦ M-Sa, lunch and dinner. 1933 Rue Ste-Catherine W (between Rues St-Marc and du Fort). 935.4436

19 KOJAX

★$ The original—and best—Greek souvlaki restaurant in the citywide chain is located here on Rue Ste-Catherine. Order the chicken souvlaki, a taco, and a draft. This is one of the best fast-food franchises in Montreal. On Saturday and Sunday, the place stays open till 4AM. ♦ Greek ♦ Daily, lunch and dinner. 1389 Rue Ste-Catherine W (between Rues Crescent and Bishop). 844.1644. Also at Place Montreal Trust (at Rue Ste-Catherine and Ave McGill College). 499.9703; Olympic Stadium (at Ave Pierre-de-Coubertin). 251.3583

20 LES HALLES

★★★★$$$$ Long regarded as one of Montreal's finest restaurants, this venerable 30-year-old retains the flavor of the old Paris marketplace for which it is named. Recently renovated, the bright, open main dining room is done in beige and lush green; two other smaller rooms allow for more intimate dining. Owner Jacques Landurie and his wife, Ita, have updated the menu, boosting the number of selections on the wine list to more than 300 and replacing the three-course luncheon with an à la carte menu. Highlights include the superb veal sweetbreads au pineau des Charentes served on puff pastry in a raspberry-vinegar sauce and topped with fresh raspberries, followed by a spectacular, refreshing dessert of mango, strawberries, raspberries, poached pears, kiwi, and a mango coulis over coconut sherbet. The adventurous can choose the gastronomic du patron menu—a surprise meal with something different for each guest. ♦ French ♦ Tu-F, lunch and dinner; M, Sa, dinner. 1450 Rue Crescent (between Rue Ste-Catherine W and Blvd de Maisonneuve W). 844.2328 ᬑ

21 THURSDAY'S (LES BEAUX JEUDIS)

★$$ This classic Crescent club is a combination restaurant, bar, and disco on three floors that can accommodate up to 900 people. At one of the most notorious cruising bars in the city, customers toss around pickup lines along with the peanut shells that cover the floor. The disco, which can hold 300 gyrating dancers, attracts the young and athletic, who can watch themselves groove in the mirrors surrounding the dance floor. Occasionally, such celebrities as David Bowie and Paul McCartney pop in for a visit. Although the food isn't great, the terrace offers the best people watching on Crescent. ♦ French ♦ Daily, lunch and dinner; bar daily, 11:30AM-

One of the saviors of Old Montreal is former *Montreal Star* and *Gazette* music critic Eric McLean, who acquired the Papineau House at 440 Rue Bonsecours in 1961 and began the long, arduous job of restoring this former home of Louis-Joseph Papineau, a member of the legislative assembly and leader of the 1837–1838 Patriots Rebellion. The Papineau House, dating from the second half of the 18th century, was home to six generations of Papineaus, until it was sold and became a flophouse. In purchasing the house, McLean became the first Montrealer to move into the neighborhood and reclaim a historic piece of it.

The first automobile to tootle down Montreal's streets was imported by real estate developer Ucal-Henri Dandurand around the turn of the 19th century. By 1903 he owned four cars; the speed limit at the time was 14 miles per hour.

One of Old Montreal's most famous visitors was Charles Dickens. In 1842, he stayed at Rasco's Hotel (281 Rue St-Paul E) while one of his plays was performed at the Théâtre Royale.

Restaurants/Clubs: Red | Hotels: Purple | Shops: Orange | Outdoors/Parks: Green | Sights/Culture: Blue

THE BEST

Jean-Gilles Jutras

Gastronomic and Wine Writer-Counselor

The **Musée de la Civilisation** and the **Musée du Québec**—exceptional places for cultural information.

The **Château Frontenac**, a luxurious hotel that gives an international image of Quebec City.

National Battlefields Park, a historic site on a vast plateau overlooking the **St. Lawrence River**, where you can relax, walk, practice sports, and observe nature. Especially noteworthy: the **Jeanne d'Arc Garden**, at the entrance to the park.

Montmorency Park, near the waterfall of the same name—a marvelous natural site.

Île d'Orléans, where you'll find the most beautiful old homes and a superb natural setting, around which winds the St. Lawrence River.

3AM; disco daily, 10PM-3AM. 1449 Rue Crescent (between Rue Ste-Catherine W and Blvd de Maisonneuve W). 288.5656

21 SIR WINSTON CHURCHILL PUB

Twenty-five years young, this bar and restaurant attracts a diverse crowd. **Sir Winnie's**, as it's known, offers casual lunchtime dining on its famous streetside terrace, and the pub inside, a large, comfortable room with several bars, booths, and tables, is always jam-packed. There's also an adequate dance floor. ◆ Daily, 11:30AM-2:45AM. 1459 Rue Crescent (between Rue Ste-Catherine W and Blvd de Maisonneuve W). 288.0616

Within the Sir Winston Churchill Pub:

WINNIE BAR

Upstairs from the pub, this club with a tiny dance floor draws a crowd similar to the one at **Thursday's**, though the pace is a little slower. ◆ Daily 11:30AM-3AM. 288.0623

22 OGILVY

Catering to the well-heeled and the fashion conscious since 1866, this department store is still a favorite stomping ground for the elite from the wealthy residential enclaves of Westmount and Outremont. The five-floor store was thoroughly overhauled and is now divided into top-name boutiques, among them **Adrienne Vittadini**, **Jones New York**, **Liz Claiborne**, **Jean-Claude Poitras**, **Alfred Sung**, and **Guy Laroche**. Designs by Christofle Paris, New Man, Lacoste, and Jaeger and George Kiss leather clothing can also be found. The **Nicholas Hoare** bookstore on the mezzanine is excellent, and you can buy **Godiva** chocolates downstairs or a light lunch at **Café Sifon**. Furs, antiques, and furniture reign on the top floors, and regular concerts and art exhibitions are held in **Tudor Hall**. Although the white-gloved elevator ladies are gone, some traditions at Ogilvy have not fallen by the wayside: A bagpiper marches through the main floor at noon and at closing, just like in the old days. ◆ M-W, Sa; Th-F, 9:30AM-9PM; Su, noon-5PM. 1307 Rue Ste-Catherine W (at Rue de la Montagne). 842.7711

22 HENRI POUPART

Quebec is a smoker's paradise, with the highest percentage of smokers in the country and a general disdain for no-smoking bylaws, so it's no wonder this tobacconist has been thriving since 1905. This is the place in Montreal to buy Cuban cigars, pipes, cigarettes, and loose tobaccos. The pen selection is good too. ◆ M-W, Sa; Th-F, 9:30AM-9PM. 1385 Rue Ste-Catherine W (between Rues de la Montagne and Crescent). 842.5794

23 CHAPTERS

Three packed floors of books on every imaginable topic in French and English make this Montreal's largest bookstore. There's also a good selection of magazines and a knowledgeable staff. ◆ M-Th, 10AM-10PM; F-Sa, 10AM-11PM; Su, 10AM-9PM. 1171 Rue Ste-Catherine W (at Rue Stanley). 849.8825

24 LA SALSATHÈQUE

One of the first Latin-American clubs in Montreal, this disco features live salsa and taped hard-core dance music for a young crowd. With its cruising atmosphere, this is not the place to go if you want to be left alone. The clientele is hip, and lots of mirrors and lights surround the huge dance floor. ◆ Cover on Friday and Saturday. W-Su, 9PM-3AM. 1220 Rue Peel (at Rue Ste-Catherine W). 875.0016

24 PEEL PUB

$ Cheap beer and food and loud rock videos make this place a favorite with students. The food is bland, and the ambiance approaches that of a high school cafeteria, but at night the beer flows so heavily that no one cares. When crowded, it gets unbelievably noisy. ◆ Canadian ◆ Daily, breakfast, lunch, and dinner. 1107 Rue Ste-Catherine W (between Rues Peel and Stanley). 844.6769. Also at 1106 Blvd de Maisonneuve W. 845.9002; 870 Blvd de Maisonneuve E. 849.8715

25 ROOTS

This trendy clothing store is a Canadian favorite, with the ubiquitous beaver logo plastered on a wide range of clothing—T-shirts, sweatshirts, baseball hats, and warm-up pants, plus leather jackets with **Toronto Maple Leafs** or **Montreal Canadiens** logos. The store's famous shoes, which began in the 1960s as inverted platforms, are now more conservative but equally popular ♦ M-W, Sa; Th-F, 10AM-9PM; Su, noon-5PM. 1035 Rue Ste-Catherine W (between Rues Metcalfe and Peel). 845.7995

25 AU PAIN DORE

Possibly the best baguettes in Montreal can be found at this shop, which sells about 25 varieties of crusty breads, as well as wonderful cheeses, salmon pies, quiches, and pastries. ♦ Daily. 1415 Rue Peel (between Rue Ste-Catherine W and Blvd de Maisonneuve W). 843.3151

27 LA MAISON SIMONS

The buyers at this bustling, street-hip department store must be doing something right, because everyone who enters the wide glass doors emerges noticeably more fashionable and often happier than they were before. The bright, attractively designed store is chock-full of the kinds of clothes you would be more likely to associate with a hip shop in SoHo—and come with an unbeatable price-to-quality ratio. Simon's even has its own fashion-forward labels, such as Twik for women's ready-to-wear and 31 for men's. There's clothing for men, women, and children, as well as fashion accessories galore, on the first floor. The mezzanine-level men's department truly shines: You can find items by the likes of Jean-Paul Gaultier, Versace, and DKNY at prices that will have you grabbing garments off the rack and racing to the fitting rooms. More women's fashions plus a bedding department are located on the third floor. Note: Simon's shares an address with the **Cinema Famous Players Paramount** multiplex. ♦ M-Sa, 9:30AM-9PM; Su, 12PM-5PM. 977 Rue Ste-Catherine W (at Rue Mansfield) 282.1840

27 AVENUE McGILL COLLEGE

Back in the mid-1980s, former Mayor Jean Drapeau almost agreed to a commercial development deal that would have covered over this avenue off Rue Ste-Catherine with buildings. But in a rare show of unity, preser-

vationists teamed up with other developers and successfully persuaded the city to realize a longtime dream: to widen the avenue and create Montreal's version of the Champs-Elysées. This once-narrow street is now lined with glitzy high-rises all the way to the **Roddick Gates** of **McGill University**. And although it isn't the Champs-Elysées—sterile office towers don't quite lend the right ambiance, and the avenue ends at the parking garage of **Place Ville Marie**—it does offer the most spectacular view of **Mont-Royal** from downtown. The lovely flowers and trees that line the avenue are privately maintained, as are the bright decorations at Christmas. Of the many sculptures added outside several buildings, *The Illuminated Crowd* by Raymond Mason is perhaps the favorite photo-op with visitors. Located on the plaza of the **Banque Nationale de Paris** building (1981 Avenue McGill College, between Boulevard de Maisonneuve W and Rue Sherbrooke W), the sculpture consists of a group of people pointing either in wonder or disgust at something, perhaps the skyscraper across the street or one baseball cap–clad tourist too many.♦ Between Rues Cathcart and Sherbrooke W

28 CABAN

Fashion retailer Club Monaco makes its dramatic foray into the world of home décor with this bi-level emporium, which is nevertheless perhaps more impressive on account of its size than the originality of its wares. Still, if you're looking for expensive knickknacks with which to spruce up your home—from linens to scented candles—you're bound to find something here that fits the bill. ♦ M-W, 10AM-6PM; Th-F, 10AM-9PM; Sa, 10:30AM-5PM; Su, noon-5PM. 777 Rue Ste-Catherine W (at Ave McGill College). 844.9300

29 CINÉMA LE PARISIEN

If you're weary of Hollywood blockbusters, come to one of the only true repertory movie theaters in downtown Montreal. Foreign films and low-budget independent classics, as well as the better first-run hits, are shown here. Films are in English or a foreign language with English subtitles. Pick up a free monthly schedule outside the entrance. ♦ Daily, 1:30PM-closing; showtimes vary. 480 Rue Ste-Catherine W (at Rue City-Councillors). 866.3857

30 HÔTEL DU FORT

$$$$ Located at the side entrance of the **Complexe du Fort** office tower, this convenient European-style hotel's 130 rooms offer kitchenettes, small microwaves, mini-fridges,

---

and coffeemakers, and each is decorated with Louis XV–style furniture. The phone message system is computerized, and breakfasts are complimentary. There is no restaurant in the hotel, but a few operate within the complex. ♦ 1390 Rue du Fort (between Rue Tupper and Rue Ste-Catherine W). 938.8333, 800/565.6333; fax 938.2078

31 COCK 'N' BULL

A decidedly maritime bar with heavy weather-beaten wood tables and a large-screen TV for sports, this is the place for a friendly round of darts and beer on tap. They serve pub grub and occasionally book Celtic, folk, or rock bands. ♦ Daily, 11AM-3AM. 1944 Rue Ste-Catherine W (between Rues St-Marc and du Fort). 933.4556

32 ALPENHAUS

★★$$ The unassuming entrance to this Swiss restaurant just around the corner from Rue Ste-Catherine is easy to miss. The old standby has two dining rooms, including the more formal **Heidi** room, which features a pianist, a fireplace, and wagon wheels hanging from the ceiling. Appetizers range from minced veal steak and sirloin steak with a *café de Paris* sauce to beef and cheese fondue. The *roesti*, a Swiss potato specialty, is a potato pancake with a difference. Also don't miss the fried potatoes, crunchy on the outside and smooth and creamy inside. Chocolate fondue is a good choice for dessert. ♦ Swiss ♦ M-F, lunch and dinner; Sa-Su, dinner. 1279 Rue St-Marc (at Rue Ste-Catherine W). 935.2285 &

33 LE FAUBOURG STE-CATHERINE

Before 1987, this was a drab brick building housing an auto showroom, warehouses, and the legendary **Toe Blake's Tavern**. Now it's Montreal's version of Boston's Faneuil Hall, an open bazaarlike market with a slew of merchandise on display and just about every kind of fast-food outlet and specialty-food store imaginable. Fountains and plants add a calming touch, and the terraces are great for people watching. Unlike many of the struggling malls in Montreal, this one is always crowded. Big draws are **La Fine Gueule**, which has a fine selection of cheeses; **Scoops**, for its tremendous assortment of bulk candies, nuts, and chips; and **Monsieur Felix and Mr. Norton**, makers of gourmet cookies in such flavors as rich cappuccino, amaretto, and Black Forest (try the *ménage à trois*, a mixture of milk chocolate, dark chocolate, and white chocolate, or the Magnummm of Biscuits—30 cookies in a champagne bottle). The Société des Alcools, the Quebec liquor board outlet, has one of the best selections in the city. Watch Montreal-style bagels baking in a wood-burning oven at **Bagel du Faubourg**, where they also make fresh matzo, or pick up game meats and venison,

from fresh bison and caribou to pheasant and duck, at **Boucherie Toscano**, which also carries prepared frozen meals like veal cordon bleu and beef Stroganoff. Take-out places include **Le Gourmet Hot & Spicy**, with an extensive menu of everything from Szechuan shrimp with crispy spinach to Thai curry beef. Low-fat, low-cal pastries (60 calories a pop) are the specialty at **Gâterie de Sophie**. Upstairs in the international fast-food court, choose from German sausages, Greek souvlaki, Louisiana Cajun crawfish, or English fish and chips. Four **Cineplex Odeon** movie theaters are located in the basement. ♦ Daily, 9AM-10PM. 1616 Rue Ste-Catherine W (at Rue Guy). 939.3663

34 RUE CRESCENT

Montreal's beautiful people meet and greet on this street, which is undeniably *the* place to be. Once considered the Anglo version of Rue St-Denis, it now attracts its share of French-speaking locals as well. In summer, grab a table outdoors at one of the clubs or bars on the street to be in the center of the action. The Crescent atmosphere spills over onto much of Rues Mackay and Bishop and parts of Rues de la Montagne, Drummond, Stanley, and Peel. ♦ Between Blvd René Lévesque W and Rue Sherbrooke W

35 YORK

Looking for a good used 35-millimeter camera, a new watch, and perhaps some bongos? You'll find them all under one roof here. This store is a combination of one of the best-stocked camera shops in the city, a jewelry and musical instrument store, and an old-fashioned pawnshop. Some of the cameras are collectors' items, and there's a good selection of watches, sound systems, guitars, and percussion instruments. ♦ M-W, Sa; Th-F, 9:30AM-9PM; Su, noon-5PM. 1344 Rue Ste-Catherine W (between Rues de la Montagne and Crescent). 874.0824

36 LE CHÂTEAU

Designer knockoffs of men's and women's clothes are this shop's specialty. The trendy garb is in style one day and out the next, and the quality is generally low. ♦ M-W, Sa; Th-F, 9:30AM-9PM; Su, noon-5PM. 1310 Rue Ste-Catherine W (between Rues de la Montagne and Crescent). 866.2481

37 MISTER STEER

★★$ Stop by for a Mister Steerburger, a char-broiled concoction with a choice of toppings that some argue is the best hamburger in Montreal. Choose from homemade french fries, a baked potato, or baked beans on the side. ♦ Canadian ♦ Daily, breakfast, lunch, and dinner. 1198 Rue Ste-Catherine W (between Rues Stanley and Drummond). 866.3233 &

THE BEST

Bruno Bernard

President, Les Appartements Touristiques du Centre-Ville

Montreal must-sees include **Old Montreal**, the **Parc Mont-Royal**, **Rue Ste-Catherine** for its boutiques, **Rue St-Denis** for its café terraces and the restaurant **Toqué**, **Rue Sherbrooke West** for the galleries and museums, **Rue Mont-Royal** for its funk, and **Boulevard St-Laurent** for its chic restaurants.

Then for fun you should take a stroll in the labyrinths of the Underground City.

The **Ex-Centris** film center, on Boulevard St-Laurent, presents excellent avant-garde and underground movies.

A visit to the **Botanical Garden**, one of the world's foremost gardens, followed by a drink atop the **Tour de Montreal**, just across from it.

Between two free newspapers in French, *Voir* and *Ici*, and two in English, *Hour* and *Mirror* (also free), getting clued in to the culture and arts scene is a snap. The papers are published Thursdays and widely distributed.

The **Museum of Contemporary Art** enjoys an excellent reputation and is well worth a visit. The restaurant **Chez Gauthier**, at the corner of Avenue du Parc and Rue Milton, is a winner for its French-bistro ambiance, quality of cuisine, and reasonable prices.

For strolling, there is Rue de la Montagne and Rue Crescent, whereas farther west is Rue Green. Farther afield in peaceful, leafy Outremont, there are the luxurious boutiques along Rue Laurier. For *moules et frites*, check out **La Moulerie** on Rue Bernard. For a contrast to Outremont visit the *très* English town of Westmount, with its huge houses flanking the Mont-Royal and aristocratic charm.

Montreal is, above all, a city where you can take time out in a café and watch the world go by, with its people from everywhere and nowhere, a mélange of races, languages, and cultures, from yuppie to punk, united by the desire to live richly to the beat of one of the most fascinating cities in North America.

38 HMV

The Montreal flagship of a British music store chain, it lets customers listen to anything before buying. With three levels of rock, jazz, New Age, French, and classical music, it has one of the largest selections in Montreal. The knowledgeable staff members can offer advice on everything from opera to heavy metal. ♦ M-F, 9:30AM-9PM; Sa, 9AM-5PM; Su, 10AM-5PM. 1020 Rue Ste-Catherine W (between Rues Metcalfe and Peel). 875.0765

39 SHERLOCK'S

★★$$$ If you want a good meal, a beer, a game of pool, and a lot of company, head to this huge restaurant, bar, and pool hall with seating for 650. Located in the **Dominion Square Building**, it's decorated in posh Victorian style with comfortable, deep-red velour banquettes and 14 billiard tables. The roast beef is superb, as is the chocolate opera, a divine dessert. ♦ Continental ♦ M-Sa, lunch and dinner. 1010 Rue Ste-Catherine W (between Rues Metcalfe and Peel). 878.0088 &

40 A. L. VAN HOUTTE

★$ You can't go far in Montreal without finding another café in this chain. On a sunny day, order a cappuccino and a French pastry and sit on the large outdoor terrace. Salads, sandwiches, croissants, and other light fare are also served. ♦ Café ♦ Daily, breakfast, lunch, and dinner. 1255 Ave McGill College (between Rue Cathcart and Rue Ste-Catherine W). 861.5260. Also at 1187 Place Phillip. 879.1498; 1615 Rue St-Denis. 845.9919

40 LE COMMENSAL

★★$ This is unquestionably Montreal's most popular vegetarian restaurant, serving fresh salads, cold pastas, breads, and quiches cafeteria style. And you pay by the pound—pile up as little or as much as you want, in any combination. Even though the food is prepared in a central kitchen and then delivered to the various restaurants in the chain, it's always fresh. Desserts are also weighed, so you can take tiny slivers of several different cakes and pay the same as you would for one dessert anywhere else. They're all good, but the chocolate cake is irresistible. ♦ Vegetarian ♦ Daily, lunch and dinner. 1204 Ave McGill College (between Rue Cathcart and Rue Ste-Catherine W). 871.1480 & Also at 1720 Rue St-Denis. 845.2627; 3715 Chemin Queen Mary. 733.9755 &

41 LE VIEUX DUBLIN

Despite its name change from **The Old Dublin**—thanks to Quebec's infamous language laws—this pub is an island of Celtic mirth and merriment among a sea of downtown skyscrapers. A clutch of old snapshots on the walls, live entertainment nightly—sometimes directly from Ireland—and imported Irish stouts and bitters on tap make

---

Restaurants/Clubs: Red | Hotels: Purple | Shops: Orange | Outdoors/Parks: Green | Sights/Culture: Blue

LITTLE BURGUNDY

Hemmed in on the north by the Mont-Royal and the south by the St. Lawrence River, and traversed from east to west by Highway 720, Montreal's downtown is relatively compact. It may come as a surprise, then, that other neighborhoods exist just a few blocks south of the highway. One of these, **Little Burgundy**, is a former working-class quarter that grew up around the **Canal de Lachine**, built in 1825 as a way for ships to skirt the St. Lawrence rapids. Unlike the bustling St. Catherine area, the neighborhood's character is more gritty than polished, but that's changing somewhat as former factories are converted to condos and young professionals move in. One of the most interesting walks here is on Rue Notre-Dame West, one of the oldest streets in Montreal, originally laid out in 1660. With some 30 antiques shops, the stretch between Rues Guy and Atwater is known as the **rue des antiquaires**. Most of the shops are located in renovated 19th-century commercial buildings on the southern side of the street.

The other highlight of the 'hood is **Atwater Market**, one of Montreal's oldest marketplaces. Housed in a somewhat brutalist Art Deco building designed by architects Ludger and Lemieux in 1933, it boasts 10 butcher shops, 3 cheese shops, a fish shop, 12 boutiques, and—in season—outdoor fruit and vegetable vendors. There's also a **Premiere Moisson** bakery, a favorite stop among bicyclists who load up their picnic baskets before taking a spin along the paths that line the adjacent Lachine Canal. The market is located at 138 Atwater Ave (just south of Rue Notre-Dame). M-W, Sa-Su, 8AM-6PM; Th-F, 8AM-9PM. 937.7754. Access Little Burgundy via Metro stations Lucien-L'Allier or Lionel Groulx.

this pub authentic enough to solace even Irish expats. As you might expect, the beer flows green on St. Patrick's Day. ♦ Daily, 11AM-3AM. 1219A Rue Université (between Rue Cathart and Rue Ste-Catherine W). 861.4448

42 INFO-TOURISTE

Across from **Dorchester Square** in the **Dominion Square Building** is the city's largest tourism office, with extensive travel information about the city and the province, a reservation service, and currency exchange. It also sells souvenirs and tickets for bus tours. ♦ Daily. 1001 Rue du Square Dorchester (between Rues Metcalfe and Peel). 873.2015, 800/363.7777

43 ACTUEL

★★$$$ Crispy Belgian french fries served with mayonnaise and mussels prepared 14 ways are two of the main draws at this busy and noisy restaurant. Other good bets are the steak tartare, well-prepared salads, and excellent chocolate mousse. ♦ Belgian ♦ M-Sa, lunch and dinner. 1194 Rue Peel (between Rue Cypress and Rue Ste-Catherine W). 866.1537

44 SUN LIFE BUILDING

Constructed in three periods, starting in 1914 and ending in 1933, this 26-story building was the largest in the British Commonwealth when it was completed. The giant Corinthian and Ionic columns lining the interior and exterior add to the monumental character of the imposing structure. Once the center of Anglo-Saxon business in Montreal and head-quarters of the Sun Life Assurance Company, the building was chosen by British authorities as the repository for the crown jewels during World War II. But all of this changed in the late 1970s, after the election of the separatist Parti Québécois government. Sun Life was probably the largest of the Anglo companies to move to Toronto, declaring that the Quebec government's attempts to separate from Canada were creating a negative business climate. The building now serves as Sun Life's regional headquarters and as headquarters for the **National Hockey League**. The bronze-and-marble interior is definitely worth a visit. To mark the end of business hours, chimes are rung every afternoon at 5PM. ♦ 1155 Rue Metcalfe (between Blvd René Lévesque W and Rue Ste-Catherine W)

45 CANADIAN CENTRE FOR ARCHITECTURE

Conceived by Phyllis Lambert, one of the daughters of Seagram's founder Samuel Bronfman, this museum of architecture is considered the only one of its kind in the world. It houses Lambert's extensive and ever-growing collection of architectural prints, drawings, books, photographs, plans, models, toys, and other artifacts, and exhibitions of the center's treasures are held regularly. Visitors can tour the library or shop at the bookstore. The museum is also a study center devoted to the preservation of architectural documents and to scholarly research, and much of the research facility, including a huge underground storage vault, is closed to the public. The center incorporates the beautiful old **Shaughnessy House**, built in 1874. The house was almost demolished a century later, but Lambert bought and restored it in 1988 and now uses its rooms for offices and reception areas. If you're an architecture fan, you'll delight in this place. ◆ Admission. June-Sep: Tu-W, 11AM-6PM; Th, 11AM-9PM; F-Su, 11AM-6PM. Oct-May: W, 11AM-6PM; Th, 11AM-8PM; Fri, 11AM-6PM; Sa-Su, 11AM-5PM. 1920 Rue Baile (between Rues St-Marc and du Fort). 939.7026

45 SHAUGHNESSY VILLAGE

The unofficial moniker for a neighborhood once full of run-down boardinghouses now connotes a more gentrified area where, over the past several years, new life has been given to many of the Victorian graystones. This pleasant residential neighborhood is home to property owners who take matters into their own hands when they see fit. When the city of Montreal refused to turn a vacant lot into a park, for example, residents created a park of their own. They also hold an annual beautification contest, awarding prizes for the best gardens. From the **Canadian Centre for Architecture**, stroll along the roads of the village. ◆ Rues Baile, St-Marc, Tupper, and Towers and Aves Seymour and Hope

46 UPSTAIRS JAZZ CLUB

★★★$$ An elongated yet cozy room with exposed brick walls, black café tables, and a glowing aquarium where there was once a fireplace greet patrons of this downstairs (despite the name) jazz and supper club. A mixed crowd of McGill students and somewhat older, more upscale folks contribute to an easygoing ambiance, and performers mix easily with diners in between sets. Friday and Saturday feature headline jazz combos (the best show is usually the third set on Saturday), Sunday is up-and-comer night, and Wednesday and Thursday are cabaret nights, featuring a vocalist. To accompany the musical menu—which typically starts around 9PM—there are tapas appetizers as well as a full menu with steak, chicken, and fish dishes, often with Southwestern accents. Delicious fresh-cut french fries and jazz-themed cocktails are extra details that make this club a cut above others in the neighborhood. ◆ Canadian/American ◆ M-F, lunch and dinner; Sa-Su, dinner. 1254 Rue MacKay St (between Blvd René Lévesque and Rue Ste-Catherine W). 931.6808

47 DA VINCI'S

★★★$$$ Set in a 146-year-old Victorian mansion, this Italian restaurant, owned by the Mazzaferro family, receives accolades from the **Montreal Canadiens** and other local sports figures, as well as **Los Angeles Dodgers** manager Tommy Lasorda. Aldo Mazzaferro serves advice on what ails the Canadian economy, along with great food and service. Mahogany furnishings, Venetian artwork, and a marble antipasto bar set the mood for your culinary trip back to the Old World. Start with an appetizer of sausages, red peppers, and mushrooms, then move on to the seafood linguine, with shrimp, scallops, mussels, and clams. The homemade cannoli is not to be missed. ◆ Italian ◆ M-F, lunch and dinner; Sa, dinner. Reservations recommended. 1180 Rue Bishop (between Blvd René Lévesque W and Rue Ste-Catherine W). 874.2001 &

47 COMEDY WORKS

On any given night, the comedy at this casual club can range from hilarious to downright pathetic. But also booked are some relatively big names who perform at the club's annual **Just for Laughs Festival**. Tuesday night features improvisational comedy. There's more craziness on Wednesday night with the On the Spot Players, who perform the hilarious *Improv Madness*. ◆ Cover. Daily, 7PM-3AM. Reservations recommended. 1238 Rue Bishop (between Blvd René Lévesque W and Rue Ste-Catherine W). 398.9661

47 GRUMPY'S

"Men—also journalists and politicians," reads the sign on the men's room in this basement institution, a favorite hangout for journalists from the *Gazette*, the city's only English daily, and various federal and provincial politicians. The cartoons on the wall are of Nick Auf der Maur, the former city councilor for downtown and a noted boulevardier who makes the bar a second home. Great munchies served at happy hour. ◆ Daily, 11AM-3AM. 1242 Rue Bishop (between Blvd René Lévesque W and Rue Ste-Catherine W). 866.9010

48 ROSALIE

★★$$$ Though this newcomer to the downtown scene is named for attentive owner David McMillan's Italian grandmother, it's anything but old-fashioned. Waitresses sporting black midcalf boots and miniskirts keep the buzz going in the spacious dining room, where the walls are outfitted with odd-sized wood-grain panels and mirrors and white globe lights run the length of the ceiling. Happily, the best thing about this hip canteen is the food, which leans toward updated versions of French classics. Try the roast chicken with wine gravy and mashed potatoes or the "merveilleux" steak and fries. Desserts such as roast pineapple with pound cake and vanilla ice cream provide a tasty finishing touch. ◆ Canadian ◆ M-F, lunch and dinner;

Restaurants/Clubs: Red | Hotels: Purple | Shops: Orange | Outdoors/Parks: Green | Sights/Culture: Blue

Sa, Su, dinner. 1232 Rue de la Montagne (between Blvd René Lévesque W and Rue Ste-Catherine W). 392.1970

49 HOTEL EUROPA ROYALE

$$ This is one of the few moderately priced (and still well-maintained) hotels in the downtown area. Don't expect a whirlpool in your bathroom, but the 180 rooms are clean and comfortable. The hotel contains a fitness center and a **Red Lobster** restaurant. ♦ 1240 Rue Drummond (between Blvd René Lévesque W and Rue Ste-Catherine W). 866.6492, 800/361.3000; fax 861.4089

Within the Hotel Europa Royale:

TERRA

★★★$$$ This airy, luxurious restaurant is as much a feast for the eyes as it is for the palate. The big off-white dining chairs are almost too comfortable, but the attentive waitstaff will make sure you don't fall asleep. But Chef Denis Payen's savory, studied Mediterranean-inspired cuisine may well send you to cloud nine. The Sunday brunch is not to be missed. ♦ Mediterranean ♦ Daily, breakfast, lunch, and dinner. 866.8910

50 METROPOLITAN NEWS

For almost 8 decades, this newsstand was a landmark on Rue Peel near Rue Ste-Catherine. But a few years ago, when rents climbed, it moved to a tiny side street around the corner. You can find Montreal's best selection of foreign newspapers and magazines here. ♦ Daily. 1109 Rue Cypress (between Rues Peel and Stanley, one block south of Rue Ste-Catherine W). 866.9227

51 DORCHESTER SQUARE

ⓟ A public park since 1873, this is the largest square in the downtown area, sprawling over an entire city block. Once called **Dominion Square**, it was renamed when Boulevard Dorchester became Boulevard René Lévesque after the 1987 death of the much-loved former separatist premier of Quebec. Lord Dorchester was a governor general of Canada in the 18th century. The park contains several monuments to former prime ministers and war heroes. In 1992, the *Sir John A. MacDonald Monument*, honoring the father of the Confederation who was also Canada's first prime minister, had its head lopped off by vandals, who were ostensibly advocating Quebec independence. But Parti Québécois leader Jacques Parizeau denied involvement, saying the vandals might have been agents provocateurs out to discredit the separatist movement. The statue has since received a new head. ♦ Rue Peel (between Rues de la Gauchetière and du Square Dorchester)

52 RUE PEEL

The street is named after politician Sir Robert Peel, who created the London police force and after whom the bobbies are named. The Peel and Ste-Catherine corner has been dubbed the crossroads of the nation. If you wait long enough, the story goes, you're bound to see somebody you recognize. ♦ Between Blvd René Lévesque W and Rue Sherbrooke W

53 PHAYATHAI

★★★$$ Unlike other Asian restaurants in Montreal that have toned down their dishes to suit timid North American palates, this Thai eatery is not at all restrained with its spices. If you like, the chef will be happy to turn up the heat even higher. This was the first Thai restaurant in downtown Montreal, and the dishes remain first rate. ♦ Thai ♦ M-F, lunch and dinner; Sa-Su, dinner. 1235 Rue Guy (between Blvd René Lévesque W and Rue Ste-Catherine W). 933.9949

53 CHEZ LA MÈRE MICHEL

★★★$$$ A pioneer of French cuisine in Montreal, this restaurant is located in a lovely old bow-front house that survived the wrecker's ball in the 1950s and 1960s. Settle into the pretty garden room with its atrium and fireplace and enjoy the simple French country food. A special *menu de dégustation* is available on weekends. The lobster soufflé Nantua and the veal sweetbreads in pastry are noteworthy, and the wine cellar has an excellent selection. ♦ French ♦ Tu-F, lunch and dinner; Sa, dinner. Reservations recommended for dinner on Fridays and Saturdays. 1209 Rue Guy (between Blvd René Lévesque W and Rue Ste-Catherine W). 934.0473

53 BAR-B-BARN

★$ Big, noisy, and always crowded, this is the place where families and businesspeople chow down on chicken and spareribs in three sizes—whole hawg, half hawg, and baby hawg. The dining room is lined with thousands of business cards. This is a great place to bring kids, because everyone is making a mess. ♦ Chicken and ribs ♦ Daily, lunch and dinner. 1201 Rue Guy (between Blvd René Lévesque W and Rue Ste-Catherine W). 931.3811

54 LA CAGE AUX SPORTS

Sports fanatics gather here to watch their beloved **Montreal Canadiens** and the **Montreal Expos** on a big-screen TV. Like most sports bars, memorabilia is everywhere. The food is mostly fried and greasy—chicken wings, onion rings, cheese nachos, and spareribs—and unlimited free popcorn is served. When there are no sports on the tube, you can play trivia games linked to a North America–wide computer network. ◆ M-F, Su, 11:30AM-closing; Sa, noon-closing. 1437 Blvd Réné Lévesque W (at Rue Mackay). 878.2243

55 LE CENTRE SHERATON MONTREAL

$$$$ At 37 stories, this is one of Montreal's largest hotels. Originally due to open for the **1976 Olympic Games**, financial troubles delayed construction until Sheraton took over several years later. Of the 824 rooms, nearly half are deluxe—done in floral themes, with soft shades of rose and green—and located on the upper nine club floors. The indoor pool, sauna, and fully equipped business center are popular with business folk. The third-floor restaurant, **Le Boulevard**, offers an eclectic menu, with such daily specials as chicken with curry, fish and chips, fajitas, and vegetable stir-fry. The reasonably priced lunch buffet is worth a try. ◆ 1201 Blvd René Lévesque W (between Rues Stanley and Drummond). 878.2000, 800/325.3535; fax 878.3958 ⑆

56 LA TOUR CIBC

The plaza of this 45-story office tower, one of the city's tallest buildings, contains the Henry Moore sculpture *Reclining Figure in Three Pieces*. ◆ 1155 Blvd René Lévesque W (at Rue Peel)

56 LE WINDSOR

This luxury office building was formerly an annex to the 1878 **Windsor Hotel**, which hosted British royalty on their trips to Montreal before the time of the **Queen Elizabeth Hotel**. When the hotel was destroyed by fire in 1957, all that remained was the annex, built in 1906. Abandoned and almost in ruins, the annex was restored to its original condition and reopened in 1987 as this eight-story office complex, with a copper roof, refurbished stone-and-brick façades, and a curved interior skylight that caps a tremendous atrium. The ballroom was modeled after New York's Waldorf-Astoria. ◆ 1170 Rue Peel (between Blvd René Lévesque W and Rue Ste-Catherine W)

Within Le Windsor:

LE PIMENT ROUGE

★★★★$$$$ Large and elegant, "The Red Pepper" offers some of the best Szechuan and northern Chinese cuisine in the city. Try the crispy beef with sesame seeds or order the beggar's chicken a day in advance. The refined cuisine matches the plush décor. ◆ Chinese ◆ Daily, lunch and dinner. Weekend dinner reservations recommended. 866.7816 ⑆

57 MARY, QUEEN OF THE WORLD CATHEDRAL

No, you haven't landed in Vatican City by mistake. But this church *is* a scale model—one third the size—of St. Peter's Basilica in Rome. Completed between 1885 and 1894 in the center of an English Protestant residential district, it was conceived by Bishop Ignace Bourget as a reminder that the pope reigned supreme. Montreal is still a bastion of Roman Catholicism in the middle of Protestant North America, but the good bishop wanted to turn the entire city into a "fourth Rome." Statues atop the cathedral recall the patron saints of the archdiocese at the time the church was built. ◆ 1085 Rue de la Cathédrale (at Blvd René Lévesque W)

58 RESTAURANT JULIEN

★★★$$ Being in the heart of downtown but just slightly off the beaten path adds to the allure of this cheerful, airy Parisian bistro—and that's before you even get to the secluded garden terrace in the rear. Chef Olivier Bouton hails from Strasbourg and brings a light and inventive touch to the menu. Salads are generous and eclectic; try the marinated chicken salad with cranberries, licorice, and cinnamon yogurt sauce, or the lobster salad with mango and avocado. Among the dozen specialty entrées are pepper-crusted caribou steak with mustard and grape sauce; polenta-crusted Arctic char served with *"fleur de bière"* sauce; and sea bass prepared with a tomato and Champagne sauce. Desserts lean toward the traditional but are very good; the homemade sorbets and ice creams are particularly toothsome. One drawback: Service can be on the slow side. ◆ French ◆ Daily, lunch and dinner. 1191 Ave Union (between Blvd René Lévesque W and Rue Cathcart). 871.1581

Nineteenth-century Montrealers living in the lavish grand mansions southwest of Mont-Royal never called their neighborhood the "Golden Square Mile." To them, this enclave of architectural splendor in the shadow of the mountain was simply "uptown" or "new town." The name *Square Mile* was coined, in print at least, in *Two Solitudes*, the renowned 1945 novel about English–French tensions in Quebec. Its Canadian author, Hugh MacLennan, claimed that the expression dated back to residents of the area after World War I. In any event, the name stuck, becoming the favored way to refer to the historic region now bounded by **McGill University** to the east, an old Indian trail called **Chemin de la Côte-des-Neiges** to the west, **Rue Sherbrooke** to the south, and **Avenue Docteur Penfield** to the north.

The Square Mile didn't acquire the *Golden* modifier until the mid-1950s when (the story goes) a journalist conferred it in reference to a long-gone era of glittery opulence. Instantly, the romantic adjective caught on with guides squiring visitors on walking tours around the city. Today, the term is once again appropriate, because the area's central artery, Rue Sherbrooke—a street lined with some of the city's most exclusive galleries, finest hotels, and priciest shops—is considered Montreal's answer to Manhattan's Fifth Avenue.

The streets of the Square Mile once *were* paved with gold in a figurative sense. During the neighborhood's prime a century ago, it was home to more millionaires per square mile than anywhere else in Canada (these "merchant princes" owned more than 70% of the country's wealth). The majority were self-made entrepreneurs from Scotland, and many were poor and uneducated when they arrived in Montreal in the 1760s after the British conquest of New France (now Quebec), seeking opportunities denied them back

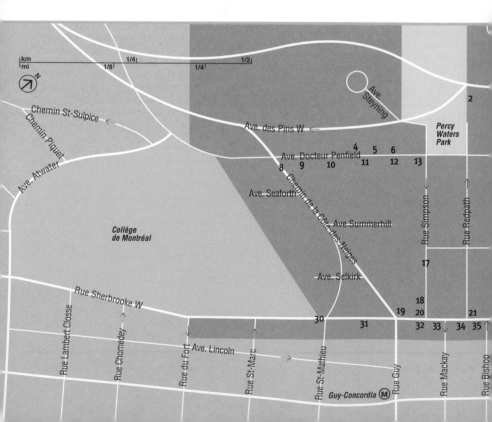

home. For 150 years, Scots were the most powerful citizens in the Montreal business community, though a smattering of English, Irish, Jewish, and French-Canadian businesspeople were comparably well-to-do.

Initially the Scottish newcomers settled in the walled city of Old Montreal, but as they prospered—first in the fur trade (the McGills and McTavishes) and later in wholesale provisions (the Torrances), shipping (the Allans), and construction and sugar refining (the Redpaths and Drummonds)—they sought to escape the waterfront squalor. It was then that they began building their now-legendary "country" homes on vast plots about a mile north, closer to Mont-Royal. These estates, many of them encircled by stone or wrought-iron gates, were erected on a palatial scale indicative of their occupants' new station in life. Several featured elaborate gardens, conservatories, terraces, stables, and servants' quarters; some also boasted ballrooms and art galleries; and the Sherbrooke estate of French-Canadian senator-stockbroker Louis Forget contained even a private chapel. As these prominent locals carved out a neighborhood, they even named the roads after themselves. By the turn of the century, Rue Sherbrooke—named for Sir John Coape Sherbrooke, governor general of Canada between 1816 and 1818—had grown from a modest country lane to an elegant residential thoroughfare veiled by a canopy of elms.

This sylvan splendor flourished undisturbed until the 1920s, when a few small businesses sprang up along Sherbrooke and began to change its residential character. In 1931, the city passed a bylaw meant to protect that ambiance, but although it prohibited some commercial activity, it allowed the construction of clubs, banks, hotels, and eventually the office towers that would alter the street beyond recognition. Then, in 1953, came a crucial blow: Developers were given the green light to build high-rise apartments. Scores of Square Mile mansions were torn down, and by the 1960s, only about 30 of the venerable

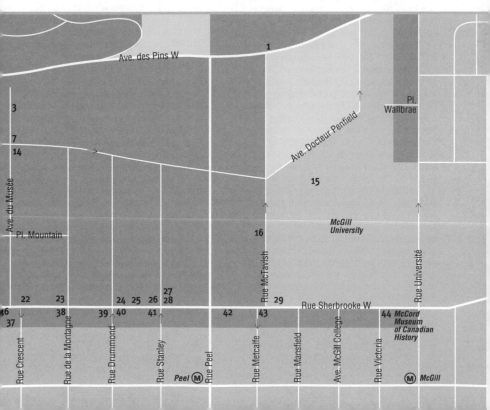

old homes remained; of these, many were owned by **McGill University** or other institutions and businesses, which drastically altered the interiors.

From that point on, the Square Mile's golden days were undeniably a thing of the past. The spacious lawns were gone, the shade trees had been all but destroyed by Dutch elm disease, and mansions were surrounded by high-rises. The public didn't seem to mind this eradication of their city's architectural heritage at first. But indifference turned to indignation on 7 September 1973, when the magnificent 52-room estate of **Canadian Pacific Railway** president William Van Horne was demolished by a developer overnight. The ruination of this aesthetic treasure by a few strokes of the wrecker's ball—it was built at the corner of Sherbrooke and Stanley in 1870, then enlarged and redecorated two decades later by Eugene Colonna, the partner of Louis Comfort Tiffany—aroused a call to action, spurring an influential preservation movement called Save Montreal. The results can be seen in the Heritage plaques on cherished sites along Rue Sherbrooke and in the city's now-steadfast commitment to retain what's left of its bygone grandeur. Today, enough of the Square Mile's stately homes are still standing—albeit tucked between high-rises or scattered amid hotels, shops, and office buildings—to evoke the past. Although visitors can tour only some of the estates (usually by appointment), their gracious exteriors give a vivid glimpse of Montreal's golden past.

1 RAVENSCRAG

Although the spectacular castle conceived by Sir Hugh Allan (1810–1888) is technically outside the Square Mile's boundaries, it's a highly visible, awe-inspiring feature of the local landscape. Situated up the hill from the venerable **Baumgarten House**, the castle boasts an enormous, imposing edifice of rock-faced stone (used here for the first time on a Montreal home), which ambitious visitors may find well worth the climb to inspect. But less hardy types can still admire the view from below. Sir Allan came to Montreal from Glasgow at age 16 and built a shipping company that made him the richest man in Canada. The Tuscan-style villa he called **Ravenscrag**—after the marquis of Lorne's residence in Scotland—was built in 1863 by leading Montreal architect **J. W. Hopkins** on land formerly owned by fur merchant Simon McTavish. The spread included a ballroom, conservatory, caretaker's house (still here), and stable displaying a magnificent stone horse's head over the entrance. That's still here, too, as is Allan's motto *Spero* ("I hope"), chiseled in stone above the front door. In Allan's lifetime, the villa entertained so many visiting dignitaries and statesmen that it was considered a second Parliament, and his son, Sir Hugh Montagu, continued to host a whirl of social activity after Allan's death. In 1943, Montagu and his wife deeded the house to the **Royal Victoria Hospital**, which turned it into a psychiatric facility within the **Allan Memorial Institute**. The name of the institute has been tarnished by the revela-

tion that between 1957 and 1964 its founder, Dr. Ewen Cameron, used monies from the Canadian government and the CIA to perform radical sleep, electroshock, and drug therapy on unwitting subjects. Recently the Canadian government agreed to compensate victims for the abuse. The facility is not open to the public, as it is still in operation as a psychiatric hospital. ♦ 1025 Ave des Pins W (at Rue McTavish)

2 CORMIER HOUSE

Visible to the north (toward **Mont-Royal**) from the corner of Avenue Docteur Penfield and Rue Redpath is the rear façade of an important Square Mile landmark. Though geographically outside the district's present-day borders, this house (circa 1931) is noteworthy for many reasons: It is probably the last single-family dwelling to be built in the area, thus marking the end of the grand mansion era; almost everything in it, from furniture to ashtrays, was designed by famed architect **Ernest Cormier**; it is one of the most important Art Deco houses in the world; and last but by no means least, ex-prime minister Pierre Elliot Trudeau moved in in 1980. The house can be distinguished from its next-door neighbor, **Gillespie House**, by its rectangular window. If you have a chance to see the place from the front, don't be deceived by its small and rather innocuous exterior. Inside, three of the four stories are tucked under the entrance level; the floors are covered in variously hued marble and terrazzo; and the walls range from dark walnut to marble to pure gold leaf in the

THE BEST

Phyllis Lambert

Founding Director, Canadian Centre for Architecture

Old Montreal is the finest, most coherent quarter in North America, with a rich variation of graystone architecture from the 17th century through the 19th century.

Place d'Armes in Old Montreal holds the earliest building in the city—the 1685 **Sulpician Seminary**—as well as the vast **Notre-Dame Basilica** with its early neo-Gothic exterior of 1824 and richly carved 1880s interior. Across the square is the neoclassical 1830 **Bank of Montreal**. The church and the bank subsume Montreal's dialectical history of religion and commerce, as well as its two major cultures, French and English.

Fine restaurants are everywhere—superb French food at **La Maree** in old Montreal; in nearby Chinatown; at the **Witloof** across from **Square St-Louis**; and at **L'Express**, the quintessential bistro farther north on **Rue St-Denis**. Fine Italian food with great wines can be found at **Le Latini** near **Place des Arts**, home of the internationally acclaimed **Montreal Symphony Orchestra**. Notice the graystone buildings (Trenton limestone) throughout the city—row houses, churches, convents, government buildings, stores, railroad stations, and new museums.

The **Canadian Centre for Architecture** is the world's leading architectural museum, with works of art and documents forming a continuum from the Renaissance to today. Its award-winning building and garden have set international standards.

The **McCord Museum of Canadian History**, in a finely renovated building, provides a rich introduction to the daily life, costumes, and art native to Quebec. Vestiges of the town's 18th-century fortifications may be seen at the **Museum of Archaeology** near the **Old Port** and at the **Champ-de-Mars** behind **City Hall**.

The Old Port has been elegantly revitalized to evoke its history. It is a people place, not a consumers' mall, and a great spot to stroll and snack, see holograms and three-dimensional IMAX films, or take off by bicycle (in summer) or on cross-country skis (in winter) 11 miles westward along the **Lachine Canal**.

Mont-Royal Park is one of Frederick Law Olmsted's great parks and certainly the most rugged. Walk it or take a horse-drawn carriage or sleigh, and look at the panorama of the city below. Smoked meat at **Bens** should not be missed.

A variety of excellent restaurants serves as an introduction to Montreal's genius loci—linking the old and the new around major interior public space—at the **Centre de Commerce Mondial de Montréal** and the **Hotel Inter-Continental** in Old Montreal; in the heart of downtown, **Le Windsor**, formerly a hotel associated with **Bruce Price**'s nearby **Windsor Station**; and on **Rue Sherbrooke** near the **Ritz-Carlton**.

library. ♦ 1418 Ave des Pins W (off Rue Redpath)

3 RODOLPHE FORGET HOUSE

This former private home, now part of the Russian consulate (along with **Molson House**), originally belonged to the nephew of French-Canadian stockbroker Louis Forget. Rodolphe Forget (1861–1919) had a business partnership with his uncle until tensions drove them apart. Rodolphe then built his own financial empire, founding the Banque Internationale du Canada, presiding over the **Montreal Stock Exchange** (1908–1911), and heading or serving on the boards of some 20 companies. Drawn to his French roots, Forget wanted that influence reflected in his home. He hired architect **J. Omer Marchand**, the first French-Canadian to graduate from the Ecole des Beaux-Arts de Paris, to build a residence in the French Classical Revival variant of the Beaux Arts style. The house, completed in 1912, remained privately occupied until 1984, when it was bought by a distinctly less capitalistic master: the Soviet Union. ♦ 3685 Ave du Musée (between Aves Docteur Penfield and des Pins W)

4 GREENSHIELDS HOUSE

Now a condominium, this elegant English Classical Revival house was built in 1911 for four brothers of the well-to-do Greenshields family, who lived together in the house for about 20 years. Two were brokers and two were attorneys; of the latter, the more famous was James Naismith Greenshields, who defended Louis Riel, leader of the indigenous people's movement called Métis, in his 1885 trial for treason. ♦ 1513 Ave Docteur Penfield (between Rue Simpson and Chemin de la Côte-des-Neiges)

5 RAYMOND HOUSE

The discriminating occupant of this 1929 house, hotelier Joseph-Alderic Raymond, was owner of Montreal's **Windsor Hotel** and part-owner of New York's celebrated Waldorf-Astoria. Architects **Robert** and **F.R. Findlay**

Restaurants/Clubs: Red | **Hotels: Purple** | Shops: Orange | **Outdoors/Parks: Green** | Sights/Culture: Blue submitted 286 design plans before Raymond finally approved. The house, with its elegant balustrade, is still in family hands. ♦ 1507 Ave Docteur Penfield (between Rue Simpson and Chemin de la Côte-des-Neiges)

6 BENJAMIN TOOKE HOUSE

Many fine houses still stand on the original portion of Avenue Docteur Penfield, clustered between Rue Simpson and Chemin de la Côte-des-Neiges, just as they used to be. Among them is the beautiful red sandstone mansion built for shirt manufacturer Benjamin Tooke. Incorporating elements from all periods of Scottish architecture, the house is as aesthetically pleasing from the side as from the front. In more recent years, the German consulate occupied the building until it was converted into four luxury condos in 1984 under architectural standards set by Quebec's Ministry of Cultural Affairs. ♦ 1501 Ave Docteur Penfield (between Rue Simpson and Chemin de la Côte-des-Neiges)

7 HERBERT MOLSON HOUSE

The section of Avenue Docteur Penfield near Avenue du Musée, with its numerous reserved-parking signs marked for diplomats, has long been dubbed **Embassy Row**. That's a misnomer. All the embassies are in Ottawa, the nation's capital; the foreign-government offices based in this enclave of former Square Mile mansions are actually consulates, and of these, many have relocated to high-rise office towers for security reasons. One of the hangers-on, oddly enough, is the consulate for the former Soviet Union, which still occupies two grand mansions on Avenue du Musée—and whose hush-hush doings intrigue locals and government officials. Half a century ago, however, one former occupant made no secret of what was brewing: Herbert Molson, great-grandson of the founder of Molson Breweries and company president between 1911 and his death in 1938, lived in what is now the Russian consulate office closest to

Avenue Docteur Penfield. That the Molson family now runs the oldest continually operating beer-making operation in North America is partly a testament to the ingenuity of the patriarch, John Molson, who came to Canada from England in 1782. In addition to establishing his brewery on the shores of the St. Lawrence, he invested in real estate and built the country's first steam-powered ship. Over the years, the Molson family helped finance the first Canadian railroad, purchased hotels, and founded Molson's Bank, which merged with the **Bank of Montreal** in 1925. Square Miler Herbert Molson was extremely patriotic— so much so that he didn't have time to enjoy his impressive home; he moved in just as World War I was declared, then almost immediately departed for the front. He left behind something of an anomaly among Beaux Arts buildings: Rather than the typical pale façade, the 1911 house's exterior is composed of bright red brick with sandstone accents. ♦ 3617 Ave du Musée (at Ave Docteur Penfield)

8 CHEMIN DE LA CÔTE-DES-NEIGES

This old Amerindian trail, one of the original streets laid out by land surveyor Dollier de Casson when he planned the Square Mile's topography at the end of the 17th century, is still the best route for driving from downtown to **Mont-Royal Park**. It is probably the route that Catholic missionary Sieur de Maisonneuve used on 2 January 1643, when he kept his pledge to carry a cross to the top of Mont-Royal if the mission outpost of Ville Marie, which he had founded 1 year earlier, was spared from a Christmas Day flood. More than 2 centuries after Maisonneuve's trek, in the heyday of the Golden Square Mile, the Côte-des-Neiges hill enjoyed a more secular use as a prized winter toboggan run. On Saturdays, the fashionable Square Milers put on their furs, piled into horse-drawn sleighs, and promenaded through the city on Sherbrooke and on up to Mont-Royal via this thoroughfare. The cream of society slowly ascended the hill while snowflakes fell, a spectacle akin to the elegant sleigh rides of czarist St. Petersburg. ♦ Between Rue Sherbrooke W and Ave Docteur Penfield

9 JAMES CRATHERN HOUSE

Famed Canadian architect **Edward Maxwell**, whose credits also include work on the **Château Frontenac** in Quebec City, designed more than 30 houses in the Square Mile; this one was the first, completed in 1892. Faced in red sandstone, the house was built for James Crathern, director of the **Bank of Commerce**. The Swiss consulate has occupied the house for more than 35 years. ♦ 1572 Ave Docteur Penfield (at Chemin de la Côte-des-Neiges)

Shearer Street in Montreal was named for the father of Norma Shearer, a Hollywood star of the 1920s, 1930s, and 1940s.

Montrealers rent an average of 72 videos per year, 6% below the national average.

In addition to French, more than 100 languages and dialects are spoken in the Greater Montreal area, including English, Italian, Spanish, Greek, Arabic, Chinese, Portuguese, and Vietnamese (in that order).

10 LEARMONT HOUSE

Built in 1893, this graystone-faced building with its Anglo-Norman roof (now owned by Cossette Communication Marketing) was originally the imposing home of Joseph Bowles Learmont, a hardware wholesaler who was self-taught in philosophy and literature. Considered an eccentric because of his passion for old books, Learmont had a second-floor library stocked with dozens of rare Bibles, engravings, and letters signed by famous people. ◆ 1564 Ave Docteur Penfield (between Rue Simpson and Chemin de la Côte-des-Neiges)

11 JOHN AULD HOUSE

John Auld was an original Square Mile pioneer—one of the first prosperous residents to leave Old Montreal in 1850 for what was then farmland close to Mont-Royal. After he died, his farmhouse was handed down to his son. Tragically, it burned to the ground in 1897, and the young heir's wife perished in the blaze. Soon, however, John Auld Jr. built a new house on the same site. With its distinctive hipped roof, V-shaped dormers, and New Brunswick sandstone façade, the house leaves a lasting impression. Since the younger Auld's death in 1918, the estate has had various occupants, including the US consulate, which in 1953 acquired both this building and the neighboring **Learmont House** and linked them with an aerial passageway. The consulate moved out in 1977, and in 1984 a major Montreal ad agency, Cossette Communication Marketing, bought and restored both structures. ◆ 1558 Ave Docteur Penfield (between Rue Simpson and Chemin de la Côte-des-Neiges)

12 SLESSOR HOUSE

Although little information is available about its original owner, James Slessor, local historians do know that this 1891 gray limestone home, a combination of the Victorian and Roman styles, was once part of a double house, the other half of which was demolished in the 1960s. Subsequent residents changed almost nothing—not even the 1930s bedroom telephone—but many magnificent Art Deco objects on the premises were donated to the **McCord Museum** after one occupant's death in 1983. Given that the house itself (with its ornate roof turrets and triangular stone archway) is squeezed between two apartment high-rises, it's a wonder that any of it survived the 1960s demolition craze at all. ◆ 1538 Ave Docteur Penfield (between Rue Simpson and Chemin de la Côte-des-Neiges)

13 STEARNS HOUSE

Scottish-born architect **Robert Findlay**, who had a fondness for red brick, designed this 1905 house. Its first owner, Harold E. Stearns, was president of a carriage upholstery firm; the next occupants, stockbroker Paul-Emile Ostiguy and his family, lived here for 40 years until the 1960s, when they objected to being scrutinized by dwellers in the new high-rise apartments nearby. The building is now owned by a law firm headed by Raymond Robic. ◆ 1514 Ave Docteur Penfield (at Rue Simpson)

14 WILSON HOUSE

Since 1975, the Polish consulate has occupied the house built in 1910 for wine-and-spirits magnate (and later senator) Joseph Marcelin Wilson. Born to a French-Canadian mother and an English father, Wilson was one of the few French-speaking inhabitants of the Square Mile and somewhat out of his element in this predominantly British enclave. His home, displaying both British and French influences, reflects his mixed heritage. Wilson lived here until his death in 1940; his wife stayed on 9 years longer. Part of his land was ceded to the city for the extension of Avenue Docteur Penfield, known as MacGregor at the time. ◆ 3501 Ave du Musée (at Ave Docteur Penfield)

15 REDPATH MUSEUM

Sugar heir Peter Redpath donated the money for this nature and history museum on the McGill Campus. Built in 1882, it was the first structure in Canada designed specifically as a museum, and it now holds the country's second-largest collection of Egyptian antiquities (a mummy lies in a glass viewing case near the entrance), along with numerous displays of extinct creatures. Temporary exhibits stress an ecological theme. Outside, just steps away from the museum, is another Peter Redpath gift to the school: **Redpath Hall**, a former library reading room restored for use as a concert hall. ◆ Free. M-Sa; Su, 1-5PM. 859 Rue Sherbrooke W (west side of campus, near Ave Docteur Penfield). 398.4086

16 BAUMGARTEN HOUSE

In the first half of the 1900s, **McGill University** acquired a number of Square Mile mansions west of the main campus. This one, obtained in 1926 and now home to the McGill Faculty Club, is in the best condition. (Visits are limited to organized group tours, by appointment only.) A native of Dresden, Alfred Baumgarten (1842–1919) was introduced early to palatial living, when his father was personal physician to the German monarch. Alfred grew up to become president of the St. Lawrence Sugar Refinery in Montreal, where he built a mansion as austere on the outside as it was posh on the inside. His was the first Montreal residence with an indoor swimming pool (it no longer exists), and he personally designed the ballroom floor to rest on springs, lending an extra lift to the festivities. Many of these features have since been altered (the two-story grand salon, for example, is now divided horizontally). But the house is still replete with grand old comfortable chairs, billiard tables, and oil paintings. And with McGill faculty members coming here for dining and leisure, it's still being used in keeping with the original owner's intent. In lieu of admission, groups are asked to purchase coffee or a bite to eat at the Faculty Club dining room. ♦ M-F, 11AM-10PM, 11 Aug-19 June. 3450 Rue McTavish (between Rue Sherbrooke W and Ave Docteur Penfield). 398.6391

17 RUE SIMPSON

One of the most beautiful streets in the Square Mile, Rue Simpson is named after Sir George Simpson (1786–1860), a Scottish fur trader who headed the Hudson's Bay Company when it controlled all the British North American fur trade. Simpson was also a prominent landholder who developed a block of eight elegant town houses on Rue Sherbrooke for local denizens who lacked either the motivation or the means to build on a grand scale. The project, called the **Prince of Wales Terrace**, was torn down in 1973 to make way for **McGill University**'s **School of Management**. A bit farther down Simpson is Avenue Docteur Penfield, which both literally and figuratively marks an important intersection in the neighborhood's history. The avenue itself (named for a world-renowned neurologist at the **Royal Victoria Hospital**, but

Way back when "Old Montreal" was just Montreal, the city was surrounded by a wall, complete with ramparts and fortifications. To enter, you had to be allowed in through one of three gates. The wall was torn down in the early 1800s, after the threat of attack from hostile outsiders diminished. Some segments of the wall were recently uncovered by archaeologists.

When Canada's first transcontinental train left for Vancouver from Montreal's Dalhousie Station in 1886, it achieved the goal Canadians had aimed for with confederation: to bind the country together physically as well as politically (confederation, which created the self-governing Dominion of Canada, occurred in 1867).

originally called MacGregor) was formerly a cul-de-sac ending on Simpson; then, in 1956, the city extended it—radically changing the northernmost portion of the Square Mile and demolishing a number of mansions in the process. Across the street on Penfield is **Percy Walters Park**, whose gates once encircled the erstwhile stately home called **Rosemount**, where Scottish lawyer and legislator Sir John Rose entertained the Prince of Wales (the future King of England) during that monarch's first visit to Canada in 1860. Opposite the park at the same intersection is **Trafalgar School for Girls**, established in 1871 by Scottish merchant Donald Ross in honor of his wife. ♦ Between Rue Sherbrooke W and Ave Docteur Penfield

18 MOUNT VIEW

So obscured from view on the Sherbrooke side that even some locals aren't aware it exists, this once-sumptuous mansion originally stood amid verdant, rolling grounds—land now occupied by **Linton Apartments**. The grand house was built around 1867 for David Lewis, an importer of dry goods, who sold the property 5 years later to James Linton, a manufacturer of boots and shoes. When the Linton family eventually constructed its large apartment building on the portion that fronted Sherbrooke, the home's entrance porch was remodeled to face Simpson. Despite a succession of subsequent owners, who turned the home into a rooming house, a clinic, and a club by turns, the mansion's original exterior and interior (now owned by the Linton Apartments management) are virtually intact. ♦ 3424 Rue Simpson (at Rue Sherbrooke W)

19 ROBERT STANLEY BAGG HOUSE

Since 1892, this house has been a striking focal point for the intersection of these two historic thoroughfares (Rues Sherbrooke and Guy). Constructed of red sandstone and rock-faced graystone, the home was the property of Robert Stanley Bagg (1848–1912), a cultivated man whose family had been wealthy for generations. His widow remained in the home after he died. Though it was divided into two units in the 1920s and the distinguishing western tower that crowned the original conical roof was damaged by fire, Mrs. Bagg stayed on until her death in 1946. The **Bagg House** has since been occupied by several commercial enterprises, including two banks. ♦ 1541 Rue Sherbrooke W (at Rue Guy)

20 LINTON APARTMENTS

One of the city's finest examples of the Beaux Arts style, and one of the few remaining local structures with terra-cotta cladding, this building was literally a massive achievement when it was built in 1907. The 90 apartments

THE POWER OF THE PUCK

The **Montreal Forum**, former home of the perennially powerful **Montreal Canadiens**, was sacred (albeit slippery) turf in the eyes of professional hockey players and their fans. Twenty-four Stanley Cup banners, inspiring both awe and envy, hung high above the ice, as symbols of the dynasty's dominance of the sport. Montreal has captured the ultimate championship more often than any club in **National Hockey League** history. Now the old Forum is the **Pepsi Forum Entertainment Center** and the team plays in the new **Molson Center**. It remains to be seen whether it will hold the same place in Montrealers' hearts.

It's no understatement to say that the Canadiens epitomize the game of ice hockey. Organized in 1909, eight years before the National Hockey League was formed, its players have always been noted for their flamboyant style and exceptional speed. They were long ago dubbed the Flying Frenchmen, a moniker that underscores Quebecers' provincial pride. No inhabitant of La Belle Province is unaware of the Canadiens' fortunes; newspapers devote page on page to hockey coverage, even in the off-season, when almost as much ink is spilled in speculation and second-guessing.

The club's management boasts a similarly prestigious pedigree. The team and the Molson Center are owned by Molson Companies Limited, which runs the oldest continually operating brewery in North America. Founded in 1786 by John Molson, an English immigrant, the business has spanned seven generations, making it the second-oldest corporation in Canada. Over the years, the family's interests expanded beyond beer to include shipping (the first steamboat to run between Montreal and Quebec City), investments in the railroad, a sugar factory, and **Molson Bank**. But what really established the Molson name in Canada's collective consciousness was their 1957 purchase of the Canadiens and the Forum, as well as their corporate sponsorship of *Hockey Night in Canada*, a television institution that keeps

millions of passionate puckwatchers glued to their sets every Saturday evening.

Though the Canadiens have moved to new, more commodious quarters, the memories of events that took place on the Forum's ice (and off) accompanies the team and their fans to the new digs. Here's an example of an unforgettable moment that is perennially retold (and relived in the telling). St. Patrick's Day, 1955: Four days earlier, NHL Commissioner Clarence Campbell had suspended Canadiens superstar Maurice Richard for the remainder of the season, including the playoffs. The call? Roughing up a Boston Bruins defenseman and an official. Canadiens supporters were incensed: Not only was Richard on track for the NHL scoring title that year, but Montreal's bid for the Stanley Cup would be severely impaired by his absence. On 17 March, when Montreal faced the Detroit Red Wings at the Forum with Campbell in attendance, fans picketed the arena and heaped verbal abuse on the commissioner at game time. Then one fan slapped him, and somebody tossed a tear-gas bomb, sending everyone scrambling to the exits. Once out on the streets, the fracas that became known as the "Richard Riot" raged. Every window in the Forum was shattered, and for 4 hours looters rampaged down **Rue Ste-Catherine**; 37 adults and 100 juveniles were arrested before peace was restored.

Of course, Richard is now enshrined in the Hockey Hall of Fame, as are many of his Canadiens contemporaries, including his younger brother, Henri, and Jean Beliveau, Bernard Geoffrion, Doug Harvey, Dickie Moore, and Jacques Plante. But despite its illustrious history, the team never rests on its laurels. For the Flying Frenchmen, the goal of next year's Stanley Cup always looms large. The Molson Center is located downtown at 1250 Rue de la Gauchetière, 514/989.2841, near **Windsor Station**. Hockey season runs from September through June.

spread over 10 stories made this the largest apartment building in the city. It was erected on the lawn of **Mount View**, one of the Square Mile's oldest surviving houses—now tucked behind the building on Rue Simpson. ♦ 1509 Rue Sherbrooke W (at Rue Simpson)

21 CHURCH OF ST. ANDREW AND ST. PAUL

A work of art in itself, this enormous church flanking the oldest wing of the **Montreal Museum of Fine Arts** was created in 1932, several years after the merging of two Presbyterian congregations from the **Church of**

St. Andrew (founded in 1803) and the **Church of St. Paul** (founded in 1832). Designed by architect **Harold Lea Featherstonhaugh**, the building is noteworthy for the main entrance, with its deeply recessed archway and canopied niches displaying statues of the patron saints, and for incorporating the older churches' original stained-glass windows in the design plan. This is also the official military church of the Black Watch (Royal Highland Regiment) of Canada, whose colors are displayed in the sanctuary. ♦ Open only for Su services. 3415 Rue Redpath (at Rue Sherbrooke W). 842.3431

Restaurants/Clubs: Red | Hotels: Purple | Shops: Orange | Outdoors/Parks: Green | Sights/Culture: Blue

22 ERSKINE AND AMERICAN UNITED CHURCH

Worshipers at this Presbyterian church, built by **A.C. Hutchison** in 1894, were among those early Square Milers who moved here from the old city. Many had previously attended the **Scottish Secession Chapel** on Boulevard de la Gauchetière in Chinatown (where a Chinese Catholic church now stands). Inside the amphitheater-style chapel are windows from Tiffany Studios in New York. ◆ Open only for services. 1339 Rue Sherbrooke W (at Rue Crescent). 849.3286

23 CHÂTEAU APARTMENTS

Built in 1926, this elegant apartment house—graced with carriage entrances and gargoyles and inspired by the beauty of Spanish fortified homes and French Renaissance châteaux—affirmed the apartment house as a Depression-era alternative to the mansions of earlier Square Milers. The 12-story building is topped with a copper roof in keeping with the grand château-style hotels being built at the time. Erected on the former property of textile tycoons Andrew Frederick Gault and George Washington Stephens, the building was a business venture for Senator Pamphile-Real du Tremblay, publisher of the French-language daily newspaper *La Presse*. The architect was **Harold Lea Featherstonhaugh**, who also designed the **Church of St. Andrew and St. Paul**. ◆ 1321 Rue Sherbrooke W (at Rue de la Montagne)

24 MAISON CORBY

Completed in 1883 for businessman Thomas Craig, who almost immediately rented it out, this residence was redesigned at the turn of the 19th century by American architect **Richard Waite**, who virtually dismantled and reassembled the entire building stone by stone. In the process **Waite** maintained some decorative touches but moved the main entrance, redesigned the front staircase, and added another story for then-owner James Reid Wilson, a Montreal banker. Corby Distilleries bought the house for its headquarters in 1951. ◆ 1201 Rue Sherbrooke W (at Rue Drummond). 288.4181

25 FORGET HOUSE

Louis J. Forget, who lived from 1853 to 1911, was an aberration—a French-Canadian highly regarded in both English and French financial circles. The wealthiest French-Canadian businessman of his time and founder of the most powerful brokerage house in Canada, Forget was the first French-Canadian member—and eventually, president—of the **Montreal Stock Exchange**, and later became the first French-Canadian director of the **Canadian Pacific Railway** and a senator as well. Few changes have been made to the exterior of his imposing limestone mansion since its completion in 1884, but inside, it's a different story. His private chapel, for instance, is now used as a restaurant by the United Services Club (USC) for veterans, which made the home its headquarters in 1927 and now occupies the main floor. Still, the chapel skylight, mahogany woodwork, and a stained-glass window by **Tiffany & Co.** remain. When USC membership declined, the MacDonald Stewart Foundation bought the home and moved into the two upper floors. The building also houses offices of the St. Andrew's Society of Montreal, founded in 1834 to help Scottish immigrants settle in the city. ◆ 1195 Rue Sherbrooke W (between Rues Stanley and Drummond)

26 MONT ROYAL CLUB

Even from the outside, this old-style businessmen's club and its two neighbors to the east, **Forget House** and **Maison Corby**, give passersby a feel for the splendor of Sherbrooke around the turn of the 19th century. Legend has it that when prominent citizens George Drummond, Hugh Montagu Allan, Louis Forget, and some 30 other Square Milers decided that their downtown haunt, the St. James Club, was too noisy, they moved to create a new one. (The spurned St. James survived nicely; it has since moved from its previous location on Dorchester and Université to new quarters on Union.) Pooling their considerable resources, they bought the former home of Canada's third prime minister, John Abbott, to house what they called the Mont Royal Club—only to have it burn down 4 years later. Not long afterward, New York architect **Stanford White** happened to be in town. Over lunch, the displaced members persuaded him to design them a new club. White's finished product resembles an Italian Renaissance palace, with a long, grand entryway. Inside, opulent marble pillars reflect the wealth of the club's 300 resident and 140 nonresident members—all admitted by invitation only—who include prime ministers, cabinet ministers, heads of multinational corporations, and other professionals at the top of their fields. Unfortunately for just plain folk like the rest of us, the visiting policy is as exclusive as the membership: No one is admitted unless accompanied by a club member. ◆ 1175 Rue Sherbrooke W (at Rue Stanley). 842.5454

27 THE ALLAN HOUSES

Two nephews of shipping magnate Sir Hugh Allan (owner of the imposing **Ravenscrag** castle) built houses side by side on Rue Stanley. Andrew Alexander Allan's L-shaped home, the one closer to Sherbrooke, is best described as Victorian eclectic; his brother

MONTRÉAL MUSEUMS PASS

You can visit a total of 25 museums and historic sites with the **Montréal Museums Pass**. Valid for 2 of 3 consecutive days, the pass costs $20.00 and can result in substantial savings if you intend to take in several museums in a 2-day period. The pass is on sale in all participating museums as well as at the INFOTOURISTE center in Dorchester Square. Call 873.2015 for more information.

Hugh Andrew Allan lived next door in a medieval-looking house complete with characteristic portico and lacy brickwork. Today, both buildings are owned by the Sisters of the Congregation of Notre-Dame, who use Andrew's old house as an arts-and-crafts school and Hugh's as a sewing and cooking school. The latter has gained considerable renown due to its star teacher, Soeur Berthe, famous for her cookbooks featuring traditional Quebec cuisine. ♦ 3433 and 3435 Rue Stanley (at Rue Sherbrooke W)

28 SOFITEL

$$$ Lovers of natural light will be pleased to learn that the 258 rooms and suites at this smart address feature three-meter floor-to-ceiling windows. Each room is decorated in burnt amber accents with teak furniture, including Chesterfield chaises, and bathrooms have ochre-colored marble walls and black granite countertops. As this property is geared toward the business traveler, the rooms come equipped with three telephones and high-speed Internet access (there's also a business center). There is fine dining in the **Restaurant Renoir.** ♦ 1155 Rue Sherbrooke W (at Rue Stanley). 285.9000, 800/SOFITEL; fax 289.1155

29 RODDICK GATES/MCGILL UNIVERSITY

Across the street from the **McCord Museum** stands a prominent Montreal landmark: the curved, sentrylike stone gates to **McGill University**, long regarded as the finest institution of higher learning in Canada. Its Scottish founder, James McGill, who came to Montreal in 1766 after attending the University of Glasgow, may have been the only Square Mile settler with a college education. After marrying into a wealthy French-Canadian family, he amassed a fortune in fur trading and later became a legislator and a colonel in the Montreal militia. McGill, who died in 1813, bequeathed £10,000 and his 46-acre estate, **Burnside Place**, to the Royal Institution for the Advancement of Learning with the stipulation that a college bearing his name be erected on the site. Classes began in 1829. The gates are a memorial to Sir Thomas George Roddick, an eminent surgeon and dean of the Faculty of Medicine. Inside the gates, a stone unearthed in 1925 marks the discovery of what is thought to be the site of the Iroquois village of Hochelaga—the first settlement encountered by explorer Jacques Cartier when he landed here in 1535 and named the area Mont-Royal. Although new evidence suggests that the settlement actually may have been closer to the mountaintop, excavators did find an intriguing collection of human bones, stone axes, pipes, arrowheads, and other remnants of Iroquois life not far from here. A more recent artifact sits nearby at the top of the university's main drive: The urnlike monument in front of the **Arts Building** (framed by the Roddick Gates) is James McGill's tomb. His remains were transferred to the campus in 1875 from the city's old Protestant cemetery, which is now Dorchester Square. ♦ 801-885 Rue Sherbrooke W (at Rue McTavish)

30 CHÂTEAU VERSAILLES AND HÔTEL VERSAILLES PARK PLAZA

$$$ With its 65 bright, cheerfully decorated rooms and suites nestled in four adjacent, early 1900s townhouses, the château is a sheer delight; the 15-floor, 107-room hotel across the street is in a modern building and caters to a more business-oriented crowd. Leisure travelers may prefer the château, which succeeds in creating an atmosphere at once warm, chic, and sumptuous. Here interior designer Patricia McClintock has combined rich fabric textures with vibrant color schemes, an effect that in concert with bright, spacious bathrooms makes one want to linger. There's also a sauna, exercise room, and small but complete business center. Rooms in both properties feature in-room CD players, Fruits & Passions amenities, and daily continental breakfast—somewhat more substantial in the hotel. The **Hotel Versailles** is home to **La Maîtresse**, a contemporary French bistro and bar designed by award-winning Montreal designer Michael Joannides,

---

Restaurants/Clubs: Red | Hotels: Purple | Shops: Orange | Outdoors/Parks: Green | Sights/Culture: Blue

but guests at both the hotel and château can enjoy room service from the restaurant. (Guests at the latter can peer out their windows to see a staff member carrying their meals across Rue Sherbrooke—a charming sight.) ♦ Château Versailles, 1659 Rue Sherbrooke W (at Rue St-Mathieu). 933.3611, 888/933.8111; fax 933.8401. Hotel Versailles, 1808 Rue Sherbrooke W (at Rue St-Mathieu). 933.3611, 888/933.8111; fax 933.6967. Both properties: www.versailleshotels.com

31 PHYSIQUE SPA

This urban day spa in a loft setting offers a full range of fitness and aesthetic services for overexerted executives and tired tourists alike. In addition to a variety of massages, there are face treatments, which include the 90-minute "lady danger" and "gentleman revanche" facials, and body treatments ranging from an oxygen bath to sea-salt polish and "tutti-frutti" scrub. Fitness sessions include pilates, yoga, and spinning. ♦ 1632 Rue Sherbrooke W (between Rues Guy and St-Mathieu). 937.1632

32 PETIT MUSÉE

The name means **Little Museum**, and this antiques store is just that. Spread graciously over four floors, some 10,000 valuable artifacts are sparingly and artfully displayed with all the skill of a fine curator. According to proprietor Dan Klein, grandson of the store's founder, the building was originally a house built in 1884 and was later divided in two. Clients come from around the world in search of the precious finds that have made the place a Montreal fixture for more than 40 years. ♦ Tu-Sa. 1494 Rue Sherbrooke W (at Rue Simpson). 937.6161

33 PREMIÈRE MOISSON

This boulangerie and pastry shop is an excellent place to stop and refuel with coffee and fresh croissants, sandwiches, and the like. The fruit tarts are excellent (try lemon or pear), as are the mousses and cakes—even the danishes are uncommonly savory. There's also a (much busier) branch in the **Gare Centrale**. ♦ M-F, 7AM-8PM; Sa-Su, 7AM-7PM. 1490 Rue Sherbrooke W (at Rue Mackay). 931.6540

34 DAVIDOFF

The sole Canadian location of the worldwide store founded by Zeno Davidoff of Geneva, this shop specializes in fine cigars and pipes, along with ties, wallets, sunglasses, and other accessories for men (even its own line of cologne). ♦ M-W, Sa; Th-F, 10AM-8PM. 1452 Rue Sherbrooke W (at Rue Mackay). 289.9118

34 CANADIAN GUILD OF CRAFTS (QUEBEC)

If you want to buy Inuit art, avoid the junk sold in tourist shops and come to this nonprofit organization founded in 1906 to promote artisans in Quebec and Canada. It sells all manner of handicrafts and artwork and has temporary exhibitions, a permanent collection, and a gallery of Inuit and Indian art. ♦ Tu-F, 9:30AM-6PM; Sa, 10AM-5PM. 1460 Rue Sherbrooke W (at Rue Mackay). 849.6091

35 JEAN D'AIRE, BURGHER OF CALAIS

One of Montreal's most valuable sculptures, fashioned by Auguste Rodin in Paris, stands outside the venerable **Dominion Art Gallery**. The piece is one of several attempts by the sculptor to complete a commissioned project between 1884 and 1895. It commemorates a heroic burgher of the French town of Calais, which was besieged by the armies of England's King Edward III between 1346 and 1347. Offering the king the keys to the city if he would lift the siege, the burghers—led by Jean d'Aire—left their walled city and marched to the king's camp expecting death; inexplicably, he spared their lives. More sculpture is on display inside the Dominion Art Gallery, internationally known for its fine collection of bronzes. ♦ 1438 Rue Sherbrooke W (at Rue Bishop). 845.7471

35 IL CORTILE

★$$ Tucked away in the courtyard complex called **Passage du Musée**, this trattoria offers a variety of pasta, veal, and seafood dishes for lunch and dinner. The outdoor terrace with its linen-covered wrought-iron tables makes a delightful summer hideout, by day or under starry skies. ♦ Italian ♦ Daily, lunch and dinner. Reservations required for terrace dining. 1422 Rue Sherbrooke W (at Rue Bishop). 843.8230

JEAN-NOËL DESMARAIS PAVILION

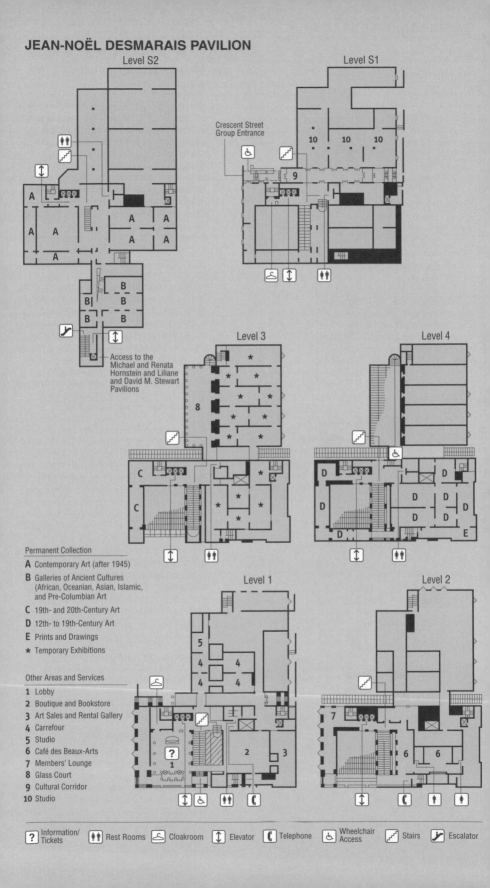

Level S2

Level S1

Crescent Street
Group Entrance

10 10 10

9

Access to the
Michael and Renata
Hornstein and Liliane
and David M. Stewart
Pavilions

Level 3

8

Level 4

Permanent Collection

A Contemporary Art (after 1945)

B Galleries of Ancient Cultures
(African, Oceanian, Asian, Islamic,
and Pre-Columbian Art

C 19th- and 20th-Century Art

D 12th- to 19th-Century Art

E Prints and Drawings

★ Temporary Exhibitions

Other Areas and Services

1 Lobby

2 Boutique and Bookstore

3 Art Sales and Rental Gallery

4 Carrefour

5 Studio

6 Café des Beaux-Arts

7 Members' Lounge

8 Glass Court

9 Cultural Corridor

10 Studio

Level 1

Level 2

? Information/
Tickets　　♦♦ Rest Rooms　　🔳 Cloakroom　　⬍ Elevator　　📞 Telephone　　♿ Wheelchair
Access　　Stairs　　Escalator

HORNSTEIN/STEWART PAVILION

Level 2

Level 1

Access to the Jean-Nöel Desmarais Pavilion

Permanent Collection	Other Areas and Services
A Canadian Art	**1** Lobby
B Inuit Art	**2** Hall of Mirrors
C Amerindian Art	**3** Rest Area
D Canadian Decorative Arts	**4** Studio
E Decorative Arts from the Renaissance to Today	**★** Temporary Exhibitions

? Information/Tickets   **††** Rest Rooms   Cloakroom   **⬍** Elevator

(Telephone   Wheelchair Access   Stairs   Escalator

36 MONTREAL MUSEUM OF FINE ARTS

No, your eyes aren't playing tricks: The oldest art museum in Canada (1860) and largest in Quebec does indeed occupy both sides of Sherbrooke. In 1991, thanks to a large-scale renovation drive, the museum (originally located on Rue Ste-Catherine at Phillips Square) expanded from the **Edward** and **William Maxwell**-designed **Benaiah Gibb Pavilion** (1860) on the north side of the street to the **Desmarais Pavilion** (1990) on the south side. The Gibb building—distinguished by its white Vermont marble and four Ionic columns and financed largely with support from prosperous Square Mile tailor and art lover Benaiah Gibb—has routinely hosted blockbuster traveling exhibitions from around the world (in 2001 it was the only North American venue for the exposition *Picasso érotique*). It also boasts collections of engravings, drawings, sculptures, paintings, furniture, and silverware. Across the street, the stunning Desmarais Pavilion, also fashioned of white Vermont marble but designed by Israeli-born architect **Moshe Safdie**, connects to the Gibb building via an underground tunnel. Safdie (whose credits include the National Gallery in Ottawa) calls this the most urban museum in any city and says he tried to reflect every facet of Montreal in the building. The airy pavilion seems to wrap itself around the city—and vice versa: When a visitor emerges from the elevators, there's Mont-Royal atop Avenue du Musée; from the glass courtyard area, Montreal rooftops stretch east and west; and all seven levels provide city views. The museum has a fine-art bookstore, a gift shop, a boutique specializing in Inuit art, and a gallery where original paintings by local artists are available for rent. ♦ Free admission for the permanent collection; admission for temporary exhibitions (half price W, 5:30PM-9PM). Daily, 10AM-6PM; W, 10AM-9PM. 1380 Rue Sherbrooke W (at Ave du Musée). 285.1600

Within the Montreal Museum of Fine Arts:

CAFÉ DU MUSÉE

★$ The service is cafeteria-style, but the fare, including muffins, sandwiches, juices, coffee, and tea, is tasty. ♦ Canadian ♦ Daily, lunch and snacks. 285.1600

CAFÉ DES BEAUX ARTS

★$$ The museum's sit-down restaurant offers a full menu of hot and cold entrées with contemporary leanings as well as daily specials consisting of appetizer, entrée, dessert, and coffee. ♦ Continental ♦ Daily, lunch. 285.1600

37 MUSEUM OF DECORATIVE ARTS

This small museum moved from the **Château Dufresne** near the **Botanical Garden** to the **Desmarais Pavilion** of the **Montreal Museum of Fine Arts** in 1997—in a space designed by architect **Frank Gehry**—but it is independent, with a separate entrance. It showcases the Lilian and David M. Stewart Collection of international decorative arts amassed between 1935 and the present. Furniture, glassware, ceramics, textiles, and graphic arts are all on display. There are also temporary exhibitions with works by Canadian and international designers. ♦ Admission. Tu-Su, 11AM-6PM; W, 11AM-9PM. 2200 Rue Crescent (between Blvd de Maisonneuve W and Rue Sherbrooke W). 284.1252

38 HOLT RENFREW

In 1937, the city's oldest and finest department store opened in this six-story building that's a textbook example of the architecture known as Streamline Moderne, a variant of Art Deco. The store began operations under the name **Henderson, Holt, and Renfrew Furriers**, making its reputation by supplying exquisite furs to British royalty. It has expanded over the years to other locations but is still known for its furs. (Denmark's Birger Christensen showroom is on-site.) ♦ M-W, 10AM-6PM; Th-F, 10AM-9PM; Sa, 9:30AM-5PM; Su, noon-5PM. 1300 Rue Sherbrooke W (at Rue de la Montagne). 842.5111

39 RITZ-CARLTON

$$$$ The grande dame of Sherbrooke is also the birthplace of the hotel chain's world-famous hyphenated name. Built in 1912 as a place where wealthy Square Milers could lodge their friends, this hotel was the dream of four men—railway engineer Herbert Holt, president of the Royal Bank of Canada; Charles Gordon, president of Dominion Textile and a director of Molson's Bank; shipping heir Hugh Montagu Allan; and Charles Hosmer, a self-made man who built up Canadian Pacific Telegrams to international status. During frequent visits to Europe, these gentlemen became captivated by the Carlton Hotel in London and decided to use it as a model for a rooming establishment of their own. They formed the Carlton Hotel Company; found a suitable piece of land; engaged New York architects **Whitney Warren** and **Charles Wetmore**, who had built New York's Grand Central Station; and solicited the endorsement of a Swiss hotelier who was then the talk of Europe—Caesar Ritz. For a fee of $25,000 and the contractual promise that the Montreal hotel would be run according to his fastidious standards, Ritz agreed, and ever since, the posh hotel has pampered and coddled kings, queens, heads of state, politicians, and entertainers. The Rolling Stones were asked, politely of course, to wear neckties when they dined at the hotel (they complied). Elizabeth Taylor married Richard Burton here (for the first time) in 1964. Queen Elizabeth and Prince Philip dropped by on short notice during the **1976 Summer Olympics**, but because the royal suite was already occupied by Liberace, the queen had to stay in slightly less palatial quarters—much to the consternation of the Ritz staff. Although it's had some competition in recent years from the **Westin Mont-Royal** and other up-and-comers, this upscale hotel, with its Edwardian elegance and distinguishing black metal parapet that shelters guests at the main entrance in inclement weather, is still the place to see and be seen. ♦ 1228 Rue Sherbrooke W (at Rue Drummond). 842.4212, 800/363.0366; fax 842.6722

Within the Ritz-Carlton:

CAFÉ DE PARIS

★★★$$$$ Power brokers do their power breakfasts here, ladies in lovely hats do lunch, shoppers enjoy high tea, and high society meets for elaborate dinners. And between May and October, this Montreal institution moves out to the garden, where sophisticated guests dine alfresco around the pond as a dozen ducklings paddle about. The indoor dining area is elegant, with fresh flowers atop tables, large gilt-edged mirrors reflecting a plethora of hanging plants, and etched-glass dividers depicting classic Parisian scenes. Delectable entrées include medallions of pork in mustard sauce and filet mignon served with Béarnaise sauce. ♦ French ♦ Daily, breakfast, lunch, and dinner. Reservations required; jacket and tie required at dinner. 842.4212 ♿

40 WALTER KLINKHOFF GALLERY

Four decades ago, Walter Klinkhoff started this gallery, specializing in Canadian artwork, in a private 1870s home. Alan and Eric, his sons, now help him run the business. The family has kept the stairwell, moldings, and other features of the old place intact, leaving the interior unembellished so as not to distract from the art. ♦ M-Sa in winter. M-F in summer. 1200 Rue Sherbrooke W (at Rue Drummond). 288.7306

41 MAISON ALCAN

When Alcan Aluminum's world headquarters debuted on Sherbrooke in 1983, the company was widely praised for a masterful recycling

---

Restaurants/Clubs: Red | Hotels: Purple | Shops: Orange | Outdoors/Parks: Green | Sights/Culture: Blue

---

THE BEST

Gaëtan Gagné

CEO, L'Entraide Life Insurance

Walking on the **Plains of Abraham**.

Lunch at the **Le Continental**.

A visit to **Musée de la Civilisation**.

Dinner at **Château Frontenac**.

A visit to **île d'Orléans**.

A cruise on the **St. Lawrence River**.

Shopping at **Place Royale** and **Place Laurier**.

Dinner at **le Graffiti** on **Avenue Cartier**.

---

effort of an architectural sort: It preserved three historic row houses and a hotel and linked them to a new glass atrium and seven-story, aluminum-clad office structure. One of the architectural trio, the **Lord Atholstan House** (1895), with its fanciful windows framed by medallion-patterned plasterwork, now houses the office of Alcan's president; the other preserved structures have been remodeled and contain shops and galleries. Several restaurants are located in the atrium, also the site of a summer concert series. In their pre-Alcan incarnations, these buildings enjoyed a somewhat checkered past. The **Atholstan House** was occupied successively by an antiques store, the Canadian Textile Association, the Jesuit Fathers' Mission, and the Iran Trade Commission. Its namesake, known as Sir Hugh Graham before acquiring his lordly

In the 1840s, 1,000 Montrealers, led by such prominent citizens as John Moison Jr. (the Moison company had been brewing beer since the 1780s), signed a petition to have Canada annexed to the United States. They were incensed by England's repeal of the corn laws that regulated the importation of grain.

Every year, Montreal organizes the longest-running St. Patrick's Day parade in North America. The first parade was held in 1824. Approximately 300,000 Montrealers are of Irish descent.

The top 10 countries from which most new immigrants come to Montreal are Haiti, Lebanon, France, China, Romania, Sri Lanka, the Philippines, India, Vietnam, and Morocco.

Montreal's four universities have a total enrollment of nearly 150,000 students and award 6,000 diplomas and degrees each year, including 650 doctorates. In Toronto, which has a higher population, 114,000 students are enrolled in universities that produce 4,000 graduates and award 580 doctorates annually.

title, was a journalist and founder of the *Montreal Star*, the city's largest English-language daily newspaper before it folded in 1979. He lived in the house until his death in 1938. The **Frederic Beique House** (1894) belonged to Senator Frederic-Ligori Beique, a lawyer, legislator, and owner of the French-language newspaper *Le Canada*, who managed to squeeze a family of 12 into half the space his next-door-neighbor Graham occupied with his family of 3. The redbrick-and-limestone **Berkeley Hotel** began life in 1928 as the **Hermitage** apartment house, and the **Elizabeth Holland House**, the oldest of the four structures, was built in 1872 when Sherbrooke was still a country lane. ◆ Daily, 7AM–midnight. 1188 Rue Sherbrooke W (at Rue Stanley). 848.8000

42 OMNI MONT-ROYAL

$$$$ One of the city's toniest hotels has vied for the same moneyed clientele as the nearby **Ritz-Carlton** since its opening in 1976. Formerly the **Four Seasons**, later a Westin, the property has 299 modern, pastel-toned, plushly carpeted rooms and suites. There's also a 6,600-square-foot health club, complete with sauna, steam room, and massage services, and an outdoor heated pool. ◆ 1050 Rue Sherbrooke W (at Rue Peel). 284.1110, fax 845.3025

Within the Omni Mont-Royal:

ZEN

★★★$$$ Montreal's most exquisite Chinese restaurant is not in Chinatown but on the lower level of the **Omni Mont-Royal** hotel. Yet this place, with its attentive staff, white linen tablecloths, minimalist glass walls, and fabulous food, still offers a terrific bargain: an all-you-can-eat sit-down dinner menu called the Zen Experience, featuring 43 dishes, from appetizers to desserts, for around $25 per person. ◆ Chinese ◆ Daily, lunch and dinner. Reservations required. 284.1110

OPUS II

★★★$$$$ Just down the hall from **Zen** is the **Omni**'s other fine restaurant, with its circular dining room in a cloudlike setting of soft pinks and blues. The atmosphere is refined but not stuffy, the service impeccable yet friendly, and the chairs and banquettes as comfortable as they are lovely. Creative menu selections marry French, Italian, and California cuisine and include choices low in calories and cholesterol. Though the tariff is steep, an exceptionally reasonable table d'hôte is offered each day; on a recent evening it included an appetizer of seasonal greens and home-smoked salmon drizzled with honey-and-lavender dressing, an entrée of grilled sea bass with crushed tomatoes and tarragon, and a rich, creamy hazelnut torte for dessert—all for under $25. ♦ Continental ♦ Daily, breakfast, lunch, and dinner. Reservations required. 284.1110 &

43 INTERNATIONAL CIVIL AVIATION ORGANIZATION (ICAO)

In this 27-floor office tower, a United Nations body sets safety standards for aviation worldwide. This is the only UN body headquartered in Canada. Guided tours of the building and of the organization's fabulous art collection—gifts from its 178 member states—are available by appointment only; call the public information office. ♦ Free. M-F. 1000 Rue Sherbrooke W (at Rue Metcalfe). 954.5855

44 MCCORD MUSEUM OF CANADIAN HISTORY

The history museum at the neighborhood's eastern edge is an ideal place to begin exploring the Square Mile—in part because it houses the Notman Photographic Archives, a one-of-a-kind visual record of residents in the area's heyday. William Notman, Canada's first internationally recognized photographer, came to Montreal from Paisley, Scotland, in 1856, and was soon in high demand for his creatively styled portraits of members of Square Mile society, who often came knocking on his studio door. An artist behind the lens (he once aspired to becoming a painter), Notman shunned formal posing, and when making house calls at the mansions, even included the servants in the picture. After his death in 1891, Notman's sons produced a trove of more than 400,000 of his negatives depicting Victorian Montrealers at work and play, inside and outside their estates. It's largely thanks to his oeuvre that you can witness the majesty of those Square Mile homes now lost to history. The museum itself, founded in the 1920s with an assemblage of Canadiana and aboriginal artifacts donated to **McGill University** by Judge David Ross McCord, today houses six permanent collec-

tions besides the Notman archives. Its gray limestone building, designed by Scottish-born architect **Percy Erskine Nobbs** as his first major commission and erected in 1906, originally housed the **McGill University** student union. The museum relocated here in 1965 and underwent a major $20 million expansion and renovation—doubling its space—between 1989 and 1992. ♦ Admission (free Sa, 10AM-noon). Tu-F, 10AM-6PM; Sa-Su, 10AM-5PM; also open in summer. 690 Rue Sherbrooke W (at Rue Victoria). 398.7100

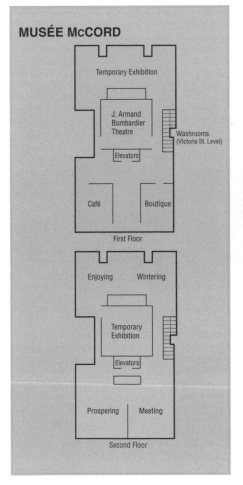

MUSÉE McCORD

Temporary Exhibition

J. Armand Bombardier Theatre

Washrooms (Victoria St. Level)

Elevators

Café

Boutique

First Floor

Enjoying   Wintering

Temporary Exhibition

Elevators

Prospering   Meeting

Second Floor

MONT-ROYAL PARK

When French explorer Jacques Cartier arrived at the Mohawk trading post of Hochelaga in 1535, he encountered a uniquely impressive setting: The village was built onto the side of a 700-foot-high glacial deposit that rose dramatically from the plains—steep on one side, gradually sloping on the other, and densely covered with lush forest. Being a true imperialist, Cartier immediately dubbed this sylvan spectacle **Mont-Royal**, or Royal Mountain, in honor of his country's then-reigning monarch, Francis I.

Today, concrete and steel cover much of "the mountain," as it's informally called. But 496 acres at the summit remain relatively pristine, thanks to the vision of US landscape architect Frederick Law Olmsted, who also designed New York City's Central Park. In the 1870s, Montreal's city fathers, concerned that residents were deforesting their prominent landmark in the quest for firewood, commissioned Olmsted to design an oasis of greenery that would preserve both the setting's tranquillity and its sweeping vistas of the city below. Olmsted accomplished that feat by cutting bridle and walking paths through the woods and instigating a moratorium on development (most of which remains concentrated near the mountain's steeper southern side).

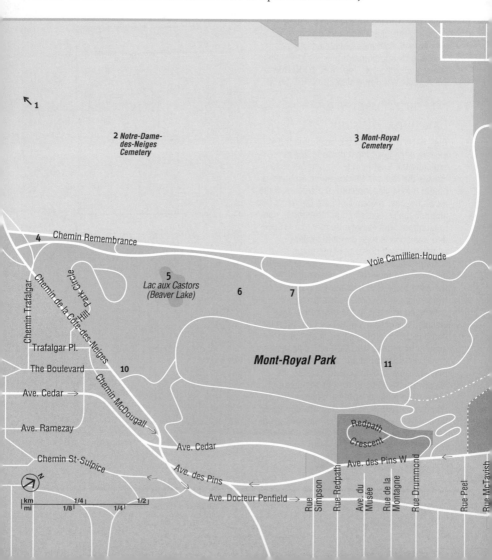

Mont-Royal Park is defined geographically by **Avenue du Parc** on the east, **Chemin de la Côte-des-Neiges** on the west, **Avenue des Pins** to the south, and the **University of Montreal** to the north. Yet its character is largely defined—as with Olmsted's Central Park—by the people who use it. The park is usually alive with pickup football games, rock bands shooting videos, and mountain bikers testing their endurance on the sloping terrain. Even outdoor concerts, like those held to celebrate the Quebecois holiday of St-Jean Baptiste in June, tend to be informal and low key. In fact, this bastion of well-preserved nature is a window on Montreal culture—present and past. From the expansive cemeteries making up the park's northern perimeter to the hilltop's illuminated cross dominating the landscape for miles around, there's a pervasive sense of the city's religious roots, along with omnipresent evidence of the population's rich multicultural mix. All strands of the city's heritage converge in the park, where tai chi masters relax cheek-by-jowl with readers of the Koran. The park, to put it simply, is huge—too vast and varied to cover in a day, especially on foot. The easiest approach is by car; ample metered parking is available in designated lots, and a primary road snakes throughout the grounds. Otherwise, bicycling lets you cover large distances while you take in the vistas from the hilly grades. You can also get a feel for the area from one of the horse-drawn calèches

for hire at **Place d'Armes** in Old Montreal, or via cross-country skis during the winter months. And for a scenic overlook, *points d'observation* are situated in the southern and eastern sectors.

As urban parks go, Mont-Royal is relatively safe (a police substation is located prominently on the grounds). The park is open daily 6AM to midnight; for more information, call 872.6559.

1 St. Joseph's Oratory

A 20-minute walk from the park's west entrance, this basilica is a must-see when you're on top of the mountain. Next only to Lourdes and Fatima, this is one of the world's most popular Catholic shrines—a fact underscored by its museum's display of thousands of cast-off crutches from faithful supplicants who came here hoping to be healed. It all began with a small chapel built to honor Joseph, Quebec's patron saint of healing, by a local monk named Brother André in 1904. The monk, who was orphaned at age 12 and worked in the New England textile mills, had chronic health problems. But he had a knack for curing others through his prayers to St. Joseph. In fact, Brother André was beatified in 1982 and is expected to be dubbed a saint soon. By the 1920s, offerings to St. Joseph were pouring in to Brother André, and in 1924 construction began on the massive basilica. When the Italian Renaissance–style dome was completed in 1955, it was the world's largest. Today the shrine includes a small museum, Brother André's tomb (he died in 1937 at age 91), his original chapel, several monuments,

KIDS ON BOARD IN MONTREAL

Riding a roller coaster at **La Ronde**, laughing at the clowns at **Cirque du Soleil**, stargazing at the **Planetarium**, tobogganing at the **Olympic Basin**— Montreal is rich with activities for children that are both fun and educational.

Tops on the list of places to go with children in tow is **Parc des Îles (Islands Park)**, a short Metro ride from the city. This revamped park encompasses **Notre-Dame** and **Ste-Hélène Islands**, Expo '67 sites. In summer, the 10-minute *Island Shuttle* ferries visitors between the park and the harbor, leaving Jacques-Cartier Basin regularly every half hour between mid-May and mid-October (514/872.4537). Among the favorite spots for kids here are the **Old Fort**, the beach, and scenic bicycle paths. Special events at the park include **La Fête des Neiges**, a free, 3-week snow festival in February with costumed skating parties, ice racing, and rides on a horse-drawn sleigh. Within the **Old Fort** on Ste-Hélène Island is the **Stewart Museum** (514/861.6701), named for the Montreal philanthropist, which began as an arsenal commissioned for the Duke of Wellington in 1822 to protect the city against naval attacks that never came. Today it houses a collection of military artifacts— muskets, pistols, model ships, globes, and maps—dating from 1608 to 1867. Inside, interpreters describe colonial life while showing off the former mess kitchen, its fireplace hung with pots and its hearth cluttered with other household articles. The museum is open daily; admission is charged. www.stewartmuseum.org

Outside, cannons announce military maneuvers by the **Compagnie Franche de la Marine** every summer. Authentically uniformed in gray coats, knee breeches, and tricornered hats, the men march in precision step to fife and drum, followed by **Fraser Highlanders** performing 18th-century Scottish drills to the skirl of the bagpipes. Shows run between 24 June and late August, Wednesday through Sunday, at 11AM, 2:30PM, and 5PM.

Also within the fort is the **Festin du Gouverneur Restaurant** (★$$$$; daily, dinner; reservations required; 514/879.1141), which promises terrific family fun. For more than 30 years, this reenactment of a French colonial banquet has attracted guests to its cavernous dining hall. The 2-hour party is hosted by costumed servers who sing operetta-style, joke, and entertain the diners as they enjoy a wholesome repast of game hen served on pewter dinnerware. Children especially enjoy the audience participation and comic sketches.

Youngsters love to run or cycle through the spray of Ste-Hélène Island's **Interactive Fountain**. The level pavement is punctuated by grilles through which jets spurt in unpredictable directions. Actually, a computer-

controlled sequence marks the time, so the fountain also serves as a clock. Stone pavilions at the site house bicycle-rental and information booths and public washrooms. The grassy field nearby is perfect for flying kites, throwing Frisbees, and playing ball.

Also in this area is the **Ste-Hélène Island Pool Complex** (514/872.6093), an Italian Renaissance—style pavilion that provides changing rooms, showers, and a snack bar. Admission is charged. Looming behind the pool complex is **Buckminster Fuller's Geodesic Dome** (514/283.5000), an acrylic globe created for Expo '67. Recently converted to a Biosphere, the 12,203-square-foot building is now a state-of-the-art, multimedia, living museum highlighting the ecosystems of the **St. Lawrence River** and the **Great Lakes**. The Biosphere is open daily, 10AM-6PM, between the end of June and the beginning of September, and Tuesday through Sunday, 10AM-5PM, between the end of September and the end of June.

Ste-Hélène Island's **La Ronde Amusement Park** (admission; June-Sept: M-Th; Su, 11AM-midnight; F-Sa, 11AM-1AM; mid-May to June and Labor Day weekend: Sa-Su, 11AM-1AM; 514/872.6222), built for Expo '67 and since renovated for $20 million, provides old-time carnival fun on 35 rides, including the Hydroid, which simulates a transoceanic subway, and the Monster roller coaster. Also featured are a small circus and traditional midway, and a children's village for toddlers with pint-size boat rides and a gentle roller coaster. La Ronde hosts the **International Fireworks Competition** between mid-June and July, with displays set to music.

The beach at neighboring Notre-Dame Island (514/872.6093) was designed with families in mind. A curve of sand skirts the shore, picnic tables dot the grassy slopes, and a Laurentian-style chalet houses a restaurant, changing facilities, and sailboarding school. Sailboards, pedal boats, canoes, and kayaks can be rented here, and parking is convenient. The constructed lake, fed by the St. Lawrence, is continuously purified by a system based on aquatic plants and recirculation. The beach is open daily mid-June to Labor Day; admission is charged.

Also on Notre-Dame Island is the **Olympic Basin**, which freezes over in winter and becomes a superb skating rink (rental skates are available at the pavilion). On the nearby hill is a giant toboggan run, and across **Cosmos Bridge**, on Ste-Hélène Island, are cross-country and snowshoeing trails. Montreal's latest snow fad, "tubing" downhill on rainbow-hued inner tires (for rent at the pavilion), got its start on these slopes. Winter activities generally run from Christmas to early March.

Back in Old Montreal, Cirque du Soleil (514/522.2324), the big hit under the big top, provides top-notch entertainment for kids as well as adults. This circus is a one-ring, high-tech affair, with state-of-the-art lighting and special effects spotlighting jugglers, contortionists, high-wire artists, and trapezists clad in costumes inspired by medieval dress (no animals are used). The clowning relies more on

audience participation and sophisticated mime than on pratfalls. The *cirque* pitches its yellow-and-blue tent at the end of Jacques Cartier Pier during the warm-weather months. It's popular, so be sure to reserve tickets.

Science students will enjoy the **Planetarium** (1000 Rue St-Jacques W, between Rues Peel and de la Cathédrale; 514/872.4530), a gift to the city from Dow Breweries in 1966. Easily recognizable by the statue of Polish astronomer Copernicus outside, the modern domed building is within walking distance of the **Bonaventure** and **Marriott Château Champlain** hotels. The dome rises 65 feet, providing an expansive backdrop for celestial effects produced by the Zeiss projector and some 100 auxiliary units. Lecture-shows on the Milky Way, quarks, black holes, and so on last for 90 minutes and change periodically, the only exception being the annual December production of *Star of the Magi*. Evening presentations reveal the sky as it is that night. Children younger than 5 years old get in for free; admission is charged for all others. English shows run Tuesday through Sunday at 2:30PM and 7:30PM; the theater is closed between shows. A gift shop sells educational games, astronomy books, and souvenirs.

Kids can handle carnivorous plants, reptile eggs, coral, and other intriguing stuff in the "interactive discovery room" of the **Biodôme**, a natural-science center (4777 Avenue Pierre-de-Coubertin; 514/868.3000). After the kids have trekked through the four ecosystems upstairs—tropical jungle, Laurentian forest, marine life of the St. Lawrence River, and polar worlds—they may want to learn more about the living plants and animals they have just seen. The Biodôme's staff is happy to help visitors discover how flora and fauna adapt to water, dryness, darkness, and gravity and how they reproduce, protect themselves, and communicate. The center is open daily and charges admission. Youngsters needn't be warned, "Don't touch" at the special hands-on gallery for children at the **Montreal Museum of Fine Arts** (1380 Rue Sherbrooke W, between Rues Crescent and Bishop; 514/285.1600). Here, kids can explore color and design through artworks and shapes designed especially for that purpose at the gallery in the *Carrefour*. (The don't-touch rule, though, applies to the rest of the galleries.) The museum also hosts weekly family activities during major exhibitions. These programs vary from film screenings to workshops where budding young artists may reproduce works from the ongoing show, paint paper plates, or try their hand at origami. The museum is open Tuesday through Saturday and charges admission; toddlers younger than 2 years old get in for free.

THE BEST

Charles Ploem

Former Maître d'Hôtel (38 Years), Beaver Club, Queen Elizabeth Hotel

What I like most about Montreal are the two cultures—English and French—and that I can walk anywhere in town day or night and feel safe in a completely bilingual atmosphere.

A walk on **Rue Sherbrooke** between **Rues Peel** and **Guy** while visiting some art galleries (particularly **Dominion Gallery**) and shopping at **Holt Renfrew**. On a beautiful summer day, have lunch in the garden of the **Ritz-Carlton Kempinski** nearby on Sherbrooke.

If you're in town on the third Friday of January, try to get an invitation to the annual **Beaver Club Dinner** at the **Queen Elizabeth Hotel**. It's the greatest party of the year in Canada.

A stroll along the wonderful **Rue St-Denis** (between **Rues Sherbrooke** and **Maisonneuve**). See and feel the action on **Rues Crescent** and **Mountain** at 3AM.

The best smoked-meat sandwich is at **Schwartz's Deli** on **Boulevard St-Laurent**.

A visit to the second-largest **Botanical Garden** in the world and the **Biodôme** natural science museum.

A walk (or a jog) on our mountain, **Mont-Royal** (which is located in the middle of the city).

For Chinese food, **Le Piment Rouge** in the beautiful **Old Windsor Hotel** on **Dorchester Square**.

The best shiatsu massage is by Leo Legris at **Le Centre Sheraton Montreal**.

Montreal is the home base of **Cirque du Soleil**—a must when it is in town.

In summer take the subway to **Olympic Stadium** to see the **Expos** play in the most expensive ballpark in the world. And in winter take the same subway to the shrine of the **National Hockey League**, the **Forum**, to see the **Montreal Canadiens** play the **Boston Bruins** or the **L.A. Kings**.

White-water rafting on the **Lachine Rapids** (in summer, of course). What a ride!

---

a 56-bell carillon, and stations of the cross in a sculpture garden. ♦ Oratory: free; museum: donation appreciated. Oratory: daily, 7AM-5PM, Sept-May; daily, 7AM-10:30PM, June-Aug. Museum: daily, 10AM-5PM. 3800 Chemin Queen Mary (at Chemin de la Côte-des-Neiges). 733.8211

The Canadian parliament, now in Ottawa, was situated in what is today Old Montreal until 1849, when the building was burned to the ground by an angry mob—led by the city's fire chief. The law that enraged them had established compensation for those whose property had been damaged during a rebellion 12 years earlier. Some of the property belonged to the rebels, and Anglo Loyalists didn't want to pay taxes to aid them.

In 1876, George Stephen, a president of the Bank of Montreal and Canadian Pacific Rail (whose former home is now occupied by the Mount Stephen Club in downtown Montreal), turned down a budding inventor who was looking for financial backers for his projects. The young man was Alexander Graham Bell, inventor of the telephone.

In August 1940, Montreal Mayor Camillien Houde was arrested by the Royal Canadian Mounted Police for taking a public stand against the federal Conscription Act, which marked Canadian involvement in World War II. He spent 4 years in an internment camp.

2 NOTRE-DAME-DES-NEIGES CEMETERY

The long, parallel rows of sun-bleached markers in this enormous Catholic graveyard resemble the war cemeteries of Belgium and France. More than a million Montrealers are buried here, including Calixa Lavallée (1842-1891), the music teacher who composed Canada's national anthem. ♦ Northwestern perimeter of park

3 MONT-ROYAL CEMETERY

Established in 1854, this Protestant and primarily Anglo graveyard—the smaller of the two cemeteries that form the park's northern perimeter—actually predates the park by 20 years. Burials no longer take place in either yard, but visitors can explore on foot and by car. Although **Cimetière Mont-Royal** holds the graves of many early Canadian politicians, explorers, and entrepreneurs, the most famous headstone belongs to Anna Leonowens, the English governess to the king of Siam whose autobiography inspired the musical *The King and I*. ♦ Northern perimeter of park

4 MOUNTED POLICE STATION

Don't be surprised if children think the best thing about the park is the police officers who ride horseback. Kids are naturally drawn to the tall black steeds the officers use to patrol the woods and parking areas. The adjacent stables are open for family visits. ♦ Daily.

Near the park's west gate (at Chemin Remembrance)

5 LAC AUX CASTORS (BEAVER LAKE)

This tiny artificial lake is the park's social center. In summer, toy boats bob on the water, urban picnickers barbecue under the trees, and sunbathers stretch out on the nearby grassy slope. When winter sets in, the slope becomes a practice run for novice downhill skiers with the help of a small rope-tow. Year-round, the adjacent **Pavilion** has a snack bar and changing facilities with lockers and washrooms. ♦ Southwest corner of park (near Chemin Remembrance)

6 INTERNATIONAL SYMPOSIUM OF SCULPTURE

In 1964, 10 leading contemporary sculptors from other nations traveled to Montreal to take part in the first sculpture symposium in North America. Today, the pieces they created—abstract works of wood and other materials—form a landscape-harmonizing cluster on the grassy rise beside one of the park's well-trod bridle and jogging paths near the **Grand Chalet**. ♦ Southern section of park (near Beaver Lake)

7 SMITH HOUSE

From this 1858 stone structure (originally a private residence), cross-country ski enthusiasts can follow 7 miles of beginner, intermediate, and expert trails, distinguished with colored markers throughout the park grounds. The house also contains a small, free museum featuring displays of local wildlife. ♦ Daily. Southern section of park (near Voie Camillien-Houde)

8 MONTREAL CROSS

Beaver Lake may be the park's social center, but this is the spiritual one. The cross marks the legendary trek up the mountain by the city's founder, Paul de Chomedy, Sieur de Maisonneuve. In January 1643, Maisonneuve carried a rough-hewn oak cross to the summit to offer thanks for the community's having been spared from a Christmas Day flood. In the early 1920s, well after the original emblem of faith and hope had decayed, local children took up a collection to replace it, and on Christmas Eve in 1924, officials erected an 83-foot-tall cross of steel bedecked with colored lights. It's now a major landmark, visible throughout the city and some 60 miles beyond. At the foot of the steep stone steps nearby, a parking lot and observation area

provide an impressive cityscape view east, highlighted by the **Olympic Stadium**. ♦ Southeast corner of park (near Hôpital Royal Victoria)

9 GEORGES ETIENNE-CARTIER MONUMENT

One of Canada's founding fathers—a provincial prime minister who was the driving force behind the **Canadian-Pacific Railroad**—is honored with an elaborate statue that's either the zenith or nadir of monument art, depending on your taste. Aesthetics aside, children love to climb on the four bronze lions that guard the wily old politician. The natural amphitheater behind him makes a perfect place to relax on summer days and listen to the congas and drums played by the city's West African residents from Togo and the Ivory Coast. ♦ Eastern edge of park (near Ave du Parc)

10 WESTMOUNT HOUSES

The traditional "two solitudes" of Montreal (a phrase made famous by the Hugh MacLellan novel of the same name describing a cross-cultural romance) were the working-class French and the moneyed English. Here, overlooking Beaver Lake, you can catch a glimpse of how opulently the latter half lived (and begin to see why the French often despised their English bosses). The Art Deco mansions on streets like **Parkside** and **Trafalgar Place** are among Canada's most expensive residences. ♦ Southwest section of park (near Chemin de la Côte-des-Neiges)

11 GRAND CHALET

Built in 1931 and 1932 as a city meeting place for the then-astronomical cost of $200,000, this Swiss-style chalet in the south central area of the park remains a favorite venue for civic functions and exhibitions. The well-preserved features of the original décor include a massive fireplace and murals depicting Montreal's early history as a trading and shipping town. Nowadays the snack bar, washrooms, and public phones make this a popular rest stop for visitors. But the building's charming interior is eclipsed by the stunning panorama from its balustraded terrace. On clear days you can see well beyond the south shores of the St. Lawrence River to the communities that extend to the US border some 60 miles away. The nearby **Centre de la Montagne** is a nature interpretation and education center where visitors can pick up informative literature and a walker's map of the park. ♦ Daily. South central section of park.

ST-LAURENT/ ST-DENIS/PLATEAU MONT-ROYAL

Surrounded by a pair of parks and two streets of boutiques and cafés closed off to cars, Plateau Mont-Royal is best appreciated *à pied*, and the trendier the footwear, the better. This lively quarter is favored by students, academics, and other bohemian types, who frequent the multicultural restaurants, bookstores, and nightspots. Though technically bounded by **Rue Sherbrooke** and the **Canadian Pacific Railroad** tracks and by **Rue Frontenac** and **Avenue du Parc**, Plateau Mont-Royal's heart and soul belongs to the quadrant formed by **Parc Lafontaine**, **Boulevard St-Laurent**, Rue Sherbrooke, and **Avenue Mont-Royal**.

Though the Plateau wears a very French face, a full 40% of the residents were born outside of Canada. Walk a few blocks on Boulevard St-Laurent and you'll travel the globe, from Brazilian samba halls and Polish sausage stands to sushi bars and souvlaki parlors. Commonly called "The Main" by natives, Boulevard St-Laurent is Montreal's spine, demarcating the east (*est*) side addresses from the west (*ouest*).

On weekends, Parc Lafontaine is filled with trendy locals who bundle into funky retro furs in winter, kids and toboggans in tow, and whiz around on bicycles and in-line skates or gather at **Théâtre de la Verdure** to take in a free concert under the stars in summer.

The pace in nearby **Parc Jeanne-Mance** is much more frenetic. Once a military parade ground known as **Fletcher Field**, today the park is an open stage for African drummers, table players, and castanet clackers who crowd around the **Sir George-Etienne Cartier Monument** and jam. The scene is a dead ringer for Haight-Ashbury in the 1960s, with self-styled entrepreneurs hawking handmade jewelry and clothing.

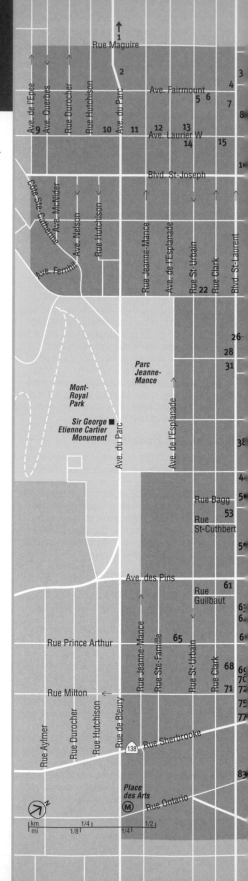

Rue St-Gregoire

Rue Maguire

Rue Boucher

Rue Masson

Parc
Sir Wilfrid-
Laurier

Rue St-Denis

Ave. Laurier E

Ⓜ Laurier

Rue Gilford →

Rue Gilford

Ave. Villeneuve

17
18
19 20

Rue de Bienville

Ave. Christophe-Colomb

Ave. Brebeuf

Rue de Lanaudière

Rue Marquette

Ave. Papineau

23   21
Ave. Mont-Royal   Ⓜ 24
Mont-
Royal

25

27
29 30

Rue Marie-Anne

Rue de Bullion

Ave. Hôtel de Ville

32 33
34

Rue Rachel

Ave. Bureau

35 36
39 40

37   Rue Rachel E

Ave.
Coloniale

41 42   43
Rue Duluth E

Jardin des
Merveilles

45   46

47
49
48

Parc
Lafontaine

Rue Gauthier ←

Rue
Napoleon

51 52
54 55
56

Rue Rivard

Rue Berri

Rue St-Hubert

Rue St-Christophe

Rue St-André

Rue Mentana

Ave. Parc La Fontaine

Ave. Emile-Duploye

Rue Roy

57 58
60

Ave. Laval

Ave. Henri-Julien

Rue Drolet

62

Ave. Calixa-Lavallée

Carré
St-Louis

67
Rue Cherrier

73 74
76
78

Rue de
Rigaud

Ⓜ Sherbrooke

335

79
80

81

82
84

Rue
Emery

Rue Sanguinet

Rue St-Denis

Ave. Savoie

85 86
87
Berri-
UOAM

Rue Beaudry

Rue Panet

Rue La Fontaine

Rue Robin

Rue Logan

Rue Champlain

Parc

Ⓜ St-Laurent
Blvd. de Maisonneuve

Ⓜ

88 89

Ⓜ Beaudry

Ⓜ Papineau

Rue St-Denis between Boulevard de Maisonneuve and Rue Sherbrooke marks Montreal's Latin Quarter. In true Quebecois tradition, this street's history encompasses both the bourgeoisie and the proletariat. Originally the private property of Louis-Joseph Papineau and Denis-Benjamin Viger, two leaders of the 1837 patriot rebellion, this street earned its identity early as the main drag of the posh **Faubourg St-Laurent** district, one of the city's first suburbs. In the 1920s, it was regarded as the intellectual and cultural capital of Canada, and in the late 1960s and early 1970s, the street's bars and bistros harbored nationalist and separatist activists. Now it's a focal point for Quebecois arts, crafts, and innovative clothing shops, along with nightclubs, bistros, bookstores, and galleries, which still attract the town's intelligentsia. From Rue Sherbrooke north, the vibe is a bit more sophisticated but still, in true Montreal style, very easygoing.

Rue Duluth, the four-block pedestrian promenade that links Parc Lafontaine to the Mountain (as **Mont-Royal** is popularly known), and **Rue Prince Arthur,** another urban walkway, are BYOW (bring your own wine) zones. These streets are lined with dozens of intimate ethnic eateries—Vietnamese, Greek, Italian, and more—that don't offer wine lists but instead invite diners to bring a bottle from home or buy one from a store nearby.

Situated beside the flowerbeds of **Carré St-Louis,** Rue Prince Arthur is named in honor of Queen Victoria's third son, who served as governor general of Canada between 1911 and 1916. Today, the street is better known for revelry than royalty, and scepters have been replaced by shish kebabs. Street performers and musicians entertain a captive audience of diners at the sidewalk tables.

Dollars are easy to drop on Avenue Mont-Royal, the Plateau's main shopping strip, and definitely worth a few hours of leisurely exploration. One of its culinary and cultural landmarks is **La Binerie Mont-Royal** (The Beanery), which is described in telling detail in Yves Beauchemin's novel of Montreal street life, *Le Matou* (*The Alleycat*).

1 LE PETIT MILOS

★★$$ This gourmet market and casual eatery is like a sunnier, if considerably smaller, edition of its big brother down the street, the seafood emporium **Milos.** Here you can buy savory olive oils, Greek specialties, and fresh pre-prepared dishes to go, or order something from the menu (which changes daily) for dining on the premises. With its spacious windows, tables set amidst the gourmet offerings, and pleasant atmosphere, this place rivals Chez l'Epicier, in Old Montreal, for all-around appeal. ♦ Greek ♦ Daily, lunch and dinner. 5551 Ave du Parc. 274.9991

2 MILOS

★★★$$$$ Year in and year out this glamorous Greek restaurant stays hot, not only because it is favored by international pop stars and actors when they swing through Montreal but on account of the kitchen, which knows how to keep them pleased. It does so by focusing on essentially one thing: the freshest of fresh grilled fish. From French bass to Dover sole, the list is long and varied. Other entrées and accompaniments are served, including a fabulous taramasalata, but seafood is what keeps this upscale seaside-style taverna going strong. Descend the staircase under a faux Mykonos windmill to arrive at the sleek bathrooms, which apparently have won design awards. Service here, unsurprisingly, is smooth and professional. ♦ Greek ♦ Daily lunch and dinner. Reservations recommended. 5357 Ave du Parc (between Aves Fairmount and St-Viateur). 272.3522

3 ROYAL CARI

★★$$ You can't miss the two large carved-wood elephants, covered with brightly painted fabric, guarding the entrance. This colorful little restaurant lays claim to the spiciest Indian cooking in town. Start with *reshmi* (beef marinated in yogurt and mint chutney) or the lamb shish kebab. If the huge aquarium stirs a desire for seafood, try shrimp *bhoona* sautéed with green peppers and onion in a spicy curry sauce for the main course. *Kulfi* (mango ice cream) is a delicious finale. ♦ Indian ♦ M-Sa, lunch and dinner; Su, dinner. Reservations recommended. 5215 Blvd St-Laurent (between Ave Fairmount and Rue Maguire). 278.8211 ♿

4 KILO

$ Famous for its rich desserts and pastries, this busy bistro also has good sandwiches and hearty soups. ◆ Bistro ◆ M-Th, breakfast, lunch, and dinner; F-Su, lunch and dinner. 5206 Blvd St-Laurent (between Ave Fairmount and Rue Maguire). 277.5039 ♿

5 AU PAPIER JAPONAIS

At this charming boutique somewhat off the beaten path, you can browse among 500 kinds of papers from Japan and other countries. Stationery, journal books, photo albums, and origami are among the selections to be found. ◆ M-W, 10 AM-6PM; Th, 10AM-9PM; F-Sa, 10AM-6PM. 24 Rue Fairmount W (between Rues Clark and St-Urbain). 276.6863

Boulangerie   Bakery

L'authentique
The Original

6 FAIRMOUNT BAGEL

$ This bagel shop sells perhaps the best bagels in Montreal. Those used to New York bagels will easily adapt to the smaller size and larger holes of their northern cousins once they take a taste: The secret is in the dough, which counts eggs among its ingredients and is dipped in honey water before being baked in a wood-burning oven. Fairmount bakes 15 varieties of bagels, from classic sesame to aromatic everything and lots in between. ◆ Open 24 hours. 74 Rue Fairmount W (between Rues Clark and St-Urbain). 272.0667

7 ATELIER 68

A variety of Canadian artists are represented at this gallery in posters, prints, and art books. ◆ M-F, 10AM-9PM; Sa, 9AM-5PM; Su, noon-5PM. 5190 Blvd St-Laurent (between Aves Laurier W and Fairmount). 276.2872

8 CAFÉ CINÉ-LUMIÈRE

★★$$ Fans of films from the 1930s and 1940s delight in the nightly showings of screen gems at this café (patrons get free use of infrared headphones). Watch W.C. Fields while supping on marinated salmon, pot-au-feu, or steak tartare complemented by imported beers and wines. ◆ French ◆ M-F, lunch and dinner; Sa-Su, brunch and dinner. 5163 Blvd St-Laurent (between Aves Laurier E and Fairmount). 495.1796

9 LEMÉAC

★★$$$ Thanks to its airy interior and an irresistible menu, this contemporary bistro in the chic Outremont district has become one of Montreal's most popular restaurants, and as such is a veritable magnet for the local beau monde. The large, high-ceilinged room is spare yet improbably intimate, and in summer a bee or two may buzz in from the awning-covered terrace, piercing any veneer of formality. Starters can be a bit uneven, but entrées are where the kitchen truly shines: the short ribs are delicious, as are the roast Icelandic cod with fennel purée and fish and chips. The latter comes with french fries that are positively scrumptious; happily, they can be ordered separately. The wine list is solid and service friendly, if a bit too leisurely. ◆ French ◆ M-Sa, lunch and dinner; Su, brunch and dinner. Reservations recommended. 1045 Ave Laurier W (at Ave de l'Epee). 270.0999

10 RÔTISSERIE LAURIER

★$$ Established in 1936, this family-run restaurant's mocha dessert earns praise from far and wide, and the lemon tart was a favorite of Canadian Prime Minister Pierre Trudeau. The casual cuisine—quiches, poached salmon, and hearty soups—is straight out of a Quebecois home kitchen. ◆ Quebecois ◆ Daily, lunch and dinner. 381 Ave Laurier W (between Ave du Parc and Rue Hutchison). 273.3671 ♿

11 LES PETITS PLAISIRS D'ANDREA

This is a gourmet shop low on frills and high on flavors. Stop in to stock up on Quebec-made preserves, imported fine foods, or (perhaps best of all) Andrea's amazing artisanal ice creams, varieties of which include double pear, mango and Szechuan pepper, fresh thyme with strawberry, and orange chocolate. ◆ 273 Ave Laurier W (between Rue Jeanne-Mance and Ave du Parc). 495.3999

12 ORCHIDÉE SAUVAGE CARMEN BOUTIQUE

The fashion-forward stance of Quebecois designers Carmen Belanger, Beverly Salsky, and Marc Levrault make this boutique avant-garde central for cotton, linen, silk, and leather womenswear. ◆ M-W, 11AM-6PM; Th-F, 11AM-8PM; Sa-Su. 207 Ave Laurier W (between Ave de l'Esplanade and Rue Jeanne-Mance). 271.5274

13 ESCALE À SAIGON

★★$$ Devotees of Vietnamese cuisine will find a few surprises here—unusual dishes like grilled pork liver, partridge eggs, prawn rolls, and grilled fillet of monkfish in dill and peanut sauce—as well as tamer entrées based on chicken and beef. ◆ Vietnamese ◆ M-F, lunch and dinner; Sa-Su, dinner. 107 Ave Laurier W (between Rue St-Urbain and Ave de l'Esplanade). 272.3456 ㅎ

14 LE CLUB DES PINS

★★$$ Satisfying and flavorful cuisine from the south of France—specifically Gascony and Provence—gets top billing at this restaurant, featuring such dishes as garlic duck with fresh basil and fish cooked with a Mediterranean flair. ◆ French ◆ Tu-F, lunch and dinner; Sa, dinner. 156 Ave Laurier W (between Rue St-Urbain and Ave de l'Esplanade). 272.9484 ㅎ

15 RESTAURANT CHAO PHRAYA

★★$$ This is considered to be one of the best Thai restaurants in Montreal. Chicken in pungent peanut sauce with fried spinach (*phra ram gai*), duck salad with mint (*larb peb*), and seafood tossed in curry, basil, and coconut milk are a few of the enticing dishes served here. A tumbler of sweet Thai iced tea is guaranteed to take the heat off the spicy fare. ◆ Thai ◆ M-W, Sa, Su, dinner; Th-F, lunch and dinner. 50 Ave Laurier W (at Rue Clark). 272.5339. Also at 4088 Rue St-Denis (at Ave Mont-Royal). 843.4194

16 PARISH ST-ENFANT-JESUS

Take a break from hip Boulevard St-Laurent to visit this 1857 Baroque church, resplendent with trumpeting cherubim and seraphim. The frescoes were done between 1917 and 1919 by celebrated Quebec painter Ozias Leduc. ◆ M-Th, 1PM-4:30PM; other times by appointment. 5039 Rue St-Dominique (between Blvd St-Joseph and Ave Laurier E). 271.0943

17 LE NAUTILUS

Alain Vadon and his entomologist wife Sylvie (who's also a spider specialist) collect rare specimens on their travels to Africa, Malaysia, and Mexico. The mounted butterflies are fascinating, but perhaps you'd prefer a preserved piranha, teeth and all, or a giant staghorn beetle. Rounding out the selection are fossils, petrified wood, and coral samples. ◆ M-W, 11AM-6PM; Th-F, 11AM-9PM; Sa, 10AM-5PM. 4840 Rue St-Denis (between Rue Gilford and Ave Villeneuve). 849.7409

18 PIZZAIOLE

$$ This old-fashioned diner (circa 1952) was trucked to Montreal from a Boston scrapyard and restored. Now it's a gleaming stainless-steel eatery. Formerly the **Galaxie Diner**, it has been transformed yet again, this time into an upscale pizzeria where your pie can come with anything from artichokes and Italian sausage to goat cheese and onion. ◆ Italian ◆ Daily, lunch and dinner. 4801 Rue St-Denis (at Rue Gilford). 499.9711 ㅎ

19 THÉÂTRE RIDEAU VERT

The theater's green curtain lifted for the first time on 17 February 1949. Beginning with the premiere of Michel Tremblay's *Les Belles-Soeurs* in 1968, it's been a forum for contemporary Quebecois playwrights. ◆ 4664 Rue St-Denis (between Rues de Bienville and Gilford). 844.1793

20 LE PERSIL FOU

★★$$ French fare is prepared with fresh pasta and innovatively spiced veggies. Try the pasta with salmon, ginger, citronelle, and fleur de sel, a delicately textured salt from France. ◆ French ◆ Tu-Sa, dinner. 4669 Rue St-Denis (at Rue de Bienville). 284.3130

21 LE DIABLE VERT

Despite its name, the décor is all red at this large, self-described "groovy bar." ◆ Su-Tu, 8PM-3AM; W-Sa, 4PM-3AM. 4557 Rue St-Denis (between Ave Mont-Royal and Rue de Bienville). 849.5888

22 BEAUTY'S

★$ Hymnie and Freda Sckolnick opened this popular brunch spot back in 1942. Nearly 60 years later, it's still a Plateau hot spot. After a hard night of clubbing, do as other neighborhood residents do and plop yourself on one of the comfy blue banquettes in this bright (but circa 1942) diner and refuel with a hearty fried breakfast of delicious omelettes, pancakes, or Beauty's Special: smoked salmon on a bagel with cream cheese, tomato, and onion. Wash it down with a fresh-fruit smoothie. Though it gets busy here, particularly in the morning, Hymnie and son Larry oversee service that's swift and courteous. ◆ Daily, breakfast and lunch. 93 Ave Mont-Royal (at Rue St-Urbain). 849.8883

23 LA BINERIE MONT-ROYAL

★$ This family-owned enterprise serves 27 tons of *fèves au lard* (baked beans and bacon) a year, along with such old favorites as *ragout de pattes et de boulottes* (meatball and pig's feet stew) and *lard salé* froid (salted pork boiled in pea soup). Truck drivers and politicians, pensioners and *artistes*, secretaries and CEOs crowd the counter and booths, where containers of ketchup and maple syrup reign supreme. ◆ Quebecois ◆ M-F, breakfast, lunch, and dinner; Sa, breakfast and lunch. 367 Ave Mont-Royal (between Rues St-Denis and Drolet). 285.9078

24 LES FOLIES

★★$ As much a café as it is a restaurant, this relaxed Plateau hot spot is perhaps more distinctive for its retro-futurist décor of white plastic seats and flat screens beaming images of nature than its food. The latter is Californian, with salads, vegetarian wraps, pastas, and quesadillas figuring prominently on the menu. But locals are as likely to while away an afternoon over a latté—especially when the terrace is open—here as they are to chow down at lunchtime or late at night. Live DJs from 9PM every night add to the buzz. ♦ Californian ♦ Daily, lunch and dinner. 701 Ave Mont-Royal E (at Rue St-Hubert). 528.4343

25 DUBUC MODE DE VIE

If you're looking for new duds that are as far away from the Gap as possible design-wise yet not too over-the-top to wear to a fine restaurant, this could be a good place to start. Philippe Dubuc's innovative fashion designs for men and women are popular with many actors, singers, and members of Montreal's media crowd. Although styles vary season to season, of course, look for such head-turning touches as shirts that button diagonally and creative use of both natural and synthetic fabrics. ♦ M-W, 10AM-6PM; Th-F, 10AM-9PM; Sa, 10AM-5PM. 4451 Rue St-Denis (between Rue Marie-Anne and Ave Mont-Royal). 282.1465

26 LIVING

This trendy if somewhat grungy bar catering to Plateau night owls is located in a high-ceilinged onetime bank building. ♦ Daily. Call for hours. 4521 Rue St-Dominique (between Rue Marie-Anne and Ave Mont-Royal). 286.9986

27 LE VALET D'COEUR

With flamenco music in the background, peruse the eclectic selection of imported tarot and playing cards, fake tattoos, adventure comic books, fantastic figurines of griffins and dragons, Florentine masks, and hand-carved wooden bird whistles. ♦ M-W, 11:30AM-6PM; Th-F, 11:30AM-9PM; Sa, 10AM-5PM; Su, noon-5PM. 4408 Rue St-Denis (between Rue Marie-Anne and Ave Mont-Royal). 499.9970

27 CONFISERIE LOUISE DÉCARIE

In this eclectic and friendly shop you'll find a shocking-pink bonbon counter filled with equally eye-catching sweets from France, England, Italy, Switzerland, and Belgium. ♦ M-W, 11AM-6PM; Th-F, 11AM-9PM; Sa, 11AM-5PM. 4424 Rue St-Denis (between Rue Marie-Anne and Ave Mont-Royal). 499.3445

28 CLUB BALATTOU

The Tuesday- and Wednesday-night concerts of African, Cuban, Jamaican, and South American rhythms make this the hippest place in town for tropical music. The club devotes the rest of the week strictly to dancing. ♦ Cover. Tu-Su, 9PM-3AM. 4372 Blvd St-Laurent (between Rue Marie-Anne and Ave Mont-Royal). 845.5447

29 CHAMPIGNY

Even if you're not fluent in French, you'll want to browse through the largest French bookstore in North America. There is room on room of tomes that are either neatly shelved or casually stacked on antique oak tables in artful still lifes (for instance, cookbooks are displayed amid baskets of bread and grains). There's also a fine selection of European magazines. ♦ Daily, 9AM-midnight. 4380 Rue St-Denis (between Rue Marie-Anne and Ave Mont-Royal). 844.2587

30 PIERRES D'AILLEURS

Rock hounds love this mineral shop for its exhaustive stock of "stones from elsewhere." Chunks of delicate rose quartz and celestite from Madagascar make stellar paperweights. ♦ M-W, 11AM-6PM; Th-F, 11AM-9PM; Sa-Su, 11AM-5PM. 4377 Rue St-Denis (between Rue Marie-Anne and Ave Mont-Royal). 849.9311

31 BAGEL ETC.

★★$$ A mélange of marble, mirrors, pressed tin, and glass bricks surrounds diners studying the gargantuan menu, which offers everything from champagne and caviar to half-pound burgers and salads. The main event is certainly brunch, with eggs Benedict, Romanoff, and Florentine; blintzes; and, of course, bagels. ♦ Eclectic ♦ M-F, lunch and dinner; Sa-Su, brunch and dinner. Reservations recommended. 4320 Blvd St-Laurent (between Rues Vallières and Marie-Anne). 845.9462 ♿

32 MADRAS

Unusual new and retro clothing and accessories, not necessarily from Madras, are the forte of this spunky shop, which is in no short supply of attitude. ♦ M-W, 10AM-6PM; Th-F, 10AM-9PM; Sa, 10AM-5PM. 4304 Rue St-Denis (between Rues Rachel E and Marie-Anne). 286.0138

33 FONDUEMENTALE

★★$$ Set in a lovely 19th-century Victorian brick building, this Swiss restaurant specializes in fondue. Varieties include Swiss cheese, pesto, and beef, shrimp, and lamb. ♦ Swiss ♦ Daily, dinner. 4325 Rue St-Denis (between Rues Rachel E and Marie-Anne). 499.1446

THE BEST

Pierre Bourque

Mayor of Montreal and Former Director of the Botanical Garden

Everyone should take the time to discover the eastern part of Montreal, near the **Olympic Stadium**. Taking a walk in the **Montreal Botanical Garden** is like getting back to nature; you can feel a profound calmness inside the largest **Chinese Garden** in North America, enjoy the serenity of the **Japanese Garden**, or catch a whiff of the 10,000 scented roses in the

Rose Garden. Before crossing the street to the **Biodôme**, visit the **Insectarium**, where you'll discover a large collection of insects. The **Biodôme** will fascinate those concerned about the environment. Get in touch with the nature of the polar world, the tropical rain forest, the Laurentian forest, and the St. Lawrence marine ecosystem.

Also a must: a walk in Old Montreal to get in touch with the history of the city or a chance to discover the magnificent view at the top of **Mont-Royal Park**. Or simply take the time to stroll down **Rue St-Denis** and through the Latin Quarter just to get a feel for Montreal.

34 ZONE

Fragrant lemongrass potpourri scents the air of this spacious store, which offers cutting-edge European designs for the home. Sleek halogen lamps, wrought-iron plant stands, kitchen gadgets, and nifty picture frames abound. There's a good selection of high-tech desk accessories that make for great gifts or ways to perk up your home office ♦ M-Tu, 10AM-6PM; W-F, 10AM-9PM; Sa, 10AM-5:30PM; Su, 11AM-5PM. 4246 Rue St-Denis (between Rues Rachel E and Marie-Anne). 845.3530

35 ESSENCE DU PAPIER

For those weary of voice mail and faxes, this shop is an uplifting anachronism. The handmade stationery, exotic wooden pens, imported inks, rubber stamps, and sealing wax will elevate even making a grocery list to an art form. ♦ M-W, Sa; Th-F, 10AM-9PM; Su, noon-5PM. 4160 Rue St-Denis (between Rues Duluth E and Rachel E). 288.9691

35 ULYSSES

This bookshop stocks travel literature, guidebooks (half English, half French), and maps of destinations from Atlanta to Zimbabwe. The selection of guidebooks to and books about Quebec is particularly impressive. ♦ M-W, 10AM-6PM; Th-F, 10AM-9PM; Sa, 10AM-5PM; Su, noon-5PM. 4176 Rue St-Denis (between Rues Duluth E and Rachel E). 843.9447

36 CONTINENTAL

★★$$ The menu is as creative as the clientele of artists, actors, dancers, and musicians who gather under this bistro's Art Deco lamps. The adventurous can try the horse meat tartare (very popular in France); the timid opt for seviche, duck, rabbit, or salmon. This eatery is especially popular on weekends. ♦ Continental ♦ Daily, dinner. 4169 Rue St-Denis (at Rue Rachel E). 845.6842 ら

37 L'AUBERGE DE LA FONTAINE

$$ This is the insider's alternative to the huge, impersonal hotels of downtown. Its 21 guest rooms are decorated in tranquil pastel tones, and many of them face out onto **Park Lafontaine**. Breakfast is included in the room rates, the atmosphere is convivial, and there's a communal kitchen accessible to all. ♦ 1301 Rue Rachel E (at Rue de Lanaudière). 597.0166, 800/597.0597

38 OASIS OXYGÈNE

Need to de-stress after a long flight or grueling day of shopping? Or do you simply want to relax in a peaceful setting that's neither a tea salon nor a bar? Then energizing yourself with a 20-minute session of inhaling aromatized oxygenated air may be just the thing. That's the central experience at this stylish, friendly "oxy bar," the entrance of which is marked by long plastic reeds that curve up to the ceiling. Have a bottle of Fiji spring water at the bar before heading to one of the oxygen stations, where a staff member will show you how it's done (nasal tubes are involved, but don't worry, it's clean and it's fun). There are massage services, too. ♦ 4059 Blvd St-Laurent (between Rues Duluth E and Rachel). 284.1196

39 AU FESTIN DE BABETTE

Treat yourself to a bite of Belgian chocolate or a liqueur-filled bonbon (try the Cointreau or crème de menthe) at this sweets shop. ♦ M-W, Su; Th-F, 11AM-9PM; Sa, noon-midnight. 4118 Rue St-Denis (between Rues Duluth E and Rachel E). 849.0214

40 KALIYANA

This bright, airy shop for women features breezy, artistic designs that trend toward the colorful and free-flowing. There's also a small but interesting selection of shoes to pair with the outfits. ♦ M-W, Sa; Th-F, 10AM-9PM; Su, noon-5PM. 4107 Rue St-Denis (between Rues Duluth E and Rachel E). 843.0633

41 CARTON

Functional artworks by well-known Montreal artists, including Michel Harvey's ceramics, lamps, and clocks fashioned out of paper, are showcased at this shop. ♦ M-W, Sa; Th-F,

10:30AM-9PM; Su, 12:30-5PM in summer only. 4068 Rue St-Denis (between Rues Duluth E and Rachel E). 844.9663

42 SOCIÉTÉ DES ALCOOLS DU QUÉBEC

Pick your potables at this government liquor store before dining at any of the bring-your-own-wine restaurants on Rue Duluth. There's always a wide selection of vintages, and the prices are agreeable. ♦ M-W, Sa; Th-F, 9:30AM-7PM; Su, 10AM-7PM. ♦ 4053 Rue St-Denis (between Rues Duluth E and Rachel E). 873.7027

43 LE JARDIN DE PANOS

★$ Wild with hibiscus and geraniums, the beautiful terrace of this Greek restaurant is a perfect setting for the succulent shish kebab platters. ♦ Greek ♦ Daily, lunch and dinner. 521 Rue Duluth E (between Rues St-Hubert and Berri). 521.4206 &

44 SEHO PERLES D'AFRIQUE

You hear this small store of African goods before you see it. Festive world-beat rhythms blare from the outdoor speakers, luring you into the shop. The smell of incense provides an even more subtle invite. Teak and bone carvings and traditional African clothing and jewelry are for sale. ♦ M-W, Sa, 10AM-5PM; Th-F, 10AM-6PM. 4007 Blvd St-Laurent (at Rue Duluth E). 849.6373

45 TASCA

$$ Fresh fish and seafood figure prominently in the robust Portuguese fare served here. ♦ Portuguese ♦ Daily, lunch and dinner. 172 Rue Duluth E (between Ave Hôtel de Ville and Rue de Bullion). 987.1530 &

46 LA PIERRE DE LUNE

Prismatic glass panels of peacocks, angels, flowers, and more are exquisite examples of the glassmaker's art, sure to add an elegant touch to the home. ♦ M-W, 9AM-6PM; Th-F, 9AM-9PM; Sa, noon-6PM. 230 Rue Duluth E (between Aves Laval and Hôtel de Ville). 845.3429

47 AU BISTRO GOURMET 2

★★$$$ Like its counterpart in downtown, this friendly bistro serves delicious French bistro fare that's contemporary and reliably delicious. It is the larger of the two restaurants and boasts a delightful terrace that opens up on Rue St-Denis. Try any of the soups or salads, meat dishes such as roast lamb, or seafood dishes such as the Mediterranean Fish Duo. ♦ French ♦ Daily, lunch and dinner. 4007 Rue St-Denis (between Rues Roy and Duluth E). 844.0555

48 AU PIED DE COCHON

★★★$$$ Diners fill this 1930s-style French bistro for many reasons, but losing weight is probably never one of them. Chef Martin Picard rustles up the likes of gourmet *poutine*, venison tartare, and confit de canard for an eager crowd of hip thirty- and fortysomething Plateau denizens. Despite the preponderance of meat on the menu, there are some seafood offerings, too. Reservations recommended. ♦ French/Canadian ♦ Dinner, Tu-Su. 536 Rue Duluth E (at Rue Berri). 281.1114

49 BRÛLERIE ST-DENIS

$ This little Parisian-style café, perfumed to the rafters, intoxicates with the scent of coffee beans being roasted and ground. Order a cup of frothy mocha and the *Bonne Gueule* sandwich—stuffed with baked asparagus, artichokes, bleu cheese, and tomato. Finish with a crisp apple tart. ♦ Café ♦ Daily, lunch and dinner. 3967 Rue St-Denis (between Rues Roy and Duluth E). 286.9158 &

49 GIRAFFE

The owners of this shop travel to Africa twice a year to purchase traditional and contemporary art, crafts, and musical instruments from a dozen countries. Among the prizes you'll find are gorgeous hand-dyed fabrics, brass jewelry, and ceremonial masks. ♦ M-W, 10AM-6PM; Th-F, 10AM-9PM; Sa, 10AM-5PM; Su, noon-5PM. 3997 Rue St-Denis (between Rues Roy and Duluth E). 499.8436

50 SCHWARTZ'S DELI

$ Smoked meats are this beloved if somewhat overrated Montreal institution's claim to fame. It takes a committed carnivore to brave the raw lighting, crammed tables, and minimal service for the sake of a sandwich. Vegetarians take note: Sour pickles and coleslaw are about your only viable options here. ♦ Deli ♦ Daily, lunch and dinner. 3895 Blvd St-Laurent (between Rues St-Cuthbert and Bagg). 842.4813 &

51 ARTHUR QUENTIN

Serious cooks search these shelves for just the right copper caldron and are rarely disappointed. Also purveying European home accessories, this trend-setting shop has influenced the aesthetic evolution of Rue St-Denis. ♦ M-W, Sa; Th-F, 10AM-9PM. 3960 Rue St-Denis (between Rues Roy and Duluth E). 843.7513

51 CHAPOFOLIE

Style-conscious Quebecers shop here for fashion accessories and jewelry by local talents Barry Gaudreault, Mireille Racine,

---

Restaurants/Clubs: Red | Hotels: Purple | Shops: Orange | Outdoors/Parks: Green | Sights/Culture: Blue

Clarine Cormier, Annie Chouinard, Nathalie Levasseur, and Galurin. ♦ M, noon-6PM; Tu, W, 11AM-6PM; Th-F, 11AM-9PM; Sa, 10AM-5PM; Su, noon-5PM. 3944 Rue St-Denis (between Rues Roy and Duluth E). 982.0036

52 L'EXPRESS

★★$$ Cellular telephones and a yuppie clientele are much in evidence at this very French, slightly snobbish bistro with lacquered walls, tile floors, and a chic stainless steel bar. But the food is decidedly down-to-earth—crusty baguettes, octopus-and-lentil salad, and flavorful *pot au feu* (boiled beef and vegetables). It's a good place to chat long into the night. ♦ French ♦ Daily, breakfast, lunch, and dinner. Reservations recommended. 3927 Rue St-Denis (between Rues Roy and Duluth E). 845.5333 ⑁

53 S.W. WELCH BOOKSELLER

Mostly secondhand and rare English titles fill this cozy, old-fashioned bookshop. Flop on the comfy sofa and read at leisure. ♦ M-W, 11AM-10PM; Th-Sa, 11AM-midnight; Su, 11AM-10PM. 3878 Blvd St-Laurent (between Rues St-Cuthbert and Bagg). 848.9358

54 TOQUÉ!

★★★★$$$$ Chef Normand Laprise is one of the pioneers of *la cuisine du marché*, or cooking based on the freshest ingredients the market has to offer. At his signature restaurant—which has some of the most sought-after tables in Montreal—he marries organic, often Quebec-grown ingredients with a colorful but controlled culinary imagination. The result is such first courses as roasted Îles-de-la-Madeleine half-lobster with wilted sea spinach, daylily bud and bacon vinaigrette with fresh daylily shoots, and entrées the likes of Mr. Leroux's "Barbarie" duck magret roasted with licorice, celeriac, and duck confit brandade on fried bread with crunchy turnip and spring corn purée. For those who wish to eliminate menu guesswork, Laprise offers a five-course set menu. Desserts here are not to be missed: Try the caramelized chocolate brioche with creamy Manjari chocolate, clove ice milk, and a port reduction or the poached rhubarb or the rosemary-fried pound cake accompanied by vanilla-scented mascarpone, raspberry sauce, and strawberry sorbet. The restaurant also boasts a bright, eclectic décor and friendly waitstaff whose members seem to take a real pleasure in explaining the intricacies of the menu. At press time, Toqué! was due to move ro Place Jean-Paul Riopelle in Old Montreal, so definitely call to confirm its current location. ♦ Eclectic ♦ Daily, dinner. Reservations required. 3842 Rue St-Denis (between Rues Roy and Duluth E). 499.2084

55 BOULANGERIE AU PAIN DORE

Truly committed bread-lovers are known to call ahead to reserve their morning baguette at this bakery. Try the "Polish" and the "36 hours" varieties and see if you can detect the difference in the crusts. The delicious French pastries are worth the calories. ♦ M-W, Sa-Su; Th-F, 8:30AM-7:30PM. 3895 Rue St-Denis (between Rues Roy and Duluth E). 849.1704

55 BLEU NUIT

This elegant boutique stocks European bed and table linens made from natural fabrics (French damasks, cashmere throws, Egyptian cottons), as well as bath accessories ranging from creams to tortoiseshell combs. ♦ M-W, Sa; Th-F, 10AM-9PM. 3913 Rue St-Denis (between Rues Roy and Duluth E). 843.5702

56 DEBEDE

Fans of French comic books spend hours here, paging through thousands of new, secondhand, and collector's editions of *Asterix, Tintin, Spirou*, et al. ♦ M-W, 11AM-6PM; Th-F, 11AM-9PM; Sa, 10AM-5:30PM; Su, noon-6PM. 3882 Rue St-Denis (between Rues Roy and Duluth E). 499.8477

57 REVENGE

A vibrant wall mural by Quebec painter Claude Théberge (known for his surreal scenes of lovers in tall hats and with umbrellas) is the backdrop for couturier fashions for women and men. The shop features such local designers as Angela Buccaro and Marie-St-Pierre. ♦ M-W, Sa; Th-F, 11AM-9PM; Su, 1PM-5PM. 3852 Rue St-Denis (between Rues Roy and Duluth E). 843.4379

58 INÈS

This attractive second-floor shop sells an interesting selection of original women's ready-to-wear that seems inspired by the airy styles of the Mediterranean as well as reasonably priced jewelry from area designers. ♦ M-F, 10AM-6PM; Sa, 10AM-5PM. 3883 Rue St-Denis (between Rues Roy and Duluth E). 843.3004

59 LA VIEILLE EUROPE

The Quebecois equivalent to New York City's Zabar's, this gourmet grocery has one of the best cheese departments and coffee selections in town. The array of deli foods is reasonably priced. ♦ M-W, 7:30AM-6PM; Th-F, 7:30AM-9PM; Sa, 7:30AM-5PM; Su. 3855 Blvd St-Laurent (between Rues Roy and Napoleon). 842.5773

60 PSAROTAVERNA DU SYMPOSIUM

★★$$ If you missed your flight to Athens, here's the next best thing. Graze your way through a variety of traditional Greek appetizers before your waiter brings out the fresh fishes of the day on a huge platter: it's up to you to decide which one you would like to see on your plate. The whole fish is then grilled and served simply with fresh lemon–olive oil sauce on the side (one fish is more than enough for two persons). Enjoy it with a glass of *retsina* or Kouros Patras, a light and inexpensive white wine from Greece. ♦ Greek ♦ M-F, lunch and dinner; Sa, Su, dinner. 3829 Rue St-Denis (between Rues Roy and Duluth E). 842.0867

61 ANTIQUES HUBERT

Rummage through the knickknacks and bric-a-brac, lamps, furniture, and musty trunks at this antiques shop. The old *"La Belle Province"* license plates make good mementos. Pick up a copy of *Guide des Antiquaires* for information and maps locating antiques shops from Montreal to the US border. ♦ Daily. 3680 Blvd St-Laurent (at Ave des Pins). 288.3804

61 LIBRAIRIE GALLIMARD

A cheerful, quiet ambiance pervades one of Montreal's best French-language bookshops. On the first floor you'll find an excellent range of current and classic French, Canadian, and foreign literature; travel, philosophy, and children's literature is located on the basement level, where molded blue stools invite serious browsing. ♦ M-W, Sa, 10AM-6PM; Th-F, 10AM-9PM; Su, noon-6PM. 3700 Blvd St-Laurent (between Rue Guilbaut and Ave des Pins). 499.2012

62 LALOUX

★★★$$$ Chef André Besson describes his cuisine as "halfway between classic and contemporary," but wherever it falls on the culinary scale, the results are delicious. The predominantly French menu reflects Californian and even pan-Asian influences, from a simple mesclun salad with grapefruit vinaigrette to an appetizer of tangy pork and vegetables *"swi maï"* with ginger, sweet pepper, and lemon in a sweet vinegar sauce. For entrées, try the mille-feuille of vegetables with pesto and balsamic caramel sauce or red snapper fillet, served with black olives tapenade, anchovies, and tomato confit tartlet. Choice desserts include the raspberry tulipe, a delightful dish of fresh raspberries, raspberry sorbet, and whipped cream, and the "sun blast" pie made with apricot and frangipane cream and a serving of sorbet. The décor is elegant, with abundant large windows and mirrors reflecting a crowd of hip and happy Montreal diners. ♦ French ♦ Daily, lunch and dinner. Reservations recommended. 250 Ave des Pins E (between Aves Henri Julien and Laval). 287.9127

63 SCANDALE

Quebecois couturier Georges Levesque designs for dancers, and his one-of-a-kind evening dresses are theatrically feminine. Mixing bold colors and textures into luscious patchwork creations with bias cuts and plunging backs, they come in sizes 5 to 10. The mezzanine holds a great collection of postwar European leather bomber jackets; upstairs features unusual, low-priced eveningwear. ♦ M-W, Sa; Th-F, 11AM-9PM. 3639 Blvd St-Laurent (between Rue Prince Arthur and Ave des Pins). 842.4707

63 LE SWIMMING

Upscale snooker and billiards fanatics queue up for cues at this elegant bar and pool parlor. ♦ Daily, noon-3AM. 3643 Blvd St-Laurent (between Rue Prince Arthur and Ave des Pins). 282.7665

DEX - ST-LAURENT

64 DEX

Colorful street-conscious clothes for men and women are the mainstay of this bright, hip shop, which has something of the ambiance of a club (and you'll find flyers advertising the latest club happenings on a table near the entrance). There's a also a good selection of shoes and accessories, including inexpensive jewelry. ♦ June-Sept: M-W, Sa, 10AM-8PM; Th-F, 10AM-10PM; Su, noon-5PM. Oct-May: M-W, Sa, 10AM-6PM; Th-F, 10AM-10PM; Su, noon-5PM. 3651 Blvd St-Laurent (between Rue Prince Arthur and Ave des Pins). 286.3883

65 LE CAVALIER AFGHAN

★$ Afghani cooking, in all its spicy, hearty splendor, comes with a very attractive price tag at this small BYOB restaurant. The menu consists largely of aromatic meats, dumplings, and grilled eggplant with yogurt. There's live music, too. ♦ Afghani ♦ Daily, dinner. 170 Prince Arthur E (between Rues Ste-Urbain and St-Famille). 284.6662

66 EURO DELI

★$ The essence of the trendy Main (the nickname for Boulevard St-Laurent), this zingy aqua-and-orange café is distinguished by the plush red-velvet sea scallop hanging from the ceiling. It's a popular place for brunching on

---

Restaurants/Clubs: Red | Hotels: Purple | Shops: Orange | Outdoors/Parks: Green | Sights/Culture: Blue

banana French toast, apple crepes, and elaborate omelettes while sipping a Mimosa. ◆ Nouvelle ◆ Daily, breakfast, lunch, and dinner. 3619 Blvd St-Laurent (between Rue Prince Arthur and Ave des Pins). 843.7853

67 Mañana

★★$$ This restaurant garners an enthusiastic *olé!* for its succulent chicken, mariachi band (weekends only), and friendly service. Festooned with papier-mâché mobiles, it's scenically situated in front of **Carré St-Louis**. ◆ Mexican ◆ Daily, lunch and dinner. 3605 Rue St-Denis (between Rues de Malines and Cherrier). 847.1050

67 Witloof

★★$$$ This elegant bistro—with mirrored walls, white table linens, and a jungle of plants—serves an unusual mix of Belgian, Tunisian, and Quebecois cuisine. An efficient waitstaff serves such favorites as french fries with mayonnaise, mussels, wild boar, pickled herring, salmon, and goat tartare. You might meet Quebecois theater director René-Richard Cyr among the arty crowd at the bar. ◆ Belgian/Tunisian/Quebecois ◆ M-W, lunch and dinner; Th-Su, dinner. 3619 Rue St-Denis (between Rues de Malines and Cherrier). 281.0100 &

67 Café Cherrier

★$$ Because of its prime people-watching location along Rue St-Denis, the terrace of this café is jammed on sunny days. Order a glass of French wine, sample the broiled halibut with two mustards or beef *au poivre*, and soak up the scene. ◆ French ◆ Daily, breakfast, lunch, and dinner. 3635 Rue St-Denis (at Rue Cherrier). 843.4308 &

68 Multimags

Fashion magazines; newspapers from Canada, the US, and Europe; sleek gift books and hot novels: You'll find all this and more at this hip, brightly lit newsstand. ◆ Su-W, 8AM-1AM; Th, 8AM-2AM; F-Sa, 8AM-3AM. 3552 Blvd St-Laurent (between Rues Milton and Prince Arthur). 287.7355

69 Cafeteria

★★$$ A variety of sandwiches, pizzas, crepes, quiches, salads, and exotic fruit juices fill out the menu, but the towering chocolate cakes steal the show at this bustling café. ◆ Eclectic ◆ Daily, breakfast, lunch, and dinner. 3581 Blvd St-Laurent (between Rues Milton and Prince Arthur). 849.3855

70 Shed

$ In this large, dimly lit, and always busy café-bar, you can enjoy a generously portioned salad, pizza, burger, California wrap, or noodle dish—but no one really comes here for the food. The place has long been ground zero on Boulevard St-Laurent for young Montrealers to socialize and flirt with each other and (if they're up to it) the waitstaff. You can do the same, or just contemplate it, while listening to the techno music and enjoying wine by the glass or freshly squeezed fruit juice. M-F, 11AM-3AM; Sa-Su, 9:30-3AM. 3515 Blvd St-Laurent (between Rues Milton and Prince Arthur). 842.0220

70 Nevik

The name, an anagram of designer Kevin Allwood's first name, is a fair reflection of the innovative women's ready-to-wear collections to be found in this coolly sophisticated second-floor showroom. The off-street location invites leisurely browsing. ◆ M-F; call for hours. 3523 Blvd St-Laurent (between Rues Milton and Prince Arthur). 288.9706. Also at Les Cours Mont-Royal. 842.8188

71 Ex-Centris

This stunning center for independent film and digital art opened in 1999 with financing from president and founder Daniel Langlois, and ranks among the city's most resplendent cultural jewels. The graystone building, designed by **Bureau Architecture Rioppel**, is simple but refreshingly distinct from the street and sleek but spare on the inside. Original design elements include the rotating clock in the high-ceilinged lobby and a baffling digitized ticket-buying experience. Independent films from Quebec, Canada, and around the world are played in three sleek, state-of-the-art screening rooms. ◆ 3536 Blvd St-Laurent (between Rues Milton and Prince Arthur). 847.2206

Within Ex-Centris:

Café Méliès

★★★$$$ Though a part of the beautiful Ex-Centris cinema, this restaurant-café-bar more than stands on its own. It's named for George Méliès, the first director to use special effects in film. Montreal designer Michael Joannides plays the sci-fi theme to the hilt, with metal and plush purple velvet chairs, metal tables, and an almost impossibly sleek bar. All this makes for a cool feast for the eyes, but what comes out of the kitchen is even better. Star appetizers include the likes of lobster and tarragon vichyssoise, rabbit terrine with fennel and sweet wine jelly, and gourmet sandwiches with home-baked focaccia. Entrées include the likes of braised snapper with lemon and artichokes and a solid range of fish and meat dishes. Desserts are eccentric: Try the lemon cake with avocado cream and field berries, nougatine waffle with wine-braised pear and porto sabayon, or pineapple tarte tatin with coconut cream. ♦ Contemporary ♦ M-F, breakfast, lunch, and dinner; Sa-Su, brunch and dinner. 847.9218

72 PIZZÉDÉLIC

★★$ Ever tried a goat cheese pizza? Or a shrimp, mussels, and shallots combo? Here they are, thin and crisp, plus the more traditional pies: pepperoni, sausage, and vegetarian. Ask to sit at one of the semicircular booths. ♦ Italian ♦ Daily, lunch and dinner. 3509 Blvd St-Laurent (between Rues Milton and Prince Arthur). 282.6784 &

73 CHORUS

★★$$$ Hearty palates that don't mind an adventurous edge will most enjoy this relative pocket of calm on busy Rue St-Denis, in the spot previously occupied by the highly regarded **Jongleux Café**. Start off with appetizers such as duck tartare with sesame, lacquered fresh fig and crispy *papadam*, or the house smoked salmon and potato pancake. For entrées you can keep things simple with red snapper and scallops, pan-fried with sea salt; move up a notch with roasted venison chop, port, and red currant sauce; or take it all the way with braised pig cheeks in beer, served with a stew of young veggies, basil, and saffron gnocchi. ♦ Eclectic ♦ Daily, dinner. Reservations recommended. 3434 Rue St-Denis (between Rues Sherbrooke and de Rigaud). 841.8080

74 LES GÂTERIES CAFÉ-BISTRO

★★$ Movie and theater posters decorate this cozy café serving continental breakfasts, sandwiches (try the Croque Asperges, a French-inspired ham-and-cheese sandwich with tomato and asparagus), and generous bowls of steaming soup. But most people come here to fire up on the potent house coffee. The exact blend of beans is a closely guarded secret—even the manager claims not to know the ingredients; as for the owners, well, we dare you to pry it out of them. ♦ Café ♦ Daily, breakfast, lunch, and dinner. 3443 Rue St-Denis (between Rues Sherbrooke and de Rigaud). 843.6235

75 PRIMADONNA

★★$$$ Of the gaggle of see-and-be-seen eateries that line the lower end of Boulevard St-Laurent, this one is a standout for its décor and cuisine. Graceful blond-wood furniture and curving yellow walls provide a sophisticated backdrop to a split menu of Italian fare and sushi. For the latter, try the nigiri sushi, a mélange of salmon, red snapper, halibut, and tuna. All pastas are homemade and paired to house-made sauces. A good bet among many is the Chitarra Di Pasta Fresca Con Aragosta, a combination of angel-hair–style pasta with lobster chunks and shiitake mushrooms in light tomato cream sauce. The wine list is solid if expensive, and service can be slow. ♦ Italian/Japanese ♦ M-F, lunch and dinner; Sa-Su, dinner. Reservations recommended. 3479 Blvd St-Laurent (between Rues Sherbrooke and Milton). 282.6644

75 WAX LOUNGE

Despite its hip location a relaxed atmosphere prevails in this charming second-floor bar-lounge. The house specialties are cigars, scotch, and R&B. It fills up fast on weekends. ♦ Daily. 3481 Blvd St-Laurent (between Rues Sherbrooke and Milton). 282.0919

75 GLOBE

★★$$$ High ceilings, hip Jean-Pierre Viau décor, and loud music create a decidedly urban environment in which to schmooze at the bar or enjoy fresh and reliable bistro fare tableside. Most of the produce is organic and, as with free-range meats and fowl, is purchased from local farmers. Standout main courses include slow-cooked rabbit with greens, bacon, and mustard jus; crispy Peking duck with honey, greens, and roasted organic root potatoes; and seared sirloin Angus steak with spinach, tomatoes, and red wine jus; as well as any fresh fish. Items on the wine list are varied but lean toward the expensive. ♦ Canadian ♦ Daily, dinner. Reservations recommended. 3455 Blvd St-Laurent (between Rues Sherbrooke and Milton). 284.3823

restaurant
formosa
gastronomie d'asie

76 FORMOSA

★★$$ Don't let the nondescript exterior fool you: This is a large, sleek restaurant with abundant offerings of deliciously, resolutely Thai dishes. Sculptured white stone frescos of fish along with ergonomically designed gray chairs and thoughtfully spaced tables set the tone for the menu, which moves easily between basic and adventurous. There's a full range of vegetarian plates, from seitan and seaweed to Choochi soya croquettes, battered with coconut milk. Carnivores can sink their teeth into morsels of bison or ostrich sautéed with hot peppers and fresh basil leaves, or the Duck Red Curry—sliced duck simmered with pineapple, tomatoes, and peppers in a creamy curry sauce. ◆ Thai ◆ Daily, lunch and dinner. 2115 Rue St-Denis (at Rue Sherbrooke). 282.1966

77 OMORPHO

Native American–inspired rugs and pottery, cactus-shaped candles, tooled leather belts, and other designs from the desert are featured in this Southwestern shop. ◆ M-W, Sa; Th-F, 10AM-9PM. 3497 Blvd St-Laurent (between Rues Sherbrooke and Milton). 848.0812

77 MEZZE

★★$$$ *Mezze* is the Greek word for appetizers, and you can choose from more than 30 of them at this trendy, boisterous restaurant. There are grilled vegetables in olive oil, stuffed grape leaves, and fried calamari, to name but a few. If your appetite is heartier, you could also go for the fresh fish or jumbo shrimp by the pound. ◆ Greek ◆ Daily, dinner. 3449 Blvd St-Laurent (between Rues Sherbrooke and Milton). 281.0275

78 LA CAPOTERIE

Capote in French means "hood," "bonnet," "greatcoat"—and "condom." This family-friendly sex shop carries condoms galore in preposterous colors and flavors, whimsically packaged in small clay pots shaped like flowers, mice, snakes, or cats. The stock is complemented by a selection of X-rated games, and, in a semiseparate area up front, PG-rated clothes. ◆ M-Sa, 11AM-9PM; Su, noon-9PM. 2061 Rue St-Denis (between Rue Ontario and Terrasse St-Denis). 845.0027

79 AUX DELICES DE SZECHUAN

★★★$$ Labeled the best Chinese restaurant in Montreal by those who know their Hunan, the large menu offers an impressive variety of vegetarian, seafood, poultry, and meat dishes, spiced wild or mild. Cool off with a beer on the attractive terrace. ◆ Chinese ◆ M-F, lunch and dinner; Sa-Su, dinner. 1735 Rue St-Denis (at Rue Ontario). 844.5542

79 LA SILA

★★★$$$ Even in this city of sophisticated tastes, this intimate restaurant, decorated in muted Mediterranean colors, earns

outstanding reviews for its simple yet elegant Italian cruisine. Specialties are spaghetti in squid's ink, lobster ravioli, and calf's liver veneziana. ◆ Italian ◆ M-F, lunch and dinner; Sa, dinner. Reservations recommended. 2040 Rue St-Denis (between Rue Ontario and Terrasse St-Denis). 844.5083

80 MIKADO

★★$$ Everything about this traditional sushi bar is authentic: the waitresses wearing kimonos, the knives flashing behind the sushi bar where the chef assembles morsels of raw fish and vegetables, and the low tables in the tranquil tatami room. ◆ Japanese ◆ M-F, lunch and dinner. Sa-Su, dinner. Reservations required. 1731 Rue St-Denis (at Rue Ontario). 844.5705 &. Also at 368 Ave Laurier W (at Ave du Parc). 279.4809

81 JELLO BAR

This lively (and noisy) retro-style bar and lounge is popular with the martini-swilling 20-something set. Each night there are different bands, mostly swing, jazz, salsa, funk, or soul, with resident DJs taking up the slack between acts. Tuesday is Brazil night. There's a nominal cover charge on most nights. ◆ M-Tu, Sa, 9PM-3AM; W-F, 5PM-3AM. 151 Rue Ontario E (at Rue de Bullion). 285.2621

82 PIZZERIA DEI COMPARI

★★$ Wood-fired ovens imbue the 33 kinds of pizza made here with the savors of Tuscany. Toppings include anchovies, zucchini, artichokes, broccoli, crab, eggplant, escargot, capers, and smoked meats. The homemade pastas are great too. ◆ Italian ◆ Daily, lunch and dinner. 1668 Rue St-Denis (between Rues Emery and Ontario). 843.6411 &

82 RISTORANTE ITALIANO

★$ When asked why the St. Valentine's Day decorations were still up in August, a waiter explained, "Here, we are always in love. We don't wait for the fourteenth of February!" Among the unexpected specialties are Swiss, Chinese, and Italian fondue. ◆ Italian ◆ Tu-Su, lunch and dinner. 1670 Rue St-Denis (between Rues Emery and Ontario). 844.2935 &

82 BIBLIOTHÈQUE NATIONALE DU QUÉBEC, L'ÉDIFICE ST-SULPICE

Designed in 1915 by **Eugene Payette** in the Beaux Arts style, Quebec's National Library is illuminated by shimmering stained-glass windows and skylights, chandeliers, and old brass reading lamps shining across long wooden tables. The stacks house the 1844 collections of the St-Sulpicians, a copy of every book published in the province, and hundreds of precious manuscripts from around the world. ◆ M-F, 9AM-5PM. 1700 Rue St-Denis (between Rues Emery and Ontario). 873.4553

83 JUST FOR LAUGHS MUSEUM/MUSÉE JUSTE POUR RIRE

The only museum devoted to the history of laughter grew out of the largest comedy festival in the world, Montreal's Just for Laughs. Occupying the former Ekers brewery, clever high-tech displays re-create benchmarks in buffoonery: Greek satire, court jesters, and the commedia dell'arte tradition. Videos showing classic scenes from movies (silent and talkie), cartoons, radio programs, and TV sitcoms keep visitors in stitches. The museum houses the **Humour Hall of Fame**, a 250-seat cabaret, a **Comedy Research Archive** for scholars of the snicker, the **National School of Humour**, and a boutique of witty gifts. ◆ Admission. Tu-Su, 10AM-5PM. 2111 Blvd St-Laurent (between Rues Ontario and Sherbrooke). 845.4000. www.hahaha.com

84 LE COMMENSAL

★★$$ More than 100 gourmet vegetarian dishes are priced by the gram at this cafeteria, which also serves as a mecca for New Age Montrealers. Fill up on couscous or tofu marinated in ginger or one of the fabulous cakes and pies while eavesdropping on a discourse on the secrets of the *I Ching*. ◆ Vegetarian ◆ Daily, breakfast, lunch, and dinner. 1720 Rue St-Denis (between Rues Emery and Ontario). 845.2627 ප

85 L'AVENTURIER

Rugged but gorgeous clothing and gear for every season and sport from such prestigious Quebecois labels as Kanuk, Chic-Choc, and Chlorophylle are the stock in trade of this large, modern store. Look for the handsome wooden walking sticks with leather handles (a status item for a hike on Mont-Royal). If you're scouting for canoe or camping partners or feel like joining a mountain-bike tour, check out the notice board near the entrance. ◆ M-W, Sa; Th-F,

10AM-9PM; Su, 11AM-5PM. 1610 Rue St-Denis (between Blvd de Maisonneuve and Rue Emery). 849.4100

86 LE ST-MALO

★$$ Frequented by students, this bistro with its emphasis on the cuisine of Brittany has been going strong for 26 years. Specialties include mussels, couscous, and crispy, piping-hot *frites* (french fries). ◆ French ◆ Daily, lunch and dinner. 1605 Rue St-Denis (between Blvd de Maisonneuve and Rue Emery). 845.6327

87 LA BRIOCHE LYONNAISE

★★★★$$ *Ooh la la!* Even in this city of European confectioners and pastry chefs, the fabulous cakes and tartes by Guy Laffont are an epicurean's dream. Try the St-Honoré or *l'équateur*—a caramel mousse with pears—or the luscious Paris Brest. The old stone walls and lace curtains provide a pleasant setting for lingering; there's also a terrace out back. ◆ French pastries ◆ Daily, 8:30AM-midnight; Su, 9AM-midnight. 1593 Rue St-Denis (between Blvd de Maisonneuve and Rue Emery). 842.7017 ප

88 THE CINÉROBOTHÈQUE

You won't catch the projectionist napping here. A robot fetches the laser disc of your choice and pops it into the video player (sorry, it won't go for popcorn). Quebec's film archive has 22 individual screens with comfortable chairs, headphones, and THX sound, and private viewings are free. The National Film Board of Canada also projects movies from its 7,000-strong collection in its 142-seat theater. ◆ Tu-Su, noon-9PM. 1564 Rue St-Denis (at Blvd de Maisonneuve). 496.6887

88 THÉÂTRE SAINT-DENIS

Built in 1908, this 2,200-seat hall is the city's second-largest theatrical venue. It features Quebecois singers, stand-up comics, and bands, as well as international talent. ◆ 1594 Rue St-Denis (at Blvd de Maisonneuve). 849.4211

89 UNIVERSITÉ DU QUÉBEC À MONTRÉAL (UQAM)

When this university opened on Rue St-Denis in 1979, it revitalized Montreal's Latin Quarter. Instead of razing the **St. James Cathedral**, architects preserved the church's ornate Gothic Revival façade as the front of one of the university buildings. The 320-foot-high spire is the tallest in the city. ◆ Blvd de Maisonneuve (between Rues Berri and St-Denis). 987.3000

Restaurants/Clubs: Red | Hotels: Purple | Shops: Orange | Outdoors/Parks: Green | Sights/Culture: Blue

OLYMPIC PARK/BOTANICAL GARDEN

When the Montreal suburb of **Maisonneuve** set aside 21.9 million square feet of outdoor space for the development of a sports and recreation area in 1910, little did planners know that the land would one day be the site of the world's ultimate sports event: the Olympic Games. In 1970, Mayor Jean Drapeau won his bid for the **1976 Summer Olympic Games**, and the race to construct an Olympic park with sports facilities worthy of the world's greatest athletes began.

French architect **Roger Taillibert** designed the futuristic **Olympic Stadium**, with sweeping curves, a huge leaning tower, a retractable roof—and a billion-dollar price tag (which Montrealers are still paying for through a special Olympics tax). Today the stadium is home field for the **Montreal Expos** baseball team and a venue for rock concerts and other major events. The former **Velodrome**, site of cycling competitions during the summer games, was reincarnated as the **Biodôme** in 1992, with four fascinating natural ecosystems to explore. Across from the Olympic complex is the **Montreal Botanical Garden**, a top Montreal attraction that contains 30 theme gardens and more than 26,000 species of flora.

1 MAISONNEUVE PARK

This 525-acre wonderland offers everything from cross-country ski trails and an illuminated ice-skating rink to cycling paths and a nine-hole golf course. In the winter, children love tobogganing down the hills; in summer, the park is perfect for picnics. ◆ Free; fee for the golf course. Daily, 9AM-10PM. 4601 Rue Sherbrooke E (between Rue Viau and Blvd Pie IX). 872.6555

2 OLYMPIC VILLAGE

Some 9,000 Olympic athletes and 2,000 coaches were quartered at the then spanking-new pyramid-shaped village in 1976. Today, it's home to about 2,000 residents (20% of whom are seniors on low incomes)—it has been transformed into a commercial-residential complex. ◆ 5199 Rue Sherbrooke E (between Blvd de l'Assomption and Rue Viau). 252.4970

3 MONTREAL BOTANICAL GARDEN

Brother Marie-Victorin, a local priest, conceived of the idea for this assortment of theme gardens and exhibition greenhouses—each with a different environment—that opened in 1931. More than 21,000 species (36,000 specimens) of flora flourish on these 180 acres, but you don't have to be an expert on flowers to enjoy the tranquillity and sheer beauty of the place. The gardens are accessible by free shuttle from **Olympic Park** or on foot via a lower-level passage beneath Rue Sherbrooke. Walk in through the formal **Entrance Garden**, where wide beds of flowers surround an imposing central fountain. Small rubber-wheeled *balades* (trains) transport visitors through the various gardens. The garden with poisonous plants is a favorite. Two parking lots are located on the premises. ◆ Admission. Daily. 4101 Rue Sherbrooke E (at Blvd Pie IX). 872.1400

Within Montreal Botanical Garden:

INSECTARIUM

Founded in 1990 by entomologist George Brossard, who donated some 250,000 specimens from his private collection, this museum is devoted entirely to creepy-crawlies and their habits and purpose on earth. The thousands of species represented here (many of them alive) range from exceedingly large South American cockroaches and giant walkingsticks to colorful butterflies and beetles. The building itself is designed like a giant cicada, to which is attached the Butterfly House. There are insect tastings on weekend evenings in November.

FIRST NATIONS GARDEN

Inaugurated in summer 2001 by the City of Montreal to commemorate the tricentennial of the Great Peace Treaty of Montreal (a peace treaty between the French and 39 Amerindian nations), this garden evokes the close bonds between Amerindian and Inuit peoples and the plant world. The five zones include hardwood forest, mixed forest, northern territory, and an interpretation pavilion.

THE CHINESE GARDEN

Also called "Dream Lake Garden," the garden was created in China for Montreal and inspired by the Ming Dynasty's many mountain and water gardens. This 6-acre garden opened in 1991 as the largest such attraction outside Asia, with 7 beautiful pavilions and 16 landscapes. Winding pathways, water, bridges, and courtyards serve as backdrops for the lush vegetation. It is truly exquisite.

JAPANESE GARDEN AND PAVILION

Like Oriental wisdom, the design of this park is simple yet profound. Created by Ken Nakajima, it includes a Zen pebble garden, a museum, a library, and a pavilion, behind which sits a delightful tea garden where formal tea ceremonies are held. Seasonal exhibits include artistic and cultural works between May and October; and in the summer, Japanese bonsai are presented in a small garden.

THE LOVERS' BENCH

When Lea Vivot sculpted two lovers kissing on a bench in the buff, with a woman seated at the other end opening her mouth in shock, she couldn't have imagined how many times it would change hands. The work was well accepted by an amused Montreal public when exhibited outside an art gallery on Rue Sherbrooke West. But when it was sold in 1979 to Toronto, residents there were not pleased, and a major controversy broke out. Even New Yorkers objected when the sculpture was once again sold to a hotel in that seemingly shock-proof city. Finally, *The Lovers' Bench* came home when the New York hotel gave it back to the artist, and she, in turn, donated it to the garden. All this proves once again that Montrealers may be the most open-minded people on the continent, at least with regard to culture.◆ Near the Exhibition Garden and cafeteria

Restaurants/Clubs: Red | Hotels: Purple | Shops: Orange | Outdoors/Parks: Green | Sights/Culture: Blue

THE BEST

Thomas Schnurmacher

Former Society Editor for the *Montreal Gazette,* Lecturer, and Author of *Gold-Digger's Guide: How to Marry Rich*

Walking down **Rue Sherbrooke West** on a Sunday afternoon.

Late sushi at the **Mikado** on **Avenue Laurier.**

Reading on the park benches on the second floor of the **Coles** bookstore on **Rue Ste-Catherine West.**

Watching the canine parade at **Percy Walters Park.**

Driving along **Boulevard St-Laurent.**

High tea in upper **Westmount.**

Breakfast at **Hotel Vogue.**

People watching in the lobby of the **Montreal Museum of Fine Arts.**

Making friends at the **Native Friendship Center** on Côte-des-Neiges.

The Montreal skyline by night as you drive in on the **Bonaventure Expressway.**

Sticky rice on Friday and Saturday at **Chao Phraya.**

The cheap teapot gift shops in **Chinatown.**

The **Walshroom** designed by Dick Walsh at the **Royal Club** on **Rue Ste-Catherine East.**

4 TOURIST HALL

To your left as you exit the **Biodôme** is the triple-tiered 42,000-square-foot visitors' center that provides information and entry tickets to various attractions in **Olympic Park**. Located at the base of the famous **Tour de Montréal** (formerly known as the **Inclined Tower**), the hall features a souvenir shop, a 182-seat auditorium where you can see a 15-minute film about the **1976 Olympic Games** and the construction of the park (included in the guided tour of the site), and an exhibition called the *World Federation of Great Towers*, of which the **Olympic Stadium**'s record-holding **Tour de Montréal** is a proud member. If you're hungry, try one of the three snack bars for pizza, hot dogs, soup, and fries.♦ M, noon-6PM; Tu-Su. Bounded by Ave Pierre-de-Coubertin and Rue Sherbrooke E and by Rue Viau and Blvd Pie IX. 252.8687

Via the Tourist Hall:

TOUR DE MONTRÉAL

The largest inclined tower in the world hovers 890 feet above the ground and is itself a major tourist attraction. On a clear day, you can see forever (or at least 50 miles in any direction) from the top-floor observatory, which is reached by taking a 2-minute ride on a cable car. Photos and other memorabilia highlighting the history of the park are show-cased on the observatory's lower level. ♦ Admission. Daily, 10AM-5PM. 252.8687

SWIMMING CENTER

The building housing the 25-by-50-meter pool used at the **1976 Olympic Games** is acces-sible through the **Tourist Hall**. Actually, there are now six pools, including the competition pool, a wading pool for toddlers, a diving pool with three platforms, and a warm-up pool for competitors who wish to loosen their muscles before the big event. Water sports, physical-fitness programs, and special "water days" for students are held here, in addition to interna-tional meets. A water park with slides and rides is under consideration as another way to cover an Olympic deficit said to be in excess of $2 million annually. If that happens, it will become the largest indoor facility of its type in Eastern North America.♦ Admission. Call for hours. 252.4622

5 CHÂTEAU DUFRESNE

When Parisian architect **Jules Renard** built this Beaux Arts–style mansion for Oscar and Marius Dufresne in 1916, the brothers hoped that other well-heeled Montrealers would build in the vicinity—but World War I contributed to the bankruptcy of the new municipality of Maisonneuve, so the chateau is unique to this part of town. The design is a lavish mix of Tudor, Gothic, classical, Renais-sance, Second Empire, and other styles. The brothers filled their mansion with extravagant original furnishings and decorative objects. The museum is easy to overlook because of its location away from other park attractions but worthy of a detour. ♦ Admission. Th-Su, noon-5PM. 2929 Rue Jeanne d'Arc (between Ave Pierre-de-Coubertin and Rue Sherbrooke E). 259.9201

6 OLYMPIC STADIUM

Designed by French architect **Roger Taillibert**, the "Big O" is referred to as the "Big Owe" by locals disgruntled about its extraordinary cost—a billion dollars and counting for the stadium alone. The exorbitant price tag came as a surprise to Montrealers, whom Mayor Jean Drapeau had convinced would pay nothing to host the **1976 Olympic Games**. (In fact, he compared the likelihood of Montrealers' having to pay to that of a man having a baby.) But homeowners currently fork out an annual municipal Olympics tax to offset the cost of the stadium. The stadium's million-dollar "retractable" roof, which opened and closed with the aid of wires attached to its girth, was a magnificent contraption . . . when it worked. But far too often it didn't, and when the orange Kevlar material it was made of started to tear, the Olympics Installation Board (OIB) announced plans to replace it with a nonretractable steel roof, adding to the expense (and frustration) of Montrealers. In 1991, the Big O suffered another mishap when a massive chunk of concrete fell from the stadium's perimeter to the ground below. Thankfully, it happened early in the morning, when no one was inside. But the **Montreal Expos** played out the remainder of their home games on the road that season and the stadium remained closed until engineers gave it a clean bill of health months later. (Nothing has broken off since.) Still, the stadium *is* one of the most graceful (albeit extraterrestrial-like) structures ever built in the city. The statue in front of the entrance is of Jackie Robinson, who broke baseball's "black barrier" when he played for the **Montreal Royals**, then the farm team for the **Brooklyn Dodgers**. The Montreal Expos have been pennant contenders almost every year since they moved here from Jarry Park field. They played their first game on Big O AstroTurf on 15 April 1977 and won the Eastern Division title in 1981. ♦ Admission. Guided tours only: English, daily, 12:40PM, 3:40PM; French, daily, 11AM, 2PM. 4549 Ave Pierre-de-Coubertin (between Rue Viau and Blvd Pie IX). 253.3434

7 PIERRE-CHARBONNEAU CENTER

This sporting center, built in 1957, has a large gymnasium and other recreation rooms. The Greco-Roman wrestling competitions were held here in 1976, as well as the preliminary freestyle wrestling event. ♦ M-F, 8:30AM-10:30PM. 3000 Rue Viau (at Ave Pierre Charbonneau). 872.6644

8 BIODÔME

This $58.2 million world wonder—a living exhibit of 4,000 animals and 5,000 plants—is housed in what was once the **Velodrome**, where Olympic cycling competitions were held. **Roger Taillibert**, the architect of the **Olympic Stadium**, also designed this building,

which reopened in 1992. The complex puts visitors smack in the middle of four ecosystems found in North, South, and Central America: Tropical Forest, Laurentian Forest, St. Lawrence Marine, and Arctic.

Wander through a humid "jungle" with lush foliage and waterfalls in the Tropical Forest, where you'll come face-to-face with some of earth's strangest life-forms, including waterbabies (capybaras), tailless South American rodents that can grow to more than 4 feet in length and live in water for days on end, and coatis, raccoonlike tree-dwellers with long, flexible snouts. You'll also see the golden lion tamarin (a monkey with orange fur), marmosets, multicolored parrots, crocodiles, and even a dark cave with furry bats hanging from the rocks and flying overhead as they hunt mice. (Don't worry—they're behind a glass barrier.)

In the cooler Laurentian section, you'll spy on wildlife indigenous to Quebec: river otters, American beavers, ducks, birds, and even a Canadian lynx, all interspersed among conifers, maples, and other trees and plant life.

In the St. Lawrence ecosystem, representing 1,800 miles of river that begins in Canada and flows into the Atlantic Ocean, are many species of fish, birds, and other marine life, including anemones and barnacles. Watch a mother duck feed her hatchlings while seagulls soar lazily overhead. And penguins scramble comically over rock and snow in the Arctic ecosystem. You can breeze through a total of 1,640 feet of pathways in all four ecosystems in as little as 20 minutes or spend a couple of hours. Either way, it's an amazing experience. A restaurant and ecology-heavy souvenir shop are on the premises, as are resource personnel. ♦ Admission. Daily. 4777 Ave Pierre-de-Coubertin (at Rue Theodore). 868.3000

9 MAURICE RICHARD ARENA

Constructed in 1961 and named in honor of Maurice "The Rocket" Richard, legendary former right-winger with the **Montreal Canadiens**, this hockey and figure-skating arena also hosts music concerts, galas, circuses, and the like. The stands hold 4,200 spectators. The small Maurice Richard Museum is located inside the arena. ♦ Daily. 2800 Rue Viau (at Rue Pierre-de-Coubertin). 872.6666

MONTREAL DAY TRIPS

Montreal sits at the crossroads, with old French Canada to the east, English Canada to the west, New England to the south, and the Laurentian wilderness to the north. Day trips from this island city offer a grab bag of adventures that over a wide range of interests, from skiing, hiking, spa-hopping, mountain biking, and white-water rafting to antiquing, dining, architecture, and military or North American history. Six major tourist regions lie within a couple of hours' drive from Montreal: the **Laurentians**, the **Outaouais, Lanaudière, Montérégie, Coeur-du-Quebec,** and **Estrie.**

Visitors interested in finding roads less traveled can create their own itineraries by heading down any of the two-lane secondary roads fanning out from Montreal. Following the paths of Quebec's original 18th-century highways, these routes pass through quaint villages replete with the best of domestic and ecclesiastical architecture.

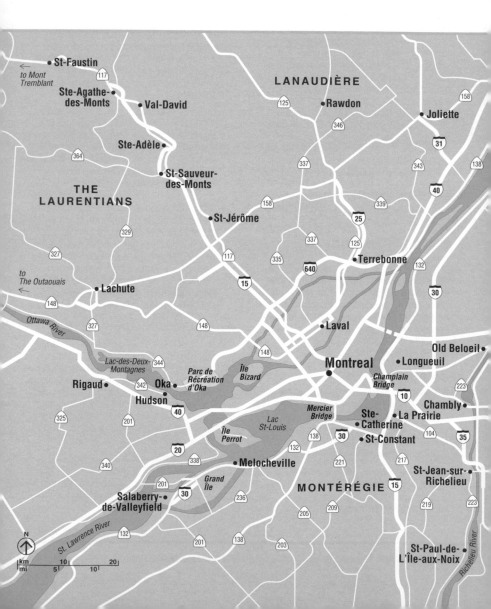

The Laurentian route (**Route 117**) runs through Quebec's "Alps" between **St-Jérôme** and **Ste-Agathe-des-Monts**, whereas **Chemin du Roy (Route 138)**, the oldest paved road in Canada, follows the north shore of the **St. Lawrence River** through hamlets of fieldstone houses with mansard roofs, inspired by those in Normandy and Brittany. Other scenic routes to try are **132** on the south shore of the St. Lawrence, and **342**, **344**, and **223**.

THE LAURENTIANS

This mountainous region 35 miles north of Montreal is a miniature Switzerland, a world-class resort area with some of the best alpine skiing in North America. Quebec's high country switches gears in the warmer months. In summer, the lakes are a colorful confetti of sails, the *boîtes-à-chansons* clubs fill with folk music, hikers climb the slopes of **Mont Tremblant**, and the wealthy old guard mingle with mountain bikers on café terraces. For general information on the Laurentians, call the **Laurentian Tourist Association** (450/436.8532 or 800/561.6673) or visit www.laurentides.com.

The **Lower Laurentians** begin with the forested mountains that flank the shores of **Lac-des-Deux-Montagnes**,

a scenic spot where the **Ottawa** and **St. Lawrence Rivers** meet. In earlier times, the lake was a canoeing highway for native North Americans and fur traders. Today, swimmers, windsurfers, and pleasure boaters come to the **Parc de Récréation d'Oka** (Paul Sauve Provincial Park) for the lake's warm, shallow waters, and landlubbers stroll along the 4.3-mile beach. Windsurfing equipment rental and instruction are available, as are hikes through the maple forests led by park naturalists. Visitors also can canoe among lily pads and beaver dams in the marsh of **Grand Bay**, bicycle, and, in winter, skate, snowshoe, and cross-country ski. **Paul Sauve Provincial Park** is located 31 miles west of Montreal, on **Chemin d'Oka** (Route 344), near the village of **Oka**. By car, take Route 15 North, then exit 21 to 640 West to the park entrance. Buses leave four times a day from the **Henri-Bourassa Metro** station, arriving at the park's entrance, a mile from Oka. Call 450/479.8337 for more information.

Oka and **Hudson**, two pretty villages set on the shores of Lac-des-Deux-Montagnes, are linked by a small, old-fashioned ferry. Oka is famous for the flat, round cheese Trappist monks make at the town's Cistercian abbey. But since Quebec's heated "Indian Summer" of 1990, Oka is better known as the site of a confrontation between developers and a local native tribe. Plans to expand a golf course that would trespass on a Mohawk burial ground sparked conflict between the Mohawk and other residents and fired up native pride throughout Canada. The burial ground is still intact. For a magnificent view recalling how this region looked before it was settled, climb to the **Oka Calvary** (**Stations of the Cross**), a popular autumn pilgrimage spot. Native Indians who were converted by missionaries built the four oratories and three chapels between 1739 and 1742. The **Cistercian Abbey of Oka** (Route 344, at 1600 Chemin d'Oka, 450/479.8361), built between 1880 and 1890, is one of the oldest monasteries in North America, founded by Trappist monks from the Bellefontaine Abbey in France. Stroll through the idyllic gardens and buy the famous cheese made here since 1893.

In good weather, a free ferry transports cars and passengers from the Oka dock on Rue des Anges over to pretty English-speaking Hudson in 10 minutes. This town is the place for tweed and afternoon tea, along with strolling, brunching, and antiquing. On Saturdays between May and late October, bargain hunters flock to **Finnegan's Market** (775 Main Street, at Côte St-Charles; 450/458.4377), Quebec's largest outdoor flea and antiques market.

Formerly located in Oka, the **Auberge Clémentine** (398 Main Street, at Cameron; 450/458.8181) moved to

In 1969, John Lennon and Yoko Ono held a "bed-in" for peace at the Queen Elizabeth Hotel on Dorchester Boulevard West (now known as René Lévesque West) in Montreal. With guests such as Timothy Leary and Tommy Smothers singing along, they recorded the anti–Vietnam War song "Give Peace a Chance" in their room.

Hudson in 1994. This place is just as cozy, with the same gaslight-and-lace-curtain ambiance. Chef Michel Beaulne and his wife, Louise, use fresh local ingredients and innovative cooking techniques to prepare traditional Quebecois recipes. Spend an evening on the seven-course *Menu Gastronomique*—starting with succulent appetizers (perhaps chicken brochettes in a subtle cream curry sauce) and moving on to such entrées as Oka pheasant and lasagna of lobster mousseline. Local cheeses and old-fashioned desserts like pure maple sugar on a hunk of homemade bread with cream are also served.

From Hudson, drive to **Rigaud** on 342 West and gorge on dishes doused in maple syrup at the old-fashioned **Sucrerie de la Montagne** (300 Rang St-Georges, at Monté Levigne; 450/451.5204). **St-Jérôme**, off **Route 117**, is the gateway to the Laurentians. Founded in 1834, the village is the first in the string of "Saints" tucked into Quebec's Little Switzerland. Next up is busy **St-Sauveur-des-Monts**, the major resort town in the Laurentians, popular for night skiing at **Mont-Habitant** and **Mont-Christie** in the winter, and for the theater and its aquatic park during *la belle saison* in the summer.

By the shores of **Lac Rond** and the slopes of **Mont Ste-Adèle** is the lovely town of **Ste-Adèle** (exit 72 off Route 15), which fills with skiers in winter and windsurfers in summer and has the restaurants and nightlife to keep energetic visitors happy when the sun goes down. A superb local restaurant specializes in the regional cuisines of France and Quebec. At **Hôtel L'Eau à la Bouche** (3003 Boulevard Ste-Adèle, at Rue Morim; 450/227.1416), Chef Anne Desjardins—one of the few female chefs in the province—sets her fresh Barbary duck off with green peppercorns and a sauce made from local raspberries picked in season. The maple ice cream is a subtle finale to the meal. The cuisine—even in this province where good kitchens are commonplace—is memorable, the service excellent, and the ambiance cozy and romantic.

The health-conscious may wish to make a detour to the **Thalaspa** (1699 Chemin Mont-Gabriel, Ste-Adèle; 450/229.1813) at the Hôtel Mont Gabriel, a beautiful and expertly run health spa that uses Phytobiodermie, a Swiss skin-care line that fuses Western and Eastern healing techniques. For a more thoroughly Oriental experience, make a detour to the nearby **Ofuro Spa** (777 Chemin St-Adolphe, Morin-Heights; 450/226.2442 or 877/884.2442), the closest Japan comes to Canada. This architectural wonder of a day spa is a most relaxing place to indulge in a massage, steam bath, or sauna.

North of Ste-Adèle on Route 117 is the **Village de Seraphin** (450/229.4777), a reproduction of the Laurentian village of the mid-1800s described in Claude-Henri Grignon's 1933 novel *Un homme et son péché* (*A Man and His Sin*). Each of the 20 buildings illustrates an episode in the life of Seraphin Poudrier, the novel's miserly protagonist, and a small train runs through the grounds. The village is open daily between mid-May and Labor Day and open on Saturday and Sunday between Labor Day and mid-October; admission is charged.

A few miles north is **Val-David**, a magnet for painters, artists, and alpinists who come to scale **Mont Condor**.

The **Passe-Montagne** (819/322.2123) climbing school

HITTING THE SLOPES

Proximity is one unbeatable selling point for the ski areas of Quebec—the resorts are all close enough for day trips from Montreal. But it's not the only plus. The rustic charm of the region's many motels, inns, and resorts makes both locals and tourists want to linger and savor the old-style ambiance and superior cuisine. The skiing is characterized by well-maintained trails, good conditions, and bracing subzero cold, so dry it's a novelty in itself. And the unrivaled quality of the northern light casts a diamondlike dazzle over it all.

Skiing near Montreal is clustered in two principal areas: the **Laurentian Mountains** to the north and the **Eastern Townships**—also known as the Estrie region—to the south. Some of the lodging facilities offer ski packages that often include half-day or full-day lift passes at the slope of your choice.

The Laurentians

Less than an hour's drive north of the city on **Highway 15** is the first of this mountain range's 19 recreation areas, offering downhill and cross-country skiing. The Laurentians originally became famous as a ski area in the 1920s, not so much for their elevation—the steepest vertical run is 2,131 feet—but for their close proximity to Montreal. Early entrepreneurs built North America's first mechanized ski tow at **Shawbridge**, and by the early 1930s, **Mont Tremblant** had the continent's first chair-lift. Today, such technology advances as halogen lighting and advanced snow-making permit skiing until midnight and for almost half of the year.

Mont Tremblant, about 1.5 to 2 hours from Montreal by car, remains the granddaddy of the region's ski areas, with 35 trails and nine lifts, as well as a ski school and day-care facilities. About an hour's drive from the city is the **St-Sauveur-des-Monts/Mont Avila** area. At 700 feet, this mountain is only one third as high as Mont Tremblant, but the 23 lighted slopes make it popular with urbanites who like to unwind on the boards after work. In the nearby town of **Piedmont**, visitors can trace the history of skiing in the Laurentians at the **Jack Rabbit Ski Museum** (220 Rue Beaulne; call for hours: 450/227.2886). The museum is named for Herman "Jack Rabbit" Johansen, a Norwegian engineering-

equipment salesman who literally blazed the trail for Nordic skiing in Canada; admission is charged. Active well into his hundreds (he died just before his one hundred twelfth birthday), he created 900 miles of cross-country trails in the Laurentian backwoods. The best known, the **Maple Leaf**, is accessible from two of the region's most popular lodges: **Far Hills Inn** (Chemin de la Gare, Val-Morin; 819/322.2014 or 800/567.6636) and **La Sapinière** (1244 Chemin de la Sapinière, Val-David; 819/322.2020 or 800/567.6635).

Estrie (The Eastern Townships)

Located on **Highway 10**, a 30- to 45-minute drive southeast of the city, the ski centers of the Eastern Townships (aka the Estrie region) have begun to rival the Laurentians for popularity in the last 10 years. One reason is their accessibility to the large population base in northern New York and Vermont; another is a joint marketing venture that combines the offerings of four recreation areas—**Bromont, Mont Sutton, Owl's Head**, and **Mont Orford**—into one attractive package called **Ski East**. Although none of the mountains match the Laurentians for height, they have nevertheless attracted many young professionals and a lot of development money in an area that retains its rural character. Unlike the Laurentians, Estrie has a sizable English-speaking population, because it was settled in the late 1700s by American loyalists who preferred British rule to life in the new republic.

Ski East offers 137 groomed downhill runs and a total of 31 lifts. Because facilities at all four ski areas are part of the same package, there's one information number (819/820.2020).

The region also has almost 500 miles of groomed Nordic trails, ranging from beginner to expert. One of the best ways to experience the area is the 22-mile **Skiwippi Inn-to-Inn Package**, which lets cross-country buffs sample the food and hospitality at three lodges: the **Hatley Inn, Hovey Manor**, and **Ripplecove Inn**. As you ski to the next inn, your luggage and vehicle are transported there in time for your arrival. For information, call 819/820.2020.

---

is based here, for those interested in tackling local peaks in Mont Tremblant, **Prevost**, and **Ste-Agathe** between April and October. Some of Val-David's traditional Quebecois stone houses with mansard roofs have been converted to charming inns and restaurants.

The resort town of **Ste-Agathe-des-Monts**, set on beautiful **Lac-des-Sables** about 60 miles north of Montreal, is the swinging metropolis of the Laurentians. In the early 1900s, the wealthy flocked to the area to build 42-room summer "cottages." Cruise around the lake on the *Bateau Alouette* (819/326.3656) to see these fabulous old estates, including the one built by Twentieth Century-

Fox tycoon William B. Fox. The lake also provides good sailing and three public beaches. Fine restaurants, cafés, and bistros fill the town, which is especially lively during Le Nord en Fête, a 10-day summer festival of popular music that draws Quebecois and international celebrities. **St-Faustin**, about 11 miles northwest of Ste-Agathe, is a tiny village in the shadow of **Mont-Blanc**. The nearby **Centre Educatif Forestier des Laurentides** (Chemin du Lac-du-Cordon, on Lac Caribou; 819/326.1606) is one of eight forestry education centers in Quebec. You can pick up maps and information on local flora and fauna at the center, then cross the lake on a boardwalk and hike along the wooded trails.

Farther north is Mont Tremblant, the highest of the Laurentian peaks (3,150 feet) and the highest skiable peak in Eastern Canada, boasting a vertical drop of 2,132 feet and Quebec's longest ski trail (3.2 miles). In autumn, you can ride a chairlift to the mountaintop and hike down through color-crazed maples. The village of Tremblant itself has been gussied up to the extent that it resembles a northern outpost of Disneyland, with spotless and bland restaurants and shops. The major resort is the very family-oriented **Fairmont Tremblant** (3045 Chemin Principal; 819/681.7000), which boasts an **Amerispa** health spa (819/681.7680) on the premises—after a day on the slopes, *the* place for a marvelous massage. The spa uses an excellent line of skin-care products, including Generium, with reputed anti-aging properties. For a spa experience that's closer to nature, visit the **Scandinave** spa (555 Montée Ryan; 819/425.5524) just outside Tremblant. Here you can have a massage, chill out in a sauna, or even experience the cool waters of the river—any time of year! **Mont Tremblant Park** is the oldest of Quebec's provincial parks, established in 1894. Summertime activities include hiking and horseback riding through forests that shelter black bears, white-tailed deer, lynx, and hundreds of species of birds. The park's 500 lakes and three major rivers create plenty of opportunities to swim, canoe, and fish. For more information, call 819/688.2281.

The Laurentians count more than 500 sugar shacks. A very well-known one is **Millette's** in Tremblant, a family affair established in 1957. The maple farm's 1,200 trees are tapped by hand; the sap is collected in buckets and put into a large horse-drawn container. The rustic "shack" itself is filled with antiques and features a dining room that can seat 300. Servers are outfitted in typical woodsman's costumes. There's also dog sledding in the forest. www.tremblant-sugar-shack.com

THE OUTAOUAIS

The source of lumber for Great Britain in the 18th century, today the Outaouais (pronounced "*Ooh*-ta-way") is Quebec's logging, hunting, and fishing country. A major attraction is the **Château Montebello**, the largest log structure in the world. When you arrive in the town of **Montebello**, stop at the kiosk at the old train station (502 Rue Notre Dame; 819/423.5689) for tourist information, local history, and a dose of train lore. Contact the **Outaouais Tourist Association** at 819/778.2222 or 800/265.7822, or visit www.outaouais-tourisme.org.

The origins of the **Château Montebello** can be traced to 1930, when US millionaire Harold Saddlemire hired

3,500 men and teams of draft horses to turn 10,000 red cedar logs into a private hunting and fishing club. As the site of his "Lucerne in Quebec," Saddlemire chose a 65,000-acre estate on the **Ottawa River** once owned by Louis Joseph Papineau, a French-Canadian insurgent leader who headed the Reform party a century earlier. Today, the log palace is the **Château Montebello**, a luxurious hotel belonging to the Fairmount chain (392 Rue Notre Dame, at Route 148; 819/423.6341 or 800/441.1414). When weather permits, stroll beside the Ottawa River, hike on 38 miles of trails, go horse-back riding, or rent tandem bicycles. Winter guests can cross-country ski, snowshoe, ice-skate, take a romantic sleigh ride, or simply relax by the fire in the lobby's 70-foot-high hexagonal fieldstone fireplace. The Château has a number of restaurants and hosts ethnic culinary festivals throughout the year. From Montreal, take Route 40 West to Route 17 to Hawkesbury, Ontario. Cross the Purley Bridge back to Quebec and turn left onto Route 148 West to Montebello. A short walk from the Château is the **Manoir Louis-Joseph Papineau** (392 Rue Notre Dame, at Route 148; 819/423.6965), built between 1846 and 1850 after the rebel leader returned from an 8-year exile. A guided tour takes you through 20 rooms of this towered and turreted mansion inspired by castles in France's Loire Valley. You may have an urge to nestle in one of the silk chairs with an old leather-bound volume by Molière and pass the afternoon gazing out at the Ottawa River. The manor is open daily between May and late October; admission is charged.

River rats claim the Outaouais region's **Rouge River**—called the Everest of white-water rafting in Canada—has some of the wildest currents on the North American continent. Even the rapids' names are intimidating: Washing Machine, Slice 'n' Dice, The Monster. Rafting guides from **Nouveau Monde** (100 Chemin de la Rivière Rouge in Calumet, off Kilmar; 819/242.7238, 800/361.5033) will brief you on bodysurfing and hydraulic action and will yank you back into the raft should you fall out. One guide per six-person raft leads day trips that include 5 to 6 hours of rafting, equipment, lunch and dinner, and *après*-rafting activities such as hot-tubbing and viewing video replays of the day's adventures. (For those who don't want to get splashed, there's bungee jumping.) To get to the base camp, take Route 40 West to Route 17 to Hawkesbury, Ontario. Cross the Purley Bridge back into Quebec and turn left onto Route 148 West. Other companies that offer day and weekend trips on the Ottawa River (Ontario side, near Beachburg) include **Owl Rafting** (613/646.2263) and **Wilderness Tours** (800/267.9166).

LANAUDIÈRE

Spanning the fertile foothills of the **Laurentians**, Lanaudière is tobacco-growing and horseback-riding country, with townships that bear such Irish names as *Kilkenny*, *Wexford*, and *Kildare*. Lanaudière has a large concentration of *cabanes à sucre* ("sugar shacks") where you can have an informal maple-syrupy feast, along with such other attractions as music festivals, hang gliding, and dogsled races. Between the end of June and early July, **Joliette**, one of the largest towns in

During Prohibition in the United States, Montreal came to be known as Sin City because of its free-flowing liquor, prostitution, and organized crime. Wealthy Americans bought summer homes around Lac Massawippi in Quebec's Eastern Townships near the US border to escape *la sécheresse*—the drought.

THE BEST

Josh Freed

Newspaper Columnist for the *Montreal Gazette*, Author, and Filmmaker

Montreal's best entertainment is found on its streets, where spring, summer, and fall are full-time celebrations of the fact that it is *not* winter. My favorite special events include

The **Montreal International Jazz Festival**, a 10-day outdoor bash that's Montreal's answer to Mardi Gras. Hundreds of thousands of people take over downtown, dancing, swigging beer, and stalling traffic until 1AM. If it happened in some cities, they'd declare martial law.

The **International Fireworks Competition**, which lights up city skies most weeks of the summer. On-site tickets are expensive, but wander down to the **Clock Tower** in **Old Montreal** and join the riverside crowds gazing for free. (Pyromaniacs can head for the **Jacques Cartier Bridge**—so close to the action they may want welder's goggles.)

Just for Laughs/Juste Pour Rire Festival, when comics from around the world take over **Rue St-Denis** and **The Main (Boulevard St-Laurent)** with outdoor routines in English and French.

St-Jean-Baptiste Day—Quebec's "national" parade on 24 June, which, contrary to rumor, is safe and exotic fun for outsiders. Listen to separatists shout, *"Le Québec aux Québécois"* and "Down with Canada!" Watch fleurs-de-lis wave. See the Canadian maple leaf burn. And yes, Virginia, you can speak English. For all the slogans, this is just a big family gathering, as warm and friendly as any on earth.

My favorite year-round activities include

The Main on Saturday morning, when it's a multicultural smorgasbord. Have a smoked-meat sandwich (medium spicy) at **Schwartz's Deli**, follow with a stand-up sausage sandwich at **Slovenia's**, then waddle down the street toward **Chinatown** ... for a *poutine*, a popular Quebec dish that features french fries covered in cheese curds and smothered in thick barbecue sauce (great for clearing your arteries of excess greenery).

Rue Prince Arthur, street-performer central, where you can bring your own bottle of wine and dine outdoors in the intimate company of a passing 12-person Peruvian flute group.

Old Montreal, a tourist spot that pays off, from "artists' alley" on **Place Jacques Cartier** to the **Old Port** area. Have a bowl of café au lait outdoors anywhere on the square or a crepe in the huge garden restaurant behind the historic **Hotel Nelson** building. Then take a hair-raising white-water raft trip around the island; it's a great way to relive the experience of the city's early explorers. Be warned: Like them, you'll wind up soaking wet.

As for nightlife, Montreal is a city of bars, many crowded onto the same streets. For English conversation, go to **Thursday's** or **Sir Winnie** on **Rue Crescent** and **Grumpy's** on **Rue Bishop**. To practice your French, try Rue St-Denis's classic bistros like **L'Express** or **Le Continental**.

---

the region, plays host to the Festival International de Lanaudière (450/759.7636), one of North America's premier celebrations of classical music. Highlights of the festival include musical Sunday brunches and performances held in the beautiful old local churches.

A walk through the narrow streets of **Vieux Terrebonne** (the oldest part of the town of **Terrebonne**) and around the **Île des Moulins (Island of Mills)** in the **Rivière de Milles Isles** goes past stone dikes, churches, historic manors, and the mill of an old landed estate granted in 1673 to Seigneur Daulier de Landes (who never left France). The mill ground flour for "sailor's biscuits" carried by canoe travelers halfway across the continent. **Laval Transport** buses leave Montreal regularly for Terrebonne from Metro station **Henri-Bourassa**, at the end of the orange line. By car, take Route 25 North to exit 17.

In the heart of waterfall country, **Rawdon** was settled by the Irish between 1815 and 1820, with the Scots arriving a few years later. Visitors are transported back to that era at the **Canadiana Village** (5750 Chemin Morgan, off Sixth Avenue; 450/834.4135), a re-created hamlet of 38 historic buildings that were moved lock, stock, and rooftop by proprietor Earle Moore onto his 150-acre property. Many movies have been filmed here.

At press time the village was closed but hoping to find a buyer by 2005. To reach Rawdon, take Route 40 to 125 North, then take the Rawdon exit. Spread a feast on a picnic table or rock near the spectacular **Dorwin Falls** on the **Ouareau River** (at the south entrance to Rawdon on Route 337) and look for the rock formation that resembles the head of the Algonquin sorcerer Nipissingue. Rejected in marriage by the maiden Hiawatha, he pushed her over the abyss and was frozen in stone by a thunderclap. **Dorwin Falls Park** is open between mid-April and mid-October. For tourist information, visit the **Rawdon Chamber of Commerce** at 3590 Rue Metcalfe or call 450/834.2282.

MONTÉRÉGIE

Apples are synonymous with Montérégie, a region graced by the Monteregian hills and steeped in the military history of Quebec. Visit **Rougemont**, 14 miles from exit 37 along **Highway 112**, in autumn to taste cider at local cellars, then learn all about apples and cider-making at the **Centre d'Interprétation de la Pomme** (11 Chemin Marieville, off Highway 112;

THE BEST

William Weintraub

Novelist and Documentary Filmmaker

A visit to the **Jean Talon Market** in **Little Italy** in early September, when the farmers offer a vast array of gorgeous crimson tomatoes, ready to be crushed into spaghetti sauce.

La Vieille Europe, the **Boulevard St-Laurent** grocery that carries more kinds of imported mustard than you ever thought could exist (to say nothing of the cheese).

The **McCord Museum of Canadian History**, a treasure trove of historic memorabilia that is everything a museum should be.

A walk through the magnificent **Mont-Royal Cemetery** to gaze on the tombstones of old robber barons like Sir Hugh Allan and Sir George Simpson, the great hockey player Howie Morenz, and Anna Leonowens, the real-life Anna from *The King and I.*

The quiet, sylvan countryside of the **Eastern Townships,** where in the summer one can escape from the cacophony of Montreal's jazz festival, film festival, comedy festival, theater festival, modern dance festival, and other orgies of culture, all based on the principle that quantity is more important than quality.

450/469.3600) and treat yourself to locally made apple pies, apple fritters, and applesauce.

The eight Monteregian hills that arc across the St. Lawrence plain were islands in the Champlain Sea 450 million years ago. Waves carved sand terraces on the slopes of **Mont St-Hilaire**, inspiring the Abnaki to name the mountain Wigwomadensis, after their wigwams of bent saplings. This highest of the Monteregian hills, which colonists rechristened Mont St-Hilaire, is still so unspoiled that UNESCO designated it the first **Biosphere Reserve** in Canada. The forest sustains oaks and pines, hundreds of mosses, 600 species of flowering plants, and 187 species of birds (bring binoculars). Mont St-Hilaire's 1,350-foot summit, sprinkled with Arctic vegetation, offers a fabulous view of Montreal (22 miles away), the **St. Lawrence Seaway**, and the **Richelieu River**. To get here by car, take Route 20 East to exit 113, then Route 133 South to Mont St-Hilaire. Walk along **Rue Richelieu** to see the presbytery built in 1772, the **Press-Vert** and **Lanctet** houses, and the 1838 **Rouville-Campbell Manoir**, which encloses a fine restaurant of the same name (2574 Bernard Pilon, at Route 106; 450/464.6060). Quebec's renowned ecclesiastical painter Ozias Leduc (1864-1955) was born in the **Correlieu House**, and the old church contains one of his frescoes. Craft boutiques, art galleries, inviting cafés and restaurants, and a pretty marina grace the town. Across from Mont St-Hilaire is picturesque **Old Beloeil**, a town on the Richelieu River that was established in 1694 as the landed estate of a seigneur. North of Old Beloeil, in **St-Marc-sur-Richelieu**, regional cooking awaits at the historic **Auberge Handfield** (555 Chemin du Prince/Route 223, off Route 20 East; 450/584.2226 or 800/667.1087). The derring-do heritage of **Richelieu Valley**, sometimes called "Valley of the Forts," includes a watercourse once known as "The River of Blood" and dungeons that imprisoned American colonial invaders and Quebec patriots; the area echoes with tales of stolen gold and haunted shipwrecks. Quebec's military history is etched in the old stones of **Fort Chambly** and **Fort Lennox**.

To start your Richelieu Valley tour, head out of Montreal on Route 20 or Highway 112 East. The pretty drive south along Route 223, past stone houses and churches dating from 1760, leads to the **Parc Historique National de Fort-Chambly**. In 1665, Captain Jacques Chambly built a wooden fortification against Iroquois attack, and the first European settlement on the Richelieu River developed around its borders, becoming the town of **Chambly**. Around 1710, the wooden fort was replaced by the massive stone fortress that stands today. After exploring the fort and military museum (658.1585), look at Chambly's old estates. The museum is open daily 10AM-5PM (until 6PM in July and August) between mid-May and Labor Day and Wednesday to Sunday, 10AM-5PM, Labor Day to November 25; admission is charged. Adventurers can go canoeing or rent a sailboat in the **Chambly Basin**. Head south on Route 223 toward the **Fort Lennox National Historic Park** (11 miles away) and stop at the historic military town of **St-Jean-sur-Richelieu**, where you can stroll past lovely Victorian houses along **Rues Jacques-Cartier, St-Charles**, and **St-Georges**, as well as the promenade along the Chambly Canal. The local museum is worth a visit too, and in August, St-Jean's skies fill with psychedelic colors during the international Hot Air Balloon Festival. From St-Jean, drive to **St-Paul-de-l'Île-aux-Noix**, from where you can take a leisurely cruise (in summer) on the *Fort St-Jean II* (450/346.2446), complete with traditional music. The 5-minute ride on the **Croisières Richelieu** passenger

---

The **Sun Life Building**, which opened in 1918, was once the bastion of English Montreal, but many Anglo institutions flew the coop when the separatist Parti Québécois came into power in 1976. Eventually, however, birds of a different feather returned to the structure: peregrines. Several years ago a project was initiated to encourage these rare falcons to remain and breed, but it did not succeed.

Eye contact in Montreal differs from that in other major cities. Whether it's because they spend more than 6 months hidden beneath winter clothes or because they are less socially inhibited than others, Montrealers do not shy away from making eye contact with strangers.

ferry (450/346.2446 or 800/361.6420) takes you to Île-aux-Noix (Island of Nuts), where the French once fought the English and the English fought the Americans for possession of Quebec. The name of the 210-acre island dates back to when hazelnuts grew wild here, and lore tells of the island having been sold for a bag of nuts. The northern end of the island is great for picnicking or hiking along the marshy riverbank populated by painted turtles, muskrats, bullfrogs, and diving kingfishers. At the southern tip of Île-aux-Noix is the impressive star-shaped Fort Lennox (1819), surrounded by a deep moat. Parks Canada guides take visitors through the guardhouse (1824), the gunpowder magazine (1823), officers' quarters, prison, and barracks. You can browse through the architectural exhibits and perhaps catch an 18th-century military skirmish (reenacted regularly during the summer). The admission price covers both the tour and exhibits. The fort is open daily between May and September. For more information, call 450/291.5700.

The St. Lawrence River rapids have deposited tons of relics and artifacts at Pointe-du-Buisson (333 Emond St, at Eighth Avenue; 450/429.7857), near Melocheville (19 miles southwest of Montreal). This 66-acre woodland was once the hunting, fishing, and burial grounds of native people, as well as a layover for explorers, missionaries, and merchants en route to the Great Lakes. University of Montreal archaeologists have excavated an Iroquois village with 7,965 objects, four fireplaces, the traces of 42 poles of an Iroquois longhouse, and stone utensils and harpoons created some 5,000 years ago. In summer you can take a guided archaeological tour, see the exhibits and laboratories, and attend workshops on Native Indian music, Iroquoian medicine, and arrowhead carving. Tours are offered daily between mid-May and Labor Day, and Saturday and Sunday between Labor Day and 7 October; admission is charged. From Montreal, take the Mercier Bridge and Route 132 West to Melocheville.

Those interested in locomotive history should head for St-Constant (from the Mercier Bridge, take Route 132 East toward La Prairie, to Route 209). Canada's first trains sped along at 25 miles an hour—an amazing sight for 19th-century eyes. Canadians called the new iron horses "smoking, clanging monsters," but they couldn't wait to ride them. The old trains now stand at St-Constant's Canadian Railway Museum (122 Rue St-Pierre, off Route 132; 450/632.2410), which has the largest collection of railway cars and memorabilia in Canada. Spread over 15 acres and housed in two giant hangars are antique locomotives, trams, trolleys, sleepers, street sweepers, boxcars, cabooses, parlor cars, diners, diesels, school cars, snowplows, horse-drawn sleighs, and a 200-car electric train. The museum is open daily between early May and early September, and Saturday and Sunday the rest of the year; admission is charged.

A few miles from St-Constant, huge tankers and other cargo ships pass through the Côte Ste-Catherine Locks into the St. Lawrence Seaway. Cyclists can pedal alongside in Côte Ste-Catherine Park (take the Champlain Bridge and follow the signs to Route 15; at La Prairie, make a right turn on Boulevard Marie-Victorian East and continue until you see signs for the park), a

narrow strip of land between the seaway and the thundering rapids. Bring binoculars to spy on the great blue herons in a nearby island refuge. The park is also a great place for views of the Montreal cityscape and Monteregian hills.

North of the small city of Sorel, about an hour's drive northeast of Montreal, the St. Lawrence River widens to form Lac St-Pierre, an archipelago sheltering 112 species of waterfowl. Seasonal flooding keeps the Sorel Islands in their naturally wild state, with marshes, canals, tall swamp grasses, and lonely beaches. The homespun Musée de l'Ecriture et Maison de Germaine Guevremont (3139 Chemin Chenal-du-Moine, at Île aux Fantômes; 450/746.1690), occupying most of the houses where novelist Guevremont once lived on the islet L'Îlette au Pée, is devoted to the lives and works of Quebec writers. Museum hours vary from May to September, so call ahead; contributions are accepted.

At Ste-Anne-de-Sorel, east of Sorel on Route 132, you can walk across a steel bridge from Chemin Chenal-du-Moine to Île aux Fantômes, then over to the tiny fishing village of Île d'Embarras, where two old icehouses have been turned into restaurants featuring gibelotte, the local fish stew. Take a cruise along the canals around Île d'Embarras, Île aux Corbeaux, and Île de Grâce, or paddle in a 12-person canoe among Lac St-Pierre's 103 islands. Croisières des Îles de Sorel Inc. ferries depart from the quay at 1665 Chemin Chenal-du-Moine. Call 743.7227 for schedules.

COEUR-DU-QUÉBEC

The region between Montreal and Quebec City is Quebec's heartland. It was once the territory of the Attikamek and Abenaki Indians, who allied with the French against the English; remnants of their culture can still be felt in the area's parks and museums. To reach Coeur-du-Québec from Montreal, take Route 20. Route 132 meanders along the St. Lawrence River, but takes twice as long.

Start your tour of Coeur-du-Québec with a visit to the Village Québécois d'Antan (1425 Rue Montplaisir, at Rue St-George, Drummondville; 819/478.1441), a reproduction of an Eastern Township from the years 1810 to 1910. This educational center attracts historians and academics, as well as Quebecois and French filmmakers. Fifty historic buildings and 30 reproductions are set on the rambling pastoral site, including log cabins, elegant mansard-roofed stone houses, a covered bridge constructed around 1878, and a vintage garage filled with antique cars. Costumed guides enliven demonstrations on the trades and crafts of colonial Quebec, including sawmill work, sash-weaving, and maple-sugar-making. The village is open daily between June and Labor Day, and on Saturdays and Sundays the rest of September; admission is charged. To reach Drummondville, take Route 20 East to exit 181.

Every July for 11 days, Drummondville hosts the Festival Mondial de Folklore, with traditional musicians and dancers from all over the world. Concerts, workshops, and informal jams provide the resonant background while colorful costumes and exotic instruments offer a visual smorgasbord. For a history lesson in how the Indians lived in the area before it was "settled," take Route 143 from Drummondville to Route 132 Northwest to **Pierreville/Odanak**; the Abenaki reserve is located at Odanak on the shores of the **St. Francis River**. The riverfront park has tepees, totem poles, and contemporary Abenaki sculpture, and the extensive 14-room **Musée des Abenakis** (Route 226; 568.2600) displays traditional dress, the scriptures in Abenaki, braided corn-husk masks, and native medicine. If you happen to be visiting on the last Sunday of July, join the powwow.

ESTRIE (THE EASTERN TOWNSHIPS)

Estrie is a French version of New England, with rambling farms, gabled houses, covered bridges, silver steeples, dusty general stores, and brightly painted barns scattered among mountains, glens, lakes, and tree-fringed rivers. In summer, the region is the place for sailing, mountain biking, and modern-day hunting and gathering at the many flea markets and shops; in winter, snow attracts legions of skiers. To get to Estrie, located between the St. Lawrence lowlands and Quebec's border

with Vermont, New Hampshire, and Maine, take the **Eastern Townships Autoroute** (Route 10) east or hop on a bus from the **Voyageur Station** (842.2281).

Though most residents of Estrie—the name comes from *est* for "east" and *patrie* for "homeland"—speak French, the region is generally referred to as the Eastern Townships because of Britain's role in its history. After the American Revolution, the British crown offered parcels of the territory to New England Loyalists fleeing the colonies. The land was divided into 11 counties and given such English names as Shefford, Stanstead, Compton, and Sherbrooke.

On the way to the village of **Knowlton** (exit 90 from the Eastern Townships Autoroute 10, then south on Route 243), a narrow winding road traces the wooded shoreline of **Lac Brome**, while groves of maples and pines shelter mansions, summer cottages, and lakeside gazebos. Knowlton is a charming spot for lunching or brunching, antiquing, and strolling beside the pond and lake (note the flocks of white ducks, Lac Brome's gastronomic specialty). The **Brome County Historical Museum** (130 Lakeside Road, at St. Paul Street; 243.6782) has nine buildings devoted to local memorabilia, archives, and Abenaki and military artifacts. The museum is open daily mid-May to mid-September; admission is charged. For hiking and bicycling maps and information on happenings around Knowlton and other

Notre-Dame-de-Bonsecours Chapel

parts of the Townships, contact **Tourism Estrie**, open Monday through Friday between 8:30AM and 6PM and Saturday and Sunday, 9AM to noon and 1PM to 6PM, at 25 Bocage Street, at King Street, West Sherbrooke; 819/820.2020.

From Knowlton, take 104 West to 215 South to **Sutton**, the soul of Estrie's cultural and countercultural life. Founded by Loyalists in 1797, this town attracts New Age entrepreneurs, artists, and other outdoor enthusiasts bound for **Mont Sutton** to ski, hike, and mountain bike. Many of Sutton's Victorian dwellings have been converted to shops, art galleries, restaurants, and cafés. In the heart of Estrie's Appalachians lies **Mont Orford Provincial Park**, a beautiful tract of wilderness, with lakes, forests, rivers, campsites, ski slopes, and hiking trails scattered around 2,750-foot **Mont Orford** (from Montreal, take Eastern Townships Autoroute 10 to exit 115, then Route 141 North). Summer pleasures in a region that is known as the **Station Touristique de Mont Orford** include swimming, windsurfing, hiking, golf, biking, and horseback riding; hiking and chairlift rides to the summit are autumn draws; and skiing, ice-skating, and snowshoeing are popular winter activities. The 222-acre **Mont Orford Arts Center** is the park's cultural treasure. Between May and September, the air rings with the sounds of music as students practice in studios on the center's grounds, preparing for the summer festival of daily concerts and recitals by up-and-coming musicians training to be professionals (for tickets and schedules, call 819/843.3981). For park information, call 819/843.6233.

The Mont Orford area has three exceptional restaurants featuring regional cuisine: **Auberge Estrimont** (44 Avenue de l'Auberge, at Route 141, Orford; 418/266.2165 or 877/778.8977), **Auberge L'Etoile sur le Lac** (1150 Rue Principale Ouest, off Highway 10, Magog; 819/843.6521 or 800/567.2727), and the **Auberge Georgeville** (71 Chemin Channel/Route 247, Georgeville; 819/843.8683 or 888/843.8686).

To reach the lively town of **Magog** from Mont Orford, take 141 South or bicycle along the 8-mile bike path from **Mont Orford Provincial Park** to the head of **Lac Memphremagog** in downtown Magog. Located at the northern tip of the narrow 30-mile-long lake that links Quebec with Vermont, Magog has a beautifully reland-scaped beachfront dotted with elegant gazebos. The lake is ideal for sailing, windsurfing, and swimming, and the downtown is filled with shops and art galleries. For information on scuba diving, contact the **Centre de plongée Memphre**, in nearby Georgeville (819/822.0302).

The west side of Lac Memphremagog is dominated by the Benedictine abbey of **St-Benoit-du-Lac** (819/843.4080), which rises like a Bavarian castle out of the mist. The monastery was designed by **Dom Paul Bellot**, a French monk who settled there in 1937 and became one of Quebec's major ecclesiastical architects. Visitors can tour the abbey's rich mosaic interior, listen to mellow Gregorian chants, and purchase cider and cheeses made by the monks.

In the protective shadow of Mount Orford sits the beautiful **Center de Santé d'Eastman** (895 Chemin des Diligences; 450/297.3009 or 800/665.5272), a destination spa recognized as one of the "100 best spas of the world" in the book by the same title (Globe Pequot Press, 2003). A two-story pavilion that opened in 1999 houses all of the treatment and relaxation rooms plus a swimming pool, Watsu pool, hammam steam room, and hydrotherapy baths. There are also several miles of hiking and ski trails on the property. Spa packages are available.

North Hatley on **Lac Massawippi** is Estrie's choicest resort village. Boutiques, antiques shops, and graceful old inns line its colorful main street, and a lovely municipal beach borders the lake. Early in the 20th century, wealthy Americans weary of Prohibition built holiday homes in North Hatley, but today it's a haven for writers, painters, sculptors, and artisans. Highlights include **The Piggery** (819/842.2431), a pig barn converted into a charming English-language theater, with shows in the summer; **Equitation Massawippi** (819/842.4249) for a day of horseback riding; and three top restaurants: **Auberge Hatley** (Route 108, exit 29 off Route 55 South; 819/842.2451), **Le Café Massawippi** (3050 Chemin Capelton, off Route 108; 819/842.4528), and **Manoir Hovey** (575 Chemin Hovey, off Route 108; 819/842.2421 or 800/661.2421). The Auberge Hatley and Manoir Hovey are also inns, beautifully situated by Lake Massawippi (Auberge Hatley, 819/842.2451 or 800/336.2451).

Nearby **Coaticook** (Route 143 South to Route 141 East) is worth a stop to explore its 230-foot gorge and walk across the world's longest suspended footbridge.

In the late 1960s, former Montreal Mayor Jean Drapeau, a lover of classical music, opened a restaurant called La Vaisseau d'Or in the former Windsor Hotel. Patrons rolled their eyes in disbelief over the restaurant's rule of silence, which was put into effect every time its 20-piece orchestra began to play. Not surprisingly, La Vaisseau d'Or closed within a few years "for renovations" and never reopened.

The first high-ranking member of the British royal family to visit Canada was the Prince of Wales, who arrived in Montreal on 25 August 1860. The future King Edward VII, then 19 years old, opened the Victoria Bridge, linking the city with the south shore of the St. Lawrence River. The bridge's mile-and-a-half span was then the longest in the world; it required the work of 3,000 men and over 10 years to complete.

Bras d'Or, the hydrofoil boat on display outside the Musée Maritime Bernier, was named after the lake near Alexander Graham Bell's summer home in Baddeck, Nova Scotia. The creator of the telephone also invented the HD-4, the world's first hydrofoil. When the craft ran its trials on Bras d'Or Lake in 1919, it reached a speed of 70 miles per hour, astonishing for the time. Other contraptions devised by Bell include the Silver Dart airplane, a machine for converting seawater to fresh water, and the "vacuum jacket," a forerunner to the iron lung.

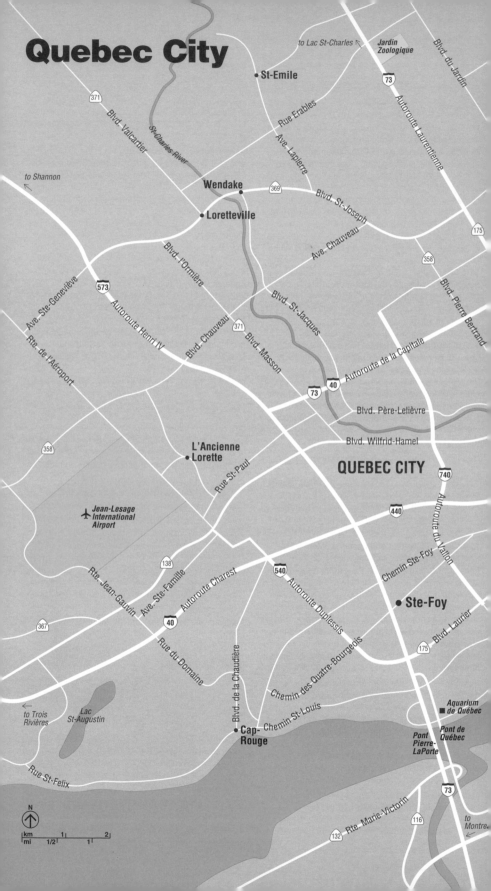

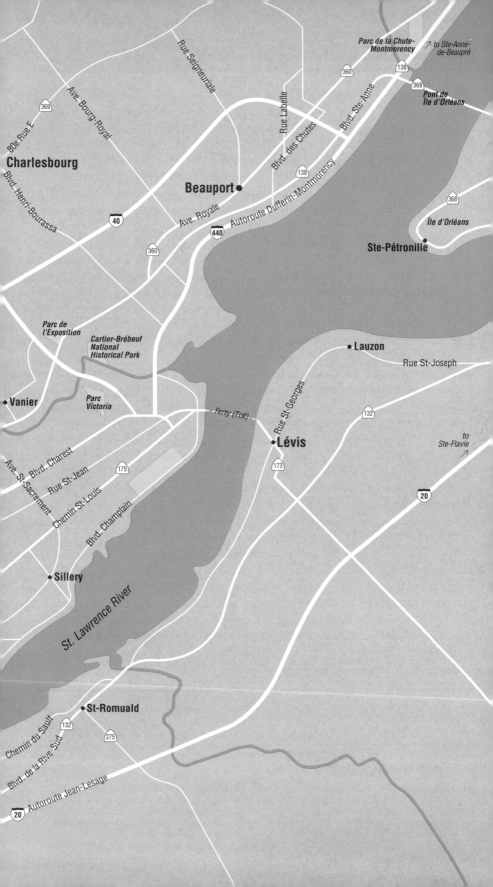

Carved into a steep cliff, Quebec City—the only walled city left in North America—is as beautiful in its natural setting as it is rich in history and Old World charm. From its 17th- and 18th-century architecture and cobblestoned streets to its French-speaking citizens and sidewalk cafés, this hilly town is undeniably European. Quebec City's French roots date back to 1608, and though it was ruled by the British—who built the walls—for 2 centuries, 95% of the more than 600,000 residents speak French, rather than English.

The 300-foot cliffs of **Cap-Diamant** abruptly split the town into two: a walled **Upper Town** on the cliffs, and **Lower Town** below. If you're so inclined, you can scale the heights on foot on the **Escalier Casse-Cou (Breakneck Stairway)** or on the steep **Côte de la Montagne**. Those less hardy often opt for a lift on the funicular.

History is palpable here. The de rigueur visit to **Old Town** usually starts with a promenade along the elegant **Dufferin Terrace**, above the waters of the **St. Lawrence River** and beneath the brick turrets and copper roofs of the fairy-tale **Château Frontenac** hotel. Other musts include meandering among the boutiques on **Rues de Petit Champlain** and **Sous-le-Fort** and visiting the **Musée de la Civilisation** and restored **Old Port**. When British General James Wolfe laid siege to Quebec City in 1759, more than 40,000 cannonballs and 10,000 bombs blew the Lower Town to rubble. A number of thick-walled, steep-gabled stone houses survived, though, and thanks to Quebec government programs, these and other significant structures have been restored to their former state.

Place Royale rests on the site of the oldest permanent European settlement north of Mexico. Three thousand years ago, this rocky point on the river was a seasonal Native Indian fishing encampment. In 1608, Samuel de Champlain established a fur-trading post on the premises, and the harbor became the commercial heart of New France. Today, it buzzes with lively street entertainers.

The attractions of Quebec City extend beyond the boundaries of the Upper Town. Among these sights are **National Battlefields Park**, with its 250 acres of woods and gardens, artillery artifacts, and the **Martello Towers**; the stately government structures at **Parliament Hill**; and the **Citadel**, an immense fortress. The largest occupied fortification in North America (Canada's Royal 22nd Regiment is in residence), the military installation was built by between 1820 and 1832 as a defense against American attack following the War of 1812. From this promontory, revel in the view of the city 400 feet below, with the **Côte-de-Beaupré** and the ever-present St. Lawrence River. When you're ready to take a break from Quebec City's historic *rues* and *ruelles*, you might motor up the Charlevoix coast to explore two islands: **Île aux Coudres** and its windmills, or **Île d'Orléans**, a bucolic area whose six villages contain many historic buildings from the French regime.

Area code 418 unless otherwise noted.

Getting to Quebec City

Jean-Lesage International Airport

Jean-Lesage International Airport (Canadian Customs, 640.3351, 800/479.9165) is located approximately 18 km (11 miles) west of downtown, about a 30-minute drive away. No matter what time of day you arrive, you're unlikely to encounter traffic problems.

Driving from the airport, take Route de l'Aéroport to Highway 540 (Autoroute Duplessis) until you reach Boulevard Laurier, which will take you straight to **Old Quebec**. Note that this street changes names: to Chemin St-Louis, then Grande Allée, and finally Rue St-Louis.

Taxis traveling from the airport to downtown will cost you $20 to $25; hail them outside any of the airport's three exits. **Autocars Dupont** (649.9226, 888/558.7668) and **Autobus La Québécoise** (872.5525) operate a shuttle bus service from the airport to the city.

BON APPÉTIT: WHAT'S COOKING IN QUEBEC

The history of Quebec's hearty farmer-and-lumberjack food is centuries old. The first 17th-century settlers from Normandy and Brittany drew on culinary traditions from France and created robust dishes that fueled them through long, laborious days in the forests and fields. *Tourtières* (meat pies), *cipaille* (deep-dish pie layered with meat, fowl, and vegetables), *fèves au lard* (pork and beans), *cretons* (squares of coarse pork pâté), *tarte au sucre* (sugar pie), and *galettes de sarrasin* (buckwheat pancakes) were among the favored dishes. These preparations were spiced with cinnamon and cloves or *herbes salées* (parsley, onions, parsnips, savory, and celery leaves preserved in coarse salt) and left to simmer in the pot or bake in the oven for the day.

Over the course of time, distinct regional cuisines developed in Quebec, based on locally available meat, game, and fish. **Lac Brome** in the **Eastern Townships** is known for its succulent duck; the **Sorel Islands** in **Montérégie** for *gibelotte*, a savory fish stew; **Lac Saint-Jean** for its unique *tourtière* (the esteemed ground meat-and-game pie that is the staple of any traditional meal) and its soup of *gourganes* (similar to fava beans) and *ouananiche* (freshwater salmon), **Beauce** for maple-syrup products and maple-flavored dishes; **Charlevoix** for lamb *pré salé*, whose tangy taste originates in the salt-sprayed meadows where the lambs feed; the **Gaspé Peninsula** for salmon and cod dishes (including cod tongues and cheeks); and the **Magdalen Islands** for snow crabs and lobsters.

As modern transportation and high-tech communications blur differences among the cultures of the world, chefs in Quebec have banded together to assure the distinctness of the province's various cuisines. *La Cuisine Regionale au Québec* is a network of restaurants established to encourage the evolution of local cooking styles that reflect the culture, history, geography, and climate of each of Quebec's 12 regions.

Chefs have also responded to modern concerns about eating healthfully. Today's cuisine features leaner meat in reduced sauces served with a variety of vegetables. Regardless of culinary fashion, however, recipes remain based on wild and domestic meat, game, and seafood. Though simple old-fashioned dishes such as beans and lard, pea soup, meat pies, and maple-sugar pie still warm the winter hearts of even the most sophisticated Quebecois gourmets, imaginative Quebec restaurants also feature smelt, eel, duck, quail, pheasant, veal, lamb, rabbit, caribou, venison, buffalo, and wild boar. Seasonal products used as garnishes or in sauces or desserts include wild mushrooms, fiddlehead ferns, goat cheese, cranberries, rhubarb, blueberries, and maple syrup. And Quebec cheeses now rival European counterparts for variety and flavor.

For a list of Quebec restaurants serving regional cuisines, contact local tourist offices or call **Tourisme Québec** at 514/873.2015 (from the Montreal area) or 800/363.7777 (from elsewhere).

If you make arrangements ahead of time, you can take a limousine to wherever you want to go in the Quebec City area. To make reservations, call **Signature Limousine** (692.3733), **Guy Samson Limo** (655.6820 or 652.7316), **Limousine A-1/Limousine Aeroport** (523.5059), or **Aristo Car Limousine** (660.5055).

AIRLINES

Air Canada 692.0770, 888/321.3652

Canadien International 692.1031, 800/665.1177

Air Nova 692.0770, 800/630.3299

RENTAL CARS

Avis.......................................523.1075, 800/879.2847

Discount 692.1244

Hertz 694.1224, 800/263.0678

Tilden 694.1727, 800/871.1224

BUS TERMINALS

For long-distance travel, the **Central Bus Station (Gare centrale des bus)** is located at 320 Rue Abraham-Martin, at Boulevard Charest, as well as in the suburb of

Ste-Foy, at 2700 Boulevard Laurier, in the Laurier shopping center. **Orleans Express Coach Lines** (525.3000) links Quebec City with the rest of the province and connections to points beyond.

TRAIN STATIONS

The greater Quebec City area has two train stations: **Gare du Palais**, 450 Rue de la Gare-du-Palais, between the post office and courthouse in downtown (692.3940), and **Gare de Ste-Foy**, 3255 Chemin de la Gare, at Rue Beaupré, in Ste-Foy (800/361.1235). Both offer excellent service heading west to Montreal and east to New Brunswick via **Rail Canada** (88/VIA RAIL).

Getting around Quebec City

BUSES

Urban Transport offers local bus service throughout downtown Quebec City as well as between suburbs. Exact change ($2.25), a daily bus pass ($5.10), or tickets, which can be purchased in convenience stores for $1.90 each, are required. For information, call **Société de Transport de la Communauté Urbaine de Québec** at 627.2511.

DRIVING

Avoid driving within the walls of the Old City: Old Quebec is filled with narrow, winding cobblestone streets and too many confusing one-way stretches. Also, some road signs are posted in French only, so it's a good idea to familiarize yourself with signage before getting behind the wheel (see page 6 in the main orientation). Parking is also a major hassle, and to make matters worse, the parking authorities are positively vigilant about handing out tickets. (A word of warning: Although towing is rare, parking citations aren't, and tourists won't get a break on violations.)

Street parking is limited in Quebec City, so your best bet may be to put your car in a garage. There are numerous pay lots and garages in town; look for green signs with a big **P** or call the **Société Parc Autos du Québec Métropolitain** at 681.4811 for information on the facility closest to your destination.

TAXIS

Hailing a cab on the street in Quebec is quasi-impossible, as most are radio-dispatched. They're easiest to find at major hotels, across from **City Hall** on Côte de la Fabrique, or on Rue Dalhousie, across from Place Royale. Otherwise, pick up the phone and call; generally, you can expect to wait 5 to 15 minutes. Taxi companies include **Taxi Coop** (525.5191), **Taxi Québec** (525.8123), and **Taxi Laurier** (651.2727).

FYI

CONSULATE

US..........2 Terrasse-Dufferin, behind Château Frontenac, 692.2095

Throughout the 17th and 18th centuries, the intrepid fur traders known as *voyageurs* in New France used Montreal as an embarkation point for their exploratory travels across North America. Most journeys aimed to extend the fur trade, but territorial expansion was another goal, pursued in particular by a famous governor, Louis Buade Comte de Frontenac, who actively encouraged land acquisition for France during his tenure between 1763 and 1782.

In the 1800s, lectures by touring authors were big events, reviewed by the local papers. Some Montrealers liked Mark Twain's lectures so much that they inducted him into their snowshoe club.

It's an architectural no-no to design a bridge with curves, but the Jacques-Cartier Bridge over the St. Lawrence River was built curved to avoid demolishing the factories on the proposed site. This curve has resulted in several accidents, earning the epithet "the Curve of Death."

HOSTELS

Youth hostels are located at **Auberge de la Paix** (31 Rue Couillard, at Rue St-Jean; 694.0735) and **Centre International de Séjour du Québec** (19 Rue St-Ursule, at Rue St-Jean; 694.0755, 800/461.8585).

HOURS

Opening hours of shops, attractions, and so on are listed with entries wherever possible. Most shops in Quebec City are open Monday to Wednesday, 10AM-6PM; Thursday and Friday, 10AM-9PM; Saturday, 10:00AM-5PM; and Sunday, noon-5PM. Winter hours can be more variable than in Montreal. To avoid disappointment, if you're in doubt always call ahead.

MONEY

Most banks are open Monday through Friday, 10AM to 3PM, with some also operating on Saturday morning. The main branches of banks and credit unions (*Caisses Populaires*) will exchange most foreign currencies and traveler's checks.

For the best rates, check with **Transchange Inc.** (43 Rue Buade, in front of the Basilica; 694.6906) or the **American Express Customer Service Centre** at the Laurier shopping center in Ste-Foy (2700 Boulevard Laurier, between Chemin de la Gare and Rue Beaupré, 658.8820). The most convenient ATM to the main **Visitors' Center** (60 Rue d'Auteuil, at the corner of Rue St. Louis) is the **Échange de devises Montréal**, at 12 Rue Ste-Anne (corner of Rue de Fort, 694.1014).

PUBLICATIONS

Quebec City's main French dailies are *Le Soleil* and *Le Journal de Québec*. The English-language newspaper is the *Chronicle Telegraph*, the oldest newspaper in North America; for news about Quebec province and Quebec City, pick up the *Montreal Gazette*. *Voir* is a free weekly tabloid about the art scene that's published in French but isn't hard to decipher if you don't speak the language. Most major newsstands carry English-language dailies from around Canada, as well as US newspapers and magazines.

TOURS

Guided tours of Quebec City range from bus outings to architectural and/or historical walks to quaint horse-and-buggy rides.

BY BUS

Old Quebec Tours, Inc.....................................664.0460

Grayline 649.9226

Quebec City Tours 836.8687

On Foot

Maple Leaf Guide Services..............................622.3677

Contact Quebec, Inc. 692.2801

Horse-and-Buggy Rides

Belle Epoque calèches....................................687.6653

Calèches du Vieux Quebec.............................683.9222

Horse-drawn trolley tours 624.3062

VISITOR INFORMATION

For the province: **Maison du Tourisme de la Province de Québec** (12 Rue Ste-Anne, across from the Château Frontenac; 800/363.7777); Labor Day to 20 June, open daily, 9AM-5PM; 21 June to Labor Day, open daily, 8:30AM-7:30PM.

For the city: **Office du Tourisme de la Communauté Urbaine de Québec** (835 Ave Wilfrid-Laurier; 649.2608, 692.2471); 24 June to Thanksgiving (second Monday of October), open daily, 8:30AM-7PM, Mid-Oct–23 June, M-Th, 9AM-5PM; F, 9AM-6PM; Sa, 9AM-5PM; Su, 10AM-4PM. Here you will find all manner of information about Quebec City and can even make free calls to local hotels.

Tourist information agents also cruise through the historical district of Old Quebec, riding green mopeds with a flag bearing a question mark (daily, 7 June-Labor Day).

To learn about historical and contemporary Quebec, visit the **Urban Life Interpretation Center** (43 Côte de la Fabrique, at Rue St-Jean; 691.4606), a museum open daily 24 June-Labor Day, 10AM-5PM; open the rest of the year Tu-Su, 10AM-5PM. Admission is charged.

Phone Book

EMERGENCIES

Ambulance/Fire/Police 911

Dental 653.5412, 524.2444

Distress Center 686.2433

Emergency Road Service (CAA/AAA Quebec)..............
....800/222.4357

Lost Passports 692.2095

Medical 648.2626

Poison Control......................656.8090, 800/463.5060

Rape Hot Line 522.2120

OTHER IMPORTANT NUMBERS

Bibliothèque (library)......................................529.0924

Convention Center 644.4000

Ferry 644.3704, 837.2408

Nonemergency Health Information 648.2626

Pharmacie Brunet 623.1571

Police (nonemergency) 800/461.2131

Postal Service 694.6175

Road Conditions 648.7766

Tides 648.7293

Veterinary Services...872.5355

Weather..648.7766

Nestled around the base of **Cap-Diamant**, the narrow cobblestone streets and buildings that form the heart of the Lower Town in Old Quebec are among Canada's oldest. This wedge-shaped area, bounded by the city wall to the west, the **Old Port** and the **St. Lawrence River** to the east, and the **St. Charles River** to the north, was the cradle of New France. Although Samuel de Champlain built his **Fort St-Louis** on a promontory overlooking the St. Lawrence, his first "habitation"—a couple of simple wooden

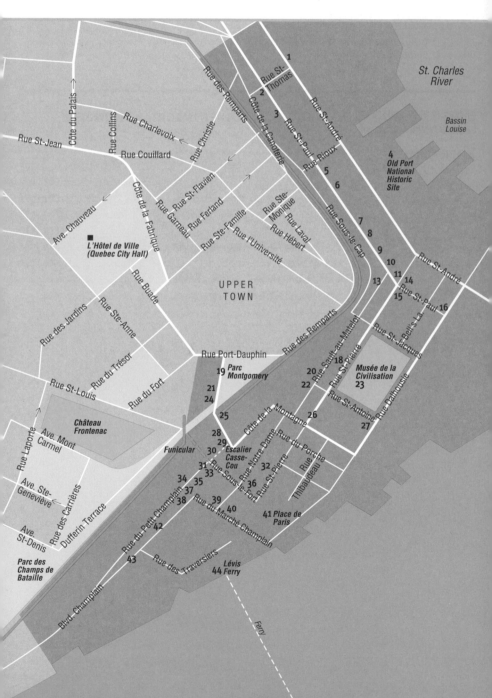

buildings comprising a trading post, fortifications, living quarters, and a garden—was constructed on the site of what is now **Place Royale**, the center of the Lower Town, near the river's edge.

In an era when boats were the primary mode of transportation in the New World, the St. Lawrence River was the "highway" to the rest of Canada. The Lower Town developed along the north shore of the riverbank and soon became a commercial and shipping hub. By 1662, more than 35 parcels of land had been granted to merchants, fur traders, and other entrepreneurs who set up shop around the base of Cap-Diamant. Twenty years later, a disastrous fire swept through the area, destroying the fragile wooden stores and warehouses. The devastating conflagration led to a revamping of the building codes, and the new structures were built of solid stone with walls up to 3 feet thick, recessed windows, and *pare-feus*—walls at the base of the chimneys to prevent future fires from leaping across the rooftops. Commerce thrived anew in the rebuilt Lower Town, and for the next 2 centuries entrepreneurs poured into the area, first to trade furs and later to become shipbuilders, brokers, and merchants. They created more land at the base of the cliffs between the promontory and the water by filling in the shoreline. In 1700, the St. Lawrence came all the way up to the site of the present-day **Musée de la Civilisation**. Fifty years later, the beach had disappeared under rows of warehouses and wharves.

The Lower Town came into its own as a departure point for oceangoing vessels carrying lumber and other raw materials destined for the motherland (by now Great Britain). **Old Port**, an 82-acre complex of warehouses, quays, and sheds, bustled with thousands of European immigrants who flocked to Canada in the early 1800s to start a new life. By the end of the 19th century, trains had overtaken sailing ships as the main mode of cargo transportation, and the port had fallen into disrepair, becoming even more of a wasteland (as did much of the Lower Town) with the advent of air travel.

But in the early 1970s, the Lower Town began to undergo a renaissance. Unsavory, run-down areas were spruced up, rebuilt, and renovated to appeal to the burgeoning

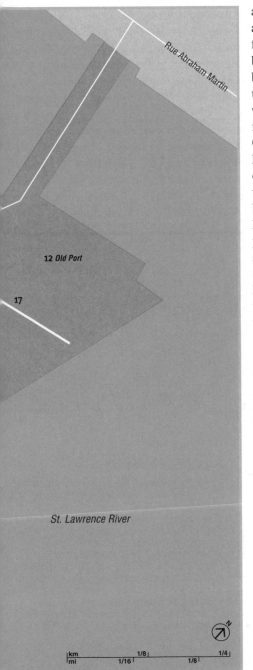

Rue Abraham Martin

12 *Old Port*

17

St. Lawrence River

km   1/8   1/4
mi   1/16   1/8

tourist trade. The federal and provincial governments poured in money and laborers to return the area to its New France heyday. Much attention was devoted to historic accuracy—from the types of materials used to the number of panes on the windows to the colors of the buildings—and the painstaking efforts were rewarded when UNESCO declared Quebec City a World Heritage Site in 1985.

Today the lively *quartier* offers a joyous mix of craft and souvenir stores, high-fashion boutiques, trendy apartments, hot restaurants, charming hotels, and fascinating museums, all housed in tiny, low-beamed structures or glitzy glass-and-steel buildings that somehow manage not to look out of place. Throughout the area, street musicians, jugglers, and other entertainers add to the festive atmosphere.

Old Port and the area to the northwest are the only less-than-bright spots on the Lower Town landscape. Much of Old Port has been renovated, but parts still have the look of an unfinished construction site—largely because of ongoing battles between developers who want to build condominiums and historical purists who don't want to build anything. Then too, part of Old Port is a working harbor with industrial warehouses, grain elevators, and storage sheds.

To reach the Lower Town, walk down—way down—the wooden stairs that lead from the **Dufferin Terrace**, in front of the **Château Frontenac**, to the left of the **Funicular Railway**—or take the funicular. The 2-minute ride to the Lower Town costs $1.50 each way; it's a welcome sight indeed when you need help getting up the hill. The funicular runs daily between 7:30AM and midnight between 20 June and Labor Day, and between 7:30AM and 11:30PM the rest of the year. Call 692.1132 for more information.

---

1 LE MARCHÉ DU VIEUX PORT

Between May and early November, this vibrant open-air market bustles with farmers and flower-growers who come from around the region to sell their fresh produce and vivid blooms. You'll find everything you need for a savory alfresco lunch—cheese, fresh fruits and vegetables, and home baked bread. If so inclined, you can buy a bottle of wine at one of the nearby *dépanneurs* (variety stores), delicatessens, or grocery stores. (Officially, you're not supposed to drink in public, but police turn a blind eye, particularly if picnickers are discreet.) If you're visiting in December, don't miss the Christmas market. ◆ Daily, May–Dec. 160 Rue St-André (past Rue St-Thomas)

2 HÔTEL LE SAINT-PAUL

$$ This small hotel has a lot going for it: 27 soundproofed, individually decorated rooms, a great location just underneath the ramparts of Old Quebec and within walking distance of the Via Rail train station, and direct access to the casual restaurant **Le Péché Véniel**. The building itself dates from the 19th century but has been completely renovated, so that even rooms that feature original brick walls and exposed wooden beams have a contemporary feel. Every room has cable TV, direct tele-

phone lines, and Internet access. There is also a selection of larger junior and executive suites. ◆ 229½ Rue St-Paul (at Rue St-Thomas). 694.4414, 888/794.4414; fax 694.0889 &

Le Péché Véniel

2 LE PÉCHÉ VÉNIEL

★$ This restaurant presents an interesting mix of casual bistro offerings in a warm, family-friendly setting with efficient service. Adults can enjoy such dishes as authentic Lac Saint-Jean meat pie, warm ginger-perfumed chicken salad, and butterflied salmon and sea pearls with lemon and leek butter while kids tuck into tasty homemade onion rings, hot dogs, or hamburgers. The list of beverages, both alcoholic and nonalcoholic, is extensive, and among the dessert choices is a selection of homemade pies. ◆ Canadian ◆ Daily, breakfast, lunch, and dinner. 233 Rue St-Paul (at Rue St-Thomas). 692.5642 &

3 RUE ST-PAUL

Once a thoroughfare connecting the wharves and warehouses that jutted onto the St. Charles River, this quaint street has become Quebec City's premier antiques district. The houses, which are tall and narrow with thick stone walls, paned windows, dormers, and steep, brightly colored roofs, are huddled cheek-to-cheek under the ramparts of the Upper Town. Over the years, many of them have been turned into trendy cafés and antiques shops, dealing in everything from junk to rare New France relics. ♦ Between Rues Dalhousie and St-Thomas

4 THE OLD PORT OF QUEBEC INTERPRETATION CENTER

Located at the far end of the Old Port, this exhibition hall contains a remarkable collection of memorabilia and archival material about the age of sailing, the lumber trade, and shipbuilding, an old and honored trade around the Old Port. At one time, four Quebec City families controlled the shipbuilding business, which was initiated by Intendant Jean Talon (1665-1672) as part of his plan for the development of New France. His mandate was to convert the small fur-trading and missionary outpost into a profitable, well-populated royal province. Talon also developed a legal framework for the colony (Quebec, unlike the rest of Canada, still operates under a French-based civil code) and encouraged agriculture, fishing, and trade with the West Indies. The central exhibit at the historic site, *Quebec, Gateway to America*, documents the importance of the lumber trade to 19th-century North America. Displays on the upper floors illustrate processes used in logging and shipbuilding. ♦ Admission. 1 Apr-1 May, by reservation; 2 May-2 Sept, daily, 10AM-5PM; 3 Sept-7 Oct, daily, 1PM-5PM; 8 Oct-31 Mar, by reservation. 100 Rue St-André (on Bassin Louise). 648.3300

5 BOUTIQUE À LA CAPUCINE

Primitively carved and painted cows, horses, and sheep, as well as decoys, old candlestick holders, church pews, and stained-glass windows abound in this enchanting shop specializing in antiques that reflect popular Quebec culture. Though it's located slightly off the beaten path, the store's wonderful hodge-podge of curios and collectibles is worth the trek. Like most of the antiques dealers along this stretch of Rue St-Paul, owner Yves Bourget keeps erratic hours, so it's a good idea to phone first to make sure someone is there. ♦ Daily. 145 Rue St-Paul (at Rue Rioux). 692.5318

5 LE RENDEZ-VOUS DU COLLECTIONNEUR

Unusual toys, Tiffany lampshades, oil lamps, antique dolls, and Depression-era glass are the specialties of this antiques store. Owner Renald Poulin is on hand to assist would-be purchasers. ♦ M-Sa; call ahead for hours. 143 Rue St-Paul (at Rue Rioux). 692.3099

6 LES CAFÉS DU SOLEIL

Specialty teas and coffees from around the world and all the paraphernalia to go with them—filters, pots, mugs, and coffee-making contraptions from France and Belgium—are sold in this cute, compact gourmet shop. ♦ Daily. 137 Rue St-Paul (between Rues St-Pierre and Rioux). 692.1147

6 ANTIQUITÉS AUX QUATRE ÉPAULES

Owner Gaetan Beaudoin is an expert in religious art, which is now very much in demand in this once-pious province. Here you'll find an intriguing collection of plaster saints, angels, and other religious articles that have been culled from various churches. Prices depend on the rarity of the piece. ♦ M-Sa. 133 Rue St-Paul (between Rues St-Pierre and Rioux). 828.2644

7 DÉCENIE

This gallery specializes in furniture and furnishings from the 1930s to the 1970s. ♦ M-F, noon-5PM; Sa-Su. 117 Rue St-Paul (between Rues St-Pierre and Rioux). 523.2544

Of the more than four million tourists who visit Quebec City each year, half are Quebecers from other parts of the province, a quarter are American, and the remainder come from elsewhere in Canada and around the world. The fastest-growing segment of the city's tourism industry is travel by cruise ships. During the summer, as many as five luxury liners are docked in Quebec's port at any given time.

Restaurants/Clubs: **Red** | Hotels: **Purple** | Shops: **Orange** | Outdoors/Parks: **Green** | Sights/Culture: **Blue**

8 BOUTIQUE AUX MEMOIRES

This venerable boutique is crammed to the rafters with grandfather clocks, folk art, silverware, and period furniture, including unusual bird's-eye maple dressers. Proprietor Louis Bolduc does appraisals too. ♦ M-Sa. 105 Rue St-Paul (between Rues St-Pierre and Rioux). 692.2180

9 GERARD BOURGUET ANTIQUAIRE

Named after owner Gerard Bourguet, this reputable establishment attracts well-heeled collectors who know what they're looking for and don't mind paying high prices to get it. New France armoires with carved wooden doors are especially hot items here. ♦ M-Sa. 101 Rue St-Paul (between Rues St-Pierre and Rioux). 694.0896

9 BUFFET DE L'ANTIQUAIRE

★$ Cheap and cheerful with a bright green décor and fake hanging foliage, this restaurant offers the likes of egg salad sandwiches, hamburgers, *poutine* (french fries with cheese and hot chicken sauce), delicious French toast, and thick sugar pies. The place is popular with local antiques dealers, shop owners, and office workers in search of simple food at decidedly nontourist prices. ♦ Continental ♦ Daily, breakfast, lunch, and dinner. 95 Rue St-Paul (between Rues St-Pierre and Rioux). 692.2661

10 LE SAINT-MALO

★★$$$ Robust French provincial fare is served in this cozy café frequented by locals. Good bets are marinated herring, rabbit, quail, and *rognons d'agneau* (lamb kidneys). The intimate ambiance and low ceilings border on cramped, so, weather permitting, opt for one of the six tables outside under the welcoming red awning. ♦ French ♦ Daily, lunch and dinner. Reservations recommended. 73 Rue St-Paul (at Rue Sault-au-Matelot). 692.2004

11 LA PIAZZETTA

$ For a posh pizza in a pleasant environment, this chain does the job nicely. Try the deluxe vegetarian, white wine-marinated onion, three cheese, or any of the other nearly 30 varieties of pizza on offer. There's a decent selection of salads and desserts too. ♦ Italian ♦ Daily, lunch and dinner. 63 Rue St-Paul (at Rue Sault-au-Matelot). 692.2962

12 OLD PORT

The 82-acre complex of warehouses, docks, grain elevators, and a yacht marina winds around the mouth of the St. Charles River where it joins the St. Lawrence River. (A lock within the Bassin Louise regulates the water level between the two rivers.) In recent years, the federal government has launched a revitalization program in an effort to turn the port into a tourist attraction, but it's still very much a working port, filled with the shouts of dock workers and the clang of ships being loaded and unloaded. Coast guard ships, tugs, ferries, freighters, firefighters, and rusty old barges are docked at the wharves, and during the summer, glitzy cruise ships, decked from bow to stern in colorful bunting, add a festive touch. So do the street musicians, clowns, and jugglers who hang out here, trying to earn a few tourist dollars. In the summer, concerts are sometimes staged at the **Agora**, a sunken outdoor amphitheater surrounded by water. ♦ 120 Rue Dalhousie (at Rue St-André).

Within the Old Port:

CAFÉ DU MONDE

★★★$$ Make the extra bit of effort required to find this welcoming Parisian-style bistro, whose friendly waitstaff and reliable cooking make it one of the surest dining bets in Quebec City. It's located on the second floor of a building in the Old Port, but once you arrive it feels very much like the center of attention. Potted palms placed against floor-to-ceiling windows afford views of the St. Lawrence River to make you swoon, and a giant map of the world (in French) on one wall adds to a decidedly stylish ambiance. From the comfort of red banquettes and cane chairs, diners enjoy such classic French bistro fare as a half farm chicken with salad and mashed potatoes, *moules et frites* (mussels with french fries), and *boudin noir* (black pudding) with apples, onions, and Calvados. There's a strong selection of wines by the glass to accompany these savory dishes. For dessert, forget about calories, pretend you're in Paris (it's not hard here), and order the *profiteroles*. ♦ French ♦ Reservations recommended. M-F, lunch and dinner: Sa, Su, brunch and dinner. Reservations recommended. 84 Rue Dalhousie (at the cruise terminal of the Old Port). 692.4455

L'ÉCHAUDÉ

13 L'ÉCHAUDÉ

★★$$$ This is one of the better French bistros to pop up in the vicinity of Rue St-Pierre, with both a menu and ambiance that strikes a pleasing balance between classical and contemporary. Try the traditional steak *frites*, roasted duck breast, the grilled red snapper

THE BEST

Richard Germain
General Manager, Hotel Dominion 1912

The best getaway within Quebec itself is **Le Vieux Port**. In the early 1900s this area was the Wall Street of Quebec City where you would find the stock exchange, all the major banks, and insurance companies. The contrast between these massive old graystone buildings and the French houses of Place Royale—where Quebec City was founded in 1608—is just amazing. The neighborhood has changed a lot—less business but more art galleries, cafés, museums, and some of the best restaurants in the city. Most importantly, this is also where you feel the local flair because many residents have made new homes here.

I spend a few nights each week at the **Hotel Dominion 1912**, a boutique hotel of 60 rooms that opened in the city's first skyscraper. After my breakfast next to the fireplace, I usually need to go shopping. The first stop might be **O'Clan**, where you will find great designer clothes either from the world but mostly from Quebec; check out www.oclan.net.

Then it's on to **Rue St-Paul**, the antiques quarter, and the **Décenie** boutique, where you shop for Wallpaper-style furniture from the '60s and '70s. Moving on to **St-Jean Street**, there is **J. A. Moisan**, the first grocery store in North America, where I buy bread, olive oil, and wines, with Edith Piaf songs playing in the background. Next stop is the **Epicerie Européenne** to choose from the best selections of local and European cheeses.

Finally, there is **Avenue Cartier**, which is one of the best areas to shop, dine, or just walk around. **Zone** is a great place to buy things for the kitchen or bathroom, as well as lamps or furniture. Great look at a low cost. You have to stop at **Krieghoff** to relax and read a paper while you are having the best coffee in town along with a quiche or a pâtisserie.

After heading back toward the hotel via the **Plains of Abraham**, now a beautiful urban park, I stop at the **Musée de la Civilisation**, one of the most acclaimed buildings in the city, built by architect Moshe Safdie. Spectacular surrounding for astonishing exhibits.

Last and not the least, my dinner will be at **L'Échaudé**, an elegant but casual French bistro with an inventive cuisine and the best wine selection in the city. It's also one of Quebec's best values.

---

fillet with olive oil and balsamic vinegar, or any of the *fruits de mer*. The wine list features 125 varieties, and there are 10 wines available by the glass. The front terrace fills up fast during the summer. ♦ French ♦ Daily, lunch and dinner. Reservations recommended. 73 Rue Sault-au-Matelot (at Rue St-Paul). 692.1299

LA CRÊPERIE de Sophie

14 LA CRÊPERIE DE SOPHIE

★★$ Here's a bright, cheerful spot to enjoy some of the best crepes in town. These can be simple affairs from the *Classiques* portion of the menu—such as egg and tomato purée with herbs—or one of the more exotic *Les Flyées*—such as the Provençale, with ratatouille, or one with chicken, sesame oil, and sweet-and-sour sauce. Salted crepes are best with buckwheat flour; sweet, with wheat flour (though you may choose). In either case, portions are generous. You might opt for one of the delicious salads, soups (try the French onion), or pastas, then order one of the scrumptious dessert crepes: the banana and chocolate and La Belle Hélène, with poached pears, chocolate sauce, and vanilla ice cream, are two standouts among the many choices available. ♦ French ♦ M-F, lunch and dinner; Sa-Su, breakfast, lunch, and dinner. 48 Rue St-Paul (between Bell's La and Rue St-Pierre). 694.9595 &

Hôtel Dominion 1912

15 HÔTEL DOMINION 1912

$$$ By any measure one of the top hotels in Quebec City, the Dominion attracts guests who value cool comfort as much as warm, friendly service. **Lemay Michaud Architecture Design** is the team behind the makeover of the old Dominion Fish and Fruit Limited office building into the kind of sophisticated urban

---

Restaurants/Clubs: Red | Hotels: Purple | Shops: Orange | Outdoors/Parks: Green | Sights/Culture: Blue

space that invites lingering. The good impressions start in the lobby, where dark wood, natural light, and contemporary art mix effectively. Here's where the complimentary continental breakfast is served (in good weather it can also be enjoyed on the terrace); guests hungry for e-mail can also avail themselves of a computer. The hotel's 60 spacious rooms and suites are outfitted with luxurious beds, immaculate bathrooms with showers and sinks featuring clear glass, and sleek work stations. Original black-and-white photographs of Old Quebec adorn the walls, and a hint of blue is a reminder of the hotel's proximity to the St. Lawrence River (for the best view of it, request a room on the eighth floor). Presiding over details great and small is affable General Manager Richard Germain, whose sister Christiane manages the Hôtel le Germain in Montreal. As an added plus, there's easy parking in a lot directly behind the hotel. ♦ 126 Rue St-Pierre (at Rue St-Paul). 692.2224, 888/833.5253; fax 692.4403

Laurie Raphaël

R E S T A U R A N T

16 LAURIE RAPHAËL

★★★★$$$$ Run by husband-and-wife team Suzanne Gagnon and chef Daniel Vézina, the restaurant, which is named after their two children, is one of the hot places to eat in Quebec City. Much of the credit goes to Vézina, who earned a province-wide reputation while he was executive chef at at **La Grand Table de Serge Bruyère**. His signature light and healthy cooking showcases fresh meats, fish, and vegetables, subtly flavored with innovative combinations of herbs and spices. Consider Atlantic halibut with drizzled

Although Quebec founder Samuel de Champlain was the first to use Montreal's natural harbor in 1611, it was the Sun King, Louis XIV, who officially created the port some 3 decades later when he granted a 20-arpent strip (roughly 1 acre) along the St. Lawrence River to the Société du Nouveau Monde for use as a port facility. This area expanded over the centuries to become one of the busiest inland ports in North America. Oceangoing freighters and cruise ships follow the river for 1,000 miles from the Atlantic Ocean to dock here. Many continue another 1,200 miles along the St. Lawrence Seaway to Lake Ontario.

citrus fruit sauce and vanilla and flower buds flavored with rice vinegar and accompanied by squash blossom prepared three ways, or roasted Inuit caribou with port and Arthabaska cranberries. Desserts are deliciously complex, such as the rhubarb extravaganza, a feast of rhubarb spring rolls, sorbet and juice, and a strawberry and rhubarb salad. The ambiance and décor are serene and sophisticated, and the waitstaff is knowledgeable and attentive. ♦ Nouvelle ♦ Daily, lunch and dinner. Reservations recommended. 117 Rue Dalhousie (at Rue St-Paul). 692.4555 ♿

17 CUSTOMS HOUSE

Behind the Agora amphitheater is this majestic neoclassical building with fluted pillars and a copper-topped dome. Designed in 1860 by English architect **William Thomas**, this grand structure is adorned with the ornate stone masonry popular during the Victorian era. Although damaged several times by fire, the building was restored to its imperial glory in the early 1980s, and today it is still used as a customs office. ♦ 2 Rue St-André (across from Old Port)

18 AUBERGE SAINT-PIERRE

$$ This lovely, modern inn in a renovated 1821 insurance company building offers guests 43 comfortable rooms with brick and stone walls, high ceilings, wood floors, and down comforters. It also boasts a great location, just opposite the **Museé de la Civilisation** in the heart of the revitalized Old Port district. ♦ 79 Rue St-Pierre (between Rues St-Antoine and St-Jacques). 694.7981, 888/268.1017; fax 694.0406 ♿

19 CÔTE DE LA MONTAGNE

The original route down Cap-Diamant to the Lower Town was hacked out of sheer rock when Samuel de Champlain needed a trail to connect **Fort St-Louis** to the port. Today the road curves under **Porte Prescott** (a replica of the original), one of four openings in the city wall, and it's still mighty steep. There was a guardhouse at the **Prescott Gate** as recently as 1871, but it was demolished to ease the traffic—a perennial problem on Quebec City's narrow streets. ♦ Between Rues Dalhousie and des Remparts

20 TOAST!

★★★$$$ On the site of the now defunct Bistro du Chef, this sexy restaurant is a true find. The front room is a modernist fantasia of red, while the large garden terrace in the back is one of the most tranquil spaces to wine and dine in town. Chef Christian Lemlin turns out updated bistro dishes such as a red tuna block with Chinese spices served on a bed of wild mushrooms, asparagus, and cherry tomatoes and rack of lamb crumbed in citrus zest with butternut squash arborio risotto. Order à la carte or, better yet, opt for the good-value table d'hôte. From a simple green salad with homemade fruit vinegar and nut oil to desserts, only the freshest ingredients are used. This is also a brunch spot nonpareil. In addition to gourmet croissants and Quebec cheeses there is a delectable French toast made with maple sugar, port wine, and sweet cream. Owner Stephane d'Anjou oversees the kind of staff you're sorry to say good-bye to. Note: Enter the restaurant through the adjacent **Hôtel Le Priori**. ♦ Contemporary/French ♦ Daily, breakfast, lunch and dinner; Sa, Su, brunch and dinner. Reservations recommended. 17 Rue du Sault-au-Matelot (at Rue St-Antoine). 692.1334

21 LE PALIER

High-quality mementos made by native North Americans, including snowshoes, costumed Indian dolls, and soapstone figurines of Inuit (Eskimo) hunters stalking polar bears and seals, are the specialty of this shop. There's also a small selection of handsome prints by such well-known Canadian artists as Benjamin Chee-Chee, a self-taught Woodlands Indian who committed suicide at age 32. ♦ Daily, 9AM-10PM. 20 Côte de la Montagne (Escalier Frontenac, halfway down the stairs on the right). 694.9307

22 HÔTEL LE PRIORI

$$ Constructed in 1741 by **Jean Baillairge**, a carpenter, sculptor, architect, and jack-of-all-trades, the building that houses this 26-room hostelry is as old as most in the Lower Town. But the hotel, which opened in 1991, is still one of the newest on the scene, and the interior has been thoroughly modernized. The décor is simple, almost stark. Rooms—ranging from small singles to a spacious suite with a living room, fireplace, double Jacuzzi, and kitchen—are furnished with low contemporary beds with shiny black headboards, spindly spotlights, leather sofas,

glass-topped coffee tables, and large pottery vases. The beamed ceilings and exposed walls make this place look and feel like a chic art gallery. ♦ 15 Rue Sault-au-Matelot (at Rue St-Antoine). 692.3992, 800/351.3992; fax 692.0883

23 MUSÉE DE LA CIVILISATION

Allow at least half a day to explore this fascinating modern museum celebrating the history and culture of Quebec. Built in 1988, the museum has won awards for its innovative design. The brainchild of renowned architect **Moshe Safdie**, best known as the creator of Montreal's futuristic **Habitat** complex (part of **Expo '67**) and the National Gallery in Ottawa, it is a harmonic arrangement of limestone and glass incorporating the old and the new. The entrance, dominated by a large angular sculpture entitled *La Debacle* (a reference to the breakup of ice in spring), by Montreal artist Astri Reusch, sets the tone for a visit.

In addition to ongoing temporary exhibits, there are four permanent presentations— *Mémoires*, *Objects de Civilisation*, *La Barque*, and *Messages*—each of which explores five main themes: the body, matter, society, language, and thought. In the *Objets de Civilisation* section (on the first floor), you'll discover a molding carved in the style of Louis XV, a 19th-century rocker from Île d'Orléans, and a Mohawk baby-carrier embellished with flowers, birds, and a beaver. Also on the first floor, *La Barque* has an entire area to itself, featuring a 250-year-old ship that measures 45 feet long by 9 feet wide. This weathered skeleton of wood, which was kept together by a cradle of iron, was found, along with two others, under the museum's foundations (the boats are believed to have been used as landfill). On the second floor, *Mémoires* gives visitors a nostalgic look at Quebec's past through a series of vignettes about the "good old days" when the family, the church, and the change of seasons dictated the cultural norms and rhythms of life in La Belle Province.

Children will love the interactive displays, located throughout the museum, which provide buttons to push, questions to answer, headsets to don, and video and computer screens to watch. (A word of warning: Save your sanity by avoiding school holidays, when the place becomes a zoo.) Benches are tucked into quiet corners for time out from all the stimulus. The museum has one minor drawback: Exhibits are labeled in French only, but you can pick up English-language brochures in bins near the beginning of each section or purchase them in the museum store. Docents who speak English are also available.

Restaurants/Clubs: Red | Hotels: Purple | Shops: Orange | Outdoors/Parks: Green | Sights/Culture: Blue

No visit is complete without a stop at the museum shop, located in the basement, where you'll find exotic crafts and objets d'art from around the world, including wooden fish from Mexico, hand-painted Russian boxes, carved elephants from Kenya, woven rugs from Tunisia, and pottery from Brazil. ◆ Admission. 24 June-Labor Day, daily, 10AM-7PM; Sept-June, Tu-Su, 10AM-5PM. 85 Rue Dalhousie (between Rues St-Antoine and St-Jacques). 643.2158

24 Boutique l'Escale

Located among a cluster of tacky T-shirt shops, this one is not as cheesy as most. If you can get past the touristy merchandise—plastic loons, stuffed toys, and the like—you'll find some fun buys, such as a cotton shirt embellished with a moose on a leash, sniffing at a fire hydrant like a big dog. ◆ Daily, 9AM-10PM. 26 Côte de la Montagne (Escalier Frontenac, halfway down the stairs on the right). No phone

25 Galerie Zanettin

Since 1885, this small art gallery has been mounting changing exhibits that run the gamut from naive oil paintings to bold, modern canvases of sun-splashed garden scenes. ◆ Tu-Su, noon-4PM; hours are erratic, so call first. 28 Côte de la Montagne (Escalier Frontenac, near bottom of the stairs on the left). 833.0456

26 Rue St-Pierre

With its prim and proper architecture and imposing façades, this street epitomizes 19th-century Quebec City, evoking the hierarchy of wheeler-dealers who ran business empires stretching to Europe and beyond. Here, you'll find banks, banks, and more banks, with a couple of insurance companies thrown in for good measure. Worth noting are the 1862 **National Bank** (No. 71); the **Post Office** (No. 105), formerly the **Molson Bank** (as in the beer company); the 1913 **Imperial Bank of Canada** (Nos. 113–115); and what used to be the **Hochelaga Bank** (No. 132). The 1900 Beaux Arts **Canadian Bank of Commerce** (No. 139), embellished with fancy stonework, domes, pediments, and monumental columns, is typical of the structures favored by the establishment at the turn of the 19th century. Also along the street is the **Dominion Building** (No. 126), Quebec City's first skyscraper, now the **Hotel Dominion**. ◆ Across from Old Port (between Rues Sous-le-Fort and St-André)

27 Auberge Saint-Antoine

$$$ Thanks to the vision of its owner, lifelong Quebecer Llewellyn Price, this is not only a sumptuous place to stay but a fascinating one, too. Archeological digs on the property turned up thousands of artifacts, from 17th-century shoes to ceramics, which are mounted in dramatic backlit displays throughout sections of the hotel. The inn's 31 original room and suites, decorated in an updated country-inn style (no two are alike), are in a rambling, renovated 1830 warehouse. The adjacent modern building houses 64 newer and decidedly contemporary guestrooms. Although the designs here differ, count on sleek, spotless bathrooms, refreshing amenities, deliciously comfortable beds, and modern touches like antique glassware embedded in the end tables. Some of the rooms and suites have arched glass doors and walk-out patios. There is a large restaurant and bar. ◆ 10 Rue St-Antoine (at Rue Dalhousie). 692.2211, 888/692.2211; fax 692.1177. www.saint-antoine.com

28 Le Vendôme

★★★$$$ This tasteful, pleasant Parisian-style bistro in an old Quebec house has been in business since 1951, longer than any other in Quebec City. A few tables in the front overlook the St. Lawrence River; but don't miss the colorful mural covering one wall, depicting such Parisian scenes as the Eiffel Tower, Montmartre, and Place Vendôme. The place owes its longevity to a faithful clientele, an extensive wine list (120 vintage selections), and a classic French menu, featuring seafood *coquilles*, snails in garlic butter, pâté, French onion soup, rabbit in mustard sauce, coq au vin, and sweetbreads. Many locals have been coming since owner Manuel Garcia arrived here from the Basque region of Spain 2 decades ago. ◆ French ◆ Daily, lunch and dinner. Reservations recommended. 36 Côte de la Montagne (Escalier Frontenac, bottom of the stairs on the right). 692.0557 ё

29 Escalier Casse-Cou

In the 17th century, this stairway was little more than a rickety shortcut from the steep cliffs to the Lower Town. Nowadays the aptly named **Breakneck Stairs** aren't nearly as hazardous. In fact, they're so stable that a couple of restaurants have set up patios with umbrella-covered tables alongside the stairs. ◆ From Côte de la Montagne down to Rue du Petit Champlain

30 Chez Rabelais

★★$$$ It's hardly surprising that owners Christian Lestriez (from Bourgogne, France) and Pierre Marceau attract a diverse crowd of passersby to this cozy spot, because you practically trip over it on the way down the stairs. The outdoor patio is nearly always filled on sunny days, but there's room for more diners inside, where typical Old Quebec décor—small cottage windows, stone walls, low-beamed doorways—is accented with soft green table linen and white porcelain crockery. Simple dishes, such as grilled salmon, broiled steak, and chicken prepared several ways, are the specialty. ♦ French ♦ Daily, lunch and dinner. Reservations recommended. 2 Rue du Petit Champlain (at the bottom of Escalier Casse-Cou). 694.9460

30 LE MARIE CLARISSE

★★★$$$$ Named after a famous wooden schooner that takes tourists on whale-watching excursions at the mouth of the Saguenay River, this inviting restaurant, owned by Quebecer Jean Michel Allain, offers an enticing array of seafood delights from around the province and the Maritimes area of Canada. Specialties include smoked sturgeon, marinated mussels, and saffron-flavored salmon. The crème brûlée is excellent. The atmosphere of this upscale, 12-table eatery is warm and intimate, with low lighting, fresh flowers atop blue linen tablecloths, and blond wood trimming 300-year-old stone walls. It's a favorite among locals, who consistently rate it one of the best seafood places in town. ♦ Seafood ♦ Daily, lunch and dinner. Reservations recommended. 12 Rue du Petit Champlain (at the bottom of Escalier Casse-Cou). 692.0857

31 RUE DU PETIT CHAMPLAIN

Believed to be the oldest shopping thoroughfare in North America, this spirited little street, which starts at the base of the **Breakneck Stairs**, is lined with some 50 craft shops, fashion boutiques, and restaurants. The first building on the right, the **Jolliet House**, was built in 1683 and is now the **Funicular Railway** station. From here, odd little glass-sided cable cars have been trundling sightseers back and forth to **Dufferin Terrace** for more than 100 years. ♦ Between Blvd Champlain and Rue Sous-le-Fort

32 PLACE ROYALE

The site of Champlain's original settlement and the "cradle of New France," this cobble-stoned square takes its "royal" name from a Bernini statue of Louis XIV that was plunked smack in the middle of the plaza in 1686. Even then, the statue was in such an awkward location that it impeded traffic, so irate residents removed it in 1689. The current statue, a copy of Bernini's original (which is now at the Palace of Versailles), was given to Quebec by France and erected in 1948.

During British General James Wolfe's siege in 1759, the buildings on this square were blasted to bits when the British hammered the town with 40,000 cannonballs and 10,000

firebombs. But although the roofs and interiors were destroyed, the stone walls remained, and the buildings were easily reconstructed. A multimillion-dollar restoration project has returned many of the square's 17th- and 18th-century structures to their original splendor.

For the historical perspective, stop by the **Centre d'Interprétation de Place Royale**. The first-floor exhibits retrace the expansion of Place Royale, whereas those on the second focus on the mercantile aspects of the neighborhood, starting with the seminal importance of the beaver. Though an ably curated salute to the 400 years of written history of the area, the center is perhaps best appreciated by families, the younger members of which may get more enjoyment from the costume shops, guides in period garb, and multimedia show than may the older. ♦ Admission. 24 June-23 Oct, daily, 9:30AM-5PM; 24 Oct-23 June, Tu-Su, 10AM-5PM. Between Rue Notre Dame and Rue St-Pierre. 646.3167

33 POT-EN-CIEL

Denise Fournier's small gallery, which highlights the work of Quebec craftspeople, presents an eclectic selection of handmade pottery, glassware, and ceramic jewelry, along with a whimsical collection of coffee mugs with webbed ducks' feet. ♦ June–Sept: daily, 9AM-10PM. Oct–May: Sa-W, 10AM-6PM; Th-F, 10AM-9PM. 27 Rue du Petit Champlain (at Rue Sous-le-Fort). 692.1743

34 LE LAPIN SAUTÉ

★★$$$ Situated in a 200-year-old stone building, this restaurant has the air of a country inn, with its floral wallpaper, intimate tables, and hanging plants. A good deal of government and insurance business is conducted in the homey space, particularly over lunch. The strong suit is the mixed grill: European sausage, pepper steak, lamb chops, and beef and chicken kebabs. There's also a limited selection of pasta, salads, and sandwiches. ♦ Daily, lunch and dinner. Reservations recommended. 52 Rue du Petit Champlain (between Blvd Champlain and Rue Sous-le-Fort). 692.5325 &

35 ZAZOU

As the snappy name suggests, this eye-catching boutique stocks trendy clothes for women. Run by France and Jean-François Blouin, it offers an appealing selection of moderately priced designer fashions from Montreal, headquarters of the Canadian rag trade. Some clothes are made especially for the boutique, such as a line of comfortable, brightly colored, oilskin-textured rainwear. ♦

Restaurants/Clubs: Red | Hotels: Purple | Shops: Orange | Outdoors/Parks: Green | Sights/Culture: Blue

M-W, Sa-Su; Th-F, 9:30AM-9PM. 31 Rue du Petit Champlain (at Rue Sous-le-Fort). 694.9990

36 ÉGLISE NOTRE-DAME-DES-VICTOIRES

The Sun King himself, Louis XIV, granted this plot of land to the good people of Quebec to build a church. The little stone church with the lone spire was erected in 1688 on the site of Champlain's second settlement, and it quickly became an adjunct to the **Basilique-Cathédrale Notre-Dame-de-Québec**, a much grander edifice. Originally dedicated to the Infant Jesus, the church was christened Notre-Dame-de-Victoire in 1690 after the failure of a 5-day siege by the British. (Quebec City's Ursuline nuns, who had prayed assiduously for deliverance, believed the town was saved because of divine intervention by the Virgin Mary.) After another unsuccessful coup attempt by the British in 1711, the church was renamed Notre-Dame-des-Victoires for the multiple victories. Around the choir, frescoes recall these historic events, and paintings throughout the interior are copies of works by Van Dyck, Van Loo, and Buyermans. A side chapel is dedicated to Ste-Geneviève, the patron saint of Paris. Hanging over the nave is a replica of *Le Breze*, the ship that brought the Carignan Regiment and Marquis de Tracy to New France in 1664 with the mandate to fight the Iroquois, who were making life difficult for new settlers. ♦ Daily, 10AM-4:30PM (closed during weddings, christenings, or funerals). Place Royale (at Rue Notre Dame). 692.1650

37 IBIZA

The name of this leather store and workshop comes from owner Juan Hernandez's birthplace, a Spanish island in the Mediterranean. Hernandez has been turning out leather belts and bags in this tiny basement for 17 years, though some of his merchandise is imported from other parts of Canada. There's a small selection of leather coats, and the fur hats (made from raccoon, coyote, and natural and sheared beaver) are favorites among Japanese and German tourists, who find the prices reasonable compared to those in their own countries. ♦ M-W, Sa-Su; Th-F, 10AM-9PM. 57 Rue du Petit Champlain (between Blvd Champlain and Rue Sous-le-Fort). 692.2103

38 LE COCHON DINGUE

★★$$$ Located in a historical stone house with 12-foot-high ceilings, this comfortable, casual restaurant is a favorite among office workers, civil servants, and families. The menu features unfussy food that's easy on the palate: steaks, quiches, salads, bagels, croissants, pasta, and baguettes. Save some room for the scrumptious homemade desserts. There's a special kids' menu too. In summer, the sidewalk terrace is a favorite spot for people watching. ♦ Continental ♦ Daily, breakfast, lunch, and dinner. Reservations recommended. 46 Blvd Champlain (around the corner, to the left, from Rue du Petit Champlain). 692.2013 &

39 MAISON CHEVALIER

Managed by the same people who run the **Musée de la Civilisation**, this museum, located in a group of three old houses—**Maison Chenaye de la Garonne** (1695), **Maison Frerot** (1675), and **Maison Chevalier** (1752)—is filled with early Canadian furniture, art, and artifacts. An exhibition hall illustrates the lives and times of the merchants who lived in the Lower Town, particularly local shipowner Jean-Baptiste Chevalier, for whom one of the houses was built. All three buildings were so solidly constructed that they survived the British bombardment in 1759. ♦ Free. Daily, 10AM-5:30PM, 24 June-Oct; Sa-Su, 10AM-5PM, Nov–Apr; Tu-Su, 10AM-5:30PM, May–June. 60 Rue du Marché Champlain (at Rue Notre Dame). 643.2158

40 RESTAURANT MONTE-CARLO

★★$$ The building that was once known as **Maison Gosselin**—constructed by Gabriel Gosselin, who came here from Normandy in 1683—opened as a restaurant in 1990. Owned by Bulgarian-born Alex Tzenev and Jean-Claude Dentinger from Cannes, this popular place is bright and airy, with wonderful views of **Château Frontenac**, the **Citadel**, and the St. Lawrence River. The menu offers something for everyone, from tortellini and veal to filet mignon and Mexican fare. Start off with a bottle of Tremblay lager, brewed in Montreal (the label depicts a wolf baying at the sky). During the summer, dine outside on the large cedar patio under a red umbrella, to the strains of accordion music. The building has two entrances: one on Rue Marché Champlain and one on Rue Sous-le-Fort. ♦ Italian/French/Mexican ♦ Daily, lunch and dinner. 21 Rue Sous-le-Fort (at Rue Notre Dame). 692.9213 &

41 PLACE DE PARIS

This square was built to commemorate the spot where French settlers first stepped onto Canadian soil in the 17th century. To the left is the **Batterie Royale**, part of Louis XIV's garrison against the British, which was destroyed during the siege of 1759 and has been rebuilt several times. Many decades later, the square became a public meeting place and a market, called the **Marché Finlay**. Today the center of the square is marked by *Dialogue with History*, a contem-

THE BEST

Stéphane D'Anjou

Co-owner of Toast! Restaurant (Quebec City)

I particularly like the Vieux-Port district of Quebec City, located just below the famous Château Frontenac bordering the Saint-Lawrence River. In summer, at the marketplace we find the best from our local agricultural producers: fresh fruit, vegetables, and fine "terroir" products. Accompanied by the chef, we find ourselves roaming the market stands daily for the restaurant's needs. The animated restaurant terraces, antiques shops, and art galleries make me feel like I'm somewhere in old Europe. During the long winter months, I love taking a drink in the cozy lobbies of the Dominion Hotel or the Auberge Saint-Antoine, a few steps away from Toast! We are always warmly greeted by all the staff.

My favorite spots:

For clothing: Oclan (Rue du Petit-Champlain) and L'Un et L'Autre (Rue Saint-Jean)

For sushi: Yuzu (corner of Charest Blvd/ Rue de l'Église)

For brunch: Le Café du Clocher Penché (Rue Saint-Joseph)

For pasta: Momento Cartier (Ave Cartier)

For fresh mussels: Mon Manège à Toi! (Rue René Lévesque, corner of Ave Cartier)

For home décor: Zone (Ave Cartier), Balthazar (Rue Saint-Joseph), M (Rue Saint-Anselme), and Villa (Rue Saint-Joseph)

For dinner and the best service in town: Bistango (Rue Saint-Germain des Près in Sainte-Foy)

Hotels: Dominion, Le Priori, and Saint-Antoine

For fine groceries: L'Épicerie Européene (Rue Saint-Jean)

For cinema: Le Clap (Chemin Sainte-Foy)

---

porary sculpture that resembles a giant pile of black-and-white bathroom tiles, capped by a smaller heap. Presented as a gift to Quebec City in 1987 by Jacques Chirac (then mayor of Paris but now President of France), the chunky sculpture by French artist Jean-Pierre Raynaud is meant to echo the geometric architecture of the buildings behind it and to form a link with the statue of Louis XIV in Place Royale. Quebecers irreverently call the sculpture "the colossus of Quebec." ♦ Across from the Lévis Ferry (off Rue Dalhousie).

42 OCLAN

Quaint may rule the *rue* in these parts, but those in need of a hip fashion fix need look no farther than this irreverent store, whose "F**k la Mode" T-shirts are perennial bestsellers. The first floor is for women, the second for men. Engage owner Jean-François in conversation and you'll come away not only with advice on which jeans are your personal *must* but hot tips on area restaurants, too. ♦ 67 Rue du Petit Champlain (between Blvd Champlain and Rue Sous-le-Fort). 692.1214

43 BOULEVARD CHAMPLAIN

A stroll to the end of the Rue du Petit Champlain brings you to this boulevard, which will take you to Rue du Marché Champlain. This stretch overlooking the St. Lawrence River used to be lined with run-down, ramshackle buildings but is now a gentrified district of museums, restaurants, and shops. ♦ At Rue du Marché Champlain

44 LÉVIS FERRY

From the end of Rue du Marché Champlain, the 10-minute ride across the St. Lawrence River is one of the cheapest tourist attractions around. Along the way, you'll be treated to a magnificent view of the Lower Town and **Château Frontenac**. ♦ One-way fare is $2.50; round-trip is $5. Daily, every half hour until 6PM, then every hour on the half hour until 2AM (schedules and prices were set to change at press time; call ahead to confirm). 10 Rue des Traversiers (off Blvd Champlain). 644.3704

44 M/V LOUIS JOLLIET

There's no better way to top off a day of strolling around the Lower Town than with a sunset cruise on the St. Lawrence River. If you can ignore the passengers who drink themselves silly (at the ship's three bars) and the DJ's insistence that you "get up and dance," the view of Quebec City's stunning skyline is well worth the trip, particularly against a backdrop of crimson-tinged clouds. Various daytime cruises, some with tour guides, are also available. ♦ Admission. Daily noon-1PM, 2PM-3:30PM, 4PM-5PM; also 8:30PM-11:30PM Sa-Su, 23 June-6 Sept. Limited sailings May-Oct, depending on the number of bookings and the weather. Reservations recommended. Chouinard Pier, Blvd Champlain (opposite Place de Paris). Reservations, 692.1159; information, 800/563.4643

Restaurants/Clubs: Red | Hotels: Purple | Shops: Orange | Outdoors/Parks: Green | Sights/Culture: Blue

Upper Town in Old Quebec is an Old World place in a New World setting, timeless and uncommonly beautiful. Located inside the Gothic portals of the city, it is brimming with antiquity. Though artists and street musicians now ply their trade on cobbled walkways lined with cafés and shops, the landscape of Upper Town, which is perched on a cliff overlooking the **St. Lawrence River** and mountains in the distance, hasn't changed much over the centuries.

The **Château St-Louis**, situated high above the river near where the imposing **Château Frontenac** hotel now stands, was the epicenter of political power in Canada for nearly 200 years. During this period, Upper Town was also the site of military might and a religious stronghold. A French town when it was founded in the 17th century, it was later controlled by the British Army, which held sway for 111 years. The **Château St-Louis** was occupied at different times by the French and the British, and both cultures had a profound impact on the area, its residents, and their descendants.

The military significance of Upper Town is still readily apparent. As soon as you enter the city's magnificent stone gate, known as **Porte St-Louis**, turn right to **Côte de la Citadelle** to reach the distinguished **Citadel**, which reigns over **Cap-Diamant (Cape Diamond)**. The **Citadel** is the city's most impressive visitors' attraction and the largest fortification still occupied by troops in North America. Nearly 3 miles of stone walls, which you can walk along, surround Upper Town. Old Quebec's **Latin Quarter** was the heart of culture and education in the 1800s, when studies were conducted in Latin, and both the **Basilique-Cathédrale Notre-Dame-de-Québec** and the **Seminary** lie within its borders. Few tourists venture as far as **Rue des Remparts**, but they should. It provides a splendid view of Lower Town and the Old Port, and the numerous cannons that point to the river are reminiscent of the early settlers' military way of life. About 50 houses in the Latin Quarter, several of which are located on **Rue Ste-Famille**, date back to the French regime. One of the oldest and best preserved is **Maison Touchet** (at No. 15), a long, rectangular home with a steep roof. The Latin Quarter was also once the city's commercial center, and signs of its former status remain on **Rue St-Jean** and **Côte de la Fabrique**. The area, and Rue St-Jean in particular, teems with restaurants, bars, and discos. Between 1820 and 1860, the era known as the town's Golden Age, Upper Town bloomed. The population tripled as the wood and shipping industries expanded and people moved away from the port area (mainly because the risk of cholera was high in Lower Town due to the arrival of immigrants). **Rue St-Denis** was constructed after the 1860s, and some of the exquisite houses built by wealthy shipowners and builders are still standing. The street, with its carved woodwork, unusual doorways, and stylized windows, is one of the most photographed in Upper Town.

In the late 1800s, the military importance of Upper Town began to diminish. The British pulled out in 1871 but left an indelible imprint, which you can trace in the younger section of Upper Town, especially along **Rue Ste-Ursule**, where Victorian-style graystone houses, balconied and turreted, abound. Yet it isn't a historic relic. An active military base carries on the traditions of the **Citadel**, and Upper Town is still the center of Quebec City's Catholic community, home to the **Ursuline** and **Augustinian** convents and the archbishop's residence. **City Hall** is also located in this vibrant residential community.

1 L'HÔTEL DU CAPITOLE

$$ This hip hotel boasts one of the most exciting addresses in Quebec, in the heart of the always bustling Place D'Youville, just outside the ramparts. It's part of a vibrant complex that includes the 1,262-seat **Théâtre Capitole**, **Le Cabaret du Capitole**, and the trendy **Ristorante Il Teatro**. The unusual lobby is narrow but dramatic thanks to an extremely high ceiling, replete with sky-and-cloud trompe l'oeil at the top. The 40 rooms and mini-suites are comfortable and contemporary. ◆ 972 Rue St-Jean (Place d'Youville). 694.4040, 800/363.4040; fax 694.1916. ♿

Within the Hôtel du Capitole:

RISTORANTE IL TEATRO

★★**$$** The contemporary Italian menu at this always abuzz eatery and bar goes well with the plush red and black décor. All of the salads are good, as is the risotto della Mamma. For entrées order a pasta, risotto, or one of the fish dishes, such as the salmon *al zafferano*, a triangle of salmon on a bed of sweet potatoes with spinach, artichokes,

---

Restaurants/Clubs: Red | **Hotels: Purple** | **Shops: Orange** | **Outdoors/Parks: Green** | **Sights/Culture: Blue**

THE BEST

Philippe Borel

General Manager, Château Frontenac, Quebec City

Quebec City's **Ursuline Convent** on quiet **Rue Ste-Ursule**, with the gray façade of the convent, an archway, and a tree. Marcel Proust could have written about the place—it's like a small time capsule. **Bar St. Laurent**, at the **Château Frontenac**, where you can have tea by the circular windows and watch the ships slicing through the mighty **St. Lawrence**, with the powerful mountains in the background. If you are attentive, you can feel the ghosts in this room: Roosevelt was here, as were Mountbatten and General George Marshall, and if you pick up the faint aroma of a great cigar, it's because Churchill was here too.

grilled peppers, and saffron sauce. This is also a cool place to come for coffee and dessert after dinner at one of the many restaurants in the area. ♦ Italian ♦ Daily breakfast, lunch, and dinner. Reservations recommended. 694.9996

1 POINTE DES AMÉRIQUES

★$ Pizzas range from the "spicy" to "thermonuclear" at this cheerful restaurant firmly anchored in the excitement of the Place d'Youville. For something on the mild side, order a pie with raw Quebec cheese, mushrooms, and thyme; on the wilder side, there's one with tomatoes, escargots, and grilled garlic. Prices are fair and there's a fun cocktail menu. ♦ Italian/Californian ♦ Daily, lunch and dinner. 964 Rue St-Jean (at Pl d'Youville). 694.1199

2 PARC-DE-L'ARTILLERIE (ARTILLERY PARK)

Ⓟ Located in the west corner of the old walled city, near **Porte St-Jean**, this large complex is a National Historic Site now maintained by the Canadian Parks Service. Four buildings, including a former iron foundry, officers' quarters, and a redoubt, have been faithfully restored, offering a glimpse of 3 centuries of military life in the walled city. Started in 1712 and finished in 1748, the **Dauphine Redoubt**, a majestic white building, is the second-oldest military structure left from the French regime. After the Battle of the Plains of Abraham, the site became the headquarters of the Royal Artillery Regiments, from which the park takes its name. After the British military withdrew from the city in 1871, the park became a federal arsenal and 1879, eventually producing cartridges for both world wars. The arsenal was closed in 1964.

For a historical overview, visit the displays in the former munitions factory, where the star attraction is a scale model of Quebec City circa 1808 that outlines with amazing detail the area's topography and the city's layout, including 100 houses and military and religious institutions. Crafted by **Duberger and By**, this model became an important working tool for designing the city's fortifications. The Dauphine Redoubt, which later became the arsenal superintendent's residence, has been transformed into a four-floor exhibit with scenes depicting various stages of Quebec's occupation. The former officers' quarters are now a hands-on museum where children can play and dress up in period costume. In summer, bread is baked in outdoor ovens every Sunday. ♦ Admission. Daily, 24 June-Labor Day. Limited hours during the spring and fall; call for times. 2 Rue d'Auteuil (near Rue St-Jean). 648.4205

3 MUSÉE DES AUGUSTINES DE L'HÔTEL-DIEU DE QUÉBEC

The highlight of this museum in the Augustine monastery is a collection of 17th-century paintings, artifacts, and furniture that were typical of early life in the province and within the Augustinian order. Located next to the **Hôtel Dieu**, the first hospital north of Mexico City (which was started by three Augustinian nuns who came from France in 1639 to tend the sick in the new colony), the museum also offers an unusual exhibit of antique medical equipment dating back to the 17th century. If you've ever been curious about bloodletting tools, anesthetic inhalers from the 1840s, or 1905-style operating tables and surgical instruments, you'll be riveted by this place. Between May and November, you can arrange for tours of the chapel (built in 1800) and the arched cellars (1695) where the nuns hid from British bombardments. Next to the chapel is the **Centre Catherine-de-St-Augustin**, an annex dedicated to **Blessed Catherine de St-Augustin**, one of the pioneers of the Catholic faith in New France. She was beatified in 1989, and her remains are kept in a hand-carved reliquary. In the annex, stained-glass windows illustrate her life, and slides and videos are shown daily. ♦ Free. Tu-Sa, 10AM-noon and 2PM-5PM; Su, 2PM-5PM. 32 Rue Charlevoix (at Rue Collins). 692.2492

4 MANOIR VICTORIA

$$ The modest street entrance of this hotel reflects neither its rambling size nor its abundant charm. Built in 1904, the hotel was

one of the classiest places in town between 1910 and 1950. It then fell from grace and eventually closed in the mid-1970s, only to reopen in 1988 after a $12 million renovation. In addition to 145 modern, spacious rooms, the hostelry now offers a complete health club, including a pool and sauna. The main hotel overlooks Côte du Palais, and one wing extends along Rue St-Jean, right in the heart of the Latin Quarter. The central location—within walking distance of all attractions—has its drawbacks, however: If you want a quiet room, be sure to ask for one that's not facing the lively street. This is a good choice for families with children, because the under-18 crowd can stay in their parents' room for free, and meals are gratis for kids 6 and younger. Indoor valet parking is available. ♦ 44 Côte du Palais (between Rues St-Jean and McMahon). 692.1030, 800/463.6283; fax 692.3822

Within the Manoir Victoria:

LE TABLE DU MANOIR VICTORIA

★★$$$ The dining room has an atrium in the center, and floral wallpaper, rose-colored tablecloths, and forest-green wainscoting complete the garden mood. Chef Nanak Chand Vig's specialties include duckling with raspberry vinaigrette, veal medallions with morel sauce, and calf sweetbreads and scampi in lobster sauce. ♦ French ♦ Daily, breakfast, lunch, and dinner. 692.1030, 800/463.6283

ST. JAMES RESTO-BAR

★$ This bistro is great for casual meals, light sandwiches, pizzas, or salads, or you can create your own pasta dish. Ten kinds of beer are on tap, and live entertainment keeps the place hopping Thursday through Saturday. ♦ Bistro ♦ Daily, lunch and dinner. 1110 Rue St-Jean (at Côte du Palais). 692.1030, 800/ 463.6283

5 L'ENTRECÔTE ST. JEAN

★$$ Food fads may come and go, but some people will never tire of steaks and french fries, the main items on the menu at this popular Parisian-style bistro from the 1930s. The steaks come in three sizes—5, 6, and 9 ounces—to match your appetite, and crispy fries, soup, salad, and dessert—usually *profiteroles au chocolat*—are included in the price of a meal. Lighter choices, such as salads and sandwiches, are also available. With lace-curtained windows, café tables, black-and-white-checkered floors, and soft jazz playing in the background, this is a mellow haven. When summer comes, you can also eat outside on the secluded terrace. ♦ French ♦ Daily, lunch and dinner, end of June-Labor Day; M-Sa, lunch and dinner, Labor Day to mid-June. Reservations recommended. 1011 Rue St-Jean (at Rue d'Auteuil). 694.0234

6 LES FRÈRES DE LA CÔTE

★★$ This pizzeria is rife with the sun-drenched herbs and flavors of Provence: fruity olive oil, aromatic thyme and rosemary, and, of course, pungent olives and garlic. There are 18 varieties of thin-crusted pizzas, as well as specialties such as *Chaussons Saleya*, a calzone stuffed with spinach and goat cheese, and *pissaladière*, an onion-and-olive tart. The menu changes daily, but dinner attractions could include such dishes as mussels Grenoise or tenderloin of horsemeat. The chefs, working in the open kitchen, wear zany straw hats and kibbitz with the young clientele, contributing to the fun, noisy atmosphere. ♦ Pizzeria ♦ Daily, lunch and dinner. Reservations required. 1190 Rue St-Jean (at Rue Collins). 692.5445

7 LE PUB SAINT ALEXANDRE

★$ High ceilings, rich mahogany, a long resplendent bar, and, best of all, an extensive selection of imported and domestic beer highlight this English-style pub. There are 20 beers on tap, including Guinness and Bass, and 175 brands of bottled brews from around the world. Will it be a Kenyan, Tusker, a German DAB, or a St. Ambroise from one of Quebec's many microbreweries? If you're hungry, you can order sausages, quiche, and salads. ♦ Daily 11AM-closing. 1087 Rue St-Jean (between Ave Chauveau and Rue St-Stanislas). 694.0015

8 CHEZ TEMPOREL

★$ If you're craving great café au lait and flaky croissants, try this coffeehouse off the beaten path. Reminiscent of a bygone era when artists and writers congregated in the Latin Quarter, this bohemian café is popular with students and staff from the architectural school nearby. The menu is simple—soups, quiches, gratinées, *croques monsieur*, well-made salads, herb teas, wine, imported beers, and hot buttered rum. ♦ Coffeehouse ♦ Daily, 7AM-1:30AM. 25 Rue Couillard (at Rue Christie). 694.1813

9 ABACA

You won't stumble over this ethnic gold mine on most walking tours, as it's tucked away from the main drag. But it's worth searching for. The owners, who concentrate on African and Asian art, travel to more than 40 countries, selecting objects and verifying their

---

Restaurants/Clubs: Red | Hotels: Purple | Shops: Orange | Outdoors/Parks: Green | Sights/Culture: Blue

authenticity. Look for Japanese porcelain from the company that supplies the imperial household; unusual jewelry from remote areas of Afghanistan, India, and Indonesia; sculptures, ritual masks, and musical instruments from Africa; and ceremonial dance shields from New Guinea. ♦ Mid-May to mid-Sept: daily, 9:30AM-10PM. Mid-Sept to mid-May: M-W, Sa-Su, 9:30AM-6PM; Th-F, 9:30AM-9PM. 38 Rue Garneau (between Rue Christie and Côte de la Fabrique). 694.9761

10 ST. ANDREW'S CHURCH

Built in 1810, this lovely building is the oldest Presbyterian church in North America. A central pulpit dominates the interior, and several flags represent the congregation's diverse heritage, including an official reproduction of the colors of the Fraser Highlanders, a regiment of Wolfe's British Army of 1759, the first Presbyterians in Quebec. In the early days of the British regime, the balcony—called the **Governor's Gallery**—was reserved exclusively for the various Presbyterian governors of Canada, including Lord Dalhousie (1819-1828). In 1900, an organ built by the renowned Casavant Frères of St. Hyacinthe, Quebec, was installed there. Call for information on church services. ♦ 5 Rue Cook (at Rue Ste-Anne). 694.1347

11 AUX MULTIPLES COLLECTIONS

Even if you can't afford the prices here, Raymond Brousseau's stellar store on Rue Ste-Anne is still worth a visit. For more than 30 years, Brousseau has been carefully selecting and showcasing items from three distinct Canadian Arctic regions, featuring the work of more than 150 artists at any time. You'll find whalebone and serpentine-stone carvings from Baffin Island, basalt sculptures from Keewatin in the Northwest Territories, and works by artists such as Mattiusi Iyaituk and Jaco Ishwlwtak of Baffin Island. There's also an impressive selection of antique and decorative duck decoys, maps from the 1750s, and original Canadian prints, as well as carved caribou antlers and woven lime grass baskets. ♦ Daily, 9AM-8PM, mid-May to Sept; daily, Oct to mid-May. 69 Rue Ste-Anne (at Rue Cook). 692.1230. Also at 43 Rue Buade. 692.4298; Galerie Brousseau et Brousseau in the Château Frontenac. 694.1828

12 L'HÔTEL DE VILLE (QUEBEC CITY HALL)

This impressive building was constructed in 1896 on the site of a former Jesuit college and church. The structure was designed by **Georges-Emile Tanguay**, who pioneered a new architectural era by adding North American touches to the traditional French Château style. ♦ 2 Rue des Jardins (between Rue Ste-Anne and Côte de la Fabrique)

13 BOUTIQUE LA CORRIVEAU

Specializing in quality Quebec crafts, this shop is chock-full of hand-knit wool sweaters, hand-painted silk scarves, and handmade jade jewelry, duck decoys, and authentic Iroquois moccasins. There are also reproductions of the traditional colorful woven blankets, rugs, and bedspreads that were used by Quebec pioneers. ♦ Daily, 9AM-10PM, mid-May to Oct; daily, 9:30AM-7PM, Nov to mid-May. 24 Côte de la Fabrique (between Rues Ste-Famille and Garneau). 694.0062. Also at 46 Rue Garneau and 49 Rue St-Louis. 692.3781

14 MUSÉE DE L'AMÉRIQUE FRANÇAISE

In the early days of the **Séminaire de Québec**, the clerical elite traveled widely and brought back an eclectic array of curiosities and religious and secular works of art. The first floor of the museum houses the permanent collection of the seminary, which includes antique silver, coins from the time of Alexander the Great, and North America's first Egyptian mummy, dating back to 3500 BC. The permanent exhibition on the second floor, *Amérique Française* (*The Settling of French America*), affords visitors an in-depth perspective on the origins and early development of French culture in North America through films, artifacts, and historical documents. It includes antique maps of New France, first editions of the *Voyages* of Cartier and de Champlain, and maps that show the spread of *la Francophonie* and the French Catholic Church in such once far-flung locales as Acadia, Louisiana, and New England. A treasure trove for scholars, the museum houses historical archives and a library of 180,000 books, newspapers, and documents that represent one of the most important assemblages of French literature in North America. ♦ Admission. 24 June-3 Sept, daily, 10AM-5:30PM; 4 Sept-23 June, Tu-Su, 10AM-5PM. 9 Rue l'Université (at Rue Ste-Famille) 692.2843

15 LE SAINT-AMOUR

★★★$$$ Whether you dine in the romantic gardenlike setting of the atrium, which has a retractable roof, or in the dining rooms of this restored Victorian mansion, bedecked with rose-papered walls and lace-curtained windows, you're bound to have a superb meal. Chef Jean-Luc Boulay, voted Quebec's best chef in 2003, specializes in inventive nouvelle cuisine with particular attention to sauces. The menu changes as a function of the market, but entrées such as seared sea scallops and fresh artichokes with virgin oil emulsion and *fines herbes* pastry and Inuit caribou steak with blueberry vinegar sauce, corn cake with wild rice flower, and butternut squash indicate that it is a document to be reckoned with (and let's not forget such fascinating appetizers as Arctic char carpaccio paired with marinated daisy buds, cattail hearts, guacamole, and taro chips *millefeuille*). And if you ever wondered what they serve for dessert in the Emerald City, look no farther: a "melting heart" of superior chocolate, creamy Manjari, and maple brandy with lavender ice cream, or a poached pear carpaccio with pistachio cake and port wine jelly, almond milk mousse and raspberry nectar, with Szechuan pepper ice cream on the side. ♦ French ♦ M, dinner; Tu-F, lunch and dinner; Sa, Su, dinner. Reservations recommended. 48 Rue Ste-Ursule (between Rues des Ursulines and Ste-Anne). 694.0667

16 HOTEL CLARENDON

$$ Established in 1870, this hotel claims to be the oldest standing hotel in Quebec City, with the oldest continuously running restaurant in Canada. But what has made it a Quebec landmark is the stunning Art Deco entrance pavilion. The foyer is a beguiling Victorian setting with antique chairs and couches; the 96 rooms, completely renovated in 1992, are decorated with a more modern touch. ♦ 57 Rue Ste-Anne (at Rue des Jardins). 692.2480, 888/554.6001; fax 692.2480

Within the Hotel Clarendon:

RESTAURANT CHARLES BAILLAIRGE

★★$$$ A comfortable place with tapestry carpets and mahogany woodwork, this restaurant serves inventive French cuisine, presenting such unusual combinations as scallops napped with pepper and saffron sauce and lamb fillets complemented by maple and oyster sauce. The menu changes every 2 weeks. The prix-fixe Sunday brunch is a strong point, featuring a cornucopia of salads, cheese trays, cold meats, pâtés, hot breakfast fare, and desserts. ♦ French ♦ M-Sa, breakfast and dinner; Sunday, brunch and dinner. Reservations recommended for brunch. 692.2480

BAR L'EMPRISE

Attracting a loyal thirty-something crowd, this Art Deco-style bar has the best jazz in town, showcasing the talents of ensembles from all over North America and Europe. The ambiance is warm and intimate, and even though it seats 60, standing room only is the norm on weekends. There's no cover charge, but a one-drink minimum is required. The favorite potation here is beer, served in 23-ounce glasses, and several Irish and Quebec brews are on tap. ♦ Daily, 11:30AM-closing. 692.2480

17 BOUTIQUE SACHEM

Shiny black argillite sculptures made by Haida carvers from British Columbia, Iroquois medicine masks, and Ojibwe porcupine quill baskets are just some of the things you'll find in this mecca for craft and folk art fans. Other standouts are wool duffel coats fashioned by Inuit designers in northern Canada, British Columbian totem poles and masks, hand-woven rugs, Inuit soapstone carvings, tomahawks from many nations, snowshoes, wolf pelts, deerskin moccasins, and mounted bison heads. ♦ Daily, 9AM-9PM, June–Labor Day; daily, Labor Day–May. 17 Rue des Jardins (between Rues Ste-Anne and Buade). 692.3056. Also at 41 Rue Sous-le-Fort. 692.3366; Comptoir du Totem, 2700 Blvd Laurier, Ste-Foy. 656.0144

18 PLACE DE L'HÔTEL DE VILLE

ⓟ A marketplace in the 18th century, this large square became a public park in the 1880s when the market was moved to Place d'Youville, outside the city walls. Dominating the square is the bronze *Cardinal Taschereau Monument*, cast by Andre Vermare in 1923 and dedicated to Canada's first cardinal and a founder of **Laval University**. ♦ Rues Buade and Ste-Famille

19 SÉMINAIRE DE QUÉBEC

One of Canada's oldest institutions, the seminary was founded in 1663 by Monseigneur de Montmorency-Laval, as a training center for priests. It soon became the hub of ecclesiastical power in New France and had a profound influence on the province's intellectual and cultural development. By the 1800s, it had become the most important boys' school in Canada; and in 1852, **Laval University**, the first French-speaking university in North America, was established here. In 1949, the university, which today has 30,000 students, moved to the suburb of Ste-Foy, but its architectural faculty has since returned to the original center, which still houses a boys' high school and a coed college in its newer (19th-century) buildings.

As you enter the courtyard through wrought-iron gates designed by **François Baillairge**, you'll face the oldest wing, an impressive stone building with fine paned windows, a steeple shaped like a lantern, and a sundial dating back to 1773. During the summer, you can visit the Romanesque **Outer Chapel**, which is now a museum with one of the most significant collections of religious artifacts outside of Rome. You can also stroll through the former refectory and the stone vaults of Bishop Laval's kitchen, where colonists took refuge during Phipps's siege in 1690. The oval-fronted building at the top of Côte de la Fabrique marks the entrance to the **Museé de l'Amérique Française** (see page 133). ◆ Admission. Tours mid-June to Labor Day; call for times. 2 Côte de la Fabrique (at Rue Ste-Famille). 692.2843

20 47TH PARALLÈLE

★★$$$ Everything about this popular restaurant, from its name to décor and menu, suggests the lure of the road. Exotic pottery, sculpture, and tables evoke Africa and Latin America by way of Europe, but the final destination is, of course, the food. And it doesn't disappoint: meat, seafood, and pasta dishes are inventive and seem to please the locals and tourists who pack the place night after night. ◆ International ◆ Daily, lunch and dinner. 24 Rue Ste-Anne (between Rues du Trésor and des Jardins). Reservations recommended. 692.1534

21 BASILIQUE-CATHÉDRALE NOTRE-DAME-DE-QUÉBEC

The oldest Catholic site of worship in North America, this baroque masterpiece is the most prominent church in Quebec City, serving as a showcase for 3 centuries of work by esteemed Quebec architects. Opened in 1650, the church was elevated to the rank of cathedral in 1674 when Monseigneur de Montmorency-Laval was appointed bishop of New France. It was enlarged in 1684 and 1697, and the King's engineer, Chaussegros de Lery, oversaw further work on the chancel, the nave, and the façades in the 1740s. Only a decade after that work was completed, it was reduced to ruins by the British Conquest of 1759. In 1768, **Jean Baillairge**, the first of four generations of the Baillairge family to contribute to the church's reconstruction, began rebuilding it. Designated a basilica at the end of the 19th century, the church was severely damaged in a 1922 fire, which insiders claim was set by an American who planned to rob the church in the

---

One display near the beginning of the permanent *Mémoires* exhibit in the Musée de la Civilisation—showing lumberjacks paddling an airborne boat—evokes an amusing bit of French-Canadian folklore about men isolated for months in the woods. It was said that when the lumberjacks wanted to visit their girlfriends, the devil would tempt them with the offer of a flying canoe.

---

ensuing bedlam. It was rebuilt a few years later using original plans and photographs. But although **Maxim Roisin**, the Paris-trained architect in charge of reconstruction, maintained the general form of the church, he made the interior much richer and more ornate by adding a glittering, gilded baldachin, the magnificent ornamental canopy over the main altar that was sculpted by André Vermare, based on designs by **François Baillairge**. Also impressive is the Casavant organ with its 5,239 pipes, and an 18th-century crypt adjoining the church, where more than 900 people, including Comte Frontenac, are buried. Monseigneur de Montmorency-Laval's tomb was relocated to a small chapel built in his honor in the Basilica. ◆ Daily, 7:30AM-3:30PM; free guided tours of the basilica and the crypt are given daily 1 May-1 Nov. Several masses are scheduled throughout the week; call for times. 20 Rue Buade (at Côte de la Fabrique). 694.0665

Within the Basilique-Cathédrale Notre-Dame-de-Québec:

"FEUX SACRÉS" SOUND AND LIGHT SHOW

This multimedia show highlights the history and culture of the **Church of Quebec**. Images are projected onto screens and computer-controlled mirrors, as viewers listen to music and commentary (in French or English) via headsets. ◆ Admission. 1 May-15 Oct, hourly, 3:30-8:30PM. 694.4000

22 HOLY TRINITY ANGLICAN CATHEDRAL

This Palladian-style cathedral, completed in 1804, served the first Anglican congregation outside the British Isles and is the oldest Anglican church in Quebec. Built on property once owned by the Recollet Fathers, who shared their chapel with newly arrived Anglicans after the British takeover, the cathedral was commissioned by King George III and is a replica of London's St. Martin-in-the-Fields. The pews and woodwork, including the beamed ceiling, are made of English oak imported from the Royal Windsor Forest, and the royal box, part of the north balcony, is still reserved for members of the royal family or their representatives. Completely restored in 1992, the church has exquisite stained-glass windows and a magnificent 2,500-pipe organ, which is played during weekday recitals and Festival Evensong in July and August. On Saturdays during summer, an outdoor market, offering jewelry, leather goods, and souvenirs, is held in the church courtyard. ◆ Free guided tours May-Aug. Evensong: M-F, 4:45PM. Services: M-F, 8:30AM; Th, noon; Su, 8:30AM and 11AM (English), 9:30AM (French). 31 Rue des Jardins (between Rues St-Louis and Ste-Anne). 692.2193

THE BEST

Witold Rybczynski
Writer and Architect

Any hot summer afternoon in the park on **Mont-Royal**.

Visiting the most attractive architecture bookstore in North America at the **Canadian Centre for Architecture**.

The view of the kooky, tilting **Olympic Stadium** tower down **Rue Mont-Royal**.

Looking at de Witte's *Woman Playing the Virginals* in the **Montreal Museum of Fine Arts**; Moshe Safdie's building has a funny ramp, but it's still worth a visit.

Smoked meat at **Schwartz's Deli**; a drink at the **Ritz-Carlton**.

Walking across the **McGill University** campus, surrounded by green lawns, earnest students, and stodgy Edwardian architecture.

Any of the long residential streets in the **Plateau Mont-Royal** district; the narrow row houses, wrought-iron balconies, and exterior stairs are unique.

Saturday-morning shopping on **Boulevard St-Laurent**.

Strolling around Old Montreal—it's corny and full of tourists, but it is still a reminder of the salad days of this once-great port city.

23 QUEBEC EXPERIENCE

This terrific multisensory, multimedia presentation will transport you back to 10 great moments in Quebec's history. You'll witness the arrival of explorers and religious institutions, and skirmishes and wars, as well as watch busy shipyards and jostling marketplaces come to life with the latest high-tech wizardry. The first of its kind in Canada, the 150-seat theater is equipped with 26 three-dimensional projectors, laser lighting, special sound effects, holographic characters, and mobile screens. Each show lasts 30 minutes, in alternating English and French versions. ♦ Admission. Daily; first English show 10:45AM, last 9:15PM. 8 Rue du Trésor (at Rue Buade). 694.4000

24 MUSÉE DES URSULINES

Located within the walls of the Ursuline monastery, this museum has three floors, dedicated to a fascinating collection of crafts, handiwork, and artifacts from 120 years of Ursuline life under the New World French regime. Also in the museum are several fine examples of French-Canadian pine armoires and cabinetry dating back to the 17th century, as well as such antique musical instruments as Erard harps, violins, and mandolins, and wood carvings, tomahawks, and other artifacts made by native North Americans. The first Ursuline nuns arrived in New France from Dieppe in 1639, and, after 3 difficult years in Place Royale, moved to their present Upper Town location. The original fireplace and indoor well of the 1644 residence of Madame de la Peltrie, the order's cofounder, can be seen in the museum. The Ursulines were a teaching order, and their Quebec girls' school, the first in North America, still operates today. ♦ Admission. May-Sept: Tu-Sa, 10AM-noon, 1PM-5PM; Su, 1PM-5PM; Oct-Apr: Tu-Su, 1PM-4:30PM. Reservations required for large groups. 12 Rue Donnacona (between Rues des Jardins and du Parloir). 694.0694

Adjacent to the Musée des Ursulines:

URSULINE CHAPEL

Built in 1902, the chapel contains much of the interior from the original chapel of 1723. Several pieces, including the pulpit and retables, were carved in the early 18th century by noted Quebec sculptor Pierre-Noel Levasseur and later gilded by the nuns. Also worth viewing are the exceptional paintings, including works by Le Brun and Phillippe de Champaigne, which were purchased in Paris by the Ursulines' chaplain in the early 1800s. A plaque commemorates General Montcalm, defeated leader of the French forces. Next to the chapel, the **Centre Marie-de-l'Incarnation** houses a bookstore and an exhibit of personal belongings of the order's cofounder. ♦ May-Oct, Tu-Sa, 10AM-11:30AM, 1:30PM-4:30PM; Su, 1:30PM-4:30PM. 694.0413

25 RUE DU TRÉSOR

For a souvenir sketch of Quebec, perhaps a vivid pastel or a watercolor, stop by this street-market-turned-gallery. Hundreds of works blanket the walls of this lively alley, where budding artists will sketch your portrait on the spot. Centuries ago, colonists trudged up this street to pay their rent at the royal treasury—hence the street's name. The treasury was located in the **Maison Maillou** (17

Restaurants/Clubs: Red | Hotels: Purple | Shops: Orange | Outdoors/Parks: Green | Sights/Culture: Blue

Rue St-Louis), a typical 18th-century building that houses the Quebec Chamber of Commerce. Though it's closed to the public, it's worth strolling by to admire the steep, slanting roof, the dormer windows, and especially the wrought-iron shutters that once guarded the king's revenues that were collected from the new colony. The house was built in 1736, and a vault with 6-foot-thick walls was added in 1799 to protect the gold bullion lodged in the treasury. ♦ Between Rues Ste-Anne and Buade

26 WALLS AND FORTIFICATIONS

Completed in 1815, the **Poudriére de l'Esplanade** (Esplanade powder magazine) serves as the reception center for Quebec's fortifications. It's located next to **Esplanade Park**, where military exercises and parades once took place. To get a sense of the city's military history, explore the gates, bastions, and polished black cannons on foot as you wander along the 3-mile walkway on top of the ramparts.

The cliff provided a natural defense where the Upper Town faces the river, but early settlers also wanted protection on the landward side, so in 1690 the French built a wooden palisade along the west side of the city. A second, more permanent wall was begun 3 years later but never completed. In 1745, with British threats of attack mounting, massive dirt and stone walls, or ramparts, were erected by the French along the west. Once the British took over, Quebec became a completely militarized city, and the walls along the north and east sides, along Rue des Remparts (then just a footpath) and Dufferin Terrace, were completed by the early 1800s.

After Confederation, the gates were demolished to allow a better flow of traffic. Lord Dufferin, Canada's first governor general (1872-1878), then initiated a beautification program to preserve and enhance the city's military fortifications. Piles of dirt, which had camouflaged the ramparts, were removed to

expose the stone walls, and the St-Louis and Kent gates were rebuilt as grand, château-style structures. The present **Porte St-Jean** was built in 1936, and **Porte Prescott** was added in 1983. Daily guided tours are conducted (in English and French) between mid-May and Labor Day. ♦ Free. Daily, mid-May to 31 Oct. 100 Rue St-Louis (at Porte St-Louis). 648.7016

27 MAISON SEWELL

This 1803 Palladian house was one of the first examples of English-style architecture in Quebec City. It was the home of Judge Jonathan Sewell, an American loyalist who fled to Canada during the American Revolution. An early advocate of confederation, Sewell was chief justice of Lower Canada for 30 years. In the rebellion of 1837, the French came here to stone his house. Sewell had 22 children. The house is not open to the public. ♦ 87 Rue St-Louis (at Rue d'Auteuil)

28 LA CARAVELLE

★$$Fresh seafood, from mussels to shrimp and fish, is the specialty of this lively Mediterranean bistro, but classic French dishes such as duck à l'orange appear on the menu, too. The restaurant is situated on the ground floor of an inn of the same name. There's a singer every night. ♦ French/Italian ♦ Daily, lunch and dinner. 68 Rue St-Louis (between Rues du Parloir and Ste-Ursule). 694.9022

29 CHEZ MARIE-CLAIRE

$$ Centrally located in the Latin Quarter, about a 5-minute walk from restaurants and attractions, this is one of the few bed-and-breakfast accommodations in Old Quebec's Upper Town. Marie-Claire Tremblay is the charming owner of the airy and attractive 100-year-old home, which has three guest rooms decorated with antiques and quilts (two have private baths). Complete breakfasts, such as omelettes or French toast with maple syrup, are served. Children are welcome here. ♦ 62 Rue Ste-Ursule (between Rues St-Louis and des Ursulines). 692.1556

30 L'OMELETTE

$ As its name indicates, this cozy restaurant specializes in omelettes, of which the selection is vast and portions generous. But there are also excellent French toast, pancakes, quiches, and other dishes that make this the perfect spot for a straightforward but solid meal. The prices are unbeatable for the Old City and service is friendly. ♦ Canadian ♦ Daily, breakfast, lunch, and (summer only) dinner. 66 Rue St-Louis (between Rues du Parloir and St-Ursule). 694.9626

In the 1630s, Samuel de Champlain issued an order prohibiting blasphemy. The penalty was having one's tongue cut out.

The Maison Jolliet, which houses the Funicular Railway, was built for Louis Jolliet, codiscoverer of the Mississippi River. Trained as a Jesuit priest, he became a highly successful fur trader and navigator, and in his later years, he was appointed hydrographer (one who studies and charts bodies of water) to Louis XIV. He lived in this house until his death in 1700.

31 AUX ANCIENS CANADIENS

★★$$ Tucked into the historic **Maison Jacquet**, the oldest house in town (1699), and extending into a former school next door, this restaurant specializes in Quebec traditions (the waitstaff even wears period costumes). Ancient tools and traditional wood sculptures fill the four low-ceilinged dining rooms. The authentic French-Canadian menu presents regional delicacies and heritage dishes, such as hearty pea soup, *tourtière*, and maple-sugar pie. But modern dishes— including lamb Charlotte with zucchini and red pepper coulis, and duck with maple syrup— are also in the chef's repertoire. And there's a children's menu. ◆ French-Canadian ◆ Daily, lunch and dinner. Reservations recommended. 34 Rue St-Louis (at Rue des Jardins). 692.1627

31 AU PARMESAN

★★$$$ You may find yourself waiting in line to get into this cheerful trattoria, where the lively ambiance is as big a draw as the generous portions of pasta, steak, and seafood. Owner Luigi Leoni plays host, and a wandering accordionist adds to the boisterous atmosphere, where tables, covered in bright red-checkered cloths, are jam-packed every night in tourist season. Thousands of odd-shaped liquor bottles and assorted ceramics add a certain eclectic charm. Valet parking is complimentary. ◆ Italian ◆ Daily, lunch and dinner. Reservations required. 38 Rue St-Louis (between Rues des Jardins and du Parloir). 692.0341

32 LA MAISON DARLINGTON

Established in 1875, this traditional clothing store is justly proud of its old-fashioned service and first-rate selection of high-quality warm and woolly items, including men's and women's hats and mitts imported from England and Scotland. The shop stocks rain gear, ranging from basic yellow slickers to designer-label coats, for cool and inclement days. You'll also find hand-smocked girls' dresses from Quebec and Ballantyne-brand lambswool, cashmere, and merino sweaters. ◆ M-Sa; Su, noon-4PM. 7 Rue Buade (at Rue du Fort). 692.2268

33 MAISON DU TOURISME DE QUÉBEC

Housed in the former **Union Hotel**, a Palladian-style building dating back to 1805, the Quebec tourist office is an excellent resource for information and brochures about travel, accommodations, and attractions throughout Quebec's 19 tourist regions. ◆ Daily. 12 Rue Ste-Anne (at Rue du Fort). 800/363.7777 (Canada and US)

34 MUSÉE DU FORT

At this very small theater, animated sound-and-light shows dramatize the six sieges of Quebec on a 400-square-foot model of the city as it was in the 1740s. The shows, both educational and entertaining, clearly and accurately portray Quebec's historical battles, including the battle of the Plains of Abraham and the American invasion of 1775. The information may be too detailed for young children. English shows every hour on the hour 10AM-6PM in summer; call for schedules at other times of the year. ◆ Admission. Daily; call ahead for hours. 10 Rue Ste-Anne (at Rue du Fort). 692.1759

Within the Musée du Fort:

GAMBRINUS

★★$$$ A stone's throw from the **Château Frontenac** and in the same building as the **Musée du Fort**, this charming mahogany-paneled restaurant has a contemporary ambiance, hanging green plants, and a guitar player who serenades diners most evenings. As you'd expect in a spot named after the Latin word for shrimp, seafood is the specialty, although owner Giovanni Venturino also serves meat and pasta dishes. Some appetizing concoctions that draw diners include salmon tartare with chives, caribou filet with hazelnuts and sour cherries in kirsch, and filet mignon with bleu cheese. During summer, the small terrace overlooking Place d'Armes is also a refreshing retreat for a cold beer. Service is excellent, and the wine list is good too. ◆ Seafood ◆ 24 June-Labor Day: daily, lunch and dinner. Labor Day-23 June: M-F, lunch and dinner; Sa-Su, dinner. Reservations recommended. 15 Rue du Fort (at Rue Ste-Anne). 692.5144

35 ANCIEN BUREAU DE POSTE (OLD POST OFFICE)

Although it's been renamed the **Louis St-Laurent** building, most locals still call this dome-roofed landmark the Old Post Office. Constructed in 1873 and enlarged in 1914, the building is now used as an exhibition hall by the Canadian Parks Service. Until 1837, there was an inn on this property called **Le Chien d'Or**, or the Golden Dog. A bas-relief from the former structure was incorporated into the newer building's entryway. ◆ 3 Rue Buade (at Rue du Fort)

Restaurants/Clubs: **Red** | Hotels: **Purple** | Shops: **Orange** | Outdoors/Parks: **Green** | Sights/Culture: **Blue**

36 LAVAL MONUMENT

The monument in front of the **Old Post Office** honors Quebec's first bishop, Monseigneur François de Montmorency-Laval (1623-1708), founder of the **Séminaire de Québec**, which later became **Laval University**. Created by Philippe Hebert, the sculpture was unveiled in 1908 to commemorate the two hundredth anniversary of the bishop's death. ♦ Rue du Fort and Côte de la Montagne

37 PARC MONTMORENCY

ⓟ Named in honor of Monseigneur de Montmorency-Laval, Quebec's first bishop, this shady park straddles Upper and Lower Town and has an exceptional view of the **Séminaire de Québec**. In 1667, Jean Talon, the intendant of New France, built the first house here. Monseigneur de Saint-Vallier, Quebec's second bishop, soon bought the structure and expanded it into a large episcopal palace. (Its neoclassical replacement, built in 1847, is across the street at 2 Rue Port-Dauphin.) In 1792, the building became home to the Legislative Assembly of Lower Canada. It was refurbished in the early 1800s to serve as Quebec's parliament, then destroyed by fire in 1883. Also in the park is the **Louis Hebert Monument**, a tribute to Louis Hebert, an apothecary who arrived in Quebec in 1617 and farmed where the seminary is today. The bronze monument, sculpted by Alfred Laliberté, depicts Hebert holding a sheaf of wheat in one hand and flanked by his daughter and son-in-law. It was presented in 1818 to commemorate the tricentennial of the arrival of Quebec's first settlers. Another monument in the park, the **Cartier Monument**, by sculptor G.H. Hill, pays homage to Georges-Etienne Cartier, one of Canada's Fathers of Confederation. A great federal politician, he headed the Quebec wing of the Conservative party and was a close ally of Sir John A. Macdonald, Canada's first prime minister. ♦ Côte de la Montagne and Rue Port-Dauphin

38 LE CONTINENTAL

★★★$$$ If you're nostalgic for the gone-but-not-forgotten days of black-tie waiters, flambées, and pampered service, this landmark restaurant, in the stately, charming home built for the Taschereau family in 1845, will feed your longing. Opened in 1956 by the Sgobba family and carried on by their sons, the restaurant has maintained its ranking as one of Quebec City's top dining spots, famous for its savoir-faire. A favorite haunt of Quebec civil servants and the bourgeois crowd, it prepares classic French meals and serves them in style: flambéed filet mignon, shrimp Newburg, or rack of lamb Victoria, and that flaming dessert classic—crêpes Suzette. Valet parking is complimentary. ♦ Continental ♦ M-Sa, lunch

and dinner; Su, dinner, Feb-Oct. Reservations recommended. 26 Rue St-Louis (between Rues du Trésor and des Jardins). 694.9995

39 ANCIEN PALAIS DE JUSTICE

Built in 1887 on the former site of the Recollet convent and church, which were razed by fire in the late 18th century, this building now houses the Ministry of Finance. Its ornate façade—featuring coats of arms and columns of fleurs-de-lis, among other motifs—was inspired by those on châteaux in the Loire Valley. ♦ 12 Rue St-Louis (at Rue du Trésor)

40 PLACE D'ARMES

ⓟ This tree-shaded park was once a military training site as well as the parade grounds for nearby **Château St-Louis**. When the **Citadel** was completed in the mid-1800s, the troops' parades were moved to **Esplanade Park**, and in the 1880s, a fountain (a high column topped with a sculpture of a child holding a fish spouting water) was installed, surrounded by a chain fence. After church services on Sundays, it became fashionable to race on horseback around the Rond des Chaînes (Circle of Chains). The present Gothic fountain, **Monument de la Foi** (**Monument of Faith**), was built to commemorate the tricentennial of the arrival of the Recollets, Quebec's first religious community, in 1615. ♦ Bounded by Rues du Fort, du Trésor, Ste-Anne, and St-Louis

41 CHALMERS-WESLEY UNITED CHURCH

Built in 1852, this beautiful Neo-Gothic church with its slender steeple now serves two congregations—one French, one English. Eight glorious floor-to-ceiling stained-glass windows and the superbly carved dark-oak woodwork create an inviting glow within the sanctuary. During summer, local artists exhibit their works on the balcony. ♦ Offerings accepted. Sunday evening recitals in summer start at 6PM. ♦ Free. 26 June-25 Aug, 10AM-5PM. 78 Rue Ste-Ursule (between Ave Ste-Geneviève and Rue St-Louis). 692.0431

42 SANCTUAIRE NOTRE-DAME-DU-SACRE-COEUR

Nestled between two buildings across from **Chalmers-Wesley**, this impeccably maintained graystone church, a replica of a Gothic chapel in Issoudun, France, was built in 1910 by architect **François-Xavier Berlinguet**. The magnificent stained-glass windows cast a lovely pool of light on the front altar, and throughout the church, old-style marble plaques are dedicated to families in the congregation. ♦ Free. Daily, 7AM-8PM. 71 Rue Ste-Ursule (between Ave Ste-Geneviève and Rue St-Louis). 692.3787

QUARTIER ST. ROCH

With its old walls, fairy-tale architecture, and pervasive sense of grandeur, you may wonder if Quebec City has anything in the way of "regular" neighborhoods. Indeed it has, and one such, the St. Roch quarter, is worth a detour if only for the contrast. Once mainly a working-class neighborhood and the place where Quebecers went to shop, St. Roch is now in full transition as television stations and high-tech firms carve cool office spaces out of old industrial lofts and a spate of new restaurants, hotels, and home décor shops move in. The quarter forms a relatively compact grid that spreads out west from the **Gare du Palais**, itself worth a look even if you don't have a train to catch (and home to two popular restaurants, **Aviatic Club** and **Charbon Steakhouse**). Walk along Boulevard Charest Est, the main east-west byway, to have a look at the architecture and the new establishments settling into old quarters. If you're hungry or need a pause, head straight to **Le Café du Clocher Penché** (203 Rue St-Joseph; 640.0597), a bistro full of character much frequented by local artists and students for its robust but creative menu, good ambiance, and decidedly untouristy prices.

43 LE CHÂTEAU FRONTENAC

$$$$ Canada's most famous castle hotel is as Canadian a trademark as the Royal Canadian Mounted Police. The upscale property began with a railway magnate's dream. Spurred by the travel boom of the late 1800s, William Van Horne, president of **Canadian Pacific**, decided to build a string of fabulous hotels to lure tourists across Canada. This hostelry was to be the crowning jewel, which he constructed on a prestigious site facing the **Château St-Louis** and marketed as the gateway to the Orient. (Travelers would disembark from steamships docked in the port, spend an extravagant night or two at the château, then depart by rail.) Van Horne named the hotel for Governor Louis de Buade, Comte de Frontenac.

New York architect **Bruce Price**, father of etiquette maven Emily Post, fashioned the hotel in the style of Loire Valley châteaux with a steeply pitched copper roof, dormer windows, spiraling chimneys, and Scottish brick, all of which lend a medieval air to the High Victorian structure. When the hotel opened in 1893, it had 170 rooms—including 93 with such luxuries as bathrooms and fireplaces—as well as a staircase copied from Marie Antoinette's palace (the Petit Trianon) and a ballroom decorated in blue and gold to resemble the Hall of Mirrors at Versailles. Designers William and Frank Maxwell of Montreal, who were dispatched to Europe to select furniture, added Victorian woodwork and thick carpets to the rich décor. The grand hotel was an instant success. By 1924, an imposing 17-story tower was added, expanding the hotel's capacity to 544 rooms.

The massive stone structure also became part of the social and political fabric of the city, with its own romantic legends. Filmmaker Alfred Hitchcock stayed here, then returned in the early 1950s to shoot *I Confess* with Montgomery Clift and Anne Baxter. (Each night during filming, Baxter stunned guests in the elegant dining room by lighting up a cigar after her meal.) Other famous guests have ranged from Charles Lindbergh to Queen Elizabeth. For 2 weeks in August 1943, Winston Churchill and Franklin Roosevelt planned the Normandy Invasion at the hotel; and in 1985 another political rendezvous took place, this time between Canadian Prime Minister Brian Mulroney and President Ronald Reagan, both of Irish ancestry, who met for what they called the Shamrock Summit.

In recent years a $60 million renovation and expansion has spruced up existing rooms and added a new wing with 66 rooms, four Entrée Gold floors with personalized concierge services, a pool, a health club, and a terrace. Currently managed by Fairmont Hotels & Resorts, the hotel now has 607 rooms (most with excellent views of the river) along with a host of shops in and below the lobby and ongoing guided tours. Not surprisingly, an atmosphere of commotion and commerciality often eclipses that of gentility, and today the hotel may be better suited to families and corporate travelers than those seeking tranquillity and true local flavor. ♦ 1 Rue des Carrières (between Ave Mont Carmel and Rue St-Louis). 692.3861, 800/441.1414; fax 692.1751

Within the Château Frontenac:

LE CHAMPLAIN

★★★$$$$ Named in honor of Quebec's founder, Samuel de Champlain, this is the city's most elegant and formal dining room.

Restaurants/Clubs: Red | Hotels: Purple | Shops: Orange | Outdoors/Parks: Green | Sights/Culture: Blue

Embellished with wood-beaded chandeliers dangling from the high ceiling, intricately carved wooden columns, and high-backed tapestry chairs, the setting is ideal for intimate meals or closing business deals. The food lives up to Château Frontenac's distinguished reputation under the talented direction of chef Jean Soulard. Such refined dishes as red snapper filet with herb *jus,* diced turnips, and pearl onions, pheasant and lobster flavored with ginger and maple, and Île-Verte lamb (naturally salted by the ocean water that bathes its fields with the rising tide) star on the classic but creative French menu. Soulard seasons dishes with fresh herbs grown in the rooftop garden. A harpist plays in the evenings. ◆ French ◆ M-Sa, dinner; Su, brunch and dinner. Jacket required. Reservations required. 692.3861

CAFÉ DE LA TERRASSE

★★$$ The pastel Art Deco interior provides a tranquil and timeless setting for this long and narrow restaurant, with expansive paned windows looking out onto Dufferin Terrace. An à la carte menu offers such dishes as spinach quiche with goat cheese or fusilli gratin with smoked salmon for lunch, and scallops with papaya coulis or veal paillard with Roquefort for dinner. Terrific well-priced buffets are set out for all meals. ◆ Continental ◆ Daily, breakfast, lunch, and dinner. 692.3861 ┗

BAR ST. LAURENT

With its cinematic view of the river, lovely rich wood tones, and elegant but relaxed atmosphere, this piano bar is the best place in town to sip a drink. When you've had your fill of sight-seeing, come here for a touch of serenity and make yourself comfortable at the large round bar or at one of the well-spaced window tables. ◆ Daily, 11AM-closing. 692.3861 ┗

44 CHAMPLAIN MONUMENT

The imposing 50-foot bronze statue of Samuel de Champlain, founder of Quebec, is the work of French sculptor Paul Chevre. The monument, unveiled in 1898, faces the St. Lawrence River and Place Royale, where Champlain arrived in 1608 to establish a French colony in the New World. ◆ Rue St-Louis and Dufferin Terr

43 UNESCO WORLD HERITAGE MONUMENT

In 1985, UNESCO classified Quebec's historic district as a World Heritage Site, making it the first urban center in North America to receive that honorary designation. The area covers 323 acres, including Upper and Lower Town, the fortified walls, military installations, and sections of the harbor. The modern bronze, glass, and granite monument, near the statue of Champlain, was erected that same year to celebrate this milestone. ◆ Rue St-Louis and Dufferin Terr

44 INFOTOURISTE

Across from the **Château Frontenac** on the **Dufferin Terrace,** by the entrance to the funicular, is the city's best information kiosk, with extensive travel information about the city and the province, a reservation service for cars and hotels, and currency exchange. It also sells souvenirs and tickets for bus tours. ◆ Daily, June 21–Labor Day, 8:30AM-7:30PM; Labor Day–June 20 9AM-5PM. 12 Rue Ste-Anne (on Dufferin Terr). 877/266.5687

45 DUFFERIN TERRACE

This elegant and expansive 2,200-foot wooden boardwalk, complete with gazebos, benches, and wrought-iron guardrails, provides a magnificent view of the St. Lawrence River and Place Royale. It was built in 1878 as part of a beautification project launched by Lord Dufferin, governor general of Canada, and named in his honor. In front of the **Château Frontenac** is a kiosk for the **Funicular,** which whisks you on a short but steep descent to the **Quartier Petit-Champlain** (nominal charge) in Old Quebec's Lower Town. During winter, there's a toboggan slide at one end, a tradition dating back to the late 1800s. In summer, street musicians and other performers stake out the terrace where they're sure to be noticed by strollers enjoying ice cream cones bought from street kiosks. ◆ Along the cliff between Ave St-Denis and Rue St-Louis

45 PROMENADES DES GOUVERNEURS (GOVERNORS' WALK)

For a blockbuster perspective on the city, the river, and the surrounding area, continue along Dufferin Terrace to this 6-foot-wide walkway. Built in 1960, it counts more than 300 steps that hug the side of a steep cliff along the outside wall from the **Citadel** to the top of **Cap-Diamant,** the highest point in the city. Together, the **Promenade** and the terrace are three quarters of a mile long, so those who aren't in shape might want to start at the top and work their way down. On sunny days the lookout at the summit provides views as far as the Quebec Bridge, Île d'Orléans, and the Laurentians. ◆ Closed in winter. Adjacent to Dufferin Terr

46 LE CHÂTEAU DE PIERRE

$ Behind this small inn's attractive graystone façade are 14 traditionally decorated, non-smoking rooms with private bathrooms ideal for those who prize location as well as value. The inn is just steps from the Jardin des

Gouverneurs and the Citadel, and some guestrooms have St. Lawrence River and garden views. Owners Richard and Lily Couturier are eager to help guests with anything from directions to restaurant tips. A selection of apartments and studios equipped with kitchenettes nearby is available for longer stays. ♦ 17 Ave Sainte-Geneviève (at Rue Laporte). 694.0429, 888/694.0429; fax 694.0153. www.chateaudepierre.com

47 JARDIN DES GOUVERNEURS

⊕ Next to the **Château Frontenac**, this serene park, surrounded by Victorian houses (many of which have been restored and converted to inns), was once the private domain of the ruling governor and his family. It is now the site of the **Wolfe-Montcalm Monument**, a 50-foot obelisk said to be the only monument in the world dedicated to both the victor and the vanquished. Wolfe, who led the British forces, died victorious on the battlefield on the Plains of Abraham, whereas Montcalm died shortly after learning of the French defeat. The tribute to the generals—commissioned by Lord Dalhousie, a governor of Canada, and unveiled in 1827—symbolized the duality of the struggling country and attempted to quell friction between the French and English. When translated, the Latin inscription reads: "Their courage gave them a common death, history a common fame, posterity a common monument." ♦ Bounded by Rues des Carrières and Laporte and by Aves Ste-Geneviève and Mont Carmel

48 AU MANOIR SAINTE-GENEVIÈVE

$$ Built as a private home, this elegant, nine-room Victorian inn is a quiet retreat in the heart of the old city. Looking out on the **Jardin des Gouverneurs**, the inn has individually decorated rooms—some with antiques and poster beds—and is close to everything. There's also a secluded terrace for guests on the third floor. There is no restaurant. ♦ 13 Ave Ste-Geneviève (at Rue Laporte). 694.1666

49 THE CITADEL

Perched high on **Cap-Diamant**, 350 feet above the St. Lawrence River, this sprawling walled fort is hidden from enemy eyes by grassy knolls. Within the complex are two buildings—a 1750 powder magazine and a 1693 redoubt, which is now one of the oldest buildings in North America. The Citadel itself was built by the British after they conquered Quebec. Their first fort on the site was erected in 1783 to protect the city from the threat of invasion by the American colonies, which had tried in 1775 to gain control of Quebec. A second American attack, in 1812, prompted the British to strengthen their fortifications, so between 1820 and 1832 the fortress walls were built as a continuation of the walls around the city.

The star-shaped plan used by the British is typical of fortifications designed by the Marquis de Vauban, a 17th-century French military engineer. Five heavily armed bastions, or points of the star, allowed for easy fire on any approaching enemies. The sole entrance to the fortress, then and now, is the narrow **Dalhousie Gate**, accessible only by Côte de la Citadelle near **Porte St-Louis**. The Canadian Artillery occupied the fort after the British garrison left in 1871, 4 years after Canada's Confederation.

Since 1920, Canada's famous Royal 22nd Regiment, or "VanDoos"— a name derived from the English pronunciation of *vingt-deux* (French for "22")—have been stationed here. Because it is still an active military base, access to the grounds is available only on a guided tour, which takes visitors by several of the 25 buildings—including the governor general's residence and the officers' mess hall—and inside two military museums run by the Royal 22nd Regiment. The museums have exhibits documenting battles from the 18th century to the Korean War, as well as uniforms, badges, medals, and weapons, including bayonets and Ross and Enfield rifles. One museum is in the old military prison, where you can see an authentic prison cell. If you time your visit right, you can catch the morning changing of the guard (including Batisse, the regimented goat) or the evening retreat of the VanDoos in their ceremonial red tunics. Parking is available inside the fortress. ♦ Admission. Daily, 10AM-4PM, Apr to mid-May; daily, 9AM-5PM, mid-May to June; daily, 9AM-6PM, July–Labor Day; daily, 9AM-4PM, Sept; daily, 10AM-3PM, Oct; Nov–Apr, by group reservation only. 1 Côte de la Citadelle (just east of Porte St-Louis). 694.2815

Restaurants/Clubs: Red | Hotels: Purple | Shops: Orange | Outdoors/Parks: Green | Sights/Culture: Blue

NATIONAL BATTLEFIELDS PARK

Although the official name of this magnificent 250-acre expanse, located on a precipice overlooking the **St. Lawrence River**, is National Battlefields Park, Quebecers and other Canadians always call it the **Plains of Abraham**. The park is named after Abraham Martin, who assumed ownership of a parcel of land between **Rue Claire Fontaine** and **Rue Ste-Geneviève** in 1646, property that now falls mainly within the park. The land later became the site of a historic 18th-century confrontation between the British and the French, who were wrestling for control of the New World.

On 17 June 1759, General James Wolfe led a British army of 9,000 soldiers and a fleet of 50 ships, mounted with 2,000 cannons, to **Quebec City**. Wolfe's men positioned themselves at Île d'Orléans, the island east of Quebec's Old Port, and at Lévis, a settlement directly across the St. Lawrence River from the Plains of Abraham. Throughout the summer, British ships bombarded Quebec City, and, finally, on the night of 12 September, Wolfe successfully led 4,000 men to the heights above the city.

The next morning the two armies—the French led by General Marquis de Montcalm—faced each other across the grassy fields, somewhere between the present-day **Musée du Québec** and **Cartier Avenue**. The actual battle lasted less than an hour, culminating in a decisive victory for the British; a few days later, the French surrendered. In the meantime, both Wolfe and Montcalm died from wounds suffered on the battlefield. (In 1760, the British and French again fought in and around the plains; the British were able to retain control over the city.)

National Battlefields Park was created in 1908 to celebrate Quebec City's three hundredth anniversary. Today it is one of North America's most beautiful city parks and

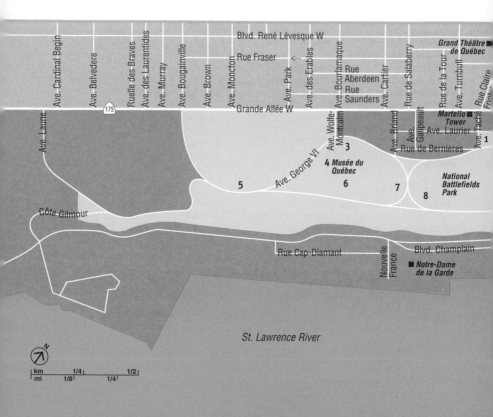

an idyllic retreat from Quebec's urban bustle. The pastoral landscape and well-maintained roads and paths make the plains a favorite place for bicycling (the city's most popular sport), jogging, walking, and even cross-country skiing in winter.

1 JEANNE D'ARC GARDEN

Designed in 1938 by landscape architect Louis Perron, this lovely two-level garden surrounds a statue of Jeanne d'Arc (Joan of Arc) on horseback, in memory of the fallen soldiers of 1759. A variety of perennials, bulbs, and annuals bloom here from spring to fall. ◆ Ave Laurier (between Pl Montcalm and Ave Taché)

2 DISCOVERY PAVILION OF THE PLAINS OF ABRAHAM

This large building, reminiscent of a French country chateau, houses a park welcome and information center and is a good place to get your bearings before setting out to explore the expansive Plains of Abraham. It is also home to a scale model of the park and *Odyssey Canada,* a multimedia show and interactive exhibition that features virtual appearances by Jacques Cartier and generals Wolfe and Montcalm as it traces the history of Canada from 1500 to the present. ◆ Pavilion open

mid-June to mid-Oct, 8:30AM-5:30PM; mid-Oct to mid-June, 8:30AM-5PM. *Odyssey Canada* exhibition is open mid-June to mid-Oct, 10AM-5:30PM; mid-Oct to mid-June, 10AM-5PM; admission. The center also runs a shuttle bus that takes visitors on tours of the park daily, Sept 1–June 14 from 10AM to 5:30PM, and on weekends in June through Columbus Day from 10AM to 5:30PM; there is a nominal fee. 835 Ave Wilfrid-Laurier. 649.6157

3 NATIONAL BATTLEFIELDS PARK INTERPRETATION CENTER

Significant moments in the history of the **Plains of Abraham** are presented in this high-tech exhibition hall. Located on the first floor of the **Baillairge Pavilion,** now part of the **Musée du Québec** complex, the center uses the latest audiovisual techniques to transport visitors from the days of bloody skirmishes between the British and the French up to the present in a 20-minute self-guided tour (an English recording is available). ◆ Daily, 10AM-5PM. Admission. 1 Ave Wolfe-Montcalm (at Ave George VI). 643.2150

MUSÉE DU QUÉBEC

4 MUSÉE DU QUÉBEC

A complex of three buildings on the **Plains of Abraham,** the museum has a collection of nearly 18,000 works—the majority of which are considered prized objects of historic significance (called the *"patrimoine Québécois"*) representing Quebec's artistic and cultural heritage. The permanent collection reflects the evolution of art in Quebec from

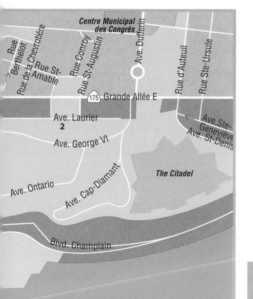

On average, the Château Frontenac hotel registers one honeymoon couple a day. Over the past century, more than 39,000 honeymooners have stayed at the grand hotel, and now many of those couples are coming back to celebrate their silver and golden wedding anniversaries.

BREAKING THE ICE: QUEBEC'S WINTER CARNIVAL

Imagine taking a bath outdoors in the snow. Then mentally bring the mercury down to subzero temperatures. Finally, picture this Siberian scenario taking place while hundreds of more sensible folks bundled up in hats, boots, and heavy coats mill around and gawk. If this notion isn't enough to give you the shivers, you might be hardy enough to endure the real thing: carnival Quebecois style. Bone-chilling thermometer readings and unpredictable weather give Quebec City's *Carnaval* its own inimitable character. Certainly the traditional polar bear swim sets the winter carnival apart from pre-Lenten amusements in balmier climes, but it is only one of the events that makes the world's largest winter celebrations different.

The city's first winter fête was an informal affair: In January 1894, a series of spirited get-togethers helped the community break the glacial monotony of life in an area blanketed with snow 6 months of the year. The revelry also had a religious role: The word *carnival* in Latin translates roughly as "to remove meat." The winter party provided an excuse for Quebecers to feast and frolic in anticipation of Lent's 40 days of fasting and abstinence. Participants were secure in the knowledge they could atone for any excesses in the weeks ahead.

After this inaugural carnival, the celebration was held at irregular intervals until 1954, when it was formally declared an annual event with a budget of $38,000. Nowadays the tab comes to slightly more than $3 million. For the Quebec City business and hospitality industry, though, the investment pays off handsomely: The 11-day diversion, which always begins the first

Thursday in February, pumps roughly $28 million into the local economy.

Despite its high financial profile, the festive essence of *Carnaval* hasn't strayed far from its origins. Several spectacles from a century ago are still vital elements of the event, prime among them the building of a full-scale snow palace on **Parliament Hill** and the elaborate processions that herald the beginning and end of the celebration. Floats for the parade are created in a special workshop by 60 part-time artisans, and more than a dozen ice sculptors devote a full 2 months to fashioning the palace.

The last day of the carnival is marked by a canoe race across the **St. Lawrence River** from Quebec City to **Lévis**. Because the river is partially frozen, the five-person teams must alternately push, pull, and haul their 250-pound vessels to shore, navigating ice floes, battling the currents, and avoiding any slushy traps that might plunge them into the frigid waters—hardly smooth sailing. The race, like much else at the carnival, has its roots in the area's rugged past. Although the canoes used today may be made of fiberglass instead of pine, the natural forces faced by the crews on the mighty St. Lawrence have not changed since the early days. And confronting the elements is what differentiates *Carnaval* in Quebec from its sister shindigs around the globe. Here, the occasion isn't only a celebration—it's a challenge. For more information on *Carnaval*, contact **Quebec Carnaval**, 290 Rue Joly, Quebec City G1L 1N8; 418/626.3716, or go to www.carnaval.qc.ca.

the late 17th century to the present, with a variety of artistic media, including paintings, sculpture, drawings, antique furniture, decorative works, and folk art. Also here are special exhibits of Quebec's sacred art, invaluable to a culture whose history is so closely tied to the Catholic Church, as well as temporary exhibits of some of the finest work by Quebec, Canadian, and international artists.

In 1987, Quebec's provincial government undertook a major expansion of the museum, taking its original home, a three-story neoclassical granite building that had served as the provincial museum since 1933, and linking it with the nearby 1870 Baillairge building, an imposing, fortresslike structure that had been used as a jail for nearly 100 years. The original museum, designed by Quebec architect **Wilfred Lacroix**, is now called the **Pavilion Gerard-Morisset**, where works from the permanent collection are displayed. Quebec architects **Charles Dorval** and **Louis Fortin** designed a third structure to link the

old jail to the pavilion. Called the **Great Hall**, the stunning newer building is crowned by a cross of skylights that resemble gigantic quartz crystals shooting out of the ground. It houses a 100-seat restaurant that opens onto an inviting terrace with a spectacular view of the **Plains of Abraham** and the St. Lawrence River. Opposite the restaurant is the museum's book and gift shop.

The **Baillairge Pavilion** retains many of the original features of the old jail, including a cell block that's open to visitors. More than a third of the building contains exhibition galleries, and there's a large art library in the building's restored vaults. A must-see is the former prison tower, where a specially chosen permanent exhibit by Dublin-born artist David Moore is showcased. A circular staircase leads to the first level of this modern, larger-than-life wooden installation; on the second level, wooden figures dangle their legs over a ledge. Self-guided audio tours are available in English; guided tours are available by arrange-

THE BEST

Jean-Louis Tremblay

University Professor, Theater Critic, and Restaurant Reviewer

Going to the **Martello Towers** on the **Plains of Abraham** at twilight, to watch the lights come on across the **St. Lawrence River** and the ships going by, or just to sit and read.

On a rainy day, taking in the same view from just a few steps away, in the cheerful comfort of **L'Astral** bar at the top of **Loews Le Concorde** hotel.

Escaping from the walled part of the old city and venturing down **Rue St-Jean** to drink in the vibrant atmosphere of the **Quartier St-Jean-Baptiste**, with its used bookstores, gourmet food stores, and original boutiques.

A musical evening at **Le Capitole**, a fabulous theater built in 1903 in the typical rococo style of the period and recently refurbished.

Walking through the city after a big snowstorm.

A trip across the river and back on the ferry that runs between **Quebec City** and **Lévis**. The view of Quebec City is wonderful. A particular treat is a trip during the winter when the boat cracks the ice, filling the air with an almost musical explosion of sound.

For a traditional dinner, try **Le Continental**, near the **Château Frontenac**.

Brunch at the **Café de la Terrasse** at the **Château Frontenac**, an unforgettable experience not only because of the fine food but also because of the lovely surroundings.

---

ment. There is limited visitor parking behind the old jail. ♦ Admission. 1 June-Sep, daily, 10AM-5:45PM (W until 9:45PM); 8 Sep-31 May, Tu-Su, 11AM-5:45PM (W until 8:45PM). 1 Ave Wolfe-Montcalm (at Ave George VI). 643.2150; fax 646.3330

5 EARL GREY TERRACE

This terrace, dedicated to Albert Henry George, the governor general of Canada between 1904 and 1911, is one of the most picturesque spots in **National Battlefields Park**. It sits atop the cliff, offering a dazzling view of the St. Lawrence River, and is situated across from the playing field and the jogging track. The **Price Guns**, the most important group of cannons in the **Plains of Abraham** from 1711 to 1890, are near the terrace. ♦ Ave George VI (between Aves Bourlamaque and Bougainville)

6 CROSS-COUNTRY SKI TRAILS

When weather permits, the park becomes a mecca for cross-country ski buffs. Six groomed trails run the length of the plains, and a well-maintained waxing room and a heated rest area are located just west of the playing field. There is free parking off Avenue Montcalm. ♦ Daily. South of Ave Wolfe-Montcalm. Ski conditions, 648.4212

7 KIOSK EDWIN-BELANGER

Located in the middle of the park, this copper-roofed bandstand is used for outdoor concerts during the summer. The kiosk is near numerous commemorative plaques dedicated to the 1759 battle on the plains, including

one honoring British General James Wolfe, and is walking distance from the museum. Contact the **Interpretation Center** for a schedule of events. ♦ Southeast of the Musée du Québec. 648.4071

8 MARTELLO TOWERS

After the American Revolution, the British feared the rebels would again attempt to annex Canada. (The American colonies had tried to claim control of Quebec in 1775.) From 1808 to 1812, by order of Governor Sir James Craig, the British built these four circular forts of masonry around the city, where troops would be stationed to watch for attacks from the river. The towers' name comes from Cape Mortella on the island of Corsica, where a structure of this type—originally of Genoese construction—was taken by British forces in 1794. The British built 196 Martello towers in the 19th century and three of these are now standing in Quebec (the fourth was demolished in 1904). Tower 1 is located on the Plains of Abraham near Avenue Ontario and houses a three-floor exhibit on the towers and a soldier's life. Tower 2, also open to the public, is at the corner of Avenues Laurier and Taché, overlooking the park. Tower 4 (closed to the public) is located outside the park, off Rue Laviguer. Also worth noting: the horse fountain on Avenue Taché was erected by the **Christian Women's Temperance Society** in the 19th century. Even today, the calèches (horse-drawn buggies that are for hire throughout the city) stop here for water. ♦ Admission. Tower 1, daily June 14-Columbus Day, 10AM-5:30PM.

Restaurants/Clubs: Red | Hotels: Purple | Shops: Orange | Outdoors/Parks: Green | Sights/Culture: Blue

GRANDE ALLÉE/PARLIAMENT HILL

Often called the Champs-Elysées of Quebec City, Grande Allée isn't nearly as long as the famous Parisian boulevard, but it's certainly as elegant. The name *Grande Allée* can be traced back to French rule when people west of the city traveled this road to sell their furs and goods. During the late 19th century, just after the complex of government buildings was completed along Parliament Hill, Quebec's elite moved here and began building opulent, turreted homes.

Before long, a unique style of "row house" sprang up along the first few blocks of Grande Allée. Known locally as *les maisons en terrasse*, these were mansions placed side by side. The farther west one moved away from the **Porte St-Louis**, an entrance to the walled **Upper Town**, the greater the distance between homes. Where Grande Allée East becomes Grande Allée West, the magnificent single homes take on an eclectic Victorian style so popular in the early 1900s.

Until World War II, Grande Allée remained the most fashionable district in Quebec City. But after the war, lifestyles changed, families grew smaller, and many who lived between **Rue St-Augustin** and **Rue Berthelot** moved farther west. Their homes were converted to small professional office buildings, and at night the strip resembled a ghost town.

In the late 1970s, however, an influx of restaurants and hotels brought new life to the street. Today, Grande Allée is one of Quebec's busiest thoroughfares, as well as one of the most popular streets to walk. Nearby is **Avenue Cartier**, an architectural hodgepodge of 19th-century cottages, three-story apartment buildings, and even a small indoor mall. The stretch running north to **Boulevard René Lévesque** has some of the city's best bars and restaurants.

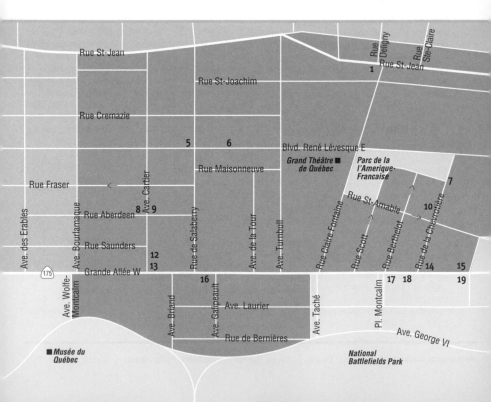

RESTAURANT
Carthage

La Playa
BAR MARTINI

1 CARTHAGE

★$ With Quebec City's plethora of quality French restaurants, it can be easy to overlook its ethnic restaurants. This one serves up robust Tunisian cooking in the improbable setting of a former bank building, appropriately outfitted with homespun North African décor. As for the food, come hungry and feast on such dishes as Couscous Royal with chicken or vegetables, tajine, meat shish kabobs, and *chorba*, a Tunisian soup. For dessert there's traditional baklava, which you can enjoy with genuine Tunisian mint tea. Belly dancers strut their stuff Fridays and Saturdays. The only drawback here is an inexplicably limited beverage menu. ◆ Tunisian ◆ Daily, dinner. 399 Rue St. Jean (between Rues Deligny and Ste-Claire). 529.0576

2 TUTTO GELATO

This attractive place serves up a tantalizing variety of homemade Italian gelatos and sorbets that you can eat on the premises or carry away. Try the chocolate, raspberry, chocolate chip, or all three at once. ◆ Daily. 716 Rue St-Jean (between Rues St-Augustin and Ste-Geneviève). 522.0896

3 LA PLAYA

★$$ The owner of this cheerful place has a passion for California, a fact which infuses the cuisine with a light, healthy touch. The pastas—all of which are homemade—are consistently good. Somewhat less healthy are the martinis; there are some 60 varieties from among which to choose. ◆ Californian ◆ Daily, lunch and dinner. 780 Rue St. Jean (between Rues St-Augustin and Ste-Geneviève). 522.3989

4 LA DRAGUE

This cavernous, centrally located nightspot caters to a mostly gay male clientele. There are two sizable bar areas, rather somber, plus an Internet corner on the main floor and a disco one flight below. Though it's open every night, Fridays and Saturdays tend to be the busiest and most fun, but on any night the atmosphere tends to be more mellow than hip. There are drag shows Thursdays and Sundays, but that's not how the place got its name (if you're not sure what *la drague* means in English, ask a habitué, who will likely be willing to help with the translation). ◆ Daily, 10PM-3AM. 815 Rue St-Augustin (between Rues St-Joachim and St-Jean). 649.7212

5 LE COCHON DINGUE

★$ A branch of the Lower Town restaurant of the same name, this cozy, casual spot is a good bet for family dining. Generous portions of simple, tasty dishes, including steaks, french fries, and quiches, are served, and there's a special children's menu too. The dining rooms are attractive, and three outdoor terraces are open in the summer. ◆ Canadian ◆ Daily, breakfast, lunch, and dinner. 46 Blvd René Lévesque W (at Rue de Salaberry). 523.2013

6 IZBA SPA

With its authentic Russian *banya* (steam bath), body treatments (from oxygen facials to algae body scrubs and Vichy shower rain massages), and full range of salon services, this world-class pampering pavilion may be the most comprehensive day spa in Quebec. It is also beautifully appointed, with hand-painted murals interspersed with exposed stone walls, and immaculately clean. Whether it's a simple manicure or mud bath you're looking for, the friendly, professional Izba staff members are ready to revitalize you to take on the world—or just another round of sight-

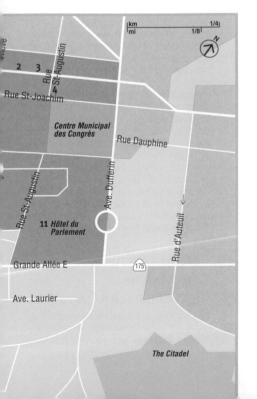

THE BEST

May Cutler

Publisher of Tundra Books and Former Mayor of Westmount

Westmount Park, just after dawn in summer, when the grass is sprinkled with white gulls—before the gray pigeons arrive to drive them away; in the fall, when the sun shines on the great old trees; on a winter night during a snowstorm; in spring, when teams of 4-year-olds play soccer.

For snacking, wander through the top floor at **Le Faubourg** and be tempted with international offerings, from German sausage to rôti.

Then there are those Montreal foods you can't find anywhere else on earth. Ex-Montrealers beg you to bring them Montreal bagels all the way across the continent to Vancouver and Los Angeles. (They can't be imitated anywhere, I'm told, because they must be flavored with Montreal water.) As for smoked meat,

where else but at **Schwartz's Deli?** For french fries I go to little holes-in-the-wall where you have to wait in line for a seat at the counter. The potatoes are freshly peeled and come to you in a brown paper bag—hot, greasy, calorically delicious, and ready to be sprinkled with vinegar.

And for extravagant occasions, nothing's more wonderful than dinner at **Les Halles** on a cold winter night, starting with the gloriously crusted *soupière des marins,* or in the garden at the **Ritz-Carlton Kempinski** hotel on a warm summer evening.

Streets worth strolling: **St-Laurent, Laurier, St-Denis,** and **Ste-Catherine,** on a Saturday afternoon.

Extra special: a walk through the islands where there's a breeze even on the hottest day, bringing back memories of the great **Expo '67.**

Montreal audiences at the opera and at French theater: so warmly appreciative they seem to elicit the better-than-best from the performers.

seeing in Old Quebec. The spa is for men and women and offers a range of half-day and full-day packages as well as nutrition and fitness consultations. ♦ Daily. 36 Blvd René Lévesque E (between Ave Turnbull and Rue de Salaberry). 522.4922

7 L'OBSERVATOIRE DE LA CAPITALE

Tucked into the top (thirty-first) floor of a government office building, this spectacular observatory is the highest point in Quebec City—a spectacular vantage point from which you can take in a panoramic view of the city and its surroundings: Île d'Orléans, landmarks such as the **Château Frontenac** and the **Price** building, and the old walled city of Quebec, laid out like a scale model. You can also see the **Citadel,** Lower Town, and the Laurentian and Appalachian Mountains. There are also a variety of informative displays about ancient and modern Quebec architecture. Guided tours are available. ♦ Admission. Daily, 10AM-5PM (closed Mondays 16 Oct-23 June). Edifice Marie Guyart, 1037 Rue de la Chevrotière (between Rue St-Amable and Blvd René Lévesque E). 644.9841

8 MOMENTO RISTORANTE

★★$$ This charming Italian restaurant is one of the friendliest on bustling Avenue Cartier. A contemporary but restrained décor is the backdrop for such delicious fare as giant shrimp in a creamy rosé sauce with red peppers and sun-dried tomatoes, veal scallopini, and pizza topped with pesto, spinach, fresh tomatoes, bocconcini, goat cheese, and

black olives. ♦ Italian ♦ M-F, lunch and dinner; Sa, Su, dinner. 1144 Ave Cartier (at Rue Aberdeen). 647.1313

9 CAFE KRIEGHOFF

★★$ Named after one of Quebec's most popular painters, Cornelius Krieghoff, who depicted the city's day-to-day life (he lived two blocks from here during the middle of the 19th century), this smoky, noisy, crowded café is a favorite among artists, students, intellectuals, and residents of the neighborhood. Diners sit elbow to elbow in four sectioned rooms furnished with upholstered benches and simple wooden tables and chairs. Thirteen types of coffee are served; the *café maison* has become so popular that the place now sells it by the pound. If you come for breakfast, start with the wonderful apricot, peach, or pear nectar, followed by Norwegian eggs—a poached egg and smoked salmon on an English muffin, covered with hollandaise sauce. Of course, the café au lait is a must. Two terraces are open in the summer. ♦ Canadian/Continental ♦ Daily, breakfast, lunch, and dinner. Reservations recommended for lunch and dinner. 1089 Ave Cartier (between Rues Aberdeen and Fraser). 522.3711

10 CHAPELLE HISTORIQUE BON-PASTEUR (GOOD SHEPHERD CHAPEL)

Built in 1866, this neoclassical chapel is a testament to the architectural versatility of **Charles Baillairge,** who also designed the old prison, now part of the **Musée du Québec** on the **Plains of Abraham**. The chapel was built for the Good Shepherd Sisters, whose mission was to aid prostitutes, though the nuns also taught the local children. In 1910, architect **François-Xavier Berlinguet** extended the front of the building toward the street, removed the single steeple, and replaced it with two turrets, each with its own bell tower. The chapel's interior blends the basic Romanesque structure—thick walls, a barrel-vaulted ceiling, and round-arched windows—with Baroque ornamentation, such as rosettes, decorative foliage, and cherub heads. Between 1868 and 1910, the sisters also painted 32 tableaux, reflecting 19th-century religious art in the province. Between October and June, the chapel offers a series of concerts, along with a musical artists' mass each Sunday at 11AM. ◆ Free. Guided visits July and August, Tu-Sa, 1:30PM-4:30PM; on request other months. 1080 Rue de la Chevrotière (between Rue St-Amable and Blvd René Lévesque E). 641.1070

11 HÔTEL DU PARLEMENT (PARLIAMENT BUILDING)

For Quebec, this building is a standing reminder that democracy is a cornerstone of the province's political life, in spite of the political turbulence that has often rocked this part of Canada. In 1867, the Dominion of Canada was created, joining what was then Lower Canada (Quebec) with Upper Canada (Ontario), and Quebec City was named the capital of Lower Canada. A decade later, the construction of the new **Parliament Building** began under the direction of architect **Eugène-Étienne Taché**; the project took 9 years to complete. The floor of the Quebec legislature, known as the National Assembly, has seen more political intrigue and drama than in any other legislative assembly in the country. (As recently as the last decade, the political party that was in power, the Parti Québécois, initiated a movement to separate the province from the rest of Canada, and the results of a Quebec-wide plebiscite came close to proclaiming Quebec its own country.) The legislative building consists of four wings (each more than 328 feet long) surrounding an inner courtyard, a configuration that was typical of late-16th-century French architecture. Using only Quebec artisans, Taché's aim was to pay tribute to the most important explorers, military and ecclesiastical figures, and governors in Quebec's history. On the building's façade are bronze statues of General Wolfe and General Marquis de Montcalm, who settled their fight on the **Plains of Abraham**, as well as Champlain, Frontenac, and others. The main tower, dedicated to

Jacques Cartier, who discovered Canada, is decorated with rose patterns in honor of England, a fleur-de-lis for France, and a maple leaf, Canada's emblem. Inside, walnut panels are engraved with the gilded coats of arms of England, Scotland, Ireland, and France, and works by Quebec painters grace the walls. On the ceiling of the main chamber is a painting by Quebec artist Charles Huot entitled *Je me souviens* ("I remember"—Quebec's provincial slogan and rallying cry; you'll notice the phrase on license plates), depicting Quebec history between 1534 and 1867. Guided tours are available in English or French. ◆ June–Labor Day: M-F, 9AM-4:30PM; Sa-Su, 10AM-4:30PM; Labor Day–23 June: M-F, 9AM-4:30PM. 1020 Rue St-Augustin (between Grand Allée E and Blvd René Lévesque E). 643.7239

Within Hôtel du Parlement:

LE PARLEMENTAIRE

★★$$ An exquisite stained-glass tunnel serves as the entrance to this elegant Beaux Arts–style restaurant, which has been frequented since 1917 by dignitaries, public figures, members of the National Assembly, and their guests. But it's also open to the public. The food is traditional French fare, and each month the menu features an item from a different region of the province. Considering the location, prices are quite reasonable. ◆ French ◆ Tu-F, lunch. Reservations recommended. 643.6640

12 GRAFFITI

★★★★$$$ A warm and airy setting for an elegant meal, this outstanding restaurant boasts a 5,000-bottle wine cellar recognized as one of the world's best. (Ironically, co-owner Adolfo Bernardo knew little about wine when he opened the place in 1984. Nevertheless, the popular, upscale eatery won the prestigious Award of Excellence from the *Wine Spectator* in 1992.) To accompany the fine wine selection, Chef Robert Saulnier and his assistant Pascal Borne create exquisitely flavored dishes that are steeped in the best

---

Restaurants/Clubs: Red | **Hotels: Purple** | **Shops: Orange** | **Outdoors/Parks: Green** | **Sights/Culture: Blue**

traditions of French and Italian cooking. The menu changes often to reflect the fresh seasonal produce but always includes game, poultry, meat, fish, seafood, and pasta. Scallops over light pastry with ginger sauce, veal scallops with mustard and green pepper sauce, and salmon topped with raspberry vinaigrette are typical of the restaurant's signature cuisine. Desserts—even their apple pie, a thin pastry crust covered with warm, crisp green apple slices and topped with real maple syrup—are exceptional. ♦ French/ Italian ♦ Daily, lunch and dinner. Reservations recommended. 1191 Ave Cartier (between Grande Allée W and Rue Saunders). 529.4949

12 LE TURF

★★$$ Downstairs is a typical English pub with wood-tone décor, serving imported beer and smoked-meat sandwiches until 2:30AM. Upstairs, there's a full menu as well as an elaborate happy hour for the famished. ♦ Canadian ♦ M-F, lunch, dinner, and happy hour; Sa-Su, breakfast. 1175 Ave Cartier (between Grande Allée W and Rue Saunders). 529.9567

13 LA MAISON HENRY-STUART

One of the few Palladian-style colonial cottages left in Quebec City, this 1849 house epitomizes bourgeois life at the turn of the 19th century. Sculpted metal medallions highlight the exterior, and inside, the furnishings date back to the 1850s, although the décor and furniture arrangement are more representative of the 1930s. For decades, the house was rented by a succession of judges and other members of Quebec's elite, before being purchased in 1917 by Mary Adele Stuart, granddaughter of Phillipe Aubert de Gaspé, one of Quebec's most famous authors. Stuart lived here until 1987, when the home was bought by a local developer, who leased the building to Quebec's historical

Throughout the years, there has been much speculation about the meaning of the Legend of *Le Chien d'Or* (the Golden Dog). Over the entrance to the Old Post Office is an intriguing image of a dog chewing a bone with the accompanying verse in gold letters:

I am a dog that gnaws his bone
I crouch and gnaw it all alone
A time will come, which is not yet
When I'll bite he who once bit me.

English-born author William Kirby immortalized the Golden Dog hotel in his romantic 18th-century novel of the same name.

council, which plans to preserve it. ♦ Admission (includes tea). Daily, 11AM-5PM, 24 June-4 Sept; Su, 1PM-5PM, 10 Sept-23 June; other days by reservation. Grande Allée W and Ave Cartier. 647.4347

14 PARIS BREST

★★★$$$ Step into a world somewhere between Paris and 1920s Berlin. This restaurant serves classic French cuisine, but the black-leather décor, with three-legged designer Art Deco chairs, mahogany paneling, ivory table linens, and elegant oversize tableware, are more in line with the mood of a hidden cabaret. One of the first gourmet restaurants on Grande Allée, it has managed to keep its reputation intact over the years. Popular house specialties include steak tartare, beef Wellington, and lamb noisettes in pastry with fresh garlic; for the health conscious, there are daily lower-calorie specials emphasizing fresh produce. Valet parking is available. ♦ French ♦ Daily, lunch and dinner. Reservations recommended. 590 Grande Allée E (at Rue de la Chevrotière). 529.2243

15 LOUIS HÉBERT

★★★$$$ Situated in a stone building dating back to 1758, this lovely restaurant is a favorite among senior civil servants, politicians, and journalists who work nearby. Chef Hervé Toussaint's inspired menu showcases fresh seafood as well as such seasonal specialties as lamb, lobster, and game. The appetizer of lobster ravioli with mustard in tarragon cream sauce is succulent, as is the main course of shrimp sautéed with sesame seeds and red and green peppers. Seating fills two dining rooms—one is an airy, glassed-in setting overflowing with plants and the other is a warm, intimate room with wood ceilings—and an outdoor terrace, a prime people-watching spot during the summer. Valet parking is available. ♦ French/nouvelle ♦ May–Sept: daily, lunch and dinner. Sept–May: M-F, lunch and dinner; Sa-Su, dinner. 668 Grande Allée E (at Rue Conroy). 525.7812

16 RELAIS CHARLES-ALEXANDRE BED AND BREAKFAST

$$ This three-story house, once a residence for military officers, has been transformed into a homey bed-and-breakfast on the quiet side of Grande Allée. Each of the nine rooms is tastefully appointed in a romantic country style with antique furnishings, wicker chairs, hardwood floors, a large pine cabinet concealing a TV, and beautiful window coverings. Owner Gaetan Drolet started decorating each room with a basic color, then expanded from there. All of the rooms have air conditioning, and seven have modern, private

bathrooms. A small, sparkling kitchen with an adjacent covered porch is a perfect place to enjoy a healthy breakfast that may include fruit and yogurt, croissants, cheese, ham, and coffee. Free parking is available. ♦ 83 Grande Allée E (at Ave Galipeault). 523.1220

17 LOEWS LE CONCORDE

$$$$ When this 30-story hotel first went up in the 1970s, it was extremely controversial. Not only was it the only high-rise to straddle the Grande Allée and the **Plains of Abraham**, but its odd shape—two buildings stuck together, one straight and one sloping—brazenly called attention to itself. Despite all the initial hoopla, the modern monolith has since been embraced by city residents, mostly because of **L'Astral**, the revolving bar and restaurant that caps the hotel. All of the 410 rooms—decorated in warm earth tones and boasting Australian marble bathrooms—offer a sprawling view of the city. An entire floor with added security is reserved for women traveling alone; another two floors are designed for travelers with disabilities. There are also three restaurants, a business center, and a heated outdoor pool, along with a health club featuring Nautilus equipment and a sauna. ♦ 1225 Cours du General de Montcalm (at Grande Allée E). 647.2222, 800/463.5256; fax 647.4710

Within Loews Le Concorde:

L'ASTRAL

★★$$$ From 29 floors up, this slowly revolving restaurant offers a dazzling vista of the city—especially at night—through bay windows. It makes a complete circle every 90 minutes, allowing you plenty of time to finish your meal and enjoy the full panorama from every angle. Or, if the restaurant isn't busy, you can come here to simply enjoy a drink while watching the sun set. At lunch, order from the à la carte menu, and on Saturday evening dig into the sumptuous Grand Buffet, a smorgasbord of cold cuts, fresh vegetables, and prime cuts of beef, fresh fish, and seafood. Highlights on the seasonal dinner menu include wild game, mussels, lobster, shrimp, and oysters. The Sunday brunch is also very popular. ♦ Continental ♦ M-Sa, lunch and dinner; Su, brunch and dinner. Reservations recommended. 647.2222

18 VOODOO GRILL

★★$$$ Its business card refers to it as a "resto-museum," and with a décor featuring sumptuously lit African and Polynesian-looking sculptures—call it tiki chic—that's a fairly accurate assessment. The menu casts its spell with the likes of Île d'Orléans Voodoo chicken and wild Nunavut salmon and, from the wok, lacquered duck and chicken with spiced lemon. The large second-floor restaurant is part of a complex that also includes the **Charlotte** bar, **Maurice** nightclub, and a cigar bar. ♦ Exotic ♦ Daily, lunch and dinner. 575 Grande-Allée E (at Cours du General de Montcalm). 647.2000

19 LE MANOIR LAFAYETTE

$$ In 1980, the Girrard family acquired what was then a 100-year-old manor house with 10 immense echoing chambers and gussied it up from top to bottom. Behind the old-fashioned façade is a surprisingly large five-story hotel with many modern amenities. All 67 guest rooms have air conditioning, color TV sets, and private bathrooms. The hotel also has free parking and conference rooms with computers and fax machines. There is no restaurant within the hotel, but there are plenty right outside the door. ♦ 661 Grande Allée E (between Rues Conroy and de la Chevrotière). 522.2652, 800/363.8203; fax 522.4400

Restaurants/Clubs: Red | Hotels: Purple | Shops: Orange | Outdoors/Parks: Green | Sights/Culture: Blue

QUEBEC CITY DAY TRIPS

When you've had enough of the city and long for wide-open spaces, explore the countryside along the **North** or **South Shores** of the St. Lawrence River, where quaint villages, picturesque farms, and small *auberges* (inns) recall the early days of New France. These day trips are long on scenery and history, ideal for those more interested in a leisurely drive through rural Quebec than in heading for a specific destination.

A drive along the North Shore will take you to such places as **Île d'Orléans**, where the fertile land continues to sustain residents; the spectacular **Montmorency Falls**; the pilgrimage site of **Ste-Anne-de-Beaupré**; the artists' community of **Baie-St-Paul**; and the whale-watching mecca of **Baie-Ste-Catherine**.

Day-tripping along the South Shore might include a stop at one of the good restaurants in **Montmagny**; a visit to a wood-carving shop in **St-Jean-Port-Joli**; a look at the unique architecture in the village of **Kamouraska**; bird watching near the village of **l'Isle-Verte**; and perhaps a ferry ride to **Île Verte**, one of the **St. Lawrence Islands**. Be sure to check the tide tables and ferry schedules before leaving the mainland, however; the St. Lawrence beyond Quebec City is considered the ocean, and ferry times vary according to the tides. A word of warning: outside of Quebec City, many locals don't speak English, although they are tourist-oriented—to French-speaking tourists, that is. Booklets on these areas, distributed by the government, make handy travel companions; write to the **Greater Quebec Area Tourism and Convention Bureau**, 835 Avenue Wilfrid-Laurier, Quebec, Quebec G1R 2L3, or call 418/649.2608.

Area code 418 unless otherwise noted.

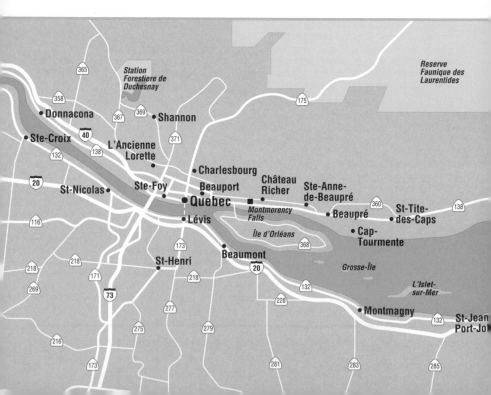

THE NORTH SHORE

ÎLE D'ORLÉANS

Connected to the mainland by a bridge off Route 440, Île d'Orléans is just a short jaunt (a 20-minute drive) from Quebec City. Today, the island is largely a bedroom community for senior civil servants and other stalwarts of the Quebec City establishment, but it remains a peaceful, slow-paced world apart. Touring the island and its charming historic villages is an easy drive, because the circumference is a mere 64 km (40 miles). You can pick up information at the **Tourist Office** (195 Chemin Royale; 828.9411), to the right at the top of the hill after the bridge.

Île d'Orléans has always been known for its fertile soil. When Jacques Cartier landed here on 7 September 1535, he found so many wild berries, fruits, and flowers that he nicknamed it the Island of Bacchus. Later he changed its name to Île d'Orléans in honor of the Duke of Orléans, son of King Francis I of France.

Traveling west around the island, **Route 368** takes you past manicured farmland toward **St-Petronille**, the island's smallest village, which was the site of General James Wolfe's headquarters in 1759. One of the best things about the village is the **Chocolaterie de l'Île** (150 Chemin Royal; 828.2252), a gourmet chocolate shop. In summer you can enjoy homemade ice cream on the bucolic terrace, underneath the towering treetops. Also in the village is **La Chasse Galerie** (6 Chemin Royal; 828.0598), a delightful emporium where you'll find Quebec maple and farm products as well as

artwork, clothes, and jewelry. Overlooking the river is **Auberge la Goéliche** (22 Rue du Quai, directly after the Prevost intersection; 828.2248), a glass-walled dining room featuring good, reasonably priced nouvelle cuisine, but service at a snail's pace (which isn't unusual on Île d'Orléans). The plaque outside the inn is dedicated to Horatio Walker, one of Canada's foremost turn-of-the-19th-century painters, who lived on the island.

The bucolic countryside, replete with churches, wayside shrines, grand manor houses, and flour mills, has a long farming history of which the island's 7,000 residents are extremely proud. Many families have been here for 15 generations—a plaque on a granite boulder by the side of a field on the way to the village of **St-Laurent** notes that "Gabriel Gosselin from Normandy came as a pioneer in 1652"—and the fertile land continues to nourish the locals. Stop by a roadside stand for fresh strawberries, raspberries, apples, or corn, when in season, or roll up your sleeves and pick your own at one of the island's numerous farms (June is best for strawberries, July for raspberries). For a light lunch, try **Le Moulin de St-Laurent** (754 Chemin Royal; 829.3888), located in a 1635 building used as a flour mill until the 1930s. The restaurant is owned and operated by a group of islanders who serve inventive, flavorful combinations of French cuisine.

At one time, St-Laurent was the center of a thriving boat-building trade where about 20 shipyards turned out 300 to 400 rowboats a year. At the **Parc Maritime de St-Laurent** (120 Chemin Royal, St-Laurent; 828.9672) a maritime museum documents that era with exhibits of tools and historical displays; entrance is free.

En route east from St-Laurent to **St-Jean** is a shabby-looking building called **Manoir Mauvide Genest** (1451 Chemin Royal, St-Jean; 829.2630), which houses a

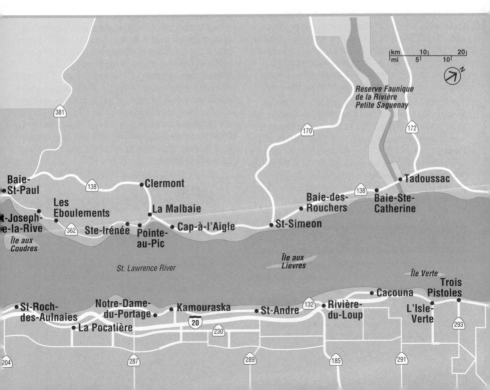

THE BEST

Gordon Atkinson

Former Member of the Quebec National Assembly

For myself, the garden of the **Ritz-Carlton Kempinski** hotel on **Rue Sherbrooke** has been a favorite for more than 50 years—a small enclave of civility in a world that sometimes seems to have gone mad. Again, it's only a question of what might tease your palate at the moment. The menu is extensive, but my favorites are the Dover sole, the dore amandine, and the poached salmon. However, you must not overlook the moose entrée served at the Christmas lunch and dinner. The wine list is catholic in presentation, with wines from around the world but, I hasten to add, only the better wines. Plonk is not the essence of the Ritz.

Strolling is a Montreal pastime, and the small restaurants and bars that line **Rue Crescent**—a primarily English-speaking enclave—and **Rue St-Denis**—a primarily French-speaking enclave of bistros (don't panic: the waiters and waitresses speak both French and English)—are suited to the tastes of anyone who fully recognizes the uniqueness of Montreal. Interspersed with boutiques and major department stores, strolling is an adventure that you'll find well worth the 3 or 4 hours it consumes. For something totally different, the hot dogs on **Boulevard St-Laurent** (the Main) are like no others in the world. Slathered with a distinctive blend of coleslaw, they tingle the palate. If after strolling you'd care to rest your feet, then there are no better places than either the indoor skating rink, near the **Central Railway Station**, or the **Botanical Garden**. These are easily accessible on the Metro, our underground transport system. If history interests you, then a walk or a calèche ride to the top of the mountain that bestrides Montreal is in order. The cross on the mountain, although now steel and festooned with lights, was originally a wooden cross planted on the mountaintop by Sieur de Maisonneuve, the founder of Montreal, in thanks to God for saving the original settlement called Ville Marie from the floodwaters in the winter of 1642.

A number of seigneuries that line both banks of the **St. Lawrence River** have been converted to restaurants, and they serve lunch and dinner ranging from nouvelle French cuisine to the meals of the farmers who originally settled Quebec, with dishes such as beans with maple syrup, and sugar pie. Whatever you choose, it will be stunning for the eyes and served with elegance. By trying these restaurants, you'll be privy to the history of Canada. There are also a number of restored 17th-century fur-trading posts and mills that ground flour and maize.

If you visit Montreal between October and April, you must take in a hockey game at the **Molson Centre** with the **Montreal Canadiens**, Stanley Cup winners more often than any other club in the 100-year history of the sport.

Montreal is a modern city that reflects its past in vivid colors, with a citizenry that exudes joie de vivre.

---

small collection of antique artifacts and a restaurant. This handsome—if worn—Norman-style house was erected in 1734 for King Louis XV's surgeon. As you round the eastern end of the island, stop and climb the steps of the wooden lookout tower just beyond **St-François** for views over the Charlevoix region on the mainland and the imposing peak of **Mont Ste-Anne**.

Just beyond **St-François**, apple orchards and maple syrup operations herald the **Church of Ste-Famille**, the oldest on the island (built in 1749). Before leaving the island, drop by the craft co-op in the **Old Church of St-Pierre** (Chemin Royal, St-Pierre; turn left at the bridge's traffic lights and continue 1 km/.62 miles; 828.9824). Here you'll find reasonably priced hand-knit baby clothes, painted baskets, handwoven bedspreads, and sweaters and scarves made by local craftspeople.

STE-ANNE-DE-BEAUPRÉ

To reach the pilgrimage site of Ste-Anne-de-Beaupré, 40 km (25 miles) from Quebec City, head east along **Route 138**. Stop along the way at the spectacular **Montmorency Falls**, only 15 minutes from downtown. The centerpiece of a park, the huge, stunning waterfall cascades 272 feet downward (one and a half times as high as Niagara Falls). During the winter, the waterfall freezes into a giant cone of ice. The site also offers scenic lookout points, a picnic area, and a glimpse of General James Wolfe's redoubt, where he planned the assault on the **Plains of Abraham** in 1759. In the small village of **Château Richer** is **Christorama, Albert Gilles Copper Studio** (7450 Blvd Ste-Anne, 10 minutes after the Montmorency Falls; 824.4225), a gallery of religious art, providing a clue of things to come. Also en route to Ste-Anne-de-Beaupré, 19 km (12 miles) past the bridge of Île d'Orléans, is the free **Musée de l'Abeille** (8862 Blvd Ste-Anne, 824.4411), a quirky little museum documenting everything you wanted to know about bees.

Ste-Anne-de-Beaupré, dedicated to the mother of the Virgin Mary, attracts almost two million visitors a year. The **Cyclorama of Jerusalem** (8 Rue Regina, just before the Basilica; 827.3101), a Disneyesque mosque, contains the world's largest panoramic painting of the crucifixion of Christ. The 88-foot-high canvas, which was completed in Munich in 1878, surrounds viewers who stand in the middle of a vast hall, listening as a Ben Hur–like voice thunders out a commentary about the Holy City. Within walking distance of the Cyclorama is a complex of religious sites, including the **Redemptorist Monastery**, **St. Alphonse's Seminary**, **Memorial Chapel**, the **Holy Stairs** (which the devout climb on their knees), and a garden bedecked with life-size cast-iron figures. The complex's centerpiece is the towering 325-foot neo-Roman Basilica (10018 Ave Royale; 827.3781), built of sparkling silver granite and embellished with beautiful mosaics and stained-glass windows. Although the Basilica was constructed as recently as 1923, the town has been a "miracle" site since 1658, when it's believed Ste-Anne saved numerous sailors who were shipwrecked off nearby Cap-Tourmente.

Across the street from the Basilica is **Café du Pelerin** (10041 Rue Royale, directly in front of Hôpital Ste-Anne-de-Beaupré; 827.4421), a greasy spoon with no-frills décor but tasty food, where waitresses will tell you, in no uncertain terms, what they think of the pilgrimage business.

BEAUPRÉ

As you approach the town of Beaupré along **Route 138**, the countryside starts sprouting hills. This is part of **Côte-de-Beaupré**, an area of great natural beauty where numerous waterfalls tumble off escarpments and out of deep fissures in the rock. The **Canyon Sainte-Anne** (827.4057) is remarkable for its seething mass of water plunging 400 feet. Walking paths and a nerve-jangling suspension bridge, dangling 180 feet above the chasm, allow visitors to explore the site. Take a slight detour off Route 138 and onto **Route 360** for a look at another impressive waterfall, **Chutes Jean Larose** in the **Mont-Ste-Anne Park**. The park, which is dominated by a 2,699-foot-high mountain carved with trails, is an internationally known ski center that has hosted several World Cups. This is also a prime spot for golf, mountain biking, hiking, and horseback riding. Don't miss taking a cable car to the summit of Mont-Ste-Anne for a breathtaking view of the **St. Lawrence River** and the Beaupré coastline.

Heading east again along Route 138, follow signs to the right to the **Cap-Tourmente National Wildlife Area** (827.4591), a bird sanctuary and wildlife preserve—open between April and November—featuring 16 kilometers (10 miles) of walking trails. During the spring and fall, the escarpment at the edge of the St. Lawrence is one of the main stopover points for more than 300,000 greater snow geese that descend, like giant, noisy snowflakes, as they migrate north to Baffin Island and south to Virginia. If you're unlucky enough to miss the geese, the next best thing is going to an exhibition center that explains it all. Scores of other birds can also be seen with the help of local naturalists. Be sure to bring binoculars. Farther east along Route 138, **St-Tite-des-Caps** heralds the beginning of **Charlevoix**, one of the most scenic and historic regions in Quebec. It was named after Jesuit priest François-Xavier de Charlevoix, who traveled through the area in 1719 and became New France's first historian.

BAIE-ST-PAUL TO LA MALBAIE

Although Charlevoix extends beyond Baie-St-Paul and La Malbaie, the roads that link them **Route 138** inland and **Route 362** along the coast) encircle the region's main attractions—sleepy villages, art galleries, plummeting views of cliffs and the ocean, and small antiques-filled, family-run *auberges*. The roller coaster Route 138 plunges into the art colony of Baie-St-Paul before coming to a halt at the main street. Here the **Centre d'Art de Baie-St-Paul** (4 Rue Ambroise-Fafard, at Rue St-Jean Baptiste; 435.3681) has become a significant regional arts center filled with landscapes by local artists. One section highlights the works of Swiss-born painter René Richard, who was a trapper before he became famous. (His studio and former home is at 58 Rue St-Jean-Baptiste, at Rue Clarence Gagnon; 435.5571.) An annual symposium for young painters from around the world is held at the center in August and September, and the gallery store sells quilts, wooden toys, and hand-knit sweaters.

Across the street is the **Centre d'Exposition de Baie-St-Paul** (23 Rue Ambroise-Fafard, at Rue St-Jean Baptiste; 435.3681), another gallery that's run by the art center. The ultramodern, award-winning building displays contemporary works by international sculptors and houses a gallery store that sells prints and posters. More than 20 other galleries can be found along the same street, on Rue St-Jean Baptiste, and on Rue Ste-Anne, which runs perpendicular to Rue Ambroise-Fafard. For a relaxing break, drop by **Café des Artistes** (27 Rue St-Jean Baptiste; 435.5585) for a cup of coffee or a panini and hang out with the artsy crowd.

The winding coast road (Route 362) takes you to **Les Eboulements**, a lovely, scenic community perched 948 feet above the **St. Lawrence River**. Named for violent landslides that devastated the area in 1663, this *seigneurie* (estate) was granted to Pierre Tremblay in 1770. Before leaving Les Eboulements, visit the **Old Mill**, the **Manoir de Sales-Laterriere**, and **Atelier d'Art**

In some parts of Quebec, an obsolete French form of land measurement, the arpent, is used instead of acres or hectares. The exact size of an arpent varies, ranging from 0.625 acre to 1.25 acres.

Throughout Upper and Lower Town, the Citadel, and the Plains of Abraham, there are 173 polished black British cannons, dating from 1790 to 1830, souvenirs of Quebec's military past.

SUMMER FUN

Quebec City is famous for its Winter Carnival, but summer is hopping too, thanks largely to the **Quebec City Summer Festival**. For 11 days during the first half of July, nearly 500 musical performances transform much of the old city into an open-air stage. World beat and French-language music usually get top billing, but there's also international jazz, baroque, hip-hop, and classical in the programming. Though many names will be unfamiliar to American ears, much of the fun of the festival is simply strolling from stage to stage—most of which are clustered in **Place d'Youville** and on **Parliament Hill**, just beyond the walls of the old city—and seeing what band the crowds are cheering on. Past performers have included Celine Dion, Cecilia Bartoli, and Youssou N'Dour, and festival organizers have a reputation for uncovering new musical talent. To access the stage areas, you must buy a festival badge, available for $8 at locations throughout the city before and during the festival. For more information, call 888/992.5200 or visit www.infofestival.com.

Claude Chiasson, all on Main Street, for a taste of local customs and culture.

Route 362 plunges downhill again at **St-Irénée**, birthplace of poet Adolphe-Basile Routhier, who wrote the French lyrics to "O Canada," the national anthem. Nineteenth-century politician and stockbroker Sir Joseph-David-Rodolphe Forget built **Domaine Forget** (398 Chemin Les Bains, in front of quai St-Irénée; 452.3535), a country estate that now serves as a cultural center and a summer music camp. Between mid-June and mid-August, concerts and musical brunches are held here. Overlooking St-Irénée's wide, sandy beach is the **Auberge des Sablons** (223 Chemin Les Bains, east of Domaine Forget; 452.3594), a quintessential Charlevoix inn, featuring pâtés, pastas, and salads with artistic presentations and exquisite sauces.

At the nearby village of **Pointe-au-Pic** is **Fairmont Le Manoir Richelieu** (181 Ave Richelieu; 800/441.1414), a grand golf resort, spa, and casino that was erected at the turn of the 19th century during the heyday of luxury liners that brought the crème de la crème of New York society here on vacation. William Howard Taft, then president of the US, built a holiday home nearby because, he said, "the air was as heady as champagne, but without the morning after!" His villa (and many others of its ilk) can be seen along **Chemin des Falaises**. **Musée de Charlevoix** (1 Chemin du Havre, at Blvd de la Comporte/Rte 362; 665.4411) is a regional museum that opened in 1990 and highlights local history; admission is charged. To really soak in that healthy sea air, take a spin in a motorized rubber raft out to the lighthouses around the coast; contact **Croisières aux Sentinelles du St-Laurent** (665.3666).

To the east is **La Malbaie**, thus-named in 1608 when Samuel de Champlain cursed the bay (*mal* means "bad" in French) for its perilous shoreline where his ships ran aground. English-speaking people know it as **Murray Bay**, in memory of General James Murray, who was once governor of the colony. No matter what moniker it goes by, it's a beautiful spot and marks the halfway point of the circular route. At the mouth of the **Malbaie River**, take Route 138 back toward Baie-St-Paul. The Charlevoix interior landscape is as scenic as its coast,

albeit with beautiful rolling hills, wide-open vistas, fields, and forests. Villages are perched on slopes in the distance, rather than along the highway, and attractions are limited to the occasional antique barn, craft studio, or flea market. You'll know where to find them when you see merchandise scattered haphazardly across a lawn.

ÎLE AUX COUDRES

A short turn to the right off Route 362 leads you to the village of **St-Joseph-de-la-Rive**, a tranquil hamlet with five *auberges*, an old wooden church, and a paper factory called **Papeterie St-Gilles**, an anomaly in this modern age. Here, thick parchment inlaid with local flowers and leaves is made by hand, using 17th-century techniques. A small, free museum traces the process (304 Rue Felix-Antoine-Savard, at Rue de l'Eglise; 635.2430). Across the street is the **Exposition Maritime** (305 Rue de l'Eglise, in front of the Librairie St-Gilles; 635.1131), a former shipyard that has been turned into a museum, documenting the lives and times of the men who lived aboard *goelettes*, the traditional wooden boats that hauled cargo to the coastal communities until the 1950s. Three of them are beached here, and more are scattered around the shoreline of Île aux Coudres, explorer Jacques Cartier's "island of hazelnuts." You can take the ferry from St-Joseph-de-la-Rive to the sleepy Île aux Coudres in 15 minutes; regular service is between 7AM and 11PM (438.2743). The old stranded schooners make great subjects for photographers and artists, as do the two historic mills (one of them a windmill) in **St-Louis**.

Other spots worth visiting include **Le Musée de l'Île aux Coudres** (admission; 231 Chemin des Coudriers, in front of the Caisse Populaire, St-Louis; 438.2753); the **Jacques Cartier Monument** (St-Bernard-Sur-Mer, near the ferry dock), where the explorer conducted the first Catholic Mass on Canadian soil; and **Maison Leclerc** (125 Rte Principale, La Baleine, 6.4 km/4 miles south of the Banque National de Canada; 438.2240). You can get around the entire island in a couple of hours, but it's worth lingering to rent a bike or to shop for crafts. *Catalognes*, colorful woven rag rugs, are a local specialty; at **Centre Artisanat de l'Île aux Coudres** (605 Chemin des Coudriers, at Rue Toudière; 438.2231) and **Artisanat Les Gens de l'Île** (720 Chemin des Coudriers, next to the Hôtel Roche Pleureuse; 438.2856) in La Baleine, prices are much lower than in Quebec City's tourist shops.

LA MALBAIE TO TADOUSSAC

Like Malbaie, the neighboring village of **Cap-à-l'Aigle** was a gracious summer resort favored by Americans and English-speaking Canadians in the late 19th and early 20th centuries. In 1872, **St-Peters-on-the-Rock**, a little red-and-white wooden church, was built to cater to visiting Anglicans. One of Charlevoix's best-known and most superb inns is the **Auberge des Peupliers** (381 Rue St-Raphael, 1 km/62 miles from Rte 138; 665.4423), an enchanting old farmhouse with original antiques run by Ferdinand Tremblay and his niece Anne Rochette. Tremblay's parents casually got into the tourism business by offering passing travelers a room for the night, a common practice in the 1950s and 1960s. Down the street, **Auberge La Pinsonnière** (124 Rue St-Raphael; 665.4431), a member of the prestigious Paris-based hotel association, Relais et Châteaux, serves uncommonly good food, showcasing pheasant, trout, venison, and lamb with unusual blends of flavors, herbs, and spices in elegant surroundings. Unfortunately, the lunchtime menu is limited to light meals, but they're served outside on the patio, where you can enjoy splendid, unimpeded views over the **St. Lawrence River**. A hiking trail through the woods leads to the water's edge.

At **St-Simeon**, between La Malbaie and Tadoussac, spend some time wandering around the wharf—the departure point for ferries to **Rivière-du-Loup** on the other side of the river—or stroll along the pristine beach, where anglers catch smelt, which makes a delicious, crunchy snack when fried. At **Baie-des-Rochers** there's a lovely picnic area and 6 km (4 miles) of hiking trails that wind around the rocky shoreline.

Baie-Ste-Catherine marks the border of the Charlevoix region, where the fjordlike **Saguenay River** and the **St. Lawrence** converge. The mixture of cold freshwater and warmer plankton-rich saltwater creates an ideal feeding ground for whales and other marine life. The whale watching here is among the best on the continent, and some 70,000 people make the annual trek to see belugas (native to these waters) and migrating minkes, finbacks, white-sided dolphins, porpoises, and the occasional big blue. A ferry (235.4395) links Baie-Ste-Catherine to Tadoussac, and passengers are sometimes lucky enough to spot the giant mammals from the deck. In Tadoussac, the imposing **Hôtel Tadoussac** (165 Rue Bord de l'Eau; 235.4421 or 800/561.0718; the *Hotel New Hampshire* of movie fame), a white wooden hostelry with a distinctive red roof, dominates

the sandy coastline. Here, you can book a whale-watching trip on the *Marie-Clarisse*, a romantic wooden schooner built in Nova Scotia in 1922. If you're short on time, forgo the ferry crossing to Tadoussac and instead book a whale-watching trip in Baie-Ste-Catherine through **Croisières AML** (692.4643), which operates sightseeing boats.

THE SOUTH SHORE

QUEBEC CITY TO MONTMAGNY

Across the **St. Lawrence River** from Quebec City, the South Shore was divided into large *domaines* (estates) that were run by wealthy landowners who erected manor houses, mills, barns, and farmhouses in the 18th and 19th centuries. East of **Lévis** along **Route 132**, the village of **Beaumont** has at least 20 historical homes from the New France era. The church, built in 1733, is famous because despite orders from General James Wolfe that it be burned, only the door caught fire. His soldiers posted a proclamation in 1759 that the British had conquered the area, but defiant villagers ripped it up.

Just outside the village is the restored **Beaumont Mill**, circa 1821 (2 Rte du Fleuve/Rte 132; 833.1867), a bright red building with a mansard roof—a style characteristic of the post-French era. Bread made with flour that's ground on the premises can be bought here.

At first glance Montmagny doesn't look very interesting, as Route 132 passes by a string of fast-food joints, car dealerships, and gas stations. But if you veer off the highway and into the town itself, you'll find nifty boutiques, art galleries, and craft shops. For unusual gifts, drop by **Boutique Suzette Couillard** (70 Rue St-Jean-Baptiste E, at Rue Ste-Magloire; 248.9642). For a truly memorable gourmet meal, try **Manoir des Erables** (220 Blvd Taché E, along the South River; 248.0100), a stately manor house–turned-hotel dating back to 1821. For information, stop by the local tourism office at the train station (45 Ave du Quai; 248.9196). An acclaimed annual event in Montmagny is the accordion festival held on Labor Day weekend.

MONTMAGNY TO ST-JEAN-PORT-JOLI

Just outside Montmagny, the marina at **Berthier-sur-Mer** is the departure point for **Grosse-Île**, Canada's Ellis Island. The island, one in an archipelago of more than 20, served as a quarantine station between 1815 and 1941, when more than four million people immigrated to Canada. Unlike its US counterpart, this one hasn't been gussied up for tourists—at least not yet. The place has a somber, spooky atmosphere, evoked in part by its ominously named **Cholera Bay**, where the dead were dumped unceremoniously into the water, and by the abandoned, desolate hospitals, chapels, and dormitories, where newcomers were isolated for weeks at a time. Rows of white crosses attest to the thousands who died of cholera, typhoid, and other infectious diseases, and a Celtic cross commemorates Irish immigrants who fled here after the potato famine of 1847. For information, contact the **Canadian Parks Service** at 563.4009; for ferry reservations, call **Croisières Lachance** at 259.2140.

The **Musée Maritime Bernier** (55 Rue des Pionniers E, just east of l'Eglise de l'Islet; 247.5001), in the nearby town of **l'Islet-sur-Mer**, documents a more cheerful period of Canada's history. Named after Captain Joseph-Elzear Bernier, a navigator and Arctic explorer in the early 1900s, the museum traces Canada's maritime achievements; admission is charged. On display outside is the *Ernest-Lapointe*, a sturdy icebreaker, and the *Bras d'Or*, a Canadian Navy hydrofoil. Continuing east, you'll come to the wood-carving colony of **St-Jean-Port-Joli**. Here, an old mill at the edge of the **Trois-Saumons River** once belonged to Philippe-Aubert de Gaspé, the local *seigneur* and novelist who wrote the best-selling *Les Anciens Canadiens* about the Seven Years' War. His ancestral manor burned down in 1909; the foundations are there, and the old bread oven still stands on the left side of Route 132. Once you enter the town, Route 132 becomes **Avenue de Gaspé**, the main drag. The **Centre d'Art Animalier "Faunart"** (377 Ave de Gaspé W, 598.7034), housed in an octagonal barn, showcases more than 100 paintings, photographs, and sculptures by local artists. The center charges admission. Also along this street are dozens of wood-carving studios and shops, most with telltale 10-foot-high sculptures of seagulls, fishermen, and *habitants* (peasant settlers) outside their doors. Many of the wood-carving shops along **Avenue de Gaspé** have a specialty: At **Sculpture Noel Guay** (No. 496; 598.3716), you'll find animal figures; at **Les Bateaux Leclerc** (No. 293; 598.3273), model boats; and at **Pierre and Lise Labelle Boutique Atelier** (No. 505; 598.3529), figurines.

It's not unusual for different family members to operate their own studios and shops, but the name *Bourgault* stands out. The three Bourgault brothers—Medard, Jean-Jacques, and André—launched the art colony in the 1930s, when they discovered wood carving was a way to earn a living during the Depression. Their lives and work are celebrated in the **Musée des Anciens Canadiens** (332 Ave de Gaspé W; 598.3392); admission is charged. Also, take a look at Medard's house next door, which is embellished with his handiwork. More of the brothers' carvings can be seen at the barnlike **Auberge du Faubourg** (280 Ave de Gaspé W, 598.3301), which has several original wall plaques. Don't be put off by the school-cafeteria décor; the place serves tasty, home-style cooking, including meat pies, onion soup, and seafood *coquilles*.

ST-JEAN-PORT-JOLI TO KAMOURASKA

The village of **St-Roch-des Aulnaies**, to the east of St-Jean-Port-Joli on Route 132, is graced with several ancestral homes, scattered around its twin-spired church (1849). The grandest of all the estates is **La Seigneurie des Aulnaies** (525, de la Seigneurie, exit 430 off Rte 20; 354.2800). The admission charge includes visits to a manor house (1854) with wide verandas and gingerbread trim, a mill (1842), a miller's house, and landscaped gardens. It is the oldest land concession on the South Shore. The mill, with its giant wheel and elaborate system of ropes and pulleys, has been restored to working order, and guides dressed in period costumes show visitors around.

Continue still farther east and you'll enter **Bas-St-Laurent**, the point at which the St. Lawrence begins stretching toward the Atlantic Ocean. The land is very flat on this stretch of Route 132, and a series of dikes has been built along the coast to protect the farmland from damage by saltwater. The interpretation center at **L'Aboiteau de la Seigneurie de Kamouraska** (60 Rte 132 E; 498.5410) explains the system and points out local flora as well. The village of Kamouraska—whose name means "where rushes grow by the water's edge" in Algonquin—is best known for its architecture. Several of the old wooden houses have smoothly rounded, arched eaves that resemble the hull of a schooner—a building technique borrowed from local shipbuilders. The protruding eaves prevent rainwater from seeping into the wood. To get a better sense of the ethnology and

folklore of the region, visit the **Musée de Kamouraska** (69 Ave Morel, next to l'Église Kamouraska; 492.9783); located in a former convent, it displays antiques, furnishings, and woodworking tools; admission is charged. Also take a look at the **Moulin Paradis** (154 Chemin Paradis; 492.5365), an 1804 gristmill that was in use until the 1970s; this was the backdrop for several episodes of *Cormoran*, a popular Quebec TV series.

KAMOURASKA TO ÎLE-VERTE

Fishing has been the mainstay of many villages along the South Shore, but unfortunately it's a dying industry. Nevertheless, it remains very much in evidence as a way of life. Offshore from **St-André** is a network of traditional wicker weirs, which are used to catch eels and other local fish such as herring, smelt, and sturgeon. Fish swim into the maze of netting and are trapped when the tide goes out—an ingenious system that was borrowed from the Amerindians. Watch for roadside stalls selling delicious but very salty smoked herring (*boucane*). At **Maison "Le Beluga"** (553 Rte du Fleuve, near l'Eglise de Notre-Dame-du-Portage; 862.7165), a craft shop in **Notre-Dame-du-Portage**, you can purchase nautical paintings, and wallets and belts made from fish leather. The village is reminiscent of a European spa town, largely because of its bracing sea air. Local peat, rich in minerals and salts, is used for mud treatments at **Auberge du Portage** (671 Rte du Fleuve; 862.3601), an old-fashioned inn and health center. The dining room offers a spa menu—featuring vegetable soups, healthy salads, and pasta dishes—as well as regular meals.

In 1673, the *seigneurie* of **Rivière-du-Loup** was granted to a wealthy Frenchman, but it wasn't until more than a century later that large-scale development began with the arrival of Seigneur Fraser. After the railroad opened in the mid-1800s, the town became a transportation hub for people traveling to the **Gaspé Peninsula** and the province of **New Brunswick**. Today, the pleasant town is alive with Victorian architecture, churches, parks and gardens, and an impressive waterfall, as well as a marina, a summer theater (productions are in French), and a regional museum, **Musée du Bas-St-Laurent** (admission; 300 Rue St-Pierre, at Rue Hôtel-de-Ville; 862.7547). For a self-guided tour, you can pick up a brochure at the **Tourist Office** (189 Blvd de l'Hôtel-de-Ville; 862.1981). Farther east along Route 132 is the affluent suburb of **Cacouna**, the South Shore equivalent of La Malbaie. At the turn of the 19th century, wealthy Americans and out-of-towners built sumptuous holiday homes here. You can leapfrog from the village of **l'Îsle-Verte** to the island of **Île Verte**, though it's unlikely you'll have time on a day trip. Also, ferry schedules (898.2843) are limited by the tides. But there should be time to explore the village and its shoreline. Footpaths across the saltwater marshes at the **Reserve Nationale de Faune de la Baie de l'Îsle Verte** (371 Rte 132, 2 km/1.2 miles east of l'Eglise de l'Île Verte) lead visitors through the breeding grounds of more than 130 bird species. Have your binoculars handy and be on the lookout for herons, cormorants, and eider ducks.

1500 Iroquois and Algonquin Indians settle in the area of modern-day southeastern Canada.

1534 Believing that a direct ocean passage to China still awaited discovery, French explorer Jacques Cartier sets sail. On this first of three voyages to Canada for French King Francis I, Cartier was also in search of gold.

1535 Cartier returns to Canada, discovers the **St. Lawrence River**, and follows it inland to an Indian settlement called Stadacona set on a cliff overlooking the river. The Indians call the passage where the river passes *kebec*, meaning "where the river narrows." Cartier sails farther upriver and finds another Indian settlement called Hochelaga. The village was built onto the side of a 700-foot-high glacial deposit that rose dramatically from the plains—steep on one side, gradually sloping on the other, and densely covered with lush forest. Cartier dubs it **Mont-Royal**, in honor of King Francis I. Relations between the French and the Indians are tense, and further exploration of the region waits about 80 years.

1608 French explorer Samuel de Champlain sails to New France and immediately recognizes Quebec's strategic significance. He establishes a small settlement, including a fur-trading post along the banks of the St. Lawrence at the future site of **Place Royale**. This was to become New France.

1620 Fur trade and shipbuilding activity in New France expands rapidly. To protect the vulnerable colony from Indian attack, Champlain builds **Fort St-Louis** on a cliff overlooking the St. Lawrence where **Château Frontenac** stands today.

1621 An outbreak of smallpox decimates the Indian population along the St. Lawrence.

1642 Sailing from Quebec City, a group of 53 French pioneers and missionaries land at a site near Mont-Royal where they build a small settlement consisting of a few houses, a store, chapel, hospital, and barracks. Led by Paul de Chomeday, they christen the site **Ville-Marie**. While the missionaries attempt to convert the Indians, Ville-Marie becomes a fur-trading center and embarkation point for traders and explorers heading into the country.

1646 Abraham Martin takes over a parcel of land between Rue Claire Fontaine and Rue Ste-Geneviève, an area that will become known as the **Plains of Abraham**.

1647 The church of **Notre-Dame-de-Québec** is founded in Quebec, the oldest parish in North America.

1650 Having expanded and consolidated their colonization of New England, the British begin to challenge French authority in New France.

1663 The **Séminaire de Québec** (**Quebec Seminary**) is founded by Bishop François de Montmorency-Laval as a training center for priests. It soon becomes the hub of ecclesiastical power in New France and has a profound influence on the province's intellectual and cultural development.

1685 The **Sulpician Seminary** is built in Montreal as a residence for the Sulpician priests who governed the island of Montreal. The building, the oldest in Montreal, still houses members of the Sulpician order.

1690 Tensions between the British and French grow. Admiral Sir William Phipps arrives from England to stake British claims to the French colonies in Canada. French governor Comte de Frontenac dismisses Phipps's claims, setting the stage for armed conflict.

1701 Eager to end the constant skirmishes with their Indian neighbors that limit the settlers' mobility, the French authorities sign a peace treaty with the Iroquois Indians. This allows the settlers to move beyond the fortified confines of Ville-Marie toward Mont-Royal. Increased trade leads to a period of prosperity that makes Montreal the business capital of New France.

1705 **Château de Ramezay** in Montreal is built as the home of the governor. In 1775 it becomes the headquarters for American troops seeking to conquer Canada.

1756 Tension grows between France and Britain for control of Canada. France sends Commander Louis-Joseph, Marquis de Montcalm, to secure the frontier of New France. He successfully holds back British thrusts along the border.

1759 General James Wolfe leads a British army of 9,000 soldiers and a fleet of 50 ships, mounted with 2,000 cannons, to Quebec City. Wolfe's men position themselves at **Île d'Orléans**, the island east of Quebec's **Old Port**, and at **Lévis**, a settlement directly across the St. Lawrence River from the Plains of Abraham. Throughout the summer, British ships bombard Quebec City before Wolfe leads 4,000 men to the heights above the city defended by General Louis-Joseph Montcalm. Soon after, the two armies face each other across the Plains of Abraham, and in a battle lasting less than 1 hour, the British cripple the French. A few days later, the French surrender and New France comes under British rule. In the meantime, both Wolfe and Montcalm die from wounds suffered on the battlefield.

1760 A French counteroffensive succeeds in temporarily taking back Quebec. British reinforcements arrive soon and drive the French troops back to Montreal.

1763 The Treaty of Paris ends the continental war between France and England. France cedes Canada to the British. The royal proclamation imposes British institutions on Canada, causing great resentment among Canadians. A provisional British-led government is appointed to run Canada. Although French administrators, businessmen, and landowners return to France, most of the clergy remain and exert a powerful influence on French-Canadian life. Immigrants from Scotland, Ireland, and England pour into Montreal and Quebec. The stone fortifications surrounding Montreal are torn down as the city expands. Soon the hub of commerce moves to present-day downtown Montreal.

1774 The British Parliament passes the Quebec Act, instituting a permanent government in Canada. It gives French-Canadians complete religious freedom and restores the French form of civil law. The Roman Catholic Church's authority in French Canada is maintained, leaving traditional Quebecois life fairly intact. The act also extends Quebec's borders down to Ohio and the Mississippi River. This infuriates the American colonists. Hemmed in at their northern frontiers, the colonists view the Quebec Act as an act of aggression by the British. By strengthening Canadian ties to the British crown, it helps keep Canada loyal during the American Revolution.

1775 American colonists challenge British rule and try to bring Canada into a rebellion. The American Continental Congress declares war on Canada. As the War of Independence breaks out, American Generals Richard Montgomery and Benedict Arnold march into Canada, capture Montreal, and set up headquarters in **Château de Ramezay**, home of the British governor. The Americans then move on to try to capture Quebec City, where they are held by a population still loyal to Britain. Quebec City never falls into American hands.

Colonial loyalists flee in revolt to Canada and settle in Ontario, Nova Scotia, and New Brunswick and on Prince Edward Island.

1776 British forces return and recapture Montreal from the Americans.

1779 Despite cultural ties to France, the ideals of the French Revolution leave Montreal and Quebec City largely untouched. Strong ties to the British monarchy and the even stronger influence of the antirevolutionary French Catholic clergy keep French-Canadians from supporting the revolution.

1785 The fur trade declines and threatens to drag down the fortunes of Montreal. However, European demand for Canadian lumber saves the economies of Montreal and Quebec. Montreal becomes the major trading center in British North America.

1791 Britain passes the Constitution Act of 1791 in response to pressure for greater self-representation from the Canadian colonies. The act divides Quebec into two provinces, Upper Canada (Ontario—largely Protestant and British) and Lower Canada (Quebec—largely Catholic and French), and provides for an elected legislature and assemblies.

1804 **Holy Trinity Church** is founded in Quebec. It is the first Anglican cathedral outside of the British Isles. In Montreal, **Place Jacques-Cartier** opens as a municipal market.

1821 James McGill, a wealthy Scottish-born fur trader, leaves his fortune for the founding of a university.

1829 **McGill University** opens its doors. Montreal's neo-Gothic **Notre-Dame Basilica** is built on the site of the first Notre-Dame.

1832 Montreal is incorporated as a city. It is already the financial, business, and transportation capital of the Canadian colonies.

1834 French-Canadians demand greater independence. Unhappy with the degree of colonial self-government granted by the British, French-speaking Canadians clamor for greater self-rule. Louis-Joseph Papineau, leader of the French-speaking majority in the legislative assembly, issues a list of grievances against British rule. The British ignore the demands. Clashes erupt between young French patriots and British soldiers in Montreal. The clashes spread into a general rebellion against the British.

1841 The rebellion shows no signs of abating. Unwilling to engage in another war in

North America but unwilling to grant full independence, the British Parliament issues the Act of Union, uniting Canada under one government born out of Lower Canada (Quebec) and Upper Canada (Ontario). Provisions are made for a legislative assembly allowing for greater self-rule. However, the executive office of the governor is appointed by the Colonial Office in London and answers only to the British. Canadians are not pleased.

1850 A flood of immigrants from Britain begins to transform Quebec. The newcomers' influence is felt strongly in Montreal. In contrast, Quebec City retains its Gallic flavor.

1867 There is continued pressure from Canada for a greater degree of self-rule. The British Parliament passes the British North America Act, creating the Dominion of Canada, a federation joining Quebec with Ontario and making Quebec City the capital of Quebec. Canada becomes a semi-independent member of the British Commonwealth. Although it is given great latitude on social and civil affairs, the British monarch remains the official head of state. More important, any changes to the Canadian constitution must be approved by the British Parliament. French is given status as an official language.

1878 Montreal's **Hôtel de Ville** (City Hall) is built.

1887 The **Ancien Palais de Justice** (the **Old Courthouse**) in Quebec is built in a neo-Renaissance style.

1889 **Windsor Station**, designed by New York architect **Bruce Price**, opens in Montreal.

1893 **Château Frontenac** opens in Quebec on the site of **Fort St-Louis**. Designed by New York architect **Bruce Price**, the hotel is an instant success and becomes a symbol of Quebec City.

1895 The **Maisonneuve Monument** is unveiled to commemorate the 250th anniversary of the city of Montreal.

1915 Canadians sustained severe casualties fighting for the British in World War I. A law restricting French from being spoken in schools outside of Quebec isolates the province and its two major cities from the rest of the country.

1917 Efforts to introduce conscription strain the already tense relations between French- and English-Canadians. French-Canadian participation in the war effort lags behind that of the rest of the country. French nationalists resist conscription efforts, claiming it is an effort to diminish the French-speaking population.

1936 The Union Nationale party is formed in Quebec, advocating separatism. Under its leader Maurice Duplessis, it controls politics in Quebec until 1960.

1960 The Liberal Party under Jean Lesage is swept into power promising social reform but quickly turns its attention to economic reform in an effort to help Quebec, which has fallen economically behind the rest of Canada.

1962 The mood for separatism grows in Quebec. Although Montreal is still the financial capital of Canada, nearly all economic power rests in Anglo-Canadian hands. The minister of natural resources, René Lévesque, calls for the nationalization of key industries (controlled by English-speaking Canadians), setting the stage for a confrontation between Anglo- and French-Canadians. The same year the **Place Ville Marie** office and shopping complex opens in Montreal as the first link in the **Underground City**. **Place des Arts**, home of the **Montreal Symphony**, opens.

1964 Canada adopts a new flag, the Maple Leaf, creating a symbolic distance from Britain's Union Jack.

1966 Montreal's futuristic **Metro** opens.

1967 The World's Fair (**Expo '67**) comes to Montreal.

1968 Faced with an increasingly violent separatist movement in Quebec, Prime Minister Trudeau introduces the Official Languages Bill, encouraging bilingualism in the Canadian government.

1970 The separatist movement gains momentum, pushing the issue of secession from Canada to the forefront of politics. An extremist arm of the movement, the Front de Libération du Québec (FLQ), engages in a campaign of violence, including bombs and arson, culminating in the kidnapping of Quebec Cabinet Minister Pierre Laporte. Prime Minister Trudeau, himself a French-speaking Quebecois, imposes the War Measures Act, but although the immediate crisis is over, the underlying tensions continue. National funds flow into Quebec in an effort to support French-Canadian cultural identity and diffuse the hostility.

1974 The Parti Québécois, led by René Lévesque, gains political control of Quebec and replaces English with French as the official language in government, businesses, and schools.

1976 The Summer Olympics come to Montreal, creating a construction boom.

1977 Legislation passed by the Parti Québécois to enforce the use of French and penalize noncompliance helps strengthen the widespread use of French but also drives away English-speaking business. The shift from Montreal to Toronto as the financial and business capital—a process begun just after World War II—is accelerated.

1980 The Parti Québécois proposes a referendum for the authority to vote on a separation treaty with the rest of Canada. The referendum is defeated.

1982 The Canada Act is passed by the Canadian government, making Canada fully independent from Britain by giving it the power to amend its own constitution. It includes the Charter of Rights and Freedoms. Quebec accepts neither the act nor the new Canadian constitution.

1988 Canada enters into a free-trade agreement with the US, its largest trading partner, creating the largest open border in the world.

1989 **Le Centre Canadien d'Architecture** (the **Canadian Center for Architecture**) opens in Montreal.

1990 The rift between Quebec and the rest of Canada continues. More than 95% of the almost 600,000 citizens of Quebec City are French-speaking. Montreal's population of 2.9 million makes it the largest city in the province of Quebec and the third-largest French-speaking city in the world. The Meech Lake Accord, a set of constitutional reforms, is designed by Canada's leaders in an effort to bring Quebec into the constitution by granting it status as a "distinct society." The measure is defeated because of opposition from a number of women's and native groups.

1992 Another measure to modify the constitution, called the Charlottetown Accord, also founders, leaving Quebec still outside the Canadian constitution.

1994 The Parti Québécois is once more voted into power, vowing to hold a provincewide referendum to separate from Canada.

1995 The referendum to separate Quebec from the rest of Canada is narrowly defeated by about 53,000 votes.

1996 In September, Senator Jean-Louis Roux is sworn in as the lieutenant-governor of Quebec. His nomination raises the ire of many Québécois, who feel that the government of Quebec is falling into the hands of fascists. Roux resigns on 5 November 1996, just hours after *L'Actualité* magazine revealed his support of anti-Semitism while he was a student at the University of Montreal. In December, Lise Thibault is named lieutenant-governor, becoming the first woman and the first handicapped person to hold this position.

1997 Quebec adopts a constitutional amendment to Article 93 of the Constitution of 1867 that obliged the province to maintain a school system granting religious privileges to Catholics and Protestants. This amendment allows the creation of the school commissions to be on linguistic rather than religious grounds.

1998 In August, the Supreme Court hands down its decision regarding Quebec's right to unilaterally declare itself an independent sovereign state, on the basis of articles submitted by both pro and con factions in the debate. However, the decision raises more questions than it answers, and no finality is yielded on the matter.

2001 Lucien Bouchard resigns as head of the Parti Québécois and as prime minister for Quebec but continues to assume the functions of prime ministers in the interim. Among the reasons for his resignation advanced by several analysts are the failure to gain ground on setting a referendum in the near future, as hoped for by the sovereignists, and the perceived indifference of the population vis-à-vis the federal vote. Bouchard himself ardently states that his decision is tied to his wish to devote himself to his family.

2002 Montreal merges with outlying districts on the island of Montreal to form greater Montreal.

INDEX

MONTREAL INDEX

**MONTREAL
RESTAURANTS**

Only restaurants with star ratings are listed below. All restaurants are listed alphabetically in the main (preceding) index. Always call in advance to ensure a restaurant has not closed, changed its hours, or booked its tables for a private party. The restaurant price ratings are based on the average cost of an entrée for one person, excluding tax and tip.

★	Good
★★	Very Good
★★★	Excellent
★★★★	An Extraordinary Experience
$	The Price Is Right (less than $15)
$$	Reasonable ($15–$20)
$$$	Expensive ($20–$30)
$$$$	Big Bucks ($30 and up)

MONTREAL HOTELS

The hotels listed below are grouped according to their price ratings; they are also listed in the main index. The hotel price ratings reflect the base price of a standard room for two people for one night during the peak season.

$	The Price Is Right (less than $125)
$$	Reasonable ($125–$200)
$$$	Expensive ($200–$275)
$$$$	Big Bucks ($275 and up)

QUEBEC CITY INDEX

CREDITS

*Writer and Researcher
for the Fourth Edition*
Anthony Lechtman

Editorial Director
Edwin Tan

Jacket Design
Chin-Yee Lai

Design Director
Leah Carlson-Stanisic

Map Designer
Patricia Keelin

Associate Director of Production
Dianne Pinkowitz

Senior Production Editor
Mareike Paessler

The publisher and authors assume no legal responsibility for the completeness or accuracy of the contents of this book nor any legal responsibility for the appreciation or depreciation in the value of any premises, commercial or otherwise, by reason of inclusion in or exclusion from this book. All contents are based on information available at the time of publication. Some of the maps are diagrammatic and may be selective of street inclusion.

ACCESS®PRESS does not solicit individuals, organizations, or businesses for inclusion in our books, nor do we accept payment for inclusion. We welcome, however, information from our readers, including comments, criticisms, and suggestions for new listings. Send all correspondence to: **ACCESS**®PRESS, 10 East 53rd Street, New York, NY 10022. PRINTED IN HONG KONG

Look for these other Access Guides at your local bookstore:

ACCESS Boston
ACCESS California Wine Country
ACCESS Chicago
ACCESS Florence & Venice
ACCESS London
ACCESS Los Angeles
ACCESS New Orleans
ACCESS New York City
ACCESS Paris
ACCESS Philadelphia
ACCESS Rome
ACCESS San Francisco
ACCESS Seattle
ACCESS Washington, DC

SYDNEY

BOSTON

CALIFORNIA
WINE COUNTRY

CHICAGO

NEW ORLEANS

SAN FRANCISCO

THE ONLY GUIDE THAT LEADS YOU STREET BY STREET INTO THE HEARTS OF THE CITIES

SEATTLE

ACCESS

SAN DIEGO

WASHINGTON, D.C.

NEW YORK CITY

PHILADELPHIA

LOS ANGELES

MONTREAL & QUEBEC CITY

LONDON

PARIS

ROME

FLORENCE & VENICE

HarperResource
An Imprint of HarperCollins*Publishers*
www.harpercollins.com

**Available wherever
books are sold, or call
1-800-331-3761 to order.**